series editor Tony Merry

Person-Centred Approach and Client-Centred Therapy Essential Readers is a new series of books making important and exciting contributions to international person-centred literature by authors who have already made distinguished additions to the development of the person-centred approach.

The series is edited by **Tony Merry**, Reader, Department of Psychology, University of East London, a person-centred counsellor, trainer and supervisor, and author of several person-centred books and articles.

Other books in this series:

WB 8799149 7

CONTRIBUTIONS TO CLIENT-CENTERED THERAPY AND THE PERSON-CENTERED APPROACH

NATHANIEL J. RASKIN

PCCS BOOKS
Ross-on-Wye

This collection first published in 2004

PCCS BOOKS
Llangarron
Ross-on-Wye
Herefordshire
HR9 6PT
United Kingdom
Tel +44 (0)1989 77 07 07
www.pccs-books.co.uk

**Contributions to Client-Centered Therapy and the
Person-Centered Approach**

ISBN 1 898059 57 8

Cover design by Denis Postle
Printed by Bath Press, Bath, UK

DEDICATION

This book is dedicated to the millions of human beings in the world who could benefit from psychotherapy, but don't know about it or can't afford it, who are trying to cope with basic problems like having enough to eat, receiving adequate health care, insufficient education, and battling prejudice, and to the individuals and organizations who are trying to help them.

CONTENTS

List of Tables, Figures and Appendices

PREFACE

I thought of writing this book because, over the course of more than half a century, from 1947 to 2001, I had written many chapters and articles on the history of client-centered therapy, general expositions of the approach, research I had done, my approach to teaching and learning, personal growth, my work with groups, descriptions of clients who had made a special impression on me, and the explanation of core concepts such as the nondirective attitude, empathy, experiencing, and locus-of-evaluation. I was aware that with all my writing, I had never had a book published. I thought that if I did so, by bringing together my principle work, I would fulfill a personal goal and hopefully, make a contribution to others.

I am indebted to many people for accomplishing this work, first of all Carl Rogers. I was fortunate enough, upon graduating from the College of the City of New York, to be one of his first graduate students at Ohio State University in 1940, when he wrote about and taught 'a newer psychotherapy'. This was the beginning of a 47-year association with him. I continued studying with Carl at the University of Chicago after World War II, earning my PhD in 1949. I became his associate in the authorship of articles and book chapters and in presentations at conventions of the American Psychological Association and other organizations. During the last four months of 1980 and the first four months of 1981, I obtained a sabbatical leave from Northwestern University to the Center for Studies of the Person in La Jolla, California when, working with Carl, Patrick Rice, and Lawrence Solomon at the center, I helped to design and carry out an Ongoing Learning Program in Client-Centered Therapy and the Person-Centered Approach for students in the United States and abroad. Carl's wife, Helen, had died in 1979, and he and I spent a good deal of time together after work, taking walks and going out for meals. Occasionally, he cooked for us; one of his specialties was corned beef and cabbage. Our friendship deepened, ending with his death in 1987; our communication continues in my dreams and thoughts.

None of this would have been possible without the devotion of my parents, Russian immigrants to the United States, who worked tirelessly so that my two older brothers and I would have a higher education after going through the New York City public school.

I returned to New York after getting my PhD, and taught at Hunter College and accepted a position as Director of Research Planning at the American

Foundation for the Blind. I married Nina Schultz in 1955. Nina was an artist who had gone to the High School of Music and Art and studied painting at Brooklyn College with the famous Mark Rothko. I recognized her talent immediately, saying, 'You are an artist!' but I could not talk her out of pursuing a career in Social Work.

I married Nina because I fell in love with a beautiful young girl but also because I sensed that she would strengthen my life in some vital ways. She was very shy with me when we first went out (I'm sure she was not that way with her girl friends!) but over time I have been the reserved one while she has been the person to make friends and develop the social side of our marriage. She is a devoted mother of our two daughters, and grandmother of our granddaughter and grandson. I am as good as Nina at remembering their birthdays, but she keeps track of those of our friends, other relatives and their children.

Nina has helped many people, children and adults in their late years, as a psychotherapist. She has a talent for encouraging individuals without any experience to express themselves through art, and has done this both as a paid worker and as a volunteer with social agencies. Unlike me, Nina comes from a musical family. She loves to dance, plays the piano, and takes the initiative in arranging for us to attend concerts.

We moved from New York to Chicago in 1957; I had accepted a position as Chief Psychologist at Children's Memorial Hospital with an appointment at Northwestern University Medical School. I resigned from the hospital after five years but remained on the Northwestern faculty for over thirty years until my mandatory retirement at the age of 70 in 1991, as Professor Emeritus of Psychiatry and Behavioral Sciences.

I have been a therapist, teacher, and researcher for over 50 years. In this time, I have had hundreds of clients and students. One article in 'Contributions' is about 'some memorable clients'. In another, 'Learning Through Human Encounters', I describe how students in my courses play a significant role in the determination of course content and process, and in grading. By sharing responsibility with clients and students, I have helped to create an environment in which they and I may grow. I believe that, in contrast, I would remain static if I decided what was best for them.

I have expressed my indebtedness to my wife and parents, to Carl Rogers, and to my clients and students. My colleagues have also been indispensable in the attainment of whatever success I have had. It would be too daunting a task to name them all, but they would include students and faculty at the colleges and universities with which I have been connected, members of the Association for the Development of the Person-Centered Approach, of the American Academy of Psychotherapists, of the Counseling and Psychotherapy Research Center of Chicago, and participants in the annual Warm Springs, Georgia conferences.

May, 2004

A Personal Message from Carl Rogers

I deeply regret that I am not able to attend the 1978 Annual Conference of AAP as I had planned to do. A large part of my regret is due to my desire to pay honor to Nat Raskin as he is inaugurated as the next president of the Academy.

I have known Nat Raskin since the early 1940s, when he and several other City College of New York students came to Ohio State to do their graduate work with me. They brought a feisty challenging east-coast spirit into our more placid midwestern style. Nat, however, was thoughtful and shy, an excellent student. I was very glad he was with me in the early years of the Counseling Center at the University of Chicago. He developed both his therapeutic and research skills, and was a tireless worker.

Raskin was one of the leading figures in our first major attempt to put the investigation of psychotherapy on an objective and scientific basis. He wrote the first and last articles of our 'coordinated research in psychotherapy', completed in 1948, and published in 1949, filling one complete issue of the *Journal of Consulting Psychology*. Nat drew all six studies together in a masterful way, showing statistically and graphically their interrelated and mutually supportive findings. As is typical of him and his modesty, Nat was careful to thank everyone who in any way helped his project. His footnote reads a little bit like the response of an Academy Award winner — 'Thanks to the producer, the screenwriters, the make-up man,' etc., etc.

More important to *me* is that during a time of great personal distress during my Chicago days, Nat was a person to whom I turned for help, and from whom I received much help. I still feel deep gratitude to him for being my 'helping person' during a time of painful need.

I feel that Nat Raskin has never received full recognition for all that he has done. His landmark study of six differing therapeutic orientations, based on recorded interviews, is not nearly as widely known as it deserves to be. I am pleased that the AAP has published it as a special monograph, but it contains sobering learnings for therapists, and needs to be much more widely studied.

This message was sent at the time of Nat Raskin's inauguration as the President of the American Academy of Psychotherapists at the AAP's 1978 Annual Conference in Monterey, California.

Over the years Nat has been my most loyal friend. I have come to love him very much. I have always been able to rely on him when I needed him. He and Nina have extended a warm and cordial hospitality. Nat has gone out of his way to do me honor, keeping himself in the background. The celebration of my 75th year by a series of symposiums at the annual conference of the American Psychological Association in San Francisco came into being because of Nat Raskin. He has twice in recent years brought together groups of former students and colleagues to meet with me — memorable and heartwarming occasions both. My wife Helen and I are grateful for all that he has done for us.

I am delighted that he is the next president of the American Academy of Psychotherapists. My own work and interests have drawn me away from this organization, but I keep closely in touch with its doings. I am proud of my deep involvement in its early and formative days, as we tried to find ways of bringing together therapists of all professions in one organization. It pleases me greatly that one of our innovations, the annual workshop, still continues to be a support group for many of you. Nat Raskin has helped to make that true.

So, as the first president of the AAP in 1955, I am honored to have the opportunity of congratulating the Academy on its next president — an excellent therapist, a solid and thoughtful investigator, a loyal friend, a sensitive and creative person — Nat Raskin.

Affectionately,
Carl Rogers

THE DEVELOPMENT OF NONDIRECTIVE THERAPY

1

The term 'nondirective therapy' is today commonly identified with the method and views of Carl R. Rogers and his students and associates. For some, nondirective therapy is just a new name for Jessie Taft's 'relationship therapy' and Otto Rank's 'will therapy'. Regardless of how the phrase is interpreted, it is one which now has some meaning for almost all workers in psychology, orthopsychiatry, mental hygiene, and counseling. Fifteen, ten, or even five years ago, advocates of 'passive', 'relationship', 'client-centered', or 'nondirective' therapy represented a point of view which was not well known and exerted little influence on the work of psychiatrists, psychologists, and social workers. Today, while the number of therapists or counselors who utilize a consistent nondirective approach is still quite small, it is one which is growing rapidly. Just as significant is the fact that there are few treatment interviewers of any orientation who have not taken cognizance of and considered, however briefly, this newer philosophy, and changed or justified their own procedures in the light of it.

Whenever interest in an idea spreads, curiosity as to the history of it grows as well, and the purpose of this paper is to help satisfy that curiosity. For the writer, 'nondirective therapy' may well stand for the philosophy and technique of the Rogers school of therapy. But, in tracing the development of this philosophy and technique, he has made no attempt to take the ideas of this school and trace them back to their origin. The development of an idea in an individual is a complicated process, often too complicated even for the individual himself to understand or trace, and the writer does not feel qualified to attempt it in this instance.

The alternative method, which has been chosen, represents a cross-sectional rather than a longitudinal type of study. The work of Freud, Rank, Taft, Allen, and Rogers has been examined here, not with the aim of causally relating the views of any one of them to the others, but with the goal rather of a logical comparison of their ideas. Prominent throughout has been the question, 'How does this view relate to nondirective thought?'

As a result of such treatment, and rather uniquely, it is believed, the nondirective aspects of Freud's technique have been stressed here, while conversely, attention

University of Chicago. Originally published in the *Journal of Consulting Psychology* (1948), *12,* 92–110. Reprinted with permission.

has been focused on the directive features of the work of Rank, Taft, and Allen. Generally, Freud's therapeutic methods have been accepted as subordinate to and within the framework of his own theories of personality development and of psychotherapy. With attention centered on client content, there has been little recognition of the degree to which Freud came to compromise with client attitudes in the course of psychoanalysis. With respect to Rank, Taft, and Allen, there has been, heretofore, a rather superficial acceptance of the general 'client-centered' nature of their approach, with no critical evaluation of the extent of therapist-direction in their work. Furthermore, the tendency to group Rogers' name with these three has served to obscure what are perhaps the most significant features of the former's work.

Thus, while the effect of our comparative treatment has been to give a different emphasis to the ideas of Freud, Rank, Taft, and Allen than that provided by these therapists at the time they made their contributions, it has left us in a better position to understand and evaluate the significant features of nondirective therapy as it stands today and more important, perhaps, the direction in which it is going.

Sigmund Freud

Freud's orientation to therapy was so completely 'physician-directed' that he would not appear to belong in any history of nondirective thought. On the other hand, a great debt is owed to Freud by all schools of psychotherapy for the work he did in establishing the interview (regardless of the therapist's orientation) as a recognized therapeutic measure and, of course, for his theoretical contributions in the fields of unconscious mechanisms, childhood, and the emotions, which have made human behavior far more understandable.[1] A more specific reason for including Freud in this paper has been the close relation which Otto Rank held to him. As one of Freud's closest disciples for approximately twenty years, and his favorite for at least ten, Rank's theory and practice, opposed as they were to his teacher's, grew out of his experience with orthodox psychoanalysis (Sachs, 1946).

But the most cogent reason for examining Freud's work here lies in the relationship between his therapeutic aim and the techniques he utilized to accomplish this end. Freud's goal in treatment, as is well known, was to have the patient recall as much as possible about his past, in order that the analyst might be given the means to afford him insight into his behavior, in terms of 'repressed infantile sexuality'. It is interesting to note that Freud, in order to achieve this aim, utilized procedures which are in accord with present-day nondirective philosophy. This is true from the very beginning of the analysis. The following excerpt, brief as it is, shows Freud's use of a nondirective technique while demonstrating, at the same time, his 'physician-directed' orientation.

> What subject-matter the treatment begins with is on the whole immaterial, whether with the patient's life-story, with a history of

---

1. Rogers has cited the indebtedness of the client-centered approach to Freud for his concepts of repression, release, catharsis and insight (Rogers, 1946).

the illness or with recollections of childhood; but in any case the patient must be left to talk, and the choice of subject left to him. One says to him, therefore, 'Before I can say anything to you, I must know a great deal about you; please tell me what you know about yourself.' (Freud, 1924, Ch. 31)

Freud continues to be nondirective with the patient who finds it difficult to begin: 'One must accede this first time as little as at any other to their request that one should propose something for them to speak of' (ibid.). But his bent for nondirection soon weakens. There is 'emphatic and repeated assurance that the absence of all ideas at the beginning is an impossibility'. And if this does not work,

> ... pressure will constrain him to acknowledge that he has neglected certain thoughts which are occupying his mind. He was thinking of the treatment itself but not in a definite way, or else the appearance of the room he is in occupied him, or he found himself thinking of the objects round him in the consulting room, or of the fact that he is lying on a sofa; for all of which thoughts he has substituted 'nothing.' These indications are surely intelligible; everything connected with the situation of the moment represents a transference to the physician which proves suitable for use as resistance. It is necessary then to begin by uncovering this transference; thence the way leads rapidly to penetration of the pathogenic material in the case. (ibid.)

But we are not yet ready to leave Freud, the employer of nondirective techniques. He states that while the first aim of the treatment consists in attaching the patient to the treatment and to the person of the physician, '... it is possible to forfeit this primary success if one takes up from the start any standpoint other than that of understanding, such as a moralizing attitude . . .' (ibid.).

In the field of interpretation Freud most clearly tends towards nondirection as a result of bad luck with directive techniques:

> This answer of course involves a condemnation of that mode of procedure which consists in communicating to the patient the interpretation of the symptoms as soon as one perceives it oneself, or of that attitude which would account it a special triumph to hurl these 'solutions' in his face at the first interview . . . Such conduct brings both the man and the treatment into discredit and arouses the most violent opposition, whether the interpretations be correct or not; yes, and the truer they are actually the more violent is the resistance they arouse. Usually the therapeutic effect at the moment is nothing; the resulting horror of analysis, however, is ineradicable. Even in later stages of the analysis one must be careful not to communicate the meaning of a symptom or the interpretation of a

wish until the patient is already close upon it, so that he has only a short step to take in order to grasp the explanation himself. In former years I often found that premature communication of interpretations brought the treatment to an untimely end, both on account of the resistances suddenly aroused thereby and also because of the relief resulting from the insight so obtained. (ibid.)

Freud had a similar experience in the matter of communicating repressed material to patients:

In the early days of analytic technique it is true that we regarded the matter intellectually and set a high value on the patient's knowledge of that which had been forgotten, so that we hardly made a distinction between our knowledge and his in these matters. We accounted it specially fortunate if it were possible to obtain information of the forgotten traumas of childhood from external sources, from parents or nurses, for instance, or from the seducer himself, as occurred occasionally; and we hastened to convey the information and proofs of its correctness to the patient, in the certain expectation of bringing the neurosis and the treatment to a rapid end by this means. It was a bitter disappointment when the expected success was not forthcoming. (ibid.)

Freud's treatment of the problem of overcoming resistance, which is closely connected with the problems of interpretation and of communicating repressed material, is similarly nondirective in its development:

The first step in overcoming the resistance is made, as we know, by the analyst's discovering the resistance, which is never recognized by the patient, and acquainting him with it. Now it seems that beginners in analytic practice are inclined to look upon this as the end of the work. I have often been asked to advise upon cases in which the physician complained that he had pointed out his resistance to the patient and that all the same no change has set in; in fact, the resistance had only then become more obscure than ever. The treatment seemed to make no progress. This gloomy foreboding always proved mistaken. The treatment was as a rule progressing quite satisfactorily; only the analyst had forgotten that naming the resistance could not result in its immediate suspension. One must allow the patient time to get to know this resistance of which he is ignorant, to 'work through it', to overcome it, by continuing the work according to the analytic rule in defiance of it. Only when it has come to its height can one, with the patient's cooperation, discover the repressed instinctual trends which are feeding the resistance; and only by living them through in this way will the patient be convinced of their existence and their power.

> This 'working through' of the resistances may in practice amount
> to an arduous task for the patient and a trial of patience for the
> analyst. Nevertheless, it is the part of the work that effects the greatest
> changes in the patient and that distinguishes analytic treatment from
> every kind of suggestive treatment. (Freud, 1924, Ch. 32)

The intent of the above quotations is not to make Freud out as a nondirective
therapist but to demonstrate that a therapist with his fundamentally authoritative
orientation found it necessary to reckon more and more with the attitudes of the
patient and to depend less and less upon the will of the analyst, in order to make
therapeutic progress.

Before leaving Freud, one other point will be cited which shows him as being
closer to the nondirective point of view than may be popularly supposed. This
relates to the nature of the unconscious. It is widely held that nondirective methods
are superficial and fail to bring to light material which is deeply buried in the
patient's unconscious. But Freud writes:

> The forgetting of impressions, scenes, events, nearly always reduces
> itself to 'dissociation' of them. When the patient talks about these
> 'forgotten' matters he seldom fails to add: 'In a way I have always
> known that, only I never thought of it.' (ibid.)

This passage fits very closely the experience of clients in nondirective therapy.
On the same topic, Freud writes further:

> The 'forgotten' material is still further circumscribed when we
> estimate at their true value the screen-memories which are so
> generally present. In many cases I have had the impression that the
> familiar childhood-amnesia, which is theoretically so important to
> us, is entirely outweighed by the screen-memories. Not merely is
> much that is essential in childhood preserved in them, but actually
> all that is essential. (ibid.)

Otto Rank

Rank, long Freud's closest associate and disciple (Sachs, 1946), first rebelled
openly against classical Freudian theory and practice in 1924 with the publication
of *The Trauma of Birth*. In this work, birth replaced castration as the original
trauma and the breast took precedence over the penis as the first libido object. In
addition, Rank identified the origin of fear with the birth process.

Having done this, Jessie Taft writes; 'he had pursued the Freudian path to its
inevitable conclusion and after trying out the final biological bases theoretically
and practically, was finally able to abandon content as in itself unimportant and
devote himself to the technical utilization of the dynamics of the therapeutic
process, with the patient's will as the central force' (Rank, 1945).

Rank is responsible for the initiation in psychotherapy of several extremely
significant ideas:

1. The individual seeking help is not simply a battleground of impersonal forces such as id and superego, but has creative powers of his own, a will. When the individual is threatened, when a strange will is forced on him, this positive will becomes counter-will.
2. Because of the dangers involved in living and the fear of dying, all people experience a basic ambivalence, which may be viewed in various aspects. Thus, there is a conflict between will-to-health and will-to-illness, between self-determination and acceptance of fate, between being different and being like others, etc. This ambivalence is characteristic not just of neurotics, but is an integral part of life.
3. The distinguishing characteristic of the neurotic is that he is 'ego-bound', both his destructive and productive tendencies are directed toward the self, his will is frozen and denied in a dissatisfied concentration on these ambivalences of living.
4. The aim of therapy, in the light of the above, becomes the acceptance by the individual of himself as unique and self-reliant, with all his ambivalences, and the freeing of the positive will through the elimination of the temporary blocking which consists of the concentration of creative energies on the ego.
5. In order to achieve this goal, the patient rather than the therapist must become the central figure in the therapeutic process. The patient is his own therapist, he has within him forces of self-creation as well as of self-destruction, and the former can be brought into play if the therapist will play the role, not of authority, but of ego-helper or assistant ego, not of positive will but of counter-will to strengthen the patient's positive will, not of total ego but of any part of the ego felt by the patient to be disturbing and against which he may battle; in sum, the therapist 'becomes in the course of treatment a dumping ground on which the patient deposits his old neurotic ego and in successful cases finally leaves it behind him' (ibid.). The therapist can be neither an instrument of love, which would make the patient more dependent, nor of education, which attempts to alter the individual, and so would inhibit the positive will by arousing the counter-will.
6. The goals of therapy are achieved by the patient not through an explanation of the past, which he would resist if interpreted to him, and which, even if accepted by him, would serve to lessen his responsibility for his present adjustment, but rather through the experiencing of the present in the therapeutic situation, in which he learns to will in reaction to the therapist's counter-will, in which he is using all of his earlier reaction patterns plus the present, in which the will conflict which is present in his total life situation, the denial of the will for independence and self-reliance, is most immediately felt and can therefore most easily be brought home to him. The neurotic is hamstrung not by any particular content of his past, but by the way he is utilizing material in the present; thus, his help must come through an understanding of present dynamics, rather than of past content.

7. The ending of therapy, the separation of patient from therapist, is a symbol of all separations in life, starting with the separation of foetus from womb in birth, and if the patient can be made to understand the will conflict present here, the conflict over growth towards independence and self-reliance, and if he can exercise the separation as something which he wills himself, despite the pain of it, then it can symbolize the birth of the new individual.

By setting the time of ending in advance, the therapist can early bring in the one situation in which he must act as positive will and thus arouse the patient's counter-will, and allows, without shock, a gradual growth of the patient's ability to give up the therapist as assistant ego, to take over his own self, and face reality.

These seven points seem to constitute the basis of Rank's 'will therapy'. They are not given systematically by Rank, but are ideas which are presented by him in various relationships to each other; we may regard them as the threads which are used to make up the complicated pattern of *Will Therapy*, the book, and the therapeutic method itself.

The following passage will serve to illustrate the manner in which Rank contrasts his own method with Freud's ideological therapy, also to illustrate the manner in which Rank interrelates some of the points outlined above, and finally to highlight Rank's skepticism regarding the possibility of a therapy with technical rules:

> In contrast to this ideological therapy, the therapeutic utilization of the analytic situation itself has led me to a dynamic therapy which in every single case, yes in every individual hour of the same case, is different, because it is derived momentarily from the play of forces given in the situation and immediately applied. My technique consists essentially in having no technique, but in utilizing as much as possible experience and understanding that are constantly converted into skill but never crystallized into technical rules which would be applicable ideologically. There is a technique only in an ideological therapy where technique is identical with theory and the chief task of the analyst is interpretation (ideological), not the bringing to pass and granting of experience. This method effaces also the sharp boundary between patient and therapist to the extent that the latter sinks to the level of assistant ego and no longer rules the scene as chief actor. It is not merely that the patient is ill and weak and the therapist the model of health and strength, but the patient has been and still is, even in the analysis, his own therapist, while the analyst can become a destructive hindrance to cure. If this occurs, not merely as incidental resistance, but threatens to establish itself as a situation, the therapist must possess the superior insight to let the patient go free, even if he is still not adjusted in terms of the analytic ideology in its role as a substitute for reality. For real psychotherapy is not concerned primarily with adaptation to any

>kind of reality, but with the adjustment of the patient to himself,
>that is, with his acceptance of his own individuality or of that part
>of his personality which he has formerly denied. (Rank, 1945)

Much of Rank's theory of psychology and psychotherapy is speculative and difficult, but the most obscure area of his work is the manner in which he practiced psychotherapy, as the above quotation (and point 5 above) might indicate. The aspect which is most inscrutable is the amount and manner of activity of the therapist in the treatment hour. Our clues to this activity lie in rather unsystematic references to it in *Will Therapy*. We find, despite all the venom heaped by Rank on the techniques of education and interpretation and despite all the emphasis placed on the autotherapeutic abilities of the patient, that 'I [Rank] unmask all the reactions of the patient even if they apparently refer to the analyst, as projections of his own inner conflict and bring them back to his own ego', that 'interpretation on the part of the analyst is worthless as long as it does not lead to the understanding of this denial mechanism itself and its relation to the yielding of the will under emotion', and that 'here is the place [the therapeutic hour] to show him how he tries to destroy the connections with this experience just as he does with the past' (ibid.).

As an illustration of the same point, the following passage demonstrates the clear use of interpretation in the Rankian method, despite the statement at the end which plays down the value of the technique:

>All that the therapist can do is to take over with understanding the
>role falling to his lot, and to make clear to the patient the universal
>meaning of this experience which comprehends in itself the whole
>man, yes, almost the whole of humanness. This explanation,
>however, can be given only in the individual terminology of the
>particular patient and not in a general ideology which cannot give
>him understanding, but at most, knowledge. Knowledge alone does
>not liberate but freeing through experience can bring the insight
>afterwards, although even this is not essential to the result. (ibid.)

Finally, we see a completely unambiguous managing of the therapeutic situation by Rank in the following account of end-setting:

>I make use of various means in the final situation in order to meet
>the inner dynamic of the patient, which already functions freely,
>sometimes too intensively, by a dynamic of the external situation
>which corresponds better to reality. According to the type of person
>and the situation, through postponing, leaving out, lengthening or
>shortening of the regular treatment hour, as well as through other
>alterations of the customary therapeutic situation, I bring an outer
>dynamic to bear upon the inner conflict which perhaps may irritate
>the patient, but is still perceived by him as an unburdening of his
>ambivalence and is utilized in terms of adaptation to reality. (ibid.)

All of this might be summed up with the comment that while Rank's desertion of content for dynamics, and of past for present, was complete, his renunciation of educative, interpretive, and other directive techniques was less so, and while it was totally wrong in his view to interpret content, it might be pardonable to interpret dynamics. To use the terms of his own simile, the patient is the author of this play, but the therapist retains the role of producer.

Jessie Taft

Taft, Rank's translator and later, for a short time, his associate at the Pennsylvania School of Social Work, for the main part has carried into her own work the features of Rankian theory described above. She has made some contributions of her own to Rankian theory and practice, however, which should be noted in an account of the development of the nondirective approach.

Perhaps her unique theoretical contribution has been the emphasis she places on time as representing the whole problem of living and of therapy. It would be a loss to abstract the views of one who writes such poetic prose. The deep feeling which is present in all of Taft's writing is especially present in her views on this subject, and a few quotations will reveal them concisely while allowing us to retain the feeling tone:

> Time represents more vividly than any other category the necessity of accepting limitation as well as the inability to do so, and symbolizes therefore the whole problem of living. The reaction of each individual to limited or unlimited time betrays his deepest and most fundamental life pattern, his relation to the growth process itself, to beginnings and endings, to being born and to dying. (Taft, 1933)

> The basis for believing that life can be thus accepted (as a changing, finite, limited affair to be seized at the moment if at all), beyond the fact that all of us do more or less accept it if we continue to exist, lies in this: that we are, after all, part and parcel of the life process; that we do naturally abhor not only ending but also never ending, that we not only fear change but the unchanging. (ibid.)

> Time in itself is a purely arbitrary category of man's invention, but since it is a projection of his innermost being, it represents so truly his inherent psychological conflict, that to be able to accept it, to learn to admit its likeness to one's very self, its perfect adaptation to one's deepest and most contradictory impulses, is already to be healed, as far as healing is possible or applicable, since in accepting time, one accepts the self and life with their inevitable defects and limitations. This does not mean a passive resignation but a willingness to live, work and create as mortals within the confines of the finite. (ibid.)

And finally, this most poignant passage of all:

> . . . one might fairly define relationship therapy as a process in which the individual finally learns to utilize the allotted hour from beginning to end without undue fear, resistance, resentment or greediness. When he can take it and also leave it without denying its value, without trying to escape it completely or keep it forever because of this very value, in so far he has learned to live, to accept this fragment of time in and for itself, and strange as it may seem, if he can live this hour he has in his grasp the secret of all hours, he has conquered life and time for the moment and in principle. (ibid.)

Taft reveals a keen appreciation of the separateness of the will of the therapist from that of the client by recognizing the necessity for therapists to accept the limitation on the help which it is possible to give others:

> I know in advance that no one is going to experience change, call it growth or progress if you have the courage, because I think it would be good for society, good for his family and friends or even good for himself . . . (ibid.)

> This means not only a limit put upon those seeking help but a genuine limitation in myself, an impotence which I am forced to accept even when it is painful, as it frequently is. There is a beloved child to be saved, a family unity to be preserved, an important teacher to be enlightened. Before all these problems in which one's reputation, one's pleasure in utilizing professional skill, as well as one's real feeling for the person in distress are perhaps painfully involved, one must accept one's final limitation and the right of the other, perhaps his necessity, to refuse help or to take help in his own terms, not as therapist, friends or society might choose. My knowledge and my skill avail nothing, unless they are accepted and used by the other. Over that acceptance and possible use, I have no control beyond the genuineness of my understanding of the difficulty with which anyone takes or seeks help, my respect for the strength of the patient, however negatively expressed, and the reality of my acceptance of my function as helper not ruler. If my conviction is real, born of emotional experience too deep to be shaken, then at least I am not an obstacle to the person who needs help but fears domination. He can now approach me without the added fear and resistance which active designs for his cure would surely produce and can find within the limitation which I accept thus sincerely, a safety which permits him to utilize and me to exercise all the professional skill and wisdom at my command. On the other hand, the person who seeks the domination of another in order to project

his conflict and avoid himself and his own development by resisting the efforts of the other to save him, is finally brought to a realization of the futility of his striving, as he cannot force upon me a goal which I have long since recognized to be outside my province and power. Whether such a person will ultimately succeed in taking over his own problem, since I cannot relieve him of it, can be determined only by what actually happens. There are those who are unwilling or unable to go further, an outcome every therapist must stand ready to admit and respect, no matter how much his professional ego is hurt or his therapeutic or economic aim defeated. (ibid.)

We are not surprised to find her writing later on that:
... therapy in the sense of socially desirable behavior can never be the goal of this type of analytic relationship. It is a purely individual affair and can be measured only in terms of its meaning to the person, child or adult; of its value, not for happiness, not for virtue, not for social adjustment but for growth and development in terms of a purely individual norm. (ibid.)

One of Taft's major contributions has been to record very completely two treatment cases with children. These appear in *The Dynamics of Therapy in a Controlled Relationship* and are valuable for the purposes of this paper because they give us the first definite indication of how a Rankian functions in a therapeutic situation. But before discussing them, it way be well to examine Taft's general views on the role of the therapist in a 'controlled relationship'. She does not care for the name 'passive therapy' which sometimes has been identified with her method of treatment:
As I conceive it, the therapeutic function involves the most intense activity but it is an activity of attention, of identification and understanding, of adaptation to the individual's need and pattern, combined with an unflagging preservation of one's own limitation and difference. (ibid.)

In describing her role in the case of Helen P, which appears first in her book, she writes:
The contacts . . . were carried through, as far as I was humanly able, in terms of the child as she actually was at the moment, and my recognition of her immediate will, feeling or meaning. Everything centered in her, was oriented with regard to her. This does not mean that there were no checks but that even when my response was a prohibition, it was also a seeing of her, never a denial of the nature of her impulse or her right to have it. Where my own curiosity as to her behavior symptoms or my interest in bringing out certain material got the better of me, as it did occasionally, I abandoned it, as soon

as I became conscious of my folly . . . Interpretation there was none, except a verbalization on my part of what the child seemed to be feeling and doing, a comparatively spontaneous response to her words or actions which should clarify or make more conscious the self of the moment whatever it might be. (ibid.)

The comments on Taft's case material are made with the following in mind:
1. A transcript of the words spoken in a contact is not an entirely adequate reproduction of it. Even records such as Taft's, which are descriptive in addition to containing a record of the conversation, lose much of the feeling tone which is present in the contact and which may be very important for therapy. This would be especially true of contacts in which an individual such as Miss Taft took part; her deep feeling of respect for the strengths and the individuality of the other would come through even if her statements were sometimes neutral (in the sense of not responding to feeling), or interrogative, or went beyond the expressed feeling.
2. Children do not verbalize as well as adults, and sometimes show clearly what they are feeling, even though they have not verbalized the attitude.

With these points in mind, the cases of Helen P and of John as handled by Taft seem to be characterized by the following:
1. There is only incidental attempt on the part of the therapist to bring out content material.

2. There are leading questions as to past feelings and warnings as to future feelings. E.g., during the third hour with Helen P, Helen is drawing a picture of a lady holding an umbrella:
'That's you,' she says laughingly.

'Helen, were you mad at me last week?'

'No.'

'Weren't you mad — just a little? I should have been in your place — because I wouldn't let you take the crayons home.'

'I wasn't mad. I like to come here to draw.' (ibid.)

It may be said that Taft's 'acceptance' of the child is displayed here as an attempt to show her that bad feelings as well as good ones are acceptable in this situation. It should be noted that acceptance is lacking here, however, in the sense of accepting the kind of feeling the child is able to give expression to at the moment.
    The same type of dynamic appears in the second case, that of Jackie (fourth hour):

He goes over to the steam pipes which he has found hot before, and shows extreme caution and fear. Can hardly bring himself to touch the pipe which burned him. Finally does so after much effort, and finds it cold.

'You decided to stay home on Thursday, didn't you, Jack?'

'Yes.' No further comment. 'It's hot here.' (ibid.)

Similarly future feelings are anticipated and introduced into the contact by the therapist with no indication that they form part of the present attitude of the child.

Helen P (end of third hour):
'I like to come,' she says.

'Yes, I know you do, but you may feel differently some day.' (ibid.)

Jackie (second hour):
He runs out quickly to see if the broom is there. When he comes back the story has grown. 'We took the broom away from her and chased her. She was going to chase us but we chased her.'

'And that's what you'll be doing to me some day. I see I have to look out.' (ibid.)

In the above two excerpts, there is displayed the therapist's need to prepare the child for the inevitable separation. Insofar as this is true, there is a lack of acceptance of the child's own capacities.

3. The therapist sometimes takes the lead in bringing out attitudes on the time element and on other aspects of the dynamics of the therapeutic situation.
E.g., Jack is brought in 15 minutes late for the fifth hour, after Miss Taft had been late for the third hour:
Jack comes in very cheerful and cold. 'Feel my ear. See how cold it is.'

'You are even with me now. You kept me waiting fifteen minutes.'

Quick as a flash, he answers, 'Are you mad at me?' (ibid.)

4. The main resource of the therapist here is her general attitude of understanding and respect for the child. In the absence of any specific techniques the therapist appears to respond on an intuitive emotional basis.
Before leaving Taft, it might be well to note first, her feeling, like Rank's, that therapy is 'purely individual, non-moral, non-scientific, non-intellectual'. Also,

that 'therapy is non-scientific . . . and not open to research at the moment' (ibid.). Secondly, it is revealing to note her view that relationship therapy is not equally suited for all people and that for some children, it may not do at all:

> . . . The less able the individual is to bear the pain of his own humanity, the less willing he is to sacrifice a partial unwilled response in favor of a consciousness which permits a choice by the whole self; in other words the less able he is to become emotionally self-conscious, the less suited will he prove for a kind of therapy which depends on the possibility of substituting feeling, emotion, thoughtful voluntary behavior for unconscious irresponsible projection. (ibid.)

> . . . the over-impulsive child, especially if he is old enough to be classed as delinquent, may be too unable or too slow to reach the point of feeling and self-inhibition of impulse which is essential to forming a new relation to the object, and will perhaps require a discipline which is incompatible with a strictly therapeutic relationship. With such a child there is always the problem of how far he will have to carry the destructive behavior patterns before he is able to face and bear in himself, the need, pain, and fear which they seek to relieve. (ibid.)

Frederick H. Allen

In Allen's work at the Philadelphia Child Guidance Clinic we see continued the Rankian emphases on the dynamics of the therapeutic situation, the importance of the relationship between client and therapist, the capacity of the client to effect his own changes, the need for the therapist to be aware of the use which the client is making of him, the notion that during therapy the client casts off his 'neurotic selves' on the therapist, leaving him an individuated, unified person at the conclusion of successful therapy, and the importance of the ending phase of therapy.

It may be recalled that in evaluating Rank's contribution, it was stated that while his renunciation of the past for the present and of therapeutic content for dynamics was complete, his abandonment of the Freudian techniques of therapist-direction and interpretation was not, at least where the dynamics of will in the therapeutic situation were concerned.

The same comment may be made in regard to Allen, but with more certainty, since we have a much clearer record of his therapeutic technique (Allen, 1942).

One of Allen's most complete accounts of his method is the report of the ninth hour of 'a fearful child in therapy' (ibid.). In order to bring out more clearly what transpired in the therapeutic hour, the writer has taken the liberty of separating: (1) the remarks made by the therapist during the treatment session (Th), (2) the statements and actions of the child (10-year-old) during the hour (Ch), and (3) Dr Allen's evaluative comments (Com). The account follows:

Com: The ninth hour was a climactic interview which brought to a focus all that had gone into the preceding weeks. Solomon looked languid and worried, but maintained his customary rigorous control of feeling.

Th: The therapist commented on his worried appearance

Ch: but he was evasive and withdrew into a corner with a few toys.

Th: When this need to escape was mentioned,

Ch: he shrugged his shoulders saying, 'I just know I come here.'

Com: Knowing how important it was for him to face and experience the pain of this immediate reality, if he were to move beyond this protective barrier,

Th: the therapist again opened the discussion of what he was doing and how he was feeling about coming.

Ch: 'I think there is nothing to it — it doesn't make sense.'

Th: The therapist agreed with this if Solomon had to continue putting the whole job of getting well on the doctor.

Ch: With more anxiety he said, 'I don't know how to get well.'

Th: At this point the therapist reversed the emphasis and said: 'The harder job is being well and you are frightened now because you are closer to being well.'

Com: It was true that this new responsibility he was taking for himself meant a breaking up of the dependent bond to his mother, which he had maintained through sickness. Each step he made away from sickness meant a step toward a more mature relationship with the mother; it also meant establishing his relationship with his therapist on the basis of getting well and not by remaining sick.

Ch: As Solomon withdrew into solitary play

Th: the therapist discussed the tenacious way in which he clung to the idea of sickness. To be sick was to be safe as long as others would do the worrying.

Ch: He almost agreed with this,

Th: and the therapist then commented on how he was finding this experience different in that it gave him a chance to do part of the job, not just to take a bottle of medicine.

Ch: 'That didn't do any good,' Solomon said.

Th: The therapist agreed and added that Solomon was frightened at the moment because 'this was doing him some good.'

Com: The mother reported a great deal of change in her son but added that his tics were as bad as ever. Through these difficult therapeutic hours very few tics were noticeable.

Ch: Solomon was silent after this,

Th: and the therapist withdrew saying that he was there to help him further when he was ready for it.

Com: The directness of this discussion had pushed Solomon momentarily further into his shell.

Ch: But his play had more purpose and much more feeling and he made a vehement attack on the soldiers.

Th: The therapist commented on 'those soldiers getting a real punishing' and added that probably some of that anger was meant for him.

Com: That touched off the explosion and the barrier he had established to hold back his feeling melted.

Ch: In angry crying he blurted: 'I would rather be like I was than go through this.'

Com: He summed up so much in this statement, and showed how aware he was of change in himself and of the amount of anxiety that was stirred by his movement away from his tight and undifferentiated way of living. His anxiety was now concerned with a new responsibility for himself which sprang directly from his growing relationship with the therapist.

Ch: As the boy continued his angry outbursts of 'What's the use of all this?'

Th: the therapist was very gentle in his support.

Ch: Then suddenly in a tone that was more grieved than angry, Solomon remarked: 'You said you didn't care whether I went to bed alone or not.'

Com: This had happened in an earlier interview when he was trying to prove that by going to bed alone he was doing what the therapist wanted him to do. He was trying at that time to avoid any self-initiated responsibility in that change.

Th: The therapist replied: 'You are quite right, Solomon. I said that and meant it. I also said I did care about what you wanted and were ready to do about that — so if you are going to bed alone it is because you are ready and want to do it.'

Ch: He nodded agreement but maintained this struggle against his part in the changes that had been occurring. He repeated: 'I'd rather be the way I was. People told me coming here would make me well.'

Com: The fact that he was finding some truth in this but not on the pattern he had planned activated a more significant anxiety that emerged from his change. No doubt he was baffled, as anyone would be, who, in fighting against change, found he was participating in bringing it about.

        The force Solomon had put into these interviews was clearly revealed toward the end of this dramatic hour.

Ch: Again he said he didn't know how to get well,

Th: and we discussed the more important and harder task of knowing how to be well.

Ch: Following this he said: 'What do I have here that I don't have at home?'

Th: The therapist said: 'Your relation with me.'

Com: For a boy who had no attachment to anyone but his mother, this was too much and he let go with a final blast of his determination:

Ch: 'I will always be sick, nothing can make me well.'

Com: In effect, he was trying to deny his growing relationship with the therapist and to assert his desire to recapture the safer and undifferentiated relationship with the mother from which both he and his mother were moving away.

Th: His divided feeling about being well was discussed and it was brought out that he was ready for something different but that he had to fight against that readiness at the same time.

Com: Solomon really suffered in this hour. He was cringing in a corner and hardly moved an inch, but he could share his anger and fear and it had real meaning to him when at the end of the hour,

Th: the therapist said: 'Solomon, I think you and I are beginning to get somewhere.'

End of ninth hour.

The writer would evaluate this account as follows:

1. The therapist may be accepting Solomon as an individual who can help himself get well, but he is not accepting the boy's capacity to arrive at that insight himself; he is not accepting the expressed feeling that he does not know how to get well and needs the therapist to help him.
2. The therapist plays the role of interpreter of the dynamics of the child's will-conflict, and of the relationship of the child to the therapist and to the therapeutic situation in general.
3. Solomon resists all these attempts at interpretation, and in being forced to express his counter-will against the therapist's will, is given no opportunity to assert the positive will which would make for growth.
4. Any progress made by Solomon is dependent upon the therapist's interpretation (under Comments above) and is not apparent from the boy's statements and actions themselves. In this connection, the last statements of the boy and of the therapist may be contrasted.

The same lack of acceptance on the part of the therapist is demonstrated by the handling of the ending phase of treatment with this same boy. Allen apparently does not believe in Solomon's capacity to take the initiative in an explicit manner in the matter of discontinuing contacts. At the same time, the following quotation indicates that little progress has been made between the ninth and this, the fourteenth hour, in regard to whether the boy or the therapist will effect the cure:

> In the fourteenth hour, Solomon continued to emphasize that he came to be cured and 'there is nothing to do here.' In this hour he took less initiative, and the therapist commented that he seemed to be about through coming to the clinic. (Allen, 1942)

The same pattern of interpretation is repeated during the next hour:

> In the fifteenth hour Solomon was ready to discuss a plan for ending but he approached this negatively. He wanted to paint but said 'There are no paints,' and 'There is no paper.' To this the therapist commented: 'Sounds as if you don't think there is much here you want and you probably are about finished.' (ibid.)

We soon observe that initiative-taking by the therapist leads to difficulties. We are told that the fifteenth hour concluded with Solomon's decision to use the next time to settle on a definite ending date. But in the sixteenth hour, the therapist finds that he must remind him of 'last week's decision to get something important settled today'. Solomon stalled and asked 'what?'

> The therapist suggested he answer that and he made two totally irrelevant guesses. The therapist commented that Solomon was finding it hard to settle down and act on his readiness to end. He said nothing more but he played two good games of checkers.
>
> The question of termination was reopened by the therapist who commented on Solomon's anxiety in facing this question. He tried to reassure himself and asked: 'What is there to be afraid of?' The therapist replied: 'Because you are not quite sure you can hold the feeling of being well that you have gained right here.' He assented, saying, 'I wouldn't be sure I would be well.' The therapist agreed to the risk involved, and that ending would and did activate that uncertainty. With some help Solomon then settled on four more appointments. He was intrigued and relieved with this decision and talked about what he had missed at school through coming here. When the therapist suggested, 'Suppose you call your mother on the telephone and tell her of your decision', his first impulse was to do this. As he made the move to pick up the telephone, however, he retreated from this daring act. With a little encouragement he went ahead, asking for his mother, and before she answered he exclaimed: 'Gee, I'm scared.' When his mother answered, timidly he asked: 'Mother, how much longer shall I come?' The therapist broke in and said: 'Solomon, you're just trying to get your mother to decide what you have really decided.' So he blurted out: 'I am coming four more times.' She thought that was fine, and a look of the most intense relief was on Solomon's face as he hung up, saying in a surprised tone, 'She said it was all right.' (ibid.)

Thus we see the therapist taking an active role throughout, always staying close enough to Solomon to be able to push him up the next step.

> In the nineteenth and closing hour, Solomon states that he is all over his fears, but that he is still a little afraid of stopping, and 'he talked of the possibility of returning sometime "for a visit".' (ibid.)

Carl R. Rogers

Rogers is the first individual in the line of therapists we are considering — Freud, Rank, Taft, Allen, Rogers — who did not experience a personal working relationship with his predecessor. This may help to account for the fresh advances in nondirective theory and practice which we see in his work.

1. He introduced into therapy the systematic use of the 'recognition of feeling' response (Rogers, 1942).
2. In so doing, he cut through the maze of mystery which had surrounded the work of psychotherapists in general, regardless of orientation, and gave to the Rankian 'client-as-central-figure' philosophy a definite technique, which Rank, Taft, and Allen had pronounced impossible.
3. At the same time, he gave a new, more exact, and deeper meaning to the concept of 'acceptance' of the client.[2] The following quotation from Rogers is pertinent here:

> There has, of course, been lip service paid to the strength of the client and the need of utilizing the urge toward independence which exists in the client. Psychiatrists, analysts, and especially social case workers have stressed this point. Yet it is clear from what is said, and even more from the case material cited, that this confidence is a very limited confidence. It is a confidence that the client can take over, if guided by the expert, a confidence that the client can assimilate insight if it is first given to him by the expert, can make choices providing guidance is given at crucial points. It is, in short, the same sort of attitude which the mother has toward the adolescent, that she believes in his capacity to make his own decisions and guide his own life, providing he takes the directions of which she approves.
>
> This is very evident in the latest book on psychoanalysis by Alexander and French. (Rogers, 1946)

This quotation seems applicable to the work of Rank, and Allen, and to a lesser degree, Taft, as well as to that of the modern analysts. Rogers' greatest contribution, it is believed, lies in the fact that he made acceptance over from a concept which was tenuous and incomplete to one which is clear and total. It is an acceptance not only of the individual's capacity for growth, but of his ambivalence over growth and perhaps incapacity for growth at any given time. It is an acceptance of his feelings at the moment without the need for showing him the origin of these feelings (Freud), and without the need for showing him the use which he is making of them (Rank). It is a 'nondirective acceptance'.

---

2. The work of Axline (1947) in play therapy has helped to define the concept of acceptance. While Rogers' principles have been derived primarily through experience with adult clients, Axline's work furnishes a direct comparison with that of Taft and Allen.

4. As a corollary, the function of the therapist, with Rogers, becomes in contrast to the Freudian who seeks first to discover and then interprets to the patient patterns of behavior related to repressed infantile sexuality, and to the Rankian, who alerts himself to the manner in which the patient is relating to the therapeutic situation and then responds on that basis simply to recognize and accept the attitudes of the client at the moment. Rogers writes:

> We have come to recognize that if we can provide understanding of the way the client seems to himself at this moment, he can do the rest. The therapist must lay aside his preoccupation with diagnosis and his diagnostic shrewdness, must discard his tendency to make professional evaluations, must cease his endeavors to formulate an accurate prognosis, must give up the temptation subtly to guide the individual, and must concentrate on one purpose only; that of providing deep understanding and acceptance of the attitudes consciously held at this moment by the client as he explores step by step into the dangerous areas which he has been denying to consciousness. (ibid.)

5. The result of therapists' functioning in this manner, of their putting into practice this new concept of 'acceptance', has been a growing accumulation of evidence that clients can achieve insights and a happier, better integrated adjustment to living, without guidance. 'The individual is capable of discovering and perceiving truly and spontaneously the interrelationships between his own attitudes and the relationship of himself to reality' (ibid.). Here in a sentence is Rogers' distinctive contribution, with the word 'spontaneously' signifying the difference between him and the Rankians.[3]

With this growing evidence of people's capacity for self-help, and with the participation by Rogers and by his students and associates in more and more experiences in which clients have shown their capacity for self-help, the original philosophy that gave rise to the method of nondirective acceptance has steadily deepened into a conviction that people in mental turmoil need no more than to be accepted as they are. And with this growing conviction have come significant changes in the approach of the Rogers school, even in its short history. There is now a tendency to get away from an atomistic relating of client statement to the counselor response which immediately precedes it and to evaluate instead the genuineness of the counselor's accepting attitude; structuring, the intellectual explanation to the client of the nondirective counseling relationship, is recognized as undesirable; the list of criteria for acceptance of 'cases' for therapy (Rogers, 1942) has given way to the belief that in all people there is a degree of capacity for

---

3. The writer has not mentioned Rogers' pioneering work in making psychotherapy objective and amenable to research, but this contribution follows from his more basic discoveries, which are not as widely recognized.

spontaneous self-help; the client's concept of self is now believed to be the most central factor in his adjustment and perhaps the best measure of his progress in therapy.

Current trends in nondirective therapy
The client-centered attitude
Most of the significant changes within the movement of nondirective therapy during the past five years center around a growing appreciation of the importance of the client's internal frame of reference, for counseling and for the study of personality. This has been reflected in the increased application of the term 'client-centered' to nondirective therapy, a tendency which has been criticized by exponents of other methods on the grounds that all psychotherapies center their interest in the client and are thus 'client-centered'. The nondirective point of view on this issue is that to the extent that some other frame of reference than the client's is introduced into the therapeutic situation, the therapy is not client-centered. The Freudian introduces his own frame of reference into the therapeutic hour by virtue of his belief that he has a knowledge of the unconscious which is superior to that of his patient and which must be utilized in understanding him. The Rankian brings his own frame of reference into therapy with his belief that he has a superior knowledge of the dynamics of the therapeutic situation which must govern his behavior in it; this is carried to the point of not accepting certain attitudes which the client may express, and of not accepting the nonexpression of other attitudes. The nondirective therapist believes that where the counselor is concerned with his own frame of reference, he will be unable to provide a full and deep understanding of the client's feelings and perceptions.

Because this latter fact has been more and more clearly understood, there has been a de-emphasis on nondirective *techniques*, together with an increased appreciation of the importance of a nondirective *attitude*. Once we center our attention on the client's frame of reference, we cannot stop with counselor techniques, but must study the manner in which they are perceived by the client. Experience indicates that clients will pick up attitudes such as the desire of the counselor that a certain area be explored, and will react defensively as a result. This type of attitude may be conveyed through a 'loaded', and thus inaccurate 'reflection of feeling' type of response. As the counselor learns, through increased experience, that clients can progress when they are not guided he comes to have a more genuine nondirective attitude. He then is better able to concentrate on understanding the way things appear to his clients, and to forget about the employment of techniques. As long as the attitude is not genuine, not only will 'reflections of feeling' tend to be inaccurate, but directive techniques will creep into the counselor responses, so that even when the goal of the counselor is to be nondirective, recordings of his interviews will show that he is making interpretations, giving support, and utilizing other directive techniques.

The self-concept

Inevitably, with attention centered on the internal frame of reference, has come an appreciation of the significance of the most central portion of that frame of reference, the concept of self, for understanding personality and the changes in personality which occur in therapy. The self, as viewed both externally and internally, has at various times in the history of thought been in the forefront of philosophical and psychological discussion. Today, nondirective psychotherapists, as well as many other psychologists and sociologists devoted to the study of personality, are giving increased emphasis to the internal view of the self in explaining adjustment and behavior. Using modern methods of studying personality, including recorded psychotherapeutic interviews, it is possible that theories of the self, which have formerly died in discussion, may be tested against objective clinical data, and either pass into the realm of useful knowledge, or be discarded as unsupportable belief.

A recent comprehensive treatment of the concept of self, which is little known outside of the field of nondirective counseling, is an unpublished dissertation by Raimy (1943) entitled *The Self Concept as a Factor in Counseling and Personality Organization*. The experimental aspect of the study has been summarized in the literature (Snyder, 1947b). Turning to his theory, we may list some of the hypotheses advanced by Raimy to indicate how far he went beyond older and more orthodox theories of the self:

1. The self-concept is a learned perceptual system which is governed by the same principles of organization which govern other perceptual objects.
2. The self-concept regulates behavior. The awareness of a different self in counseling results in changes in behavior.
3. A person's awareness of himself may bear little relation to external reality, as in the case of psychotic individuals. Logical conflicts may exist in the self-concept for the external observer, but these are not necessarily psychological conflicts for the person.
4. The self-concept is a differentiated but organized system, so that even negatively valued aspects of it may be defended by the individual in order to maintain his individuality. The self-concept may be more highly valued than the physical organism, as in the case of the soldier who sacrifices himself in battle in order to preserve the positively valued aspects of his self-concept, courage and bravery.
5. The total framework of the self-concept determines how stimuli are to be perceived, and whether old stimuli are to be remembered or forgotten. If the total framework is changed, repressed material may be recalled.
6. The self-concept is exceedingly sensitive in yielding to rapid restructuring if the conditions are sufficient, yet it may also remain unaltered under conditions which, to the external observer, are violent conditions of stress. In counseling, the counselor tries to create a permissive atmosphere in which the client can drop his guard and look at the parts of the self-concept which are causing difficulty.

For some time before Raimy began to formulate his theory, Prescott Lecky (1945) at Columbia University had been quietly developing and applying a theory of self-consistency to explain human behavior. In evaluating what the self-concept theory cannot do, Raimy (1943) wrote that 'it provides primarily an "anatomy" to personality and not a physiology. The self-concept in itself is only a perceptual object and cannot be used to explain behavior . . . ' Lecky, with his self-consistency principle, would appear to be supplying a 'physiological' formula which could complement the 'anatomical' self-concept. This principle is implicit in much of Raimy's dissertation. Used in a much more explicit way by Lecky, we are helped to see more clearly *how* the self-concept maintains and changes its structure, *how* it regulates behavior, and so on. Raimy's emphasis is on answering the question 'what' in personality, while Lecky stresses the 'how'.

Rogers early realized the importance for therapy of the client's view of himself. For example, in 1940, he wrote: 'In the rapport situation, where he is accepted rather than criticized, the individual is free to see himself without defensiveness, and gradually to recognize and admit his real self with its childish patterns, its aggressive feelings, and its ambivalences, as well as its mature impulses, and rationalized exterior' (Rogers, 1940).

Stimulated particularly by Raimy, Lecky, Snygg (1941) and Snygg and Combs (1948), and through seeing the process of therapy with increasing clarity himself, the concept of self has assumed a place of central significance in psychology for Rogers (1947).

Research
Research has always been a significant part of the nondirective picture. Many of Rogers' students (Coombs, 1945; Covner, 1942a, 1942b, 1944a, 1944b, 1947; Curran, 1945; Fleming et al., 1947; Gump, 1944; Hobbs and Pascal, 1946; Muench, 1947; Peres, 1947; Porter, 1943; Raimy, 1943; Reid and Snyder, 1947; Royer, 1943; Sachs, 1946; Snyder, 1945, 1947a) have made research contributions to the understanding of the therapeutic process and of the dynamics of personality. In his comprehensive article interpreting the present status of psychotherapeutic counseling, Snyder (1947b) outlines the following principles which had been subjected to investigation by nondirective counselors up to July, 1947:

1. The recorded content of counseling interviews can be reliably analyzed by certain methods of categorization.
2. Counseling can be a systematic, orderly process rather than a casual or intuitive one.
3. The client's feelings change in a consistent fashion during nondirective counseling.
4. Various types of counselor activity precede and apparently cause certain client responses.
5. Investigators can study the personality of the client through analysis of the statements he makes during counseling.
6. Interrelationships between the various problems of the client are an important

factor related to the outcome of counseling.

7. It is feasible to compare different counseling techniques.
8. An experimenter can compare the responses of various counselors to a particular speech by the client.
9. The reasons for lack of success of a treatment method can be studied experimentally.
10. The follow-up is important as an indication of measurable personality changes brought about by counseling.
11. The group therapy process may be subjected to research analysis.

Important as its role has been in the past, research has a much bigger place within the field of nondirective therapy today than ever before. An examination of the present research activity reveals that much of it constitutes a beginning test of the usefulness of the internal frame of reference as a basis for studying psychological data. The analytic method used by Raimy in his dissertation was an example of this type of investigation and proved fruitful. The reliance on the internal frame of reference in nondirective therapy and the accumulation of therapeutic material based on it has led to the hypothesis that this may be the most substantial foundation upon which to build knowledge about people. Rogers (1947) stated the issue clearly:

> If we take first the tentative proposition that the specific determinant of behavior is the perceptual field of the individual, would this not lead, if regarded as a working hypothesis, to a radically different approach in clinical psychology and personality research? It would seem to mean that instead of elaborate case histories full of information about the person as an object, we would endeavor to develop ways of seeing his situation, his past, and himself as these objects appear to him. We would try to see with him, rather than to evaluate him. It might mean the minimizing of the elaborate psychometric procedures by which we have endeavored to measure or value this individual from our own frame of reference. It might mean the minimizing or discarding of all the vast series of labels which we have painstakingly built up over the years. Paranoid, pre-schizophrenic, compulsive, restricted terms such as these might become irrelevant because they are all based in thinking which takes an external frame of reference. They are not the ways in which this individual experiences himself. If we consistently studied each individual from the internal frame of reference of that individual, from within his own perceptual field, it seems probable that we should find generalizations which could be made, and principles which were operative, but we may be very sure that they would be of a different order from these externally based judgments about individuals.

This hypothesis received its first comprehensive formulation by Snygg (1941) in 1940, and is presently being elaborated by Snygg and Combs (1948). It is being tested in many of the research studies being carried on or recently completed by students of nondirective therapy. Some of these investigations, on the other hand, utilize an external frame of reference while a special research project being coordinated by the University of Chicago Counseling Center combines both external and internal measures of a group of ten completely recorded cases with pre- and post-test data and with follow-up information. There are presently about forty individual studies, in the following areas: analyses of the individual therapeutic process through the classification of client responses, analyses of changes produced in therapy through objective measures of the client before and after, evaluation of the counseling experience by the client, studies of counselor methodology, counselor personality, and the effect of training on counselors, studies which objectify group situations, and the application of nondirective principles to other fields.

Application to other fields
The usefulness of being able to see things from another's point of view obviously transcends the field of psychotherapy. Covner (1947) has recently described a systematic approach to the problems of an industrial psychologist which is based on an awareness of the attitudes of both management personnel and workers. The extension of the client-centered principle to the classroom, making for 'student-centered' teaching, represents an applied situation of extreme interest to nondirective people. Blocksma and Porter (1947) have described a training program for personal counselors which relied heavily on student initiative and on a continual awareness of student attitudes on the part of the instructors.

These are illustrations of how individuals who have been trained in nondirective therapy have been stimulated to transfer some of their attitudes to other situations in which human interrelationships are a factor. Much difficulty is encountered in carrying through this transfer because of the different factors operating in these 'applied' areas. But the conviction that the principle of recognition and acceptance of another's point of view is a potentially powerful one for the betterment of human relations supplies the motivation for continuing to seek the answers to the puzzling questions which surround application.

Summary
A cross-sectional study of the development of nondirective therapy has been attempted. Freud, within a fundamentally authoritarian framework, found it necessary to respect client attitudes to an increasing degree in order to make progress in therapy. Rank focused his attention on the phenomenon of resistance, and developed a theory of will and dynamics which completely displaced Freudian content as the factor of importance in psychotherapy. At the same time, Rank utilized directive methods in an effort to impress the dynamics of the therapeutic situation on the client. Taft and Allen have carried on the Rankian tradition in this country, and have published clear accounts of their therapeutic method. Rogers has given Rank's client-centered philosophy a definite technique and has made it

more meaningful and complete by accepting the client's expressed feelings at the moment in therapy and eliminating directive features of the Rankian method. Accompanying this more complete acceptance has been a greater concentration on the client's internal frame of reference. This has led to an increased emphasis on a nondirective *attitude* as opposed to nondirective *techniques*, to an appreciation of the importance of the self-concept as a factor in adjustment, to a greater stress on phenomenological methods of studying personality, and to the application of nondirective principles to other areas of human interrelationships.

References

Allen, F. H. (1942) *Psychotherapy with children*. New York: Norton.

Axline, V. (1947) *Play therapy*. Boston: Houghton Mifflin.

Blocksma, D. D. and Porter, E. H. Jr. (1947) A short-term training program in client-centered counseling. *Journal of Consulting Psychology*, *11*, 55–60.

Combs, A. W. (1945) Follow-up of a counseling case treated by the nondirective method. *Journal of Clinical Psychology*, *1*, 145–54.

Covner, B. J. (1942a) Studies in phonographic recordings of verbal material: I. The use of phonographic recordings in counseling practice and research. *Journal of Consulting Psychology*, *6*, 105–13.

Covner, B. J. (1942b) Studies in phonographic recordings of verbal material: II. A device for transcribing phonographic recordings of verbal material. *Journal of Consulting Psychology*, *6*, 149–53.

Covner, B. J. (1944a) Studies in phonographic recordings of verbal material: III. The completeness and accuracy of counseling interview reports. *Journal of General Psychology, 30*, 181–203.

Covner, B. J. (1944b) Studies in phonographic recordings of verbal material: IV. Written reports of interviews. *Journal of Applied Psychology*, *28*, 89–98.

Covner, B. J. (1947) Principles for psychological consulting with client organizations. *Journal of Consulting Psychology, 11*, 227–44.

Curran, C. A. (1945) *Personality factors in counseling*. New York: Grune and Stratton.

Fleming, L. and Snyder, W. U. (1947) Social and personal changes following nondirective group play therapy. *American Journal of Orthopsychiatry, 17*, 101–16.

Freud, S. (1924) Further recommendations in the technique of psychoanalysis. *Collected Papers*. London: Hogarth Press.

Gump, P. V. (1944) A statistical investigation of one psychoanalytic approach and a comparison of it with nondirective therapy. Unpublished Master's thesis, Ohio State University.

Hobbs, N. and Pascal, G. R. (1946) A method for the quantitative analysis of group psychotherapy. *American Psychologist*, *1*, 297. (Abstract)

Lecky, P. (1945) *Self-consistency: A theory of personality*. New York: Island Press.

Muench, G. A. (1947) An evaluation of nondirective psychotherapy by means of the Rorschach and other tests. *Applied Psychology Monograph*, No. 13.

Peres, H. (1947) An investigation of nondirective group therapy. *Journal of Consulting Psychology*, *11*, 159–72.

Porter, E. H. Jr. (1943) The development and evaluation of a measure of counseling interview procedures. *Educational Psychology Measurement*, *3*, 105–26, 215–38.

Raimy, V. C. (1943) The self-concept as a factor in counseling and personality organization. Unpublished doctoral thesis, Ohio State University.

Rank, O. (1929) *The Trauma of Birth.* Orlando FL: Harcourt Brace.

Rank, O. (1945) *Will therapy, and truth and reality.* New York: Knopf.

Reid, D. and Snyder, W. U. (1947) Experiment in 'recognition of feeling' in nondirective psychotherapy. *Journal of Clinical Psychology*, *3*, 128–35.

Rogers, C. R. (1940) The processes of therapy. *Journal of Consulting Psychology*, *4*, 161–4.

Rogers, C. R. (1942) *Counseling and psychotherapy.* Boston: Houghton Mifflin.

Rogers, C. R. (1946) Significant aspects of client-centered therapy. *American Psychologist*, *1*, 415–22.

Rogers, C. R. (1947) Some observations on the organization of personality. *American Psychologist*, *2*, 358–68.

Royer, A. (1943) An analysis of counseling procedures in a nondirective approach. Unpublished Master's thesis, Ohio State University.

Sachs, H. (1946) *Freud, master and friend.* Cambridge: Harvard University Press.

Sherman, D. (1945) An analysis of the dynamic relationship between counselor techniques and outcomes in larger units of the interview situation. Unpublished doctoral thesis, Ohio State University.

Snyder, W. U. (1945) An investigation of the nature of nondirective psychotherapy. *Journal of General Psychology*, *33*, 193–223.

Snyder, W. U. (1947a) A comparison of one unsuccessful with four successful nondirectively counseled cases. *Journal of Consulting Psychology*, *11*, 38–42.

Snyder, W. U. (1947b) The present status of psychotherapeutic counseling. *Psychology Bulletin*, *44*, 297–356.

Snygg, D. (1941) The need for a phenomenological system of psychology. *Psychology Review*, *48*, 404–24.

Snygg, D. and Combs, A.W. (1948) Book manuscript. Published in 1949 as *Individual Behaviour: A new frame of reference for psychology.* New York: Harper.

Taft, J. (1933) *The dynamics of therapy in a controlled relationship.* New York: Macmillan.

THE DEVELOPMENT OF THE 'PARALLEL STUDIES' PROJECT[1]

2

The purpose of this article is to provide the background of the 'parallel studies' project to which this issue of the *Journal of Consulting Psychology* is devoted. In the succeeding articles of this number, Seeman, Sheerer, Stock, Hoffman, Haigh, and Carr describe their individual studies while in the final paper, Raskin analyzes some of the major interrelationships discovered in the results of these investigations.

The project was begun in the autumn of 1947. Previously, there had been completed many objective studies of the process of psychotherapy, based on verbatim or near-verbatim data. Surveys of this research have been made by Rogers (1946, 1947, 1948b) and by Snyder (1947).[2] In the autumn of 1947, many new studies were getting under way. In Table 2–I are shown those of the new studies which were later to be included in the 'parallel studies' project.

Each of the investigators planned an *objective* research, involving the following steps:

1. The selection of one of more *concepts* which had proven helpful, on a subjective, empirical basis, for understanding the therapeutic process, and for communicating that understanding to others;
2. The development of an objective *measure* of the concept or concepts, so as to allow for (a) quantitative representation of the concept, and (b) investigation of the degree of agreement between different individuals using the measure;
3. The *application* of the measure to exact and meaningful clinical data, which in this group of researches meant counseling cases carried through and recorded electrically at the Counseling Center of the University of Chicago.

1. These studies could not have been made without the assistance of grants from the Social Science Research Committee of the Division of Social Sciences, University of Chicago. The grants were made from funds made available by the Rockefeller Foundation. They made possible the recording and transcription of the cases upon which these and other studies have been based, and financed the collaborative aspects of the research. This assistance is gratefully acknowledged by all concerned.
2. Recently, Rogers (1948a, 1948c, 1949) has summarized and discussed subsequent research, including the studies reported in this issue.

Originally published in the *Journal of Consulting Psychology,* (1949), *13(* 3), 154–6. Reprinted with permission.

TABLE 2–I

New Studies of the Therapeutic Process

Investigator	Concept Investigated
Hoffman	Maturity of behavior
Hogan	Defensiveness
Sheerer	Acceptance of and respect for self
	Acceptance of and respect for others
Stock	Feelings regarding self
	Feelings regarding others
Seeman	Pattern of counselor techniques in the course of therapy
(After Snyder, 1945)	Pattern of client content in the course of therapy
	Pattern of client feeling in the course of therapy

At the time that these studies were being planned, the Counseling Center had available for analysis about 20 completely recorded cases.[3] To meet their individual requirements, the investigators shown in Table 2–I were planning to analyze different combinations of these cases. For example, Sheerer wished to study seven successful cases, while Hogan was interested in an intensive analysis of two or three cases representing highly defensive clients.

It became clear that it would be advantageous to select one group of cases and subject it to each of the several methods of analysis. In this way, there would be afforded opportunities to (1) observe and measure quantitatively the relationships between different concepts, such as acceptance of self and maturity of behavior, and (2) achieve more detailed analysis of individual cases.

Accordingly, the group of cases described in Table 2–II was constituted as a 'research block' for parallel analysis by the studies shown in Table 2–I.

It has been noted above that the Counseling Center, at this time, had approximately twenty cases fully recorded and transcribed. The ten shown in Table 2–II were distinguished by the fact that they had the test data which is indicated in the last column of the table. This added the possibility of a sixth study, an analysis of the difference between the pre- and post-tests, to supplement the five researches of Table 2–I. Such an analysis, of the Rorschach tests, was subsequently carried out by Carr, and is reported in this issue.[4]

The only deliberate selective factor operating in the choice of the ten cases of the research block was completeness of data. However nine of the ten were

---

3. The total at the present time is approximately 40. In all instances the client was aware that the interviews were being recorded and agreed to this beforehand. A random procedure was followed in selecting clients to be 'research cases'.
4. An important aspect of the research program at the Counseling Center consists of follow-up interviews and tests approximately one year following the close of the . . .

TABLE 2–II

The Research Block of Cases

Name of Case	Age	No. of Inter- views	Coun- selor Rating*	Coun- selor	Pre- and Post-Tests
Miss Ban	21	9	8	A	Rorschach, Guilford-Martin
Mrs Dem	43	3	1	B	Rorschach, Guilford-Martin
Mr Far	30	7	9	C	Rorschach, Guilford-Martin
Miss Int	23	7	7	B	T.A.T.
Mr Que	30	7	5	D	Rorschach, Guilford-Martin
Mrs Sim	25	7	5	A	Rorschach, Guilford-Martin
Mr Sketch	24	3	1	E	Rorschach, Guilford-Martin
Miss Vib	28	9	9	B	T.A.T.
Miss Wab	19	3	5	A	Rorschach, Guilford-Martin
Mr Win	17	5	3	F	Rorschach, Guilford-Martin

* Scale of 1 to 9, representing over-all success in which 1 is the low and 9 the high end of the scale.

undergraduate or graduate students and the age range, correspondingly, represents a young group. Other important factors seem to be distributed randomly. It may be seen in Table 2–II that there are six female and four male clients in the group, that six different counselors were involved, and that both the length and the success of the cases are distributed quite evenly. The sixty interviews in the research block comprise a total of 6570 client statements and counsellor responses.[5]

The fulfillment of the plan to apply each of the methods of Table 2–I to the group of ten cases meant that, in most instances, other persons than the original investigator cooperated in the project in order that all of the cases might be covered. The names of the people associated with the application of each method to the research block are given in the individual reports which follow this introductory article. All of the people involved in completing the research were Counseling Center staff members or graduate students in the field of counseling.

The aim of the 'parallel studies' project may be stated as *the development of more objective ways of measuring personality organization as it may change in*

... research case. The follow-up interview is recorded, and is analyzed objectively in the same way that the original interviews were. A complete analysis of this follow-up data will be reported at a later date, although some of the follow-up Rorschachs are discussed by Carr in his article.

5. One of the sixty, the second interview in the case of Miss Wab, was damaged during the recording process, and is not included in the statistical analyses which are described in this series of papers.

psychotherapy, in such a way that different concepts which are meaningful in describing personality organization may be correlated.

Since the stress in this project is on the development of increasing objectivity in the study of the therapeutic process, it may be useful to quote the following statement made by Rogers (1948) in evaluating the objectivity of current research in nondirective therapy, of which the present project is a part:

> Since a majority of the studies upon which this paper is primarily based are as yet unpublished, a word is in order in regard to them. They are all studies based upon small numbers of cases. In several instances the analysis has been made of the hundreds of responses in but one electrically recorded series of interviews. In all instances the reliability of the objective procedures used in analyzing the material has been determined and while these reliability measures are sufficient to warrant considerable confidence in the results, they are not as high as might be desired. In general the studies bear the marks of their pioneering nature, being more satisfactorily objective than previous investigations in this field, but being still less rigorously objective than is desirable. It has been our experience in opening up the area of psychotherapy to objective scrutiny that fully scientific methodology must develop with experience.

This statement provides a good perspective in which to view the parallel studies which follow. It should be noted, however, in relation to the criteria of sample size and of degree of reliability used by Rogers in the above statement that ten cases were analyzed in each of these researches (except in Carr's Rorschach investigation, where there were nine) and that each of the five interview-analysis methods used in the project was shown to have a highly satisfactory degree of reliability, in comparison with previous attempts to analyze subjective material in an objective way.

References

Rogers, C. R. (1946) Recent research in nondirective therapy and its implications. *American Journal of Orthopsychiatry, 16*, 581–8.

Rogers, C. R. (1947) Psychotherapy. In W. Dennis (Ed.) *Current trends in psychology.* Pittsburgh: University of Pittsburgh Press, pp. 109–37.

Rogers, C. R. (1948a) The implications of recent research in therapy for personality theory. Paper read at American Psychological Association Symposium, Boston.

Rogers, C. R. (1948b) Research in psychotherapy. In Research in psychotherapy, round table 1947, *American Journal of Orthopsychiatry, 18*, 96–100.

Rogers, C. R. (1948c) The significance of the self-regarding attitudes and perceptions. Published as part of the Second International Symposium on Feelings and Emotions.

Rogers, C. R. (1949) Trends in the formulation of client-centered therapy. Paper given at the National Symposium on New Trends in Counseling and Psychotherapy at the University of Illinois, February, 25.

Snyder, W. U. (1945) An investigation of the nature of nondirective psychotherapy. *Journal of General Psychology, 33,* 193–223.

Snyder, W. U. (1947) The present status of psychotherapeutic counseling. *Psychology Bulletin, 44,* 297–386.

AN ANALYSIS OF SIX PARALLEL STUDIES OF THE THERAPEUTIC PROCESS[1]

3

In the writer's earlier article in this issue, it was pointed out that the 'parallel studies' method afforded opportunities to (1) study the relationships between different concepts, such as acceptance of self and maturity of behavior, by obtaining measurements of these in a number of cases and (2) achieve a detailed analysis of individual cases. The attempt will be made in this paper to fulfill these two objectives, in relation to the present series of investigations.

The parallel studies, in addition, have furnished three discrete ways of measuring success in therapy. These different types of estimates are based on (1) objective interview-analysis criteria represented by the measurement of concepts such as acceptance of and respect for self, understanding and insight, defensiveness, etc., (2) counselor ratings and (3) a comparison of pre- and post-Rorschach protocols. A supplementary aspect of this paper will consist of a brief comparative presentation of the results obtained by applying these three different evaluative methods to the ten cases of the research block.

The selection of measures to be correlated
For the purposes of the present paper, then, it was decided first to select from each study the one measure which appeared to be the most stable and at the same time most meaningful criterion of therapeutic progress. Table 3–I presents the

1. This integrative treatment was made possible only through the cooperative effort of the persons who originated and participated in the individual studies. They devoted time and effort much in excess of that required to complete their individual researches, in order that their results might be compared. Mr Robert L. Neville and the writer have worked together on the integrative aspects of the project from the time it began. The writer wishes to thank Dr Carl R. Rogers who has helped wisely, when and where help was needed most. Finally, to Drs Rogers and Julius Seeman, Messrs John M. Butler and Gerard Haigh, Miss Adassa Whitman of New York University, and Messrs. Daniel Casner, Sidney Fishman and Jerome Kosseff of the Veterans Administration, the writer is indebted for a careful reading of a preliminary draft of this paper, and constructive suggestions for its revision.

Originally published in *Journal of Consulting Psychology,* (1948), *13(*3), 206–20. Reprinted with permission.

TABLE 3–I

Five Different Measures of Counseling Progress selected from the Group of Parallel Studies

Concept and Investigator	*Explanation of Measure Derived from Concept*
Attitudes Towards Self* (Stock)	Each client statement included between two successive counselor responses and which referred to some aspect of self was rated on a 1 to 5 scale, as follows: 1. negative expressions, emotional in tone 2. negative expressions, objective in tone 3. objective expressions, in which it was difficult to detect either positive or negative evaluations by the client of himself. 4. positive expressions, objective in tone 5. positive expressions, emotional in tone An average score on this 1 to 5 scale was obtained for each interview.
Acceptance of and Respect for Self (Sheerer)	Each interview was divided into approximately 25 successive units to be rated on a 1 to 5 scale of acceptance and respect. A unit consisted of a single line of thought developed by the client. The scale increases in value from 1, which stands for no expression of acceptance and respect, to 5, standing for a high degree of acceptance and respect. A score was obtained for each interview by averaging the ratings given to its units.
Understanding and Insight (Seeman)	Client statements were classified according to the system devised by Snyder. A ratio was obtained for each interview as follows: $$\frac{YUI}{YUI + YSP} \times 100$$ in which YUI = the number of statements in the interview exhibiting understanding and insight** YSP = the number of statements in the interview classified as statements of problem
Maturity of Behavior Reported by the Client (Hoffman)	All references to behavior were selected from the client content of interviews. Each reference was rated C, B or A, according to whether the behavior was judged by the rater to be immature, partly mature or highly mature. Weights of 1, 2 and 4 were assigned to C, B and A references, respectively, and an average obtained for each interview.
Defensiveness (Haigh)	The number of reported and exhibited instances of defensive behavior in each interview was obtained. The following ratio was then calculated for each interview: $$\frac{Do}{De} \times 100$$

TABLE 3–I (continued)

in which

Do = obtained defensiveness, the total amount of defensive behavior in the interview. (See Haigh's Table I).

De = expected defensiveness, equal to the total number of instances of defensive behavior in the entire case divided by the number of interviews in the case.

*Hereafter, where abbreviation is desirable, this concept will be referred to as Self-Attitudes. Similarly, the other concepts will be designated as Self-Acceptance, Insight, Behavior and Defensiveness, respectively.

** The YUI category used here combines the YUI and YOC categories used by Seeman.

---

five concepts selected from the parallel studies in accordance with this principle, together with an explanation of the manner in which the concepts have been measured. Carr's Rorschach study has not been included in this procedure, because unlike the other studies, it does not provide data on each interview, and is therefore limited in the opportunities it presents for comparison with them.

The following explanation is offered for the selection of the five measures shown in Table 3–I:

Attitudes toward self

Stock measured two kinds of attitudes, those regarding *self* and those involving *others*. Summary scores of these are presented in Table 3–I of her study. Stock points out, however, that while 'there were always an adequate number of statements relating to the self' as the basis for the 'self' score, the score for 'others' was, in the case of many interviews, based on but a few references to others. Therefore, the measure of self-regarding attitudes was selected as the most stable and meaningful one in this study.

Acceptance of and respect for self

Here again the choice was between *self*-acceptance and acceptance of *others,* and the decision made in favor of the *self* measure because it was based on a consistently larger sample.

Understanding and insight

In Seeman's study a consistent drop in the course of therapy was found for the 'statement of problem' category while conversely, the insight categories revealed a consistent increase from beginning to end of therapy. Accordingly, Seeman used as an index of process a ratio involving these two types of content categories. This index was chosen for use here as the best measure of therapeutic progress to emerge from Seeman's study.

TABLE 3–II

Scores per Interview for each of the Five Parallel Measures

Case and Interview		Self-Attitudes	Self-Acceptance	Insight	Behavior	Defensive-ness
Miss Ban	1	2.0	1.7	2	1.3	3
	2	2.7	3.1	11	1.3	8
	3	2.6	2.9	0	3.3	7
	4	2.5	2.2	16	1.0	13
	5	2.9	3.8	7	1.7	7
	6	2.7	2.5	9	1.0	11
	7	2.8	3.4	16	1.2	7
	8	3.2	3.8	35	2.7	11
	9	3.0	4.1	35	1.8	20
Mrs Dem	1	2.4	2.5	19	1.0	15
	2	2.8	2.3	7	1.0	8
	3	2.8	3.1	6	1.4	8
Mr Far	1	2.5	2.0	10	2.3	20
	2	2.4	2.3	13	1.8	11
	3	3.2	3.8	91	—	5
	4	3.4	4.4	76	2.0	4
	5	2.8	2.7	27	2.3	11
	6	3.3	4.5	97	—	4
	7	3.4	4.7	80	—	7
Miss Int	1	2.5	2.1	0	1.5	15
	2	2.8	2.2	2	1.9	11
	3	2.3	1.7	0	1.4	11
	4	2.4	2.0	9	1.0	15
	5	2.8	3.6	27	4.0	4
	6	2.8	3.3	29	4.0	6
	7	3.6	4.9	100	2.5	6
Mr Que	1	2.8	2.0	16	2.0	—
	2	2.6	3.0	14	1.8	—
	3	3.0	3.5	4	2.0	—
	4	3.0	4.0	18	2.0	—
	5	2.9	4.0	0	2.0	—
	6	3.4	4.4	21	4.0	—
	7	3.2	4.6	16	—	—

TABLE 3–II (continued)

Case and Interview		Self-Attitudes	Self-Acceptance	Insight	Behavior	Defensiveness
Mrs Sim	1	2.6	2.6	0	2.3	5
	2	2.8	2.6	8	1.3	14
	3	2.6	2.8	4	1.0	18
	4	2.6	2.8	15	1.5	10
	5	2.9	3.1	27	2.0	11
	6	2.7	3.0	24	2.3	6
	7	3.0	2.9	36	2.3	6
Mr Sketch	1	2.6	2.4	6	—	12
	2	2.6	3.2	3	1.0	38
	3	2.9	3.1	36	1.2	19
Miss Vib	1	1.8	1.0	0	1.0	30
	2	2.4	1.6	0	1.0	7
	3	2.6	2.5	23	1.8	6
	4	2.8	2.2	14	1.5	5
	5	2.6	2.5	10	1.1	23
	6	2.3	2.1	10	1.0	7
	7	2.6	3.3	41	1.0	3
	8	3.1	3.7	32	1.6	7
	9	3.7	4.7	86	3.8	0
Miss Wab	1	2.8	2.9	10	1.1	11
	2 (damaged recording)					
	3	2.5	3.1	7	1.0	9
Mr Win	1	2.7	2.6	8	1.6	17
	2	2.8	2.7	4	2.4	10
	3	3.4	3.5	10	3.7	4
	4	3.1	3.4	15	—	21
	5	3.5	3.5	62	3.6	0

Maturity of behavior reported by the client
The results of Hoffman's analysis are summed up by an index of behavioral maturity, obtained for each interview. This same measure is used in this study to relate the behavior variable to the others.

Defensiveness
In the final section of Haigh's article, which deals with its limitations and

implications, he points out that a 'limitation of this study is the fact that detection of defensive behavior depends upon analysis of the values and concepts which the individual holds. But defensiveness often operates to prevent the person from revealing his most easily threatened concepts and values so that there is an unknown amount of defensiveness which we are unable to pick up via this method. Thus, for example, no defensive behavior is discerned in the case of Mr Que and yet it seems probable that Mr Que is operating consistently on a high level of defensiveness, to the extent that he never communicates any of his vulnerable values or concepts.'

The fact that clients vary considerably in the amount of defensiveness they bring to the counseling situation suggested an index of therapeutic progress in which there is a different baseline for each client, that baseline being represented by the total amount of defensiveness revealed by the client in the entire case. Such an index is described in Table 3–I.

Application of the five measures to the ten cases
Table 3–II shows the scores per interview obtained as the result of the application of the five measures defined in Table 3–I to the ten cases of the research block. The first three measures, self-attitudes, self-acceptance and insight, yielded a score for each of the 59 interviews. Six of the interviews were found to have no behavioral references. There is no defensiveness score for any of the seven interviews in the case of Mr Que, because the instrument did not bring out defensive behavior in any of them.[2] Applying the defensiveness measure of Table 3–I, a score of $^0/_0$ an indeterminate fraction, is obtained for each of Mr Que's interviews.

The first four measures may be designated as *positive* measures of counseling progress, in the sense that high scores obtained by their application are indices of good adjustment, while the defensiveness measure may be termed a *negative* one, since high scores with it mean a high level of defensiveness, which is presumed to be an index of poor adjustment.

Intercorrelations between the five parallel measures
Table 3–III presents the product-moment correlation coefficients between the five parallel interview-analysis measures. These coefficients are derived from the data in Table 3–II. All of them represent statistically significant relationships, as the correlation coefficient, in each case, is at least four times its probable error. The negative correlations which appear in the Defensiveness column are to be expected since it is the one negative measure of counseling progress in the group.[3]

---

2. See discussion above on the selection of the defensiveness measure.
3. The implications of these results for personality theory are considered below in the Discussion.

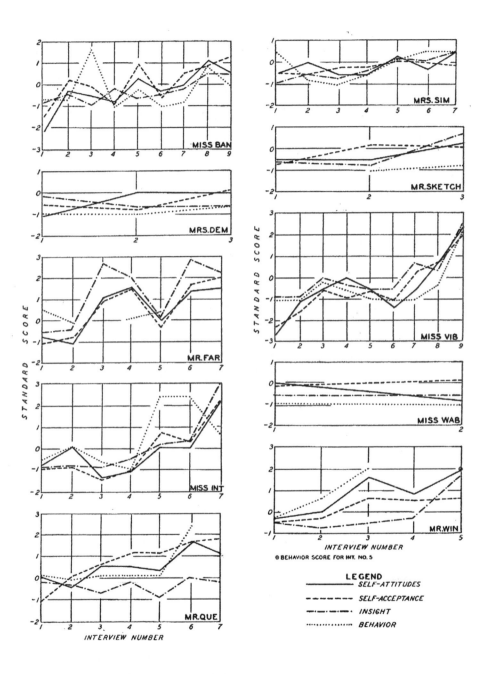

FIGURE 3–1 Four positive measures of counseling progress in the ten cases.

TABLE 3–III

Intercorrelations Between the Five Parallel Measures

	Self-Attitudes	Self-Acceptance	Insight	Behavior	Defensive-ness
Self-Attitudes		.86	.70	.61	−.40
Self-Acceptance	.86	—	—	.51	−.34
Insight	.70	.67	.67	.39	−.40
Behavior	.61	.51	.39	—	−.55
Defensiveness	−.40	−.31	−.41	−.40	—

The cases considered individually

The figures in Table 3–II were converted into standard scores, in order that each case might be represented graphically, with the five interview-analysis measures on the same scale. Figure 3–1 portrays the application of the four positive measures in each case. (The defensiveness measure is considered in a second group of graphs.) In a general way, it may be stated that these graphs evidence the high degree of correlation between the various objective measures which has been demonstrated in Table 3–III. This relationship is most striking in the cases of Mr Far, Miss Int, Mrs Sim, and Miss Vib, although in the cases of Mr Far and Miss Int, the behavior measure diverges significantly from the rest. Other instances of divergence are:

In the third interview of Miss Ban, where behavior rises to a level high above the other measures.

In Mr Que, where three of the four measures indicate definite improvement, but Seeman's (Insight) shows the client concluding at about the same point that he began, with minor fluctuations in the interval between the first and last interviews.

Other instances of divergence may be found, but on the whole, it may be said that Figure 3–1 presents a congruous picture of the level at which the clients began therapy, the level at which they concluded, and their course of progress during therapy.

The four positive measures seemed to parallel each other closely enough in Figure 3–1 to warrant their being combined and averaged to create one standard overall measure. In Table 3–IV, these overall figures are presented, together with the corresponding defensiveness scores for each interview.

Then in Figure 2 the data appearing in Table 3–IV have been graphed. Table 3–III demonstrated the negative relationship between defensiveness and the positive measures of therapeutic progress. In Figure 3–2 this relationship is shown to exist when the cases are considered on an individual basis. The cases of Mr Far, Miss Int, Mrs Sim, Miss Vib, and Mr Win give particularly striking evidence

TABLE 3–IV

Scores per Interview Obtained by Averaging the Standard Scores of the Four Positive Measures of Therapeutic Progress Compared with the Defensiveness Measure

Case and Interview		Mean of the Four Positive Measures	Defensiveness Measure
Miss Ban	1	−1.3	−1.1
	2	−.3	−.4
	3	0	−.6
	4	−.7	.3
	5	.1	−.6
	6	−.6	0
	7	−.1	−.6
	8	.9	0
	9	.6	1.3
Mrs Dem	1	−.7	.6
	2	−.6	−.4
	3	−.3	−.4
Mr Far	1	−.8	1.3
	2	−.6	0
	3	1.6	−.8
	4	1.4	−1.0
	5	.1	0
	6	2.0	−1.0
	7	2.0	−.6
Miss Int	1	−.8	.6
	2	−.4	0
	3	−1.1	0
	4	−.9	.6
	5	.8	−1.0
	6	.8	−.7
	7	2.0	−.7
Mr Que	1	−.4	—
	2	−.2	—
	3	.1	—
	4	.4	—
	5	.2	—
	6	1.4	—
	7	.9	—

Case and Interview		Mean of the Four Positive Measures	Defensiveness Measure
Mrs Sim	1	−.4	−.8
	2	−.4	.4
	3	−.6	1.0
	4	−.4	−.1
	5	.2	0
	6	.1	−.7
	7	.4	−.7
Mr Sketch	1	−.6	.1
	2	−.5	3.8
	3	.3	1.1
Miss Vib	1	−1.7	2.7
	2	−1.2	−.6
	3	−.3	−.7
	4	−.4	−.8
	5	−.6	1.7
	6	−1.0	−.6
	7	−.1	−1.1
	8	.4	−.6
	9	2.3	−1.5
Miss Wab	1	−.4	0
	2 (damaged recording)		
	3	−.6	−.3
Mr Win	1	−.4	.8
	2	−.1	−.1
	3	.9	−1.0
	4	.3	1.4
	5	1.5	−1.5

TABLE 3–IV (continued)

of this relationship, as does the cross-cutting, see-sawing picture presented in the case of Miss Ban, which brings out the existence of the relationship on an interview-to-interview basis especially well.

It will be noted, however, that while in the case of Miss Ban, there is a generally converse relationship between defensiveness and the mean of the four positive measures, both of these measures show a significant overall rise during the course of the nine interviews. This is also true in the case of Mr Sketch. On the other hand, in the case of Miss Wab, there is a slight decrease both in defensiveness and in the positive measures. Data of this type help to round out the picture of the ten cases provided by the five interview-analysis measures. It may be said that in

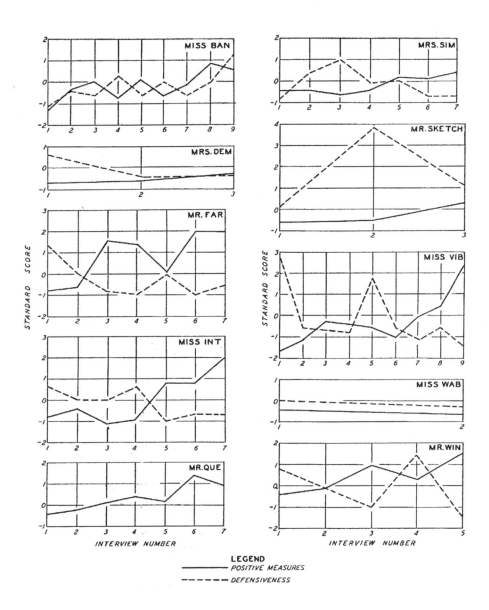

FIGURE 3–2 The mean of the four positive measures of counseling progress compared with the defensiveness measure in the ten cases.

the cases of Miss Vib, Mr Far, Miss Int and Mr Win there is a definite and significant improvement in attitudes held toward self and concomitant positive measures of therapeutic progress, at the same time that there is a sizeable decrease in defensiveness. The case of Mrs Sim follows this same general pattern, although here the increase in the positive measures and decrease in defensiveness is not of the same magnitude as is true of the first four cases. Mr Que shows a definite gain on the basis of the positive measures, but there are no data on defensiveness with which to round out the picture in this case. In Mrs Dem, there is a very slight increase in the positive measures, a rise which leaves her still on the negative side of the standard score scale, accompanied by a somewhat larger decrease in defensiveness. Then, as noted above, both Miss Ban and Mr Sketch exhibit a rise in attitudes held toward the self and concomitant positive measures together with an increase in defensiveness. By inference, it may be said that in the course of therapy in these two cases, a more integrated organization of attitudes was achieved, with the organization being of a defensive nature, designed to protect the self. Finally, in the case of Miss Wab, there is seen a decrease both in the positive measures and in defensiveness. Again, inferentially, the conclusion may be drawn that during her three interviews Miss Wab became less defensive, became more aware of negative aspects of herself, but chose not to explore them further.

The relationship between the objective measures of therapeutic progress, counselor ratings and Rorschach ratings

The data of the present study provided three different general methods of evaluating progress in the ten cases:
1. the scores yielded by the five parallel measures defined in Table 3–I;
2. the counselor rating of the case, on a 1 to 9 scale of overall therapeutic progress, with 1 representing no improvement and 9 standing for maximum improvement;
3. the comparison of the pre- and post-Rorschach protocols.

Tables 3–V through 3–VIII were computed in order to discover what relationships existed between these three different types of estimates of counseling progress.

In Table 3–V the first and last interviews of each case are compared with reference to the standard scores of each of the five parallel measures. Then in the last column is shown the mean difference between the first and last interviews of each case when all five measures are considered together. This provides a way of summing up the degree of progress in the cases on the basis of the five objective methods of interview analysis employed in the study.

In Table 3–VI these mean figures are duplicated and are shown beside the corresponding counselor ratings and the estimate of difference between the pre- and post-Rorschach protocols. This latter rating was made by an experienced Rorschach interpreter who rated each case along the following scale: Decrement — No significant change in either direction—Slight or moderate improvement—Significant or outstanding improvement.

TABLE 3–V

Differences in the Standard Scores of the Five Parallel Measures Between the First and Last Interviews of Each of the Ten Cases

Case	Self-Atti-tudes	Self-Acceptance	Insight	Behavior	Defensive-ness*	Mean
Miss Ban	2.7	2.8	1.3	.6	−2.4	1.0
Mrs Dem	1.1	.7	−.5	−.4	1.0	.5
Mr Far	2.4	3.1	2.8	—	1.9	2.6
Miss Int	3.0	3.2	3.9	1.2	1.3	2.5
Mr Que	1.1	2.9	0	—	—	1.3
Mrs Sim	1.0	.4	1.4	0	−.1	.5
Mr Sketch	.8	.8	1.1	—	−1.0	.4
Miss Vib	5.1	4.3	3.4	3.2	4.2	4.0
Miss Wab	−.8	.2	−.1	−.1	.3	−.1
Mr Win	2.2	1.1	2.1	2.2	2.3	2.0

*The direction of the defensiveness scores has here been reversed to correspond to that of the four other measures. Thus, the figure of −2.4 for Miss Ban means that she became more defensive between the first and last interviews.

TABLE 3–VI

Three Measures of the Degree of Improvement in the Ten Cases:
1. As obtained by averaging the five parallel measures (last column of Table 3–V)
2. The counselor rating of the case on a 1 to 9 scale of success, and
3. The estimate of the degree of improvement of the post-Rorschach test over the pre-Rorschach test

Case	Avg. Change in Interview-Analysis Measures Expressed in S.D.s	Counselor Rating	Rorschach Estimate
Miss Ban	1.0	8	Moderate improvement
Mrs Dem	.5	1	No improvement
Mr Far	2.6	9	No improvement
Miss Int	2.5	7	—
Mr Que	1.3	5	Moderate improvement
Mrs Sim	.5	5	Moderate improvement
Mr Sketch	.4	1	No improvement
Miss Vib	4.0	9	Moderate improvement
Miss Wab	−.1	5	No improvement
Mr Win	2.0	3	No improvement

The rating was made on the basis of the interpreter's overall impression of the differences between the pre- and post-protocols.[4] It may be noted from Table 3–VI that none of the cases was rated at either extreme of the Rorschach scale.

TABLE 3–VII

The Ten Cases Ranked for Degree of Improvement According to:
1. The five interview-analysis measures
2. Counselor ratings
(Derived from Table 3–VI)

Case	Interview-Analysis Measures	Counselor Rating
Miss Ban	6	3
Mrs Dem	7.5	9.5
Mr Far	2	1.5
Miss Int	3	4
Mr Que	5	6
Mrs Sim	7.5	6
Mr Sketch	9	9.5
Miss Vib	1	1.5
Miss Wab	10	6
Mr Win	4	8

In Table 3–VII, the cases have been ranked according to (1) the amount of difference between the first and last interviews on the basis of the five interview-analysis measures and (2) the degree of improvement indicated by the counselor ratings. There is a fairly close and consistent relationship here, the rank-difference correlation equaling .70, with a probable error of .11.

TABLE 3–VIII

Relationship between Rorschach Estimates of Improvement and the Degree of Improvement Derived from the Five Parallel Measures

	Interview-Analysis Evaluation			
Rorschach Estimate	Much Improvement	Moderate Improvement	Little or No Improvement	Totals
Significant Improvement	0	0	0	0
Slight or Moderate	1	2	1	4
No Improvement	1	1	3	5
Total	2	3	4	9

4. The manner in which these ratings were obtained is described in greater detail in Carr's article in this issue.

Table 3–VIII indicates the relationship between the Rorschach ratings and the estimate of improvement based on the interview-analysis measures. A statistically significant relationship does not exist here, the probability being great that the distribution could have been obtained by chance. Carr's article considers the relationship between Rorschach and counselor ratings.

Discussion
The project described here would seem to have considerable significance in relation to the problem of establishing psychotherapy on a scientific basis. Certain it is that these studies collectively make clear one pathway to the discovery of truth in this subjective and controversial field. This method may be seen as consisting of five steps:
1. The electrical *recording* of cases.
2. The definition of *concepts* which provide an understanding of these cases.
3. The development of objective *measures* of these concepts.
4. The *application* of these measures to the same case material.
5. The interrelating of the results of this application in order to (a) establish the relationships existing between the concepts and (b) obtain a well-rounded picture of individual cases.

The articles in this issue furnish a concrete demonstration of how these steps may be carried out. It is believed that this method of investigation is independent of the general orientation of the therapist and of the particular concepts he may employ in gaining an understanding of the therapeutic process.

The contribution of nondirective therapy to objectivity in psychotherapy
Having applied these objective procedures to cases treated nondirectively, it is now more possible to define operationally what nondirective therapists mean by a successful case. When the criteria of success are viewed together or in combined form, as they are in Table 3–V and in Figure 3–2, several preliminary generalizations concerning successful psychotherapy are suggested:

1. *On the nature of the improvement which constitutes successful psychotherapy*
   The successful client is one whose self-regarding attitudes are positive and objective, who accepts and respects himself as he is, who shows understanding of and insight into his problems, whose behavior is mature, and who is not defensive (each of these concepts being defined and having a known degree of reliability).[5]

2. *On the degree of improvement which constitutes successful psychotherapy*
   With the type of concept used in the 'parallel studies' an increase from the beginning to the end of therapy of 2½ or more standard deviations (as shown

---

5. The relationships between these concepts are discussed below.

in Table 3–V and in the graphs) represents a reorientation of the client's attitudes and behavior significant enough to be termed successful psychotherapy.

3. *On the point at which the client begins therapy in relation to success*
   There appears to be no relation between the point at which the client begins therapy (in terms of the interview-analysis measures of attitudes and behavior) and the degree of success of the therapy, judging from these cases.

4. *On the point at which the client ends therapy in relation to success*
   Clients who conclude therapy standing two or more standard deviations above the mean of objective criteria such as were used in the 'parallel studies' may be said to have achieved a satisfactory level of adjustment.

5. *On the course of successful therapy*
   In successful cases of psychotherapy, there is characteristically a dip in the client's chart of progress preceding the improvement in behavior and attitudes which ends in successful readjustment.

Let it be stated again that these generalizations are preliminary, not only for psychotherapy in general, but for nondirective therapy as well. As more cases are measured, and as they are measured more adequately, it is probable that not only the content of the generalizations, but their form will change.

The measurement of the counselor's participation in the therapeutic process has not been discussed in this paper but it has not been forgotten, as it forms an integral part of the process of introducing objectivity into psychotherapy. Porter's study (1943a, 1943b) marked the beginning of the objective study of counselor activity. Snyder (1945), Blocksma (1949) and Seeman, in his paper in this number, have continued to work in this area and have helped to refine the available measures.

If the present measurement of client and counselor activity continues, nondirective therapists will be able to state in an increasingly exact way what part they play in the therapeutic process and what results are achieved. In this way, they will be making their contribution to the establishment of psychotherapy as a scientific procedure.

The suggestion of a quantitative approach in this field at the present time may appear to be radical and to do violence to conceptions of psychotherapy which stress its subtle, subjective, attitudinal aspects. The quantitative treatment of psychotherapy described here is not in contradiction to these conceptions; it does not deny the subtleties, but proposes that they are describable, and describable in ways which can be measured.

The depth of the concepts in the present study
The concepts utilized by Stock, Sheerer, Seeman, Hoffman and Haigh constitute the basis and the limits of the objective results which emerge in this project. It

seems desirable therefore to give them at least brief consideration. One observation that may be made is that the concepts employed in the project vary in depth. Seeman observes in his paper that as the importance of the concept of self has been increasingly appreciated in nondirective therapy, individuals such as Sheerer and Hogan have come to evaluate therapeutic progress in terms of 'acceptance of self' and 'defense of self' in place of the 'understanding and insight' category used first by Snyder and now in Seeman's study. This makes possible a richer understanding of the counseling process and of the individual's personality organization. The process of developing more meaningful concepts is a continuing one, so that while the present group of parallel studies was being carried out, a deeper understanding of nondirective therapy has been achieved through the emergence and clarification of other concepts. An illustration of this is the concept of 'locus of evaluation' described by Rogers (1948a) in a paper at Harvard in the summer of 1948. As applied to the counselor-client relationship, it means that in nondirective therapy, the counselor does not set himself up as the judge of what the client should achieve, but leaves the latter free to develop his own values and standards. The phrase as applied to the process of adjustment within the client himself means that a more satisfactory adjustment is achieved as the client comes to realize and to put into practice the realization that he need not be dependent upon the expectancies and evaluations of others, but that he is capable of developing and following his own standards of behavior. This 'locus of evaluation' or 'self-responsibility' factor is one which predominates in Sheerer's definitions of 'acceptance of and respect for self'. However, Sheerer's concept of 'acceptance of and respect for self' includes at least two other factors as well, one being the willingness to accept aspects of the self formerly not seen or denied and the other being the degree of worth with which the self is regarded. All three of these factors which seem to be encompassed by Sheerer's concept, as she defines it, are important ones and have given a meaningful picture of therapeutic progress when combined, but the extent to which any one of them has influenced the score for an interview on 'acceptance of and respect for self' is unknown.

To summarize, then, it may be said that (1) some of the concepts used in this study have more depth and meaning than others, (2) those which have developed recently out of self-theory seem to be the more meaningful ones, and (3) there is some new conceptual thinking in nondirective therapy which has not as yet been tested by objective research. It may be added that there are, undoubtedly, concepts in use by therapists of other orientations which are more meaningful than some of those which make up the 'parallel studies' project, but which have not as yet been validated in objective ways.

The validity of the measures
In considering the type of study which has been presented here, it is important to evaluate not only the depth of the concepts employed, but the adequacy with which they have been measured. One could grant, for example, that defensiveness is an important variable in personality organization and yet question the use of

scores furnished by the Hogan and Haigh instrument as a measure of it. In the 'limitations and implications' section of his article, Haigh discusses the limitations of the present instrument and gives his views on the direction he believes necessary for the development of a more adequate measure of the concept of defensiveness.

Haigh raises the important question, too, of the relationship between the measure of a personality variable in the interview situation and the real value of that variable in the individual's personality organization. In the present project, this question must be faced squarely, because we wish our results to enable us to draw conclusions about the relationship, for example, between acceptance of self and defensiveness, not only in the counseling situation, but as general psychological variables in the individual's total scheme of adjustment and behavior.

On this basis the writer's estimate of the validity of the five interview-analysis measures utilized in this paper is as follows:

Self-attitudes — A very valid measure of the affect and degree of objectivity with which the individual regards himself.

Self-acceptance — A good measure of three aspects of the individual's perception of himself, combined. These three aspects are (1) the degree of worth with which the individual regards himself, (2) the degree to which the individual permits the standards and values of his behavior to reside in himself, rather than in others, and (3) the degree to which the individual is able to accept parts of himself which he would be likely to deny or distort in order to defend his status.[6] As it is likely that these three aspects correlate highly with each other, Sheerer's measure, which combines them, remains a highly useful instrument. At the same time, separate measures of the three probably would advance our knowledge and understanding of self-perception.

Insight — A good measure of the individual's degree of understanding of himself and of the degree to which he gains control over his problem-situations.

Behavior — A fair measure of the degree of maturity which the individual is exhibiting in his behavior which might be strengthened either by obtaining a more systematic report by the client of his behavior or by observation of the subject in experimental behavior situations.

Defensiveness — A fair measure of this concept, which would be strengthened considerably by the preliminary or supplementary study of the individual's values and concepts suggested by Haigh.

In general, it may be said that the data of counseling interviews are richest in material relating to the ways in which the individual perceives himself. If self-regarding attitudes and the self-concept prove to be as significant as appears now, then counseling data will be established as a very important source of raw material for the study of personality, and the discovery of better ways to analyze such data will be essential.

---

6. Rogers (1948c) also has analyzed Sheerer's 'acceptance of self' concept into these three components.

Implications for personality theory

What light, if any, is thrown on personality theory, as a result of this study? One implication of the findings presented in Table 3–III and in the analysis of the individual cases seems clear. The statistically significant correlations found to exist between all of the different concepts chosen for study represent substantial evidence for the unitary nature of personality organization and for the consistency principle in the relationship between personality and the process of adjustment. Clearly emerging from the data is the tendency for any given aspect of personality and behavior to change at about the same time as other aspects, and in an appropriate direction. Increase in understanding, attitudinal reorganization, behavior which is more mature and less defensive, proceed together.

The main approach to the study of attitudinal reorganization in this series of investigations has been via the concept of self. The demonstrated feasibility of studying self-attitudes together with the close relationship that has been shown to exist here between self-attitudes and other psychological variables constitutes another implication of this research. Attitudes toward the self seem undoubtedly to be of major importance in personality and the adjustment process. Are they more fundamental than other psychological variables? The findings suggest that this may be true; Rogers in his introduction to this group of papers states that 'it seems more than an accident that Stock's measure of self-attitudes shows the highest degree of intercorrelation with all the other methods of measuring therapy which are used in this series of studies'. A cautious interpretation of the results, however, does not allow us to go much beyond the conclusion that self-regarding attitudes, acceptance of and respect for self, understanding and insight, and behavioral maturity all tend to increase together at the same time that defensiveness decreases, without providing an answer as to which of these is most basic or fundamental or causal.

If, however, the results are utilized as a basis for speculating as to what occurs in therapy as the client moves from an unhappy state of affairs to one in which his outlook is positive, this sort of theory might be advanced: in the course of therapy, as the individual wrestles with his problems, he gains a greater understanding of his total situation. This understanding is centered around an increased appreciation of the role that he himself can play in his total adjustment. He sees that he does not have to be governed by the judgments and expectations of others, but can rely on his own values and standards. Along with this, his perception of himself as a person with little or no worth changes. At the same time that his self-regarding attitudes become more positive, they remain objective. Whereas, formerly, he needed to deny or distort certain aspects of his experience (including his experience of himself) in order to protect or bolster the self regarded as inferior, he becomes increasingly able to look realistically at and accept such experiences. He learns that he need not defend himself, but that he can be more natural and spontaneous. At the same time, his behavior becomes more mature as it becomes founded increasingly on values derived from his own experience, and less upon values introjected from others whom he had regarded as more worthy than himself.

This theory is derived from the concepts which have formed the basis of this article.[7] In three recent papers on personality and therapy, Rogers (1948b,1948c,1949) has drawn upon many other researches in addition to the 'parallel studies' and has related self-regarding attitudes, not only to the variables considered above, but to attitudes toward others,[8] physiological measurements, and many other concepts.

Summary and conclusions

1. A parallel, multi-conceptual, objective analysis has been made of one group of ten recorded counseling cases.
2. It has been found feasible to obtain for any given treatment interview, quantitative representations of such varied concepts as acceptance of and respect for self, defensiveness, maturity of behavior and insight.
3. Significant and positive relationships have been demonstrated to exist between each pair of the following concepts: self-regarding attitudes (on a positive-objective-negative scale), acceptance of and respect for self, understanding and insight, and maturity of behavior. A significant converse relationship has been demonstrated to exist between defensiveness and each of these positive measures of therapeutic progress.
4. These measures, applied to each interview of an individual case, provide an integrated and meaningful picture of the level of adjustment at which the client began therapy, the level at which he ended, and the course of therapy between these two points.
5. A significant relationship exists between the counselors' estimates of success in these ten cases and the degree of success based on the five interview-analysis measures.
6. Significant relationships were not found to exist between Rorschach results and the results of the five interview-analysis measures.
7. The 'parallel studies' approach, as exemplified by the present project, appears to establish one pathway to the establishment of psychotherapy on a scientific basis. It is a methodology which is not dependent on any particular type of therapy.
8. The concepts and measures employed in this study, while subject to the limitations of reliability and validity characteristic of new research tools, have

---

7. The Rorschach data of this study have not been utilized in this conception of the therapeutic process. It is hoped that at a later date a skilled person will fit the Rorschach data available on many Counseling Center cases into a reliable theory of adjustment. Such a task has been made considerably easier by the recent development by Reader (1948) of an instrument in which Rorschach protocols are reduced to dimensions which have been useful criteria of therapeutic progress.

8. A significant relationship between self-attitudes and attitudes toward others was found independently by Seeman, Sheerer and Stock in the present series of investigations. The profound implications of this relationship are discussed in Sheerer's paper.

yielded results which are sufficiently consistent and meaningful to suggest preliminary generalizations in quantitative and qualitative terms about successful psychotherapy, and to provide a sounder basis for the thinking about personality organization which has evolved out of experience in client-centered therapy.

References

Blocksma, D. D. (1949) An experiment in the learning of a counseling viewpoint. Unpublished PhD dissertation, Committee on Human Development, University of Chicago.

Porter, E. H. Jr. (1943a) The development and evaluation of a measure of counseling interview procedures. I. The development. *Educational Psychological Measurement, 3*, 105–26.

Porter, E. H., Jr. (1943b) The development and evaluation of a measure of counseling interview procedures. II. The evaluation. *Educational Psychological Measurement, 3*, 215–38.

Reader, N. (1948) An investigation of some personality changes occurring in individuals undergoing client-centered therapy. Unpublished PhD dissertation, University of Chicago.

Rogers, C. R. (1948a) Divergent trends in methods of improving adjustment. *Harvard Education Review, 18*, 209–19.

Rogers, C. R. (1948b) The implications of recent research in therapy for personality theory. Paper read at American Psychological Association Symposium, Boston.

Rogers, C. R. (1948c) The significance of the self-regarding attitudes and perceptions. Published as part of the Second International Symposium on Feelings and Emotions.

Rogers, C. R. (1949) Trends in the formulation of client-centered therapy. Paper given at the National Symposium on New Trends in Counseling and Psychotherapy at the University of Illinois, February 25.

Snyder, W. U. (1945) An investigation of the nature of nondirective psychotherapy. *Journal of General Psychology, 33*, 193–223.

AN OBJECTIVE STUDY OF THE LOCUS-OF-EVALUATION FACTOR IN PSYCHOTHERAPY

4

The counselor's attitude

The phrase 'locus-of-evaluation' was originated by Blocksma (1949) during an experimental study of the learning of client-centered counseling in a training course conducted for Veterans Administration Personal Counselors. Blocksma's use of the concept was an adaptation of Hartwell's (1931) thinking in his approach to the treatment of delinquent children. In analyzing samples of counseling of men in training, Blocksma differentiated, with a proven degree of reliability, between counselor responses which indicated that the counselor was *thinking for* the client, those which showed him *thinking about* the client, and those in which he *thought with* the client, or a combination of these.

How do these phrases relate to the concept of locus-of-evaluation? When the counselor thinks for or about the client, he is evaluating the client on the basis of his own system of values, a frame of reference external to the client. The locus-of-evaluation is in him, the counselor.

When, however, the counselor thinks with the client, he is attempting to leave his own values, his own frame of reference out of it. He is relying exclusively on the client's internal frame of reference; therefore, it may be said that the locus-of-evaluation is in the client, when the counselor is thinking with him.

These distinctions are illustrated and elaborated in two papers by Rogers (1948; 1949a).

The client's personality organization

In addition to being used for describing the counselor's view of his relationship to the client, the concept of locus-of-evaluation has been utilized as an important dimension of the personality organization of clients.

In the cases recorded by client-centered therapists, it is found that clients often begin counseling by reporting or exhibiting an excessive dependence on the evaluations of others. Success in therapy, as judged both by the client and

This paper is based on the dissertation of the same title submitted for the degree of Doctor of Philosophy at the University of Chicago in 1949. Published in (1952) W. Wolff and J. A. Precker (Eds.), *Success in psychotherapy,* New York: Grune and Stratton. Reprinted with permission.

counselor, is often associated with the client's coming to feel that the difference between self-evaluation and being dependent on the judgments of others is an important one. This is illustrated by the following interchange during the seventh interview of a nine-interview case with a young woman:

> Client: Well, it seems, as I look at it now, it seems that that was probably part of the whole pattern I followed of meeting expectations of others, rather than having a very firm and strong conception of what I really wanted in myself.
>
> Counselor: Perhaps it all hung together in one piece of trying to satisfy others rather than having some strong set of internal values or standards.
>
> Client: (Pause) Well, somehow, something is apparently making me ah . . . find it less important to ah . . . to measure up to the standards that other people set, or that I *think* other people have set, that's probably more it. I don't know which it is. Yet I still haven't substituted some of my own. And that's what I need.

This insight, arrived at gropingly, is one which has much meaning for the client, apparently, for she builds on it and soon (in the following interview, seven days later) reports behavior which is in line with her new attitudinal orientation:

> Client: . . . I mean I'm not doing anything drastic. I haven't taken any great steps by leaps and bounds. But, well, one of the girls lives on my floor and she would come and knock on the door and say, ah, that she wanted to eat lunch, or let's eat lunch at twelve, or all of us are going down to eat at twelve. Well, it used to be hard for me to say, 'Well, no, I would like to eat at twelve-thirty, ah, so I can have lunch and go to my one-thirty class.' And so I'd stop whatever I was doing and drag down at twelve with the group. Well, now I say, occasionally, 'Well, that isn't convenient for me. I'd rather eat later,' or 'I'd rather eat earlier.' Well, ah, before it was easier for me to say, 'OK I'll go ahead and eat, now.' And then another thing is that ah, with the group of kids that I was eating with, I felt that I had just sort of been dragged into the group, almost. They weren't people who . . . one or two of them were people that I really liked, and they had sort of pulled me in with a group of their friends that I wouldn't have picked, myself, especially. And ah, so that I found that all my time was being taken up with these people, and now I'm beginning to seek out people that I prefer myself, I mean people that I choose myself, rather than being drawn in with the bunch.

It is with this type of readjustment that the client ends therapy, feeling that she can now meet her problems independently.

An excellent generalized description of the individual at the positive end of the locus-of-evaluation dimension has been given by Sheerer (1949) as part of her 20-point definition of an individual who exemplifies self-acceptance and respect. Four of the points pertain directly to locus-of-evaluation.

1. The individual who expresses acceptance of and respect for self has internalized certain values and principles which serve as a general guide for behavior. He relies upon this guide, rather than conventions or standards of other individuals. (Note: This does not imply self-sufficiency. Nor does it imply that the internalized values and principles are necessarily different from the conventions or standards of others.)

2. He may modify his behavior in order to avoid trampling on the feelings or rights of others but he does not modify his behavior out of irrational fear of the judgment of others.

3. When he has acted on his own standards:
   a. If others pass judgment against him, although he may regret their action, he will not regret having acted on his own standards, nor will he abandon his standards merely because someone else has passed judgment against him.
   b. He does not exhibit a need to make excuses for his behavior.
   c. He does not condemn himself if he fails to meet standards for behavior which others hold if those standards are not his own, even though others may condemn him.

4. When others criticize his behavior he evaluates the criticism objectively and does not become upset by it.

The writer would like to direct attention especially to the Note contained in the first definition. The most difficult barrier in the acceptance of the locus-of-evaluation concept has been the misunderstanding that it implies a complete independence of other people and of cultural values. But Blocksma, Rogers and Sheerer do not deny that individual values develop out of interaction with other people and that healthy adjustment goes hand in hand with a positive relationship with others. It is simply that there is a difference between relating to social values objectively and creatively, and conforming to them in a slavish and dependent way, or opposing them in an emotional and aggressive fashion. Clients report such a difference and, through their experience, it appears that inner peace and a feeling of integrity are associated with the former pattern of adjustment, and that discontent and fear are the concomitants of the latter type.

The present investigation is an attempt to study objectively the locus-of-evaluation factor in the personality organization of clients as they proceed through therapy. Up to this point we have stated some beliefs about these concepts. But, can these beliefs be transformed into knowledge? Can the concept of locus-of-evaluation be reliably identified and measured? Is there in fact a shift from 'others' to 'self' in locus-of-evaluation as therapy proceeds? And if objective measures of this concept are found to be reliable, what is their relationship to measures of other variables deemed to be important in personality organization?

The population and general research plan

The population consisted of the same group of cases analyzed in the original 'parallel studies' project of the Counseling Center of the University of Chicago (Rogers et al., 1949) Table 4–I gives the characteristics of this population:

TABLE 4–I

The Research Block of Cases

Name of Case	Age	No. of Inter- views	Coun- selor Rating*	Coun- selor	Pre- and Post-Tests
Miss Ban	21	9	8	A	Rorschach, Guilford-Martin
Mrs Dem	43	3	1	B	Rorschach, Guilford-Martin
Mr Far	30	7	9	C	Rorschach, Guilford-Martin
Miss Int	23	7	7	B	T.A.T.
Mr Que	30	7	5	D	Rorschach, Guilford-Martin
Mrs Sim	25	7	5	A	Rorschach, Guilford-Martin
Mr Sketch	24	3	1	E	Rorschach, Guilford-Martin
Miss Vib	28	9	9	B	T.A.T.
Miss Wab	19	3	5	A	Rorschach, Guilford-Martin
Mr Win	17	5	3	F	Rorschach, Guilford-Martin

* Scale of 1 to 9, representing overall success in which 1 is the low and 9 the high end of the scale.

A further description of the population is given in the following quotation from the 'parallel studies' report (Raskin, 1949a):

> It has been noted above that the Counseling Center, at this time, had approximately 20 cases fully recorded and transcribed. The ten shown in the table were distinguished by the fact that they had the test data which are indicated in the last column of the table . . .
>
> The only deliberate selective factor operating in the choice of the ten cases of the research block was completeness of data. However, nine of the ten were undergraduate or graduate students and the age range, correspondingly, represents a young group. Other important factors seem to be distributed randomly. It may be seen in the table that there are six female and four male clients in the group, that six different counselors were involved, and that both the length and the success of the cases are distributed quite evenly. The 60 interviews (59 available for analysis because of one damaged recording) in the research block comprise a total of 6,570 client statements and counselor responses.

The present study consisted of the following steps:

1. A determination was made of the degree of reliability with which client statements in electrically recorded interviews could be identified as pertaining to the locus-of-evaluation factor.
2. A four-step locus-of-evaluation scale was constructed with three client statements illustrating each step. At one end of the scale were items which exhibited clearly a locus-of-evaluation residing outside of the client; at the other end were items which clearly exemplified a locus-of-evaluation residing within the client.
3. The degree of reliability of the application of the scale was determined by calculating the amount of agreement obtained between different judges in rating new items along the locus-of-evaluation scale.
4. The scale was applied to the ten cases of the research block described above, in such a manner that a locus-of-evaluation score was obtained for each of the 59 interviews.
5. The scores in the ten cases were analyzed to determine what changes occurred along the locus-of-evaluation dimension.
6. Correlation coefficients were calculated between the locus-of-evaluation scores of the same interviews for self-acceptance and respect, self-regarding attitudes, understanding and insight, maturity of behavior and defensiveness, which were obtained in the original 'parallel studies' project.
7. Evidence was obtained regarding the validity of locus-of-evaluation scores as a measure of therapeutic success by comparing them with counselor ratings, pre- and post-test results, and other objective ratings of the ten cases obtained previously.

The construction of a locus-of-evaluation scale

Prior to constructing the scale, it was thought desirable to determine the reliability of selection of locus-of-evaluation items. Three interviews were selected, each from a different case; they represented early, middle and late interviews in their respective cases. The investigator examined each client statement contained between successive counselor responses and selected those which appeared to him to help answer the question: 'In reference to his own thinking, feeling and behavior, is the client relying upon the judgments and expectations of other people, or upon his own values and standards?' Two other judges were asked to perform the same task.[1] The agreement of the investigator with each judge for the individual interviews ranged from 81 per cent to 88 per cent. Both the degree of agreement and the consistency of the results were considered to be satisfactory and to justify moving on to the next step of the research procedure. This next step is actually the construction of the scale itself.

---

1. For help in this part of the study, in constructing the scale, and in checking the reliability of application of the finished scale, the investigator is indebted to Miss Essilyn Rudikoff and Mr Eugene R. Streich.

The next step was to send a group of 22 client statements, each one representing a locus-of-evaluation item according to the unanimous opinion of the two judges and the investigator, and selected to provide a wide range of values, to 20 judges, with the following instructions:[2]

> I am enclosing 22 statements, each one dittoed on a separate card. The task is to arrange these cards in four separate piles, as follows:
>
> In the piles on the left, place those cards which indicate that in his thinking, feeling or behavior, the person making the statement is governed by the judgments and expectations of others and subordinating his own values and standards. Pile No. 1 should include statements which indicate a greater reliance upon the evaluations of others than those which are placed in Pile No. 2.
>
> Similarly, in the piles on the right, place those statements which indicate a reliance upon the values and standards of the speaker himself, rather than a dependence upon the evaluation of others.
>
> The statements should be distributed in such a way as to make the distances between successive piles approximately equal. Thus, the distances between Piles No. 1 and No. 2, No. 2 and No. 3, and No. 3 and No. 4, with respect to the 'locus-of-evaluation' dimension, should all be about the same.

The purpose of obtaining ratings in this way was to provide finally a set of items which could illustrate different points along the locus-of-evaluation dimension between 'others' and 'self', and which could represent these points in a reliable and unambiguous way. The procedure used here is an application of Thurstone's (Guilford, 1936) Method of Equal-Appearing Intervals.

On the basis of the ratings of the 20 judges, 12 of the 22 items were selected to illustrate the scale. These 12 statements, made up of four groups of three to represent each of four steps on the scale, were selected because the judges showed little disagreement in rating them, and because of the investigator's desire to have different types of items represented on the scale.

The 12 items of the scale, plus the investigator's subjective evaluation of the characteristics of each step, are shown in Table 4–II.

Table 4–II is so organized that the characteristics listed are not meant to match the illustrations on a one-to-one basis. Rather, the illustrations for each step suggested a gestalt in relation to the locus-of-evaluation concept, and the step characteristics represent the writer's attempt to describe those gestalts.

---

2. The following individuals kindly assisted in this phase of the research: Edyth Barry, Russell Becker, Paul Bergman, Paul Bowman, Daniel Casner, Paul Eiserer, Gerard Haigh, Jerome Kosseff, George Muench, Owen Otto, Robert Roessler, Essilyn Rudikoff, Julius Seeman, Elizabeth Sheerer, Bernard Steinzor, Dorothy Stock, Eugene Streich, Austin Wood, Walt Yoder and Philip Zlatchin.

With the establishment of the scale, the investigator was equipped with an instrument, substantially objective in its development and operationally defined, which could be applied to interview protocols and yield quantitative measures of the concept of locus-of-evaluation.

TABLE 4–II

The Locus-of-Evaluation Scale

Step No.	Illustrations of Step	Characteristics of Step
1	I always get very much embarrassed when I'm eating — especially cutting meat [because of a deformed hand]. If I go out anywhere, I always avoid ordering steak. I haven't had any steak in years, or anything I have to cut. I've gotten so I dislike those things. Chicken, too.	A constant or acute or unqualified reliance on the evaluations of others.
	In classes I feel that everyone's just waiting for a chance to jump on me. It's like they were breathing down my neck waiting for a chance to find something wrong. At school there were fellows like that waiting for me. I can't stand people laughing at me. I can't stand ridicule. That's why I'm afraid of kids. When I meet somebody I wonder what he's actually thinking of me. Then later on I wonder how I match up to what he's come to think of me.	No expression of dissatisfaction with the complete reliance on others. An unqualified reliance on the judgment or guidance of the counselor.
	I always felt that when people first found out that they would stiffen up around me. They would change their attitude toward me and feel sorry or something. Rather than letting them do that, I avoid ever letting them know.	
2	I go in cycles. For a long time I forget it [deformed hand], then along come several incidents — if I could just avoid — no, not avoid, but learn to handle the situation. This summer at the place where I worked, nobody said anything. They were older people, though, and I was comfortable.	A predominant concern with what others think, distinguished from Step 1, in that there is not a continuous or unqualified concern with the judgments and expectations of others.
	Well, the friendship with the girl has helped me a lot, too. She and her husband have really accepted me. They tell me I'm as bright as other people. Oh, of course, that is flattery, but it has helped me, and then just the fact that they really seem to like me, that has made a lot of difference.	An expression of dissatisfaction with the dependence on others, with no clear statement in favor of self-evaluation.

	TABLE 4–II The Locus-of-Evaluation Scale (continued)	
Step No.	*Illustrations of Step*	*Characteristics of Step*
	Yes, I've begun my plan. I'm gonna carry out my program of finding out what Robert Winsloe Smith, the fourth, really is. I'm gonna find out the ways I can better him instead of tearing him down as I have been. I'm gonna visit Arborville this weekend and I'm gonna ask everybody what *they* think my good points are, and then I'm gonna start stressing *them*.	A willingness to consider own evaluations, but with more weight given to the opinions of others, including counselor.
		An independent acceptance of the idea of being governed by the values of others.
3	I honestly don't know what to do. I think that if I could use it [deformed hand], if I could bring it out in the open and feel alright about it, I'd be all right.	A respect for own opinions at least equal to that of others, including counselor.
	Inferiority was the reason I worried about people. Inferiority was the reason that — was the reason that I worried about what people were thinking of me and it was the reason I had those irrational actions.	An appreciation of the significance of the difference between self-evaluation and being governed by the values of others.
	So I've made a decision that I wonder if it is right. When you're in a family where your brother has gone to college and everybody has a good mind, I wonder if it is right to see that I am as I am and I can't achieve such things. I've always tried to be what the others thought I should be, but now I'm wondering whether I shouldn't just see that I am what I am.	Insight into the reasons for dependence on others (or for over-compensating need to be independent).
		An emotional siding with, an apparently favorable consideration of, the idea of reliance on self-evaluation.
4	I'm pretty much like I'm going to be for the rest of my life. I can make concessions to life and I can learn to be, I think, a better husband and a more skilled worker but I'm not going to worry about a lot of things that I have in the past. People will either accept it or they will make their judgments but *I'm gonna quit trying to be all things to all men*. It's a very bad habit to get into. I don't think — at least *I* didn't realize that I was trying to do that. I, I was pretty patronizing, I think, uh, to many people. Purely — not because I had anything to gain except my own inflated ego, as I conceived it to be, but it's so different now I don't have	A clear reliance on self-evaluation expressed by: (1) a non-dependence on the judgments of the counselor. (2) reported behavior. (3) the statement of such a strong conviction in favor of self-evaluation that there is not cause to doubt its implementation in behavior.

TABLE 4–II The Locus-of-Evaluation Scale (continued)

Step No.	Illustrations of Step	Characteristics of Step

to do these things. I, I think that's, uh, — can't tell whether I read that someplace — (both laugh) this business when you're half — when you're, when you're uh —

I've gained a great deal of confidence. I don't worry about people so much. In fact, I'm having a wonderful time, just sitting around relaxing.

I just want to observe myself and if I think I'm improving, I'll take my word for it. I believe I am.

The application of the scale to the ten cases

The investigator now proceeded to select all of the client statements from the interviews of the research block which seemed to him to throw light on the locus-of-evaluation factor. Evidence has been presented for the reliability of selection of statements pertaining to locus-of-evaluation.

Following this, each of the items thus selected was given a rating of 1, 2, 3, or 4, in relation to the scale shown in Table 4–II. The average score for each interview is given in Table 4–III.

To what extent do the ten individuals in this particular population sample

TABLE 4–III

Locus-of-Evaluation Scores in the Ten Cases

Case	Interview Number								
	1	2	3	4	5	6	7	8	9
Miss Ban	1.3	2.3	2.1	1.6	2.6	1.5	1.4	3.0	2.6
Mrs Dem	1.9	1.9	1.9	—	—	—	—	—	—
Mr Far	2.3	3.0	3.0	3.2	3.5	3.0	3.4	—	—
Miss Int	1.8	1.8	1.7	1.9	2.2	2.1	3.3	—	—
Mr Que	2.7	3.0	3.0	3.0	3.1	3.0	3.3	—	—
Mrs Sim	2.5	2.7	1.9	2.9	2.0	2.6	2.4	—	—
Mr Sketch	1.7	2.5	2.4	—	—	—	—	—	—
Miss Vib	1.5	3.0	1.3	1.8	3.0	2.2	2.8	3.5	3.4
Miss Wab	1.7	—	1.3	—	—	—	—	—	—
Mr Win	2.3	2.6	3.6	2.9	3.3	—	—	—	—

experience a shift in their locus-of-evaluation? Seven of them show a higher score in their last interview than in their first. Two declined while one remained at the same level. Considering the ten cases together, the average score for first interviews is 1.97, while final interviews average 2.73. This difference was found to be significantly above chance at the one per cent level of confidence. Rogers (1951) has pointed out, 'When one takes the five cases which were judged by five objective criteria (the 'five parallel measures' shown in Table 4–V) as being most successful, the shift is even sharper. For these five cases, the average on the locus-of-evaluation scale was 2.12 for the first interview, 3.34 for the last.'

Reliability of application of the scale
Are the scores presented in Table 4–III reliable? In other words, what is the degree of reliability of the application of the locus-of-evaluation scale? To gain evidence on this question, the investigator, in random order, selected one item from each of the 59 interviews of the research block (from among those statements already chosen as pertaining to locus-of-evaluation), rated each one in relation to the four-step scale, submitted 30 of the items to one judge for comparison ratings, and the remaining 29 to another judge. In submitting the items to the judges, each one was typed on a separate card, with no indication given as to the case or interview.

The product-moment correlation coefficient between the ratings of the judges and the investigator was .91, with a probable error of .02. There was exact agreement in 45 of 59 instances, or 76 per cent, and in no instance were the investigator and judge more than one step apart in their ratings.

These results are considered to indicate that the procedure of judging new locus-of-evaluation items in relation to the scale developed in this study is a highly reliable one.

The locus-of-evaluation results in relation to previous findings
It has been noted that the research block of ten cases which formed the population of the present investigation was analyzed previously in the 'parallel studies' project of the University of Chicago Counseling Center (Rogers et al., 1949). As part of that project, the present writer calculated the intercorrelations between five of the most significant and stable measures that had emerged from the various studies (Raskin, 1949b). Since the present investigation was based on the same group of ten cases, it is now possible to add the correlations obtained between the locus-of-evaluation scores for the 59 interviews and the scores resulting from the other measures of these same interviews. All of these correlations are shown in Table 4–IV.

The only correlation in the table below which is not significantly better than chance is that between locus-of-evaluation and defensiveness. Otherwise, the results obtained here bear out the evidence furnished by the original project that personality organization and adjustment are based on a unified structure and operate on a principle of consistency. Also, the results of this study appear to

TABLE 4–IV

Intercorrelations Between Six Parallel Measures

	Locus-of-Evaluation	Self-Attitudes	Self-Acceptance	Insight	Behavior	Defen-siveness
Locus-of-evaluation	—	.67	.61	35	.45	−.19
Self-Attitudes	.67	—	.86	.70	.61	−.40
Self-Acceptance	.61	.86	—	.67	.51	−.34
Insight	.35	.70	.67	—	.39	−.40
Behavior	.45	.61	.51	.39	—	−.55
Defensiveness	−.19	−.40	−.34	−.40	−.55	—

strengthen the evidence that concepts closely related to self-structure, such as locus-of-evaluation, acceptance of and respect for self, and self-approval, are the ones which yield the closest approximations to lawful relationships in the study of personality organization. These conclusions will be amplified in the theoretic sections which follow.

Locus-of-evaluation scores as a criterion of therapeutic success
Table 4–V presents the difference between the first and last interview locus-of-evaluation scores (measured in terms of standard scores) for the ten cases, along with three other measures of success:

TABLE 4–V

Four Measures of the Degree of Improvement in the Ten Cases*

Case	Locus-of Evaluation	Five Parallel Measures	Counselor Rating	Rorschach Estimate
Miss Ban	2.1	1.0	8	Moderate improvement
Mrs Dem	0	.5	1	No improvement
Mr Far	1.7	2.6	9	No improvement
Miss Int	2.3	2.5	7	. . . .
Mr Que	.9	1.3	5	Moderate improvement
Mrs Sim	−.2	.5	5	Moderate improvement
Mr Sketch	1.0	.4	1	No improvement
Miss Vib	2.9	4.0	9	Moderate improvement
Miss Wab	−.7	−.1	5	No improvement
Mr Win	1.5	2.0	3	No improvement

* The entries in the table are explained in the text.

1. The difference between first and last scores of the five original parallel measures (self-regarding attitudes, acceptance of and respect for self, insight and understanding, maturity of reported behavior and defensiveness), combined.
2. The counselor rating of the cases on a 1 (low) to 9 (high) scale of success.
3. The estimate of the degree of improvement of the post-Rorschach test over the pre-Rorschach test.

The locus-of-evaluation estimate of improvement correlates .85 with that based on the five parallel measures and .60 with the counselor ratings. As in the original parallel studies project, there is no significant relationship with the Rorschach findings.

These statistical results are not substantial because the small number of cases may not constitute an adequate sample, but there would seem to be some evidence here, which would be worth verifying, that the locus-of-evaluation measure does have value as a criterion of therapeutic success.

Clinical illustration of the statistical findings
An increased understanding of the figures in Table IV may be conveyed by citing some of the case material from which the statistics are derived. In this section, clinical illustrations will be given of the relationship between locus-of-evaluation and three of the variables included in Table 4–IV: (1) self-regarding attitudes, (2) acceptance of and respect for self and, (3) maturity of reported behavior.

Locus-of-evaluation and self-regard
The fourth interview of the case of Miss Int supplies a good clinical illustration of the relationship between these two variables. In the portion of the interview quoted below, the client is shown struggling to achieve a new orientation based on her own values, and is seen to be hampered in this struggle by a lack of self-regard:

Client: . . . I mean, instead of trying to do something that I'd set up in advance or to copy something that someone else does or be something that someone else is, I keep trying . . . to do this: enrich what I have and where I live and with what I have.

Counselor: You feel that's one thing you've sort of gotten hold of and even though it is still vague in many ways, you feel fairly sure you don't want simply to be fourteen other guys, no matter how ideal they might be, but to really try to be yourself.

Client: And yet I think I have nothing to work on, you know. Except all this conflict, you know; I have nothing to build on at all, because everything is just gray, you know. Nothing is black or white, or definite, or sharply defined.

Counselor: When you take that attitude, you feel pretty alarmed or pretty dissatisfied with the material you have to work with.

Client: It's so inadequate, I think that's my greatest unhappiness, that
        inadequacy, you know, and not being able to do anything, I guess.
        That's back of all that I've . . . I don't know.
Counselor: You feel that back of a lot of this might be some sort of
        inadequacy. Or the fact that you felt inadequate.
Client: No, I guess it's a real inadequacy because I feel other people can
        do, can solve these things.

The translation into quantitative terms of these and the other statements made by
Miss Int in this interview is represented by a standard score of $-.9$ for the locus-
of-evaluation variable (derived from the raw score of 1.9 given in Table 4–III)
and a closely parallel standard score of -1.1 for the measure of self-regard (Raskin,
1949b).

In her final counseling hour, Miss Int is seen to have grown both in her self-
regard and in her ability to be self-contained in her evaluations.

The most important change, I guess, is considering myself, more or
less, as an individual. I used to be so disappointed in comparing
myself with others because I couldn't measure up; but instead of
being emotionally blocked by that idea, I want to think I am doing
as well as I can and [chuckles] I am sure it doesn't matter what
other people do or how much better or how much worse they are at
all. My own spirit of attainment or achievement is my own
measurement.

This change in the client's view of herself is reflected in standard scores for the
locus-of-evaluation and self-regard variables which have shifted to high positive
values, reading 1.2 and 2.2 respectively.

Locus-of-evaluation and self-acceptance
The case of Miss Vib affords us an opportunity to examine clinical material which
illustrates a shift from a low level of locus-of-evaluation and of self-acceptance
to a substantial level. The first four interviews in this case yield an average standard
score for locus-of-evaluation of $-.9$, and for self-acceptance over the same period
a correspondingly low -1.3. However, as Miss Vib looks decreasingly to others
for the evaluation of her experiences there is a growth in her self-acceptance in
the sense that she becomes better able to admit aspects of self which were formerly
unacceptable. This relationship is evidenced by the following quotation from the
seventh interview:

Client: That's what it seems, and ah, it seems that I should have, ah,
        integrity enough to ah, let people know . . . I mean acquaint people
        with, well, my shortcomings, or whatever. And, and my ah . . . If
        I ever get a new job, to ah, be myself more, instead of doing . . .
        what . . . I've been expected to do.
Counselor: You feel it would involve a very definite sort of honest feeling

of integrity if you were to try to let them know that you hadn't measured up in certain things, and that you don't expect to . . . that kind of thing.

Client: M-hm. I think so. Ah, it seems if I could take responsibility for . . . well, of course, if I just ah, accept myself, plainly and fully, and then, ah, if I could be casual about it and not be too worried and upset about it. And if someone asks me what I'm going to do next year, just say, 'I don't know,' or that I'll probably have a job somewhere, or . . . instead of being worried that they'll find out I, I'm failing in all my classes, . . . not doing too well.

In her ninth and final interview, Miss Vib goes on to develop this related theme of lessened dependence on others and increased self-acceptance. She speaks of being 'sort of tired of taking things from people and in a way having people dictate terms of how I would use my time and my life', and goes on to this expression of self-acceptance:

Client: That's another thing that I'm beginning to accept, and that is, uh, that I can have — that I have — I mean that I'm not always right on things I do, or in my reason and motives, that uh, I don't know, it seems uh, I just, well, I knew I made mistakes but I thought that fundamentally I was going along in the right direction up until things began to get too serious. Well, now I can be reconciled, or, at least I can accept the fact, uh, I'm not at all perfect in the kind of things I do and my reactions. So that, well, instead of just fighting against it, to realize that I am able to make mistakes.

The standard scores reflecting this clinical gain are .5 for locus-of-evaluation and .3 for self-acceptance, for the seventh interview, increasing to 1.4 for locus-of-evaluation and 2.0 for self-acceptance, for the ninth and final interview.

Locus-of-evaluation and behavioral maturity
Behavioral maturity is a third variable for which Table 4–IV shows a significant positive correlation with the locus-of-evaluation factor. In the case of Mr Win, we can perceive the operation of this relationship at the individual psychologic level. The first interview of this case yields standard scores of −.3 both for the locus-of-evaluation and behavioral maturity variables. The following excerpt from the interview reveals these two aspects of immaturity being expressed together:

Client: Yes, in the morning, it had no meaning, the problems. It was just, it just seemed a meaningless thing. I'd say, 'Well, why attack these problems. It's so much nicer to stay home and play cards or to uh, to go back to sleep again or to mess around for awhile. You don't have to go to class, nobody is forcing you to, nobody is going to be mad at you, nobody is going to criticize you or anything like that.'

In the third interview of this case, the behavioral maturity level has risen to 2.0 and the locus-of-evaluation score to 1.7 (standard scores). This concomitant increase is reflected in this excerpt from the interview:

Client: . . . And uh, it also was a fear of going back to classes, the ridicule perhaps. And uh, I knew that was a groundless suspicion, but it was just a creeping rationalization that I had. If you go back to classes you'll probably get the heck knocked out of you or something like that. And I knew that wasn't, that, that had absolutely no basis in actuality.

Counselor: You feel now that you have faced that much more realistically.

Client: So I just decided to solve that problem scientifically. Well, so that's why I went to classes, to see what happened. Well, what happened, I was welcomed back into the fold cheerfully. I even joked about the [few words missed] and it was that. And I can see some of my teachers for instance, my philosophy teacher. I laid my problems on the table to him, told him I hadn't been to classes, that I had missed a lot of work, told him just exactly what I had read and what I hadn't read, where I was in my work and what I was doing to catch up with my work, and he gave me a pretty square deal. There was a mid-term paper that I had missed and he said I could write it now, hand it in later. And that was pretty fine, because he told me exactly what I had missed. I mean gave me a thumbnail sketch of the work, and uh, he sat down and talked it over and I came out pretty well. And more or less with the other teachers the same thing. I just got back into the saddle to find out what I had missed, and go to it.

Locus-of-evaluation development — the attitude of parents

In the course of client-centered counseling, the client often directs his attention to the disturbance-producing circumstances of his childhood. The following hypothesis about locus-of-evaluation has emerged from this type of exploration: that the client whose difficulties center around a dependence on the judgments of others can often trace this dependence back to a childhood in which the parents systematically imposed their values upon him and provided little opportunity for self-developed values and standards.

Here is how one client, Mrs Sim, recalls this pattern:

Client: Probably it started in the home situation where, well where, probably first in relation to my mother, I don't know whether that's worthwhile — going back over that. For a long time I've accepted the idea that, uh, uh, that my mother didn't really approve of me . . . She is quite, she places quite a value on social things, people; and as I told you I was more interested in being by myself and in reading, things like that. She was constantly getting after me about that. So I suppose she started all these feelings. I mean the relationship with her. I know I never felt secure with her, never felt that she approved of me in any way. But I've been conscious of that for a long time and I've pretty well accepted it, as just the way things were.

Counselor: You are saying that in your relationship with your mother you sort of felt an inadequacy or feeling not quite at ease or not quite that you were being accepted completely for what you are, is that it?

Client: Oh, her lack of approval. I mean, I guess, oh, I remember, I have a very vivid impression of when, oh, I don't know I was 12 or 13 or so, and I remember one time somebody said, 'What nice children you have,' and she smiled and said, 'Yes, we think they are pretty nice,' and I remember feeling shocked at that, because it never occurred to me that she even liked me before. I mean I just kind of always thought that, well that she disapproved more than approved of me. And I don't know, it's just sort of the way she is . . .

Counselor: As you look back on it you have the feeling that you didn't measure up to some of the standards which she set for you.

Client: Oh, she always impressed that upon me very strongly, my, telling me I spent too much time by myself, and oh, I don't know, in school if I got good grades, if I got bad grades she didn't like it, and if I got good ones, she'd say, 'Well, now see what you can do when you try,' and 'If you'd try harder you could do this all the time.'

There are, of course, other ways for a parent to assume the locus-of-evaluation for his child. One of these ways is reported in the case of Miss Mir:

Client: . . . the thing is, he praised me when I probably shouldn't have been praised [words missing] . . . consciously looking for praise and wanting to be first. Well, I was always conscious of that; when I was in grammar school I just seemed to live for praise. And that sort of set everything off, I mean, it was so unbalanced right there. And then, he did praise me, and when I got good marks in school, he did praise me, but then when he . . . the very fact that he did, it made me even more upset, I mean, it just unbalanced things even more.

Counselor: You feel that way back there [words missing] . . . got started on the route, of just living for what others thought of what you did.

Client: That's right.

Counselor: What praise you could get.

Client: That's right. And then it just seemed as though I just lived for that . . .

Here we see one client experiencing constant disapproval, another incessant praise; in one instance, the mother is the dominant figure; in the other, it is the father; the thing they have in common is a parent who has taken over the self-evaluating function for them, and who has made them highly conscious of being evaluated. And the result in both cases is virtually similar; a self for which there is all too little regard.

The locus-of-evaluation principle in the counseling situation
A counseling formula
The moral of the preceding section might be stated thus: 'Treat the child as one who is not capable of developing his own values and standards and the child will grow up to be an individual who is dependent on the values and standards of others'. This formula is turned around in client-centered counseling where the client, child or adult, is regarded as capable of self-determination and tends to move in that direction during the course of counseling. Early in this paper it was noted that the locus-of-evaluation concept applies both to the client's personality organization and to the counselor's relationship to the client. The thesis of this section is that these two aspects of the concept can be causally related: 'In counseling, keep the locus-of-evaluation with the client and he will move in the direction of greater reliance on his own values and standards.'

The attitude of the counselor
'In the client-centered approach', writes Rogers (1948), 'the locus-of-evaluation is kept with the client. The function of responsible integration of knowledge, the evaluation of self, the function of responsible choice, of planning, of the taking of action — all these evaluative activities are lodged with the client, and he is respected as the person upon whom they rest.' 'The primary point of importance', he states in another paper (1949a), 'is the attitude held by the counselor toward the worth and significance of the individual.' He then goes on to raise the following questions:

> How do we look upon others? Do we see each person as having worth and dignity in his own right? If we do hold this point of view at the verbal level, to what extent is it operationally evident at the behavioral level? Do we tend to treat individuals as persons of worth, or do we subtly devaluate them by our attitudes and behavior? Is our philosophy one in which respect for the individual is uppermost? Do we respect his capacity and his right to self-direction or do we basically believe that his life would be best guided by us? To what extent do we have a need and a desire to dominate others? Are we willing for the individual to select and choose his own values, or are our actions guided by the conviction (usually unspoken), that he would be happiest if he permitted us to select for him his values and standards and goals?

Summary
The concept of locus-of-evaluation is defined in relation both to the attitude of the counselor and the personality organization of the client. This study presents

the development of a locus-of-evaluation scale and its application to ten counseling cases. This group made a statistically significant shift from 'others' to 'self' in its locus-of-evaluation, with a greater change in this direction occurring in those cases judged more successful by other objective criteria. Figures are presented which show the application of the scale to be a reliable procedure. In relating the results of the present study to previously obtained data on the same group of cases, it is concluded that locus-of-evaluation scores may be used as a criterion of therapeutic progress, and that this factor is correlated significantly with such other criteria as self-regarding attitudes, understanding and insight and maturity of behavior. Clinical illustrations of the relationship of locus-of-evaluation to some of these other variables are presented. The place of parental attitudes in the development of this factor is discussed, as is the role of the counselor in the readjustment process.

References
Blocksma, D. D. (1949) An experiment in the learning of a counseling viewpoint. Unpublished PhD dissertation, Committee on Human Development, University of Chicago.

Guilford, J. P. (1936) *Psychometric methods*. New York: McGraw-Hill.

Hartwell, S. W. (1931) *Fifty-five 'bad' boys*. New York: Alfred A. Knopf.

Hoffman, A. E. (1949) A study of reported behavior changes in counseling. *Journal of Consulting Psychology*, *13*, 190–5.

Raskin, N. J. (1949a) The development of the 'parallel studies' project. *Journal of Consulting Psychology*, *13*, 154–6

Raskin, N. J. (1949b) An analysis of six parallel studies of the therapeutic process. *Journal of Consulting Psychology*, *13*, 206–20.

Rogers, C. R. (1948) Divergent trends in methods of improving adjustment. *Harvard Education Review, 18*, 209–19.

Rogers, C. R. (1949a) The attitude and orientation of the counselor in client-centered therapy *Journal of Consulting Psychology*, *13,* 82–94.

Rogers, C. R. (1949b) A nonobjective introduction to a coordinated research in psychotherapy. *Journal of Consulting Psychology*, *13,* 149–253.

Rogers, C. R. (1951) *Client-centered therapy*. Boston: Houghton Mifflin.

Rogers, C. R. et al. (1949) A coordinated research in psychotherapy. *Journal of Consulting Psychology*, *13,* 149–220.

Sheerer, E. T. (1949) An analysis of the relationship between acceptance of and respect for self and acceptance of and respect for others in ten counseling cases. *Journal of Consulting Psychology*, *13,* 169–75.

STUDIES OF PSYCHOTHERAPEUTIC ORIENTATION: IDEOLOGY AND PRACTICE

5

Earlier studies

There is surprisingly little research on psychotherapeutic orientation which is based on the actual practice of therapists with diverse approaches. Meltzoff and Kornreich (1970) in the section of their comprehensive research volume which deals with the effect of 'School or Orientation of Therapist on Practices and Attitudes', cite the work of the present author (1965), Fiedler (1950a), Strupp (1955, 1958a, 1958b), Wrenn (1960), Wallach and Strupp (1964) and Sundland and Barker (1962).

Fiedler's subjects rated Q-sort items describing an ideal therapeutic relationship. Strupp's therapist subjects gave responses to standardized sound films of patient-therapist interviews and these communications constituted the data for analysis. Wrenn used a similar technique in which his counselor subjects responded by mail to thirteen excerpts from counseling interviews in which the counselor statement was left open. Wallach and Strupp utilized a seventeen-item scale of therapeutic practices. Sundland and Barker employed a 133-item Therapist Orientation Questionnaire.

While Meltzoff and Kornreich summarize these studies as indicating 'that there are apparently genuine differences in approach and techniques as a function of school or orientation of the therapist', the results are actually more mixed than this conclusion would indicate. Fiedler's well-known finding was that the description of an ideal therapeutic relationship is *not* a function of the 'school' of the therapist, be he psychoanalytically oriented, nondirective or eclectic, and Wrenn found that phenomenological, analytic and eclectic counselors all responded predominantly to feeling rather than content, gave the client primary responsibility and provided a low degree of lead. In this study, reflection was the only category of response showing a significant difference, being used less frequently by the analytic than the other two groups.

Wallach and Strupp's analysis of orthodox Freudians, general psychoanalytic, Sullivanian and client-centered therapists yielded four factors, but they were of inconclusive magnitude.

Originally published in AAP (American Academy of Psychotherapists) *Research Monograph No.1* (1974), pp. 5–33. Reprinted with permission.

On the side of the research indicating differences between orientations, Strupp found that Rogerians differed from psychoanalytically oriented psychologists in their mode of response, with Rogerians favoring reflections of feeling and the analytic group making more use of exploratory questions and interpretations.

Sundland and Barker emerged with a general factor with 'analytic' and 'experiential' poles and placed various orientations at one pole or another or at the midpoint.

The American Academy of Psychotherapists research project
In this study, the author wished to resolve not only the inconclusive results of earlier research in this area, but the ambiguities of his own experience with protagonists, often leaders and originators, of diverse orientations in the intensive workshops of the American Academy of Psychotherapists. The ambiguities consisted of impressions both of dramatic differences in therapeutic approach and of fundamental similarities.

The Academy provided two special strengths for research on 'schools' of psychotherapy. One was the availability of actual samples of therapy carried out by founders of schools or other experts; these were in the form of tape recorded interviews administered by the Tape Library of the AAP. The other outstanding resource was a pool of judges of diverse orientations, who had met rigorous standards of experience, supervision and therapy for themselves in winning membership in the AAP.

The sample which was judged

TABLE 5–I

Orientation and Therapists of Sample Being Judged

Orientation	Therapist	Code Letter
Rational-Emotive	Albert Ellis	A
Experiential	Richard Felder	B
Psychoanalytically Oriented	Abraham Levitsky	C
Jungian	Ira Progoff	D
Client-Centered	Carl Rogers	E
Direct Analytic	John Rosen	F

In selecting the size of sample to be rated, the investigator reduced his original concept of a 30 to 50-minute recording to 15 and then to approximately eight minutes. This was a subjective judgment, based on listening to the tapes, that eight minutes was sufficiently long to capture the essential style and attitudes of each therapist. Each therapist was then asked if the excerpt could be used as a representative sample of the way he worked as part of a research project in which different approaches to therapy would be systematically compared. This resulted in the substitution of one excerpt for the sample which had been chosen originally by the investigator.

In order to convey to the present readers some flavor of the material which was judged, a short excerpt will be quoted from the typescript of each of the six eight-minute tape-recorded samples:

Therapist A (Rational-Emotive)

TI6   All right, now. Let's assume that, for the moment, that you're afraid of the contact. Now let's get the exact sentence which you're saying to yourself to make yourself afraid of this contact. What are you saying is *dreadful?*

P17   Well, it sounds too simple to say, 'They won't like me,' you know —

T17   In ot —

P18   — And I'm sure that's the bottom of it.

Tl8   Yeah. In other words, you're saying, 'If I go —'

P19   But I'm inventing a lot of crap to say (sort of laughs). 'I won't — They won't like me, I guess.'

T19   Well, let's get that a little more specific. You're saying 'If I go out and meet the girls or a girl,' let us say, 'then there's a good possibility that she won't like me and that would be *dreadful —'*

Therapist B (Experiential)

T42   And you were *mad?*

P43   I told him to let go of *my* thumb.

T43   You were mad?

P44   Sure I was mad. You'd be too if your finger was sore.

T44   I *know* I would be. I didn't know *you* ever got mad.

P45   Yes, I get *mad* plenty of times, I cuss, and I throw things and I . . .

T45   I know you cuss, but I didn't know you got mad.

Therapist C (Psychoanalytically Oriented)

P5   I feel that I'm silly — I feel that I am unnecessarily susceptible to some people, some very strong people, and especially when they happen to be a man, I feel that I'm just too susceptible to them, and I feel that in other situations I'm able, somehow, to keep my feelings unraveled and somehow here I didn't do it.

T5   Don't you think that the problem we're dealing with has to do with what you're afraid might happen if you bring these 'susceptible' affectionate feelings out into the open? Aren't you afraid of what might happen?

P6   Well, sure, —

T6   Well, what do you think will happen?

P7   I don't think anything will happen. Cause really —

T7   No, I don't think you're convinced of that. If you were convinced of that, then I think you could allow yourself to bring it into the open — but you're not convinced. What *you* seem to anticipate is that if you talk about and look at whatever feelings of gratitude, affection, etc., you have experienced here, in your *own* words, this will lead to your degradation.

Therapist D (Jungian)

T20 This is a dream of when you were in that trough, in that feeling of things being almost ready, not quite being ready, not quite being ready and, uh, so you have the clothes that fit but not quite the courage to put them on and yet somehow in the dream just before there where the dog shows his teeth, then you take the strong affirmative attitude toward the other dog —

P21 Um hum.

T21 There is the sense that that strength is present.

P22 In the past few days, the form that that has taken in my thinking is this, I'm gradually becoming aware that I, maybe things have changed to the point where I don't have to worry with a backward look over my shoulder to see that something is after me—

T22 Uh huh.

P23 Chasing me, maybe —

T23 Oh —

P24 I can really take a deep breath and say, well, you know, OK now I'm really gonna go —

T24 Well, you mean you don't have to be Lot's wife anymore.

P25 Yah, um mh, I don't have to worry about this sitting, something on my shoulder —

T25 We should have a drink for that. (both laugh) We, because what a thing that means.

Therapist E (Client-Centered)

Cl15 It's just the same old story. Mothers and fathers try to tell the kids what to do, and the kids revolt. So, that's the only thing right now, that's between my parents and me.

Th15 So I guess you are saying, this is true in general but it's also true of you, that your parents try to tell you what to do and you feel, 'I won't take that.'

Cl16 Well, I don't feel it. I say it. Of course, what I say and what I do are two different things though.

Th16 Uh, huh. I am not quite clear there. You say, you say it but you don't really feel it?

Cl17 Well, let's put it this way: If my mother tells me what to do, and whether I like it or not, I have to do it. But boy I let her know that I'm not too happy about having to do it, either.

Th17 Uh, huh. Are you saying there, 'She may be able to make me behave in certain ways or do certain things, but she can't control the way I feel and I let her know how I feel.'

Cl18 That's exactly it. And about twice . . . after about two times of it straight in a row, I think she usually gives in to save the mess and bother of breaking them dishes and stuff like that.

Therapist F (Direct Analytic)

T8   And you don't look at me. You don't want to take me in at all, I can see that, but I take you in. My eyes are right on you, aren't they? My mouth doesn't shut as tight as a clam, does it? But yours does and you get silent.

P8   (pause) I don't know what to say.

T9   Well, why don't you love me? (pause) When you look at me, you wrinkle your forehead, you make your mouth as tight as a clam —

P9   (sort of sighs) I don't know it's . . .

T10 Why don't you get up and put your arms around me and give me a kiss? (slight pause) There goes your mouth again, you look away, you don't want to come near me. Now you're smiling. (laughs) And there goes that mouth again. When you smile you, you almost let me in. Are you afraid that it would mean something homosexual if you did that?

P10 No, not into the role that you explained to me.

The judge population

The original population of judges, later reduced, consisted of 100 therapists who were divided into three experience groups: Experienced (6–30 years), Moderately Experienced (2–6 years), Inexperienced (less than 2 years). They were also divided into three main orientations: Freudian, Client-Centered and Eclectic. Many of these judges had, in addition, been influenced by Experiential and Existential thought, and there was a scattering of representatives of other schools, such as Sullivanian, Adlerian, Gestalt and Transactional.

The ratings of 17 judges which were obtained during an Australian workshop in which one of the expert therapists participated were excluded from the analysis which follows, because this data reflected a statistically significant bias in favor of the therapist who was on the scene. The data in this AAP study, then, comes from 83 sets of ratings, by therapists with the three levels of experience described above. The characteristics of these judges by Orientation and Experience, are shown in Table 5–II.

The 'plus Ex' notation included in the third and fifth orientations is an abbreviation of 'plus Existential or Experiential'. These judges described themselves as primarily Freudian or Client-Centered but as having been additionally influenced by Existential or Experiential thought.

Seventy-five of the judges shown in Table 5–II are psychologists. The other eight include three psychiatrists, three social workers and two ministers.

TABLE 5–II

Orientation and Experience Level of 83 Judges

		Experience Level		
Orientation	Total	Experienced	Moderately	Inexperienced
Freudian	7	5	1	1
Non-Freudian	6	3	0	3
Freudian plus Ex	7	6	0	1
Client-Centered	12	6	0	6
Client-Centered plus Ex	11	5	1	5
Eclectic	28	8	10	10
Existential	2	2	0	0
Sullivanian	3	2	1	0
Adlerian	1	1	0	0
Experiential	2	1	0	1
Gestalt	1	1	0	0
Transactional	1	1	0	0
Experiential-Learning	1	0	1	0
'Lost'	1	0	0	1
	—	—	—	—
Total	83	41	14	28

The rating system

After a review of the literature on therapist variables and a consideration of the therapist dimensions regarded as important by the different schools of thought represented by the tapes in the project (Ellis, 1962; Whitaker and Malone, 1953; Munroe, 1955; Progoff, 1956; Rogers, 1961; Rosen, 1953), a set of 12 variables was devised as a way of describing therapists of diverse orientations. The variables were: Cognitive, Experiential, Empathic, Therapist-Directed, Equalitarian, Warm and Giving, Unconditional Positive Regard, Congruent, Emphasizes Unconscious, Systematically Reinforces, Self-Confident, and Inspires Confidence (in the judge). Space was allocated for other dimensions believed by the judge to be significant and for free descriptive comments. A separate rating sheet was furnished for each of the six therapists to be rated, with the judge circling one of four points for each variable: Imperceptible, Somewhat, Considerably, Extremely.[1]

Together with a tape containing the six therapy excerpts and the rating forms described, each judge was supplied with typescripts of the six excerpts to which he could refer as he listened to the tape and with a set of definitions of the twelve therapist variables, which had been formulated by the investigator and which is illustrated by the following:

---

1. This form, and the others described in this section, are duplicated in the Appendix.

Empathic

The therapist is trying, as sensitively and as accurately as he can, to understand the client, *from the latter's own point of view*. It is an understanding of what the client is aware of and trying to convey to the therapist, so if the latter is accurate in his empathic endeavor, the client will feel and may say, 'Yes, that's it! That's how I feel! That's what I meant! You really understand me.' This is an understanding different from the kind which relates the client's behavior to a theory of personality or adjustment which is held by the therapist and which may result in a client reaction such as, 'Let's see. Is that true? That may be right. I never thought of that.' The empathic attitude is, 'I want to know and to convey to you my understanding of how you see things, how you interpret your experience, how you feel about yourself and others.'

The judge was asked to familiarize himself with the rating method, to listen to the entire tape without making any ratings, and then to listen to the excerpts in a particular order, rating each therapist in turn. The listening sequence was varied systematically.

The therapists on the tape were identified only by a letter, as follows: Rational-Emotive, Therapist A; Experiential, Therapist B; Neo-Analytic, Therapist C; Jungian, Therapist D; Client-Centered, Therapist E; Direct Analytic, Therapist F. Expecting that many of them, being leaders of their schools, would often be recognized, each judge was asked, after he had rated each therapist, to write in the therapist's name and orientation, if he thought he had identified these.

In addition to assessing the six therapists in this manner, each judge was asked to furnish two additional sets of ratings, using the same dimensions: (a) his present behavior as a therapist and (b) his concept of the Ideal Therapist. Finally, the judge was asked to check or write in his therapeutic orientation, and to give his birth date, academic degrees, profession, and experience as a therapist.

Some of the ratings were obtained in group sessions, in which the tape was played to the group and ratings obtained from the listeners at the same time.

While 44 of the 83 judges listened to Therapists A to F in that order, the order of listening was varied for roughly half of the judges, i.e., some started with Therapist B, some with C, etc. This means that there were six different 'order of listening' groups. The ratings of these groups were compared, therapist by therapist, variable by variable, and it was concluded that order of listening did not significantly affect ratings. The effect of 'correct identification of the school of the therapist' being judged was analyzed in a similar way, and here too the effect on the overall pattern of ratings was non-significant.

TABLE 5–III

Mean Ratings by 83 Judges of the Six Therapists on the Twelve Dimensions

Dimension	A	B	C	D	E	F
Cognitive	3.5	1.2	3.2	3.1	2.3	2.9
Experiential	1.6	3.6	2.2	1.9	2.8	2.5
Empathic	2.2	2.1	2.5	2.2	3.7	2.0
Therapist-Directed	3.4	1.8	2.8	3.1	1.5	3.7
Equalitarian	1.9	3.1	2.0	2.0	2.9	1.7
Warm and Giving	1.8	2.3	2.2	2.4	2.8	2.3
Unconditional Positive Regard	1.9	2.5	2.1	2.3	3.3	1.8
Congruent	2.9	2.6	2.7	2.5	3.1	2.8
Emphasizes Unconscious	2.3	1.8	2.6	3.3	1.1	3.1
Systematically Reinforces	2.6	1.7	2.3	2.8	1.8	2.9
Self-Confident	3.6	3.0	3.2	3.2	3.1	3.7
Inspires Confidence	2.5	2.1	2.6	2.2	3.0	2.2

Overall results: the diversity of the six expert therapists as a group

Table 5-III gives the mean ratings by the 83 judges of the six expert therapists identified by the code shown in Table 5–I, on the twelve variables described above. The mean of 3.5 for Therapist A on the Cognitive dimension, to illustrate, is a high rating, halfway between Considerably (3.0) and Extremely (4.0).

Chi-square analysis was employed to evaluate the significance of the differences shown in Table 5–III. Using the ratings of the 54 experienced judges, a distribution was obtained for each of the twelve therapist behavior dimensions, and the chi-square calculated. Table 5–IV exemplifies this procedure by showing the ratings given by the 54 judges to the six therapists on the Cognitive dimension.

TABLE 5–IV

Ratings of the Six Experts on the Cognitive Dimension by 54 Experienced Judges

Cognitive Rating				Therapist			
	Total	A	B	C	D	E	F
1	73	2	44	1	1	20	5
2	55	5	7	5	1	22	5
3	100	14	2	24	26	9	25
4	96	33	1	24	16	3	19
	324	54	54	54	54	54	54

The chi-square value derived from these frequencies is 222.805, far beyond the .001 level of significance; thus, the cognitive ratings given are very much a function of the differences in the degree of 'cognitiveness' of the therapists being judged.

In this manner, it can be shown that the six expert therapists vary significantly on practically all twelve dimensions for all three groups of judges. With distributions of the Table 5–IV type being obtained on each of the twelve variables for the three classes of judges there is a total of 36 tables and derived chi-squares. Twenty-eight of these exceed the .001 level. Five others exceed .01. The three remaining are:

Judge Group	Dimension	Level of Significance
Moderately Experienced	Congruent	N.S.
Moderately Experienced	Inspires Confidence	.05
Inexperienced	Congruent	N.S.

All twelve dimensions rated by the Experienced judge group were significant at the .001 level, although it is interesting that the lowest chi-square value in this group was the one for the Congruent dimension, the same one for which a non-significant chi-square was derived for two other classes of judges. This indicates that the therapists were differentiated less in the Congruent dimension than in any of the others. The next 'most alike' dimension in the Experienced judge group is the Self-Confident one, a result supported by the relatively lower levels of significance found for this dimension by the two less experienced classes of judges. These expert therapists, then, who give themselves different labels, are experienced here as indeed different from one another, while seen as least unlike in the dimensions of genuineness (Congruence) and of self-confidence.

TABLE 5–V

'High' and 'Low' Dimensions for Each Therapist Based on the Ratings of 83 Judges

Dimension	Therapist					
	A	B	C	D	E	F
Cognitive	H	L	H	H		
Experiential	L	H		L		
Empathic					H	
Therapist-Directed	H	L		H	L	H
Equalitarian	L	H				L
Warm and Giving	L					
Unconditional Positive Regard	L				H	L
Congruent					H	
Emphasizes Unconscious		L		H	L	H
Systematically Reinforces		L			L	
Self-Confident	H	H	H	H	H	H
Inspires Confidence					H	

The largest chi-squares and hence the greatest diversity among the six therapists were obtained on Therapist-Direction, Empathic, Cognitive, Experiential, Emphasizes Unconscious and Equalitarian. The .001 level of significance was exceeded on all six of these dimensions by all three classes of judges.

A one-way analysis of variance among the six therapists on the twelve variables confirms these results. The six highest F-ratios, expressing the diversity of the therapists, were those of the same variables cited above. The lowest F-ratio was obtained for Congruence.

A more differentiated look at the six experts

Table 5–V has been adapted from Table 5–III as follows: (1) all dimensions in which a therapist has an average rating of 3.0 *(Considerably* Empathic, etc.) or more have been designated 'H' for High; (2) all average ratings of below 2.0 *(Somewhat* Empathic, etc.) have been coded 'L' for Low. This results in a distinct pattern of characteristics for each of the six therapists, e.g., the Rational-Emotive Therapist A is seen as outstandingly Cognitive, Therapist-Directed and Self-Confident, while being rated low in the qualities of Experiential, Equalitarian, Warm and Giving and Unconditional Positive Regard. A very different pattern is that of Client-Centered Therapist E who is seen as being strongly Empathic, evidencing Unconditional Positive Regard and Congruence, while being low in his Emphasis of Unconscious, Therapist-Direction and Systematic Reinforcement. Some overlap of characteristics may be observed between Therapists A and D, A and F, and between B and E.

Therapist E is the only one of the six experts who, according to these criteria, is high on Inspiring Confidence in the judges. The Client-Centered Therapist also gets the only High rating on the Empathic and Congruent dimensions.

In only one of the therapist variables, Self-Confidence, are all six experts classified alike, thus supporting one of the conclusions of the preceding section, that this is one way in which the experts are least different.

All of the qualitative differences between Highs and Lows shown in Table 5–V exceed by far the .01 level of statistical significance.

For eight of the twelve variables, a difference of .3 between any two therapists in Table 5–III is significant at the .01 level. A difference of .4 is required for the Congruent, Emphasizes Unconscious, Systematically Reinforces and Inspires Confidence variables, e.g., the difference between Therapists E (3.0) and C (2.6) in Inspires Confidence is large enough to be significant at the .01 level.

The effect of level of experience and of orientation on the ratings of the experts

For statistical convenience in assessing the effect on ratings of level of experience, the Moderately Experienced and the Inexperienced groups were combined, affording a comparison between 41 More Experienced judges and 42 Less Experienced (less than 6 years). A detailed chi-square analysis was then carried out comparing these two experience groups, therapist by therapist, variable by variable.

Table 5–VI illustrates the method employed.

TABLE 5–VI

Ratings by Two Experienced Groups of Client-Centered Therapist E on the 'Warm and Giving' Variable

'Warm and Giving' Ratings	Total	Experience Level	
		More	Less
1	4	2	2
2	21	9	12
3	44	23	21
4	14	7	7
Total	83	41	42

Chi-square for the distribution shown in Table 5–VI is .508, quite lacking in significance.

Of 72 such tables assessing the effect of experience level on ratings of the expert therapists, 70 were non-significant and two were significant at the .05 level (Empathic for Therapist E, Systematically Reinforces for Therapist F); this is a result consistent with chance.

The effect of orientation on the ratings of the expert therapists was analyzed in a similar manner, with Analytically Oriented, Client-Centered and Eclectic judges being compared. Here, as in the analyses of judge orientation which follow, the first three categories listed in Table 5–II above have been combined into one 'Analytic' classification, and the fourth and fifth into one 'Client-Centered' group. The ratings given to Therapist E on the Warm and Giving variable will again be used for illustrative purposes.

The distribution in Table 5–VII yields the non-significant chi-square of 4.683.

TABLE 5–VII

Ratings of Client-Centered Therapist E on the 'Warm and Giving' Variable by Judges of Three Major Orientations

'Warm and Giving' Ratings	Total	Orientation		
		Analytic	Client-Cent.	Eclectic
1	3	2	0	1
2	19	6	4	9
3	36	9	14	13
4	13	3	5	5
Total	71	20	23	28

Out of 72 such tables on the effect of orientation, 66 were not significant, four were significant at the .05 level, one was significant at the 0.2 level (Experiential for Direct Analytic Therapist F), and one was significant at the .001 level (Experiential for Client-Centered Therapist E). With experience held constant while assessing orientation, the results were even less significant.

The analyses reported in this section give substantial support to the conclusion that neither experience level nor orientation (Analytic, Client-Centered, Eclectic) significantly affects the ratings of diverse expert therapists.

Judges' comments
Our statistical analyses emphasize the agreement between the judges about the differences between the therapists in this study even when diversities in the experience and orientations of the judges are accounted for. The qualitative comments added to the ratings by some of the judges lend depth to the numerical assessments while also bringing out the differences of opinion that exist about the experts.

One experienced Freudian judge felt that Rational Therapist A was 'too cognitive and didactic; I just don't believe that life or therapy is *that* simple', while another experienced Freudian offered the comment that A had a 'good relationship with a disagreeable patient'.

An experienced Client-Centered judge felt that the 'client seems to have to struggle to have an opportunity to do any soul-searching; too much dogged interpretation from the Therapist', but another judge in the same category stated, 'This is a good example of Therapist A, the teacher trying to show his client how to think straight and fearlessly'.

One experienced Eclectic judge wrote, 'I was struck by two things in this excerpt. One is the therapist's strong emphasis on the patient's wording of his thoughts and feelings. The other is the therapist's neglect of the patient's behavior in the therapeutic situation, such as his nervous laughing, as material for therapeutic work.'

However, another experienced Eclectic judge described this excerpt as 'excellent, very beautifully handled, relationship very positive, but cognition also a focus of attention. Teaching but warm and client-centered.'

These thoughtful and diverse reactions to Therapist A are illustrative of the comments volunteered about each of the six therapists.

Ratings of self as therapist
The judges in this study were asked, not only to evaluate the recordings of the six experts, but to use the same set of dimensions to describe their own practice and their concept of the Ideal Therapist. Self and Ideal ratings have been compared for two Experience levels and the three major orientation groups.

On the self rating, when the two levels of experience were compared, the differences were not significant for nine of the twelve variables. They were significant at the .05 level for the Congruent variable, with the mode for the Less

TABLE 5–VIII

Self-Ratings by Two Experience Groups on the 'Self-Confident' Variable

'Self-Confident' Ratings	Total	Experience Group	
		More Exp	Less Exp
1	3	0	3
2	33	8	25
3	41	28	13
4	6	5	1
Total	83	41	42

Experienced group being 2.5, compared with 3 for the More Experienced judges.

The two Confidence variables resulted in differences exceeding the .01 level of significance. Table 5–VIII gives the distribution for the Self-Confident variable.

It is clear that the Less Experienced judges, as a group, feel less confident than the More Experienced judges. A very similar distribution for the two groups is obtained on the Inspires Confidence dimension.

When the judges are divided according to orientation, rather than experience, more differences emerge in the description of Self as Therapist. Because of the preponderance of Analytically oriented judges at the Experienced level and of Eclectics who are Inexperienced, the analyses of Self and Ideal ratings have been carried out for the different orientations within a given experience category. Table 5–IX provides an example of such a distribution.

The results of 24 such distributions of Self descriptions are as follows:

Eighteen were not significant.

Three were significant at the .05 level: Empathic–More Experienced–Client-Centered Mode 4, Other orientations 3. Therapist-Directed–More Experienced–Eclectic Mode 3, Others 2. Systematically Reinforces–More Experienced–Eclectic Median 3, Others 2.

Three were significant at the .01 level: Cognitive–Less Experienced–Client-Centered Mode 2, Others 3. Emphasizes Unconscious–Less Experienced–Client-Centered Mode 1, Others 2. Systematically Reinforces–More Experienced–Eclectic Median 3, Others 2.

We may generalize that the three orientations do not describe themselves differently on the bulk of these comparisons (no significant differences on seven of the twelve dimensions for either experience group), and that where significant differences do exist in self-description, they are in the direction of the Client-Centered judges seeing themselves as less directive and cognitive, and the Eclectic judges describing themselves as more directive and reinforcing.

TABLE 5–IX

Self-Rating on the 'Warm and Giving' Variable by the More Experienced Judges of Three Orientations

'Warm and Giving' Ratings	Total	Orientation Analytic	Client-Centered	Eclectic
1	0	0	0	0
2	11	5	3	3
3	16	7	5	4
4	6	2	3	1
Total	33	14	11	8

Ratings of the ideal therapist

When ratings of the Ideal Therapist are analyzed according to Experience level, a high degree of agreement is found among the judges. Only in respect to one of the twelve variables, Experiential, is there a significant difference, with the typical More Experienced judge favoring a 4 rating and the modal Less Experienced judge selecting the 3 point. The differences between the Experience groups on the Congruent and on the two Confidence variables which appeared in the ratings of Self practice have disappeared in respect to the Ideal.

Only three significant differences in 24 distributions in the concept of the Ideal Therapist are discovered when the ratings are broken down by orientation, while holding experience level constant. Two of these differences are at the .001 level. One occurs in the More Experienced group, on the Therapist-Directed variable, with the three orientations providing three different modes for the Ideal: Client-Centered: 1, Analytic: 2, and Eclectic: 3. The other .001 difference is in the Less Experienced group on the Emphasizes Unconscious variable, with these different modes: Client-Centered: 1, Eclectic: 2, Analytic: 3.

The other significant difference among orientations on Ideal Therapist is at the .02 level, with respect to the More Experienced judges on the Systematically Reinforces variable. Here the median for the Eclectic Judge is 3, while it is 2 for the other groups.

Relationships among the ratings of the six experts, self and ideal

Table 5–X shows the ratings given on the twelve variables to the six experts, the mean of the six experts, the Self and the Ideal Therapist, by all 83 judges.

Inspection of Table 5–X suggests the following generalizations:
1. The experts as a group inspire only a moderate amount of confidence in the judges, even though the only high rating given to the experts is on their Self-Confidence. The judges themselves feel less Self-Confident and believe they inspire somewhat more confidence than the experts have evoked in them.

TABLE 5–X

**Ratings by 83 Judges of Each Expert, of Experts Combined, of Self
and of Ideal Therapist**

Dimension	A	B	C	D	E	F	Mean A–F	S	I
Cognitive	3.5	1.2	3.2	3.1	2.3	2.9	2.7	2.7	2.6
Experiential	1.6	3.6	2.2	1.9	2.8	2.5	2.4	2.6	3.4
Empathic	2.2	2.1	2.5	2.2	3.7	2.0	2.4	3.0	3.8
Therapist-Directed	3.4	1.8	2.8	3.1	1.5	3.7	2.7	2.0	1.9
Equalitarian	1.9	3.1	2.0	2.0	2.9	1.7	2.3	2.8	3.2
Warm and Giving	1.8	2.3	2.2	2.4	2.8	2.3	2.3	2.8	3.5
UPR	1.9	2.5	2.1	2.3	3.3	1.8	2.3	2.7	3.4
Congruent	2.9	2.6	2.7	2.5	3.1	2.8	2.8	2.8	3.7
Emphasizes Unconscious	2.3	1.8	2.6	3.3	1.1	3.1	2.4	2.0	2.2
Systematically Reinforces	2.6	1.7	2.3	2.8	1.8	2.9	2.4	2.2	2.2
Self-Confident	3.6	3.0	3.2	3.2	3.1	3.7	3.3	2.6	3.5
Inspires Confidence	2.5	2.1	2.6	2.2	3.0	2.2	2.4	2.7	3.7

2. The judges see their own practice, in comparison with their view of the experts on the average, as including more of the Empathic, Equalitarian, Warm and Giving and Unconditional Positive Regard qualities and less Therapist-Direction and Emphasis on Unconscious.

3. The judges believe that the Ideal Therapist, as compared with themselves and the aggregate expert, would be more Experiential, Empathic, Equalitarian, Warm and Giving, Unconditional in their Positive Regard, and Congruent, in addition to inspiring greater confidence. They feel that ideally, they should be more Self-Confident. They see the Ideal Therapist as being less Therapist-Directed than the experts as a group.

4. In terms of the individual experts who were rated, the judges see their own way of practicing and their concept of the Ideal Therapist as being most like Client-Centered Therapist E. This is true despite the fact that only twenty-five per cent of the judges describe themselves as having a client-centered orientation.

The product-moment correlation between mean ratings of Therapist E and Ideal is .94; the only other correlation with Ideal of this order is that of the Self ratings of the judges, which is .89. The next highest correlation between Ideal and one of the experts is with Therapist B, the rating being .57. The four other experts correlate with Ideal negatively, the extreme being Therapist D, at –.66.

Consistent with the above, the principal component factor analysis run on these data yields two factors, with high loadings on Factor 1 for Therapist E (.969), Self (.939) and Ideal (.950) together with loadings on Factor 2 of –.955 for Therapist A, –.981 for Therapist C, –.754 for Therapist D and –.764 for Therapist F.

A comparison of expert therapists' own ratings and those of the judges

Three of the expert therapists provided self-ratings of their representative work samples, their practice and of the Ideal Therapist. Table 5–XI shows these ratings of Therapist A, C and E, together with the averaged scores of their work sample by the 83 judges.

Table 5–XI indicates that the therapy samples used in the study are rated by these three therapists in a way that is close to their view of how they practice generally.

The experts come quite close, in their ratings of the research sample, to those of the means of the 83 judges. Therapist A agrees with the judges within one step on all of the variables; Therapist C disagrees by one step or more on four dimensions, and Therapist E has two variables in this category.

Another generalization derived from Table 5–X is that the experts see their general practice as not far removed from their Ideal concept; a modification of this is that Therapist C's Ideal concept is 1.5 steps higher in the Experiential dimension and 2 higher in Congruence.

There are some significant differences in the Ideal profiles provided by the experts. The Cognitive-Experiential ratio is exactly reversed for Therapists A and E, with C's ratings representing still a third pattern. Therapist E values Empathy much more than the others; they value Therapist-Direction much more than he does. The Warm and Giving, Unconditional Positive Regard and Systematically Reinforces variables all receive different ratings from the three.

While these experts, then, agree in the main with the judges' ratings of their work, unlike the judges, they disagree among themselves in their concepts of what an Ideal Therapist is like. It appears, too, that Therapist E's Ideal concept is the one that comes closest to that of the Analytic, Client-Centered and Eclectic judges in this study.

Relationships among the variables

Thus far, in this paper, relationships have been analyzed among the expert therapists whose work has been judged, among the judges who vary in experience and orientation and among ratings of the experts' Self and Ideal. Inherent in all of these analyses have been the properties of the twelve variables used as parameters. The relationships among them have been studied in several different ways.

Each of the 83 judges made six ratings on each variable in judging the experts, for a total of 498 judgments on each dimension. The means of these judgments range from 2.3 on Equalitarian to 3.3 on Self-Confidence. The standard deviations range from .7 on Self-Confidence to 1.2 on Emphasizes Unconscious.

The correlation matrix derived from these 498 judgements is given in Table

TABLE 5–XI

Ratings by Therapists A, C and E of their Excerpts, their Genaral Practice and their Ideal Therapist, Compared with the Ratings of their Excerpt by 83 Judges

Variable	A				C				E			
	83 Judges	Sample	Self-Prac	Ideal	83 Judges	Sample	Self-Prac	Ideal	83 Judges	Sample	Self-Prac	Ideal
Cognitive	3.5	4	4	4	3.2	3	4	3	2.3	1	1	1
Experiential	1.6	1	1	1	2.2	2	1.5	3	2.8	3	4	4
Empathic	2.2	2	2	2	2.5	2	2	2	3.7	4	4	4
Therapist-Directed	3.4	4	4	4	2.8	4	4	4	1.5	2	1	1
Equalitarian	1.9	2	2	3	2.0	3	4	4	2.9	3	3	4
Warm and Giving	1.8	1	1	1	2.2	3	3	3	2.8	4	4	4
UPR	1.9	1	2	3	2.1	2	2	2	3.3	3	3	4
Congruent	2.9	3	3	3	2.7	2	2	4	3.1	3	3	4
Emphasizes Unconscious	2.3	2	2	2	2.6	4	3	3	1.1	2	2	2
Systematically Reinforces	2.6	2	3	3	2.3	1	1	1	1.8	2	2	2
Self-Confident	3.6	4	4	4	3.2	4	3.5	4	3.1	3	3	3
Inspires Confidence	2.5	3	4	4	2.6	3	—	4	3.0	3	3	4

TABLE 5–XII

Correlation Matrix on 498 Judgements of Six Expert Therapists on Twelve Variables

Variable	1	2	3	4	5	6	7	8	9	10	11	12
1 Cognitive	1.00											
2 Experiential	-0.55	1.00										
3 Empathic	-0.11	0.24	1.00									
4 Therapist-Directed	0.41	-033	-0.40	1.00								
5 Equalitarian	-0.41	0.45	0.32	-0.44	1.00							
6 Warm and Giving	-0.18	0.35	0.40	-0.18	0.40	1.00						
7 UPR	-0.25	0.35	0.48	-0.48	0.49	0.51	1.00					
8 Congruent	-0.01	0.23	0.28	0.04	0.25	0.32	0.22	1.00				
9 Emphasizes Unconscious	0.31	-0.23	-0.27	0.48	-0.35	-0.11	-0.32	-0.05	1.00			
10 Systematically Reinforces	0.26	-0.21	-0.16	0.50	-0.19	0.05	-0.22	0.08	0.29	1.00		
11 Self-Confident	0.16	-0.04	-0.02	0.39	-0.11	0.06	-0.12	0.29	0.20	0.28	1.00	
12 Inspires Confidence	0.03	0.17	0.50	-0.13	0.22	0.39	0.30	0.37	-0.13	-0.01	0.19	1.00

5–XII. Similar relationships among the variables emerge when only the means included in Table 5–III are correlated. The coefficients of correlation are higher, with the smaller N and the intensity of the relationships increased through the use of the means. A principal component factor analysis performed on these means on rotation yields the two factors shown in Table 5–XIII. The communality over these two factors is 10.261 as related to the total of 12.000 for 12 factors.

Factor 1 appears to be associated with the perceived Self-Confidence of the expert therapist and is highly loaded on the Cognitive, Therapist-Directed and Systematically Reinforces variables in one direction and on the Experiential and Equalitarian variables in the other. Factor 2 is associated with Inspiring Confidence in the judges and is highly loaded on Empathy and Congruence.

Consistent with the latter findings are the results of a stepwise regression between the variable of Inspires Confidence and the eleven other variables, utilizing the 498 ratings made by the 83 judges on each of the twelve dimensions. The multiple R of Inspires Confidence with Empathy alone is .50, with Empathy and Congruence is .55, with Empathy, Congruence and Warm and Giving is .57, with the addition of Self-Confidence .59 and with all twelve variables .60.

TABLE 5–XIII

Rotated Factor Matrix Based on the Six Means of Twelve Variables as Shown in Table 5–III

		Rotated Factor Matrix	
Factor Number		*1*	*2*
Sum Squares over Variables		*6.232*	*4.029*
No. and Variable Name	*Communality 2 Factors*		
1 Cognitive	0.924	−0.950	0.150
2 Experiential	0.823	0.901	−0.111
3 Empathic	0.961	0.315	0.928
4 Therapist-Directed	0.983	−0.896	−0.424
5 Equalitarian	0.962	0.953	0.232
6 Warm and Giving	0.506	0.557	0.443
7 UPR	0.905	0.700	0.644
8 Congruent	0.783	−0.094	0.880
9 Emphasizes Unconscious	0.843	−0.641	−0.657
10 Systematically Reinforces	0.891	−0.880	−0.341
11 Self-Confident	0.723	−0.844	−0.099
12 Inspires Confidence	0.955	−0.004	0.977

Summary and conclusions

This report on the Psychotherapy Research Project of the American Academy of Psychotherapists provides evidence for these generalizations:

1. Expert therapists representing different orientations actually practice differently from one another.

2. The orientation and experience level of the judges made little difference in the ratings of the experts.

3. There is a high level of agreement in describing profiles of the Ideal Therapist, regardless of orientation and experience.

4. The judges see themselves as being closer to their concept of the Ideal Therapist than they do the six experts as an aggregate. They view both their self practice and the Ideal as being most like Client-Centered Therapist E.

5. The three experts who provided Self ratings showed substantial agreement with the ratings made by the judges of their work. As a group, they disagree more than the judges in their concept of the Ideal Therapist.

6. A principal component factor analysis of the twelve variables yields two factors, one associated with the Self-Confidence of the expert and which is highly loaded on the Cognitive, Therapist-Directed and Systematically Reinforces variables in one direction and on the Experiential and Equalitarian variables in the other. The second factor is associated with Inspiring Confidence and is highly loaded on Empathy and Congruence.

7. The most general finding of the study appears to be that, while objective assessment of actual therapy samples of diverse experts reveals substantial differences in the way they practice, there is a large measure of agreement between therapists of the three main schools making up the judge population of this project (Analytically oriented, Client-Centered and Eclectic), that the Experiential aspect of therapy is more important than the Cognitive and that qualities such as Empathy and Congruence are to be given greater weight than Therapist-Direction, Emphasizes Unconscious and Systematically Reinforces.

References

Ellis, A. (1962) *Reason and emotion in psychotherapy.* New York: Lyle Stuart.

Fiedler, F. E. (1950) The concept of an ideal therapeutic relationship. *Journal of Consulting Psychology, 14,* 239–45.

Meltzoff, J. and Kornreich, M. (1970) *Research in psychotherapy.* New York: Atherton Press.

Munroe, R. (1995) *Schools of psychoanalytic thought.* New York: Dryden.

Progoff, I. (1956) *The death and rebirth of psychology.* New York: Julian.

Raskin, N. J. (1965) The psychotherapy research project of the American Academy of Psychotherapists. Proceedings of the 73rd Annual Convention of American Psychological Association, 253–4.

Rogers, C. R. (1961) *On becoming a person.* Boston: Houghton Mifflin.

Rosen, J. N. (1953) *Direct analysis.* New York: Grune and Stratton.

Strupp, H. H. (1955) An objective comparison of Rogerian and psychoanalytic techniques. *Journal of Consulting Psychology, 19,* 1–7.

Strupp, H. H. (1958a) The performance of psychoanalytic and client-centered therapists in an initial interview. *Journal of Consulting Psychology, 22,* 265–74.

Strupp, H. H. (1958b) The psychotherapist's contribution to the treatment process. *Behavioral Sciences, 3,* 24–67.

Sundland, D. M. and Barker, E. N. (1962) The orientations of psychotherapists. *Journal of Consulting Psychology, 26,* 201–12.

Wallach, M. S. and Strupp, H. H. (1964) Dimensions of psychotherapists' activity. *Journal of Consulting Psychology, 28,* 120–5.

Whitaker, C. and Malone, T. (1953) *The roots of psychotherapy.* New York: Blakiston.

Wrenn, R. L. (1960) Counselor orientation: theoretical or situational? *Journal of Consulting Psychology, 7,* 40–5.

Appendix A: Therapist Rating Sheet

Therapist being rated . . . .

Birthdate of rater . . . .
           Month   Day   Year

Date of this rating . . . .

	Degree (Circle)			
	Imperceptible	*Somewhat*	*Considerably*	*Extremely*
Cognitive	1	2	3	4
Experiential	1	2	3	4
Empathic	1	2	3	4
Therapist-Directed	1	2	3	4
Equalitarian	1	2	3	4
Warm and Giving	1	2	3	4
UPR	1	2	3	4
Congruent	1	2	3	4
Emphasizes Unconscious	1	2	3	4
Systematically Reinforces	1	2	3	4
Self-Confident	1	2	3	4
Inspires Confidence	1	2	3	4
(Other	1	2	3	4
dimensions				
you believe				
significant)	1	2	3	4

If you think you know the identity of this therapist, please give his name . . . .

If you identified this excerpt with a particular therapeutic orientation, please name it
. . . .

What is your opinion of this excerpt? (You may use the back of this form.)

N J Raskin, PhD
AAP Psychotherpist Research Project

Appendix B: Judge's Self-Description

Circle those numbers on the variables below which are most representative of your present behavior as a therapist. These variables are defined on the accompanying material. The item 'Inspires Confidence' is based on your judgment of how your clients respond to you.

	Imperceptible	*Somewhat*	*Considerably*	*Extremely*
			Degree (Circle)	
Cognitive	1	2	3	4
Experiential	1	2	3	4
Empathic	1	2	3	4
Therapist-Directed	1	2	3	4
Equalitarian	1	2	3	4
Warm and Giving	1	2	3	4
UPR	1	2	3	4
Congruent	1	2	3	4
Emphasizes Unconscious	1	2	3	4
Systematically Reinforces	1	2	3	4
Self-Confident	1	2	3	4
Inspires Confidence	1	2	3	4
(Other	1	2	3	4
dimensions				
you believe				
significant)	1	2	3	4

The Ideal Therapist

Circle those numbers on the variables below which represent your concept of the ideal therapist. The variables are defined on the accompanying material.

	Imperceptible	*Somewhat*	*Considerably*	*Extremely*
			Degree (Circle)	
Cognitive	1	2	3	4
Experiential	1	2	3	4
Empathic	1	2	3	4
Therapist-Directed	1	2	3	4
Equalitarian	1	2	3	4
Warm and Giving	1	2	3	4
UPR	1	2	3	4
Congruent	1	2	3	4
Emphasizes Unconscious	1	2	3	4
Systematically Reinforces	1	2	3	4
Self-Confident	1	2	3	4
Inspires Confidence	1	2	3	4
(Other	1	2	3	4
dimensions				
you believe				
significant)	1	2	3	4

Appendix B: Judge's Self-Description (continued)

Check or write in your therapeutic orientation:

Freudian . . . .   Client-Centered . . . .
Neo-Freudian . . . .   Existential . . . .
Adlerian . . . .   Experiential . . . .
Jungian . . . .   Rational-Emotive . . . .
Sullivanian . . . .   Eclectic . . . .
Gestalt . . . .   Other . . . .

Your birthdate: . . . .
                    Month   Day   Year

Your academic degrees . . . . Your profession . . . .

Date of these ratings . . . .

I have practiced therapy approximately . . . . . hours a week for . . . . . years.

Return to:
N J Raskin PhD, AAP Research
Northwestern University Medical School
303 East Chicago Avenue
Chicago, Illinois 60611

Appendix C: Therapist Behavior Variables — Definitions

Cognitive
The therapist is engaged in developing an *objective understanding* of the way the patient functions. He wants, for his sake and eventually the patient's, to know what makes the patient tick. The therapeutic process is centered around the concept of *insight.* Through his behavior, the therapist is saying, 'I want to understand the way you function so that I can help you to understand yourself.'

Experiential
In his behavior, the therapist is helping to create a therapeutic emotional experience for the client. He acts as if therapy for him is an *affective* rather than a cognitive process. The therapist is saying implicitly, 'This is a situation in which I would like you to experience yourself freely; I don't see you as coming here to learn lessons, but to free yourself emotionally, within you and in your relationship with me.'

Empathic
The therapist is trying, as sensitively and as accurately as he can, to understand the client, *from the latter's own point of view.* It is an understanding of what the client is aware of and trying to convey to the therapist, so if the latter is accurate in his empathic endeavor, the client will feel and may say, 'Yes, that's it! That's how I feel! That's what I meant! You really understand me.' This is an understanding different from the kind which relates the client's behavior to a theory of personality or adjustment which is held by the therapist and which may result in a client reaction such as, 'Let's see. Is that true? That may be right. I never thought of that.' The empathic attitude is, 'I want to know and to convey to you my understanding of how you see things, how you interpret your experience, how you feel about yourself and others.'

Therapist-directed
The therapist is deliberately trying to influence the direction of the interaction in the hour or the patient's behavior outside. He feels it is necessary to *intervene,* to disrupt the patient's current pattern of adjustment.
He is involved in interpreting, in teaching the patient what he has learned about him, what he feels the patient ought to know about himself, or in instructing the patient in some other manner. His attitude is, 'You have come to grief because of certain errors in the way you have been living or looking at things. I can help you correct these. I can show you how to live more happily and efficiently than you have been doing.'

Equalitarian
The therapist expresses himself as a person who is involved in an equalitarian relationship. He creates an atmosphere of mutuality rather than one in which he has a different status than the client. His attitude is, 'You have come to me for help, but as persons we have equal value, and we share the same basic human emotions, vulnerabilities and aspirations.'

Warm and giving
The therapist appears *personally* interested in the patient's problems and in what happens to him. What he does as a therapist sounds like a giving of himself rather than the employment of a professional method. He conveys the attitude, 'I care deeply about what happens to you. The way you feel and get along makes a real difference to me. I am willing to extend myself to help you. When you leave my office, I will still be thinking about you.'

Unconditional positive regard

The therapist acts in a way which sets no *conditions* on his feelings of warmth and caring for the client. There is no demand for the client to be a particular kind of person or act in some particular way in order to earn the positive regard of the therapist. The therapist states in effect, 'I respect your individuality as a person. I care for you, and you can count on my caring even if your ways, your ideas, your choices are different from mine or other people's.'

Congruent

The therapist's behavior is consistent with his feelings. He is not talking one way and thinking another. There is an *openness* about his communication which conveys the feeling that this is all of the therapist talking, not just part of him, not just a psychotherapist employing a technique, or expressing only what he thinks the client should hear.

Emphasizes unconscious

The therapist does not believe the patient can be helped unless he brings out, or communicates with, the patient's unconscious. He is saying, 'What you are aware of is superficial. There is another part of you which is much more valid, important, and powerful. This must be brought to the surface if you are to be helped.'

Systematically reinforces

The therapist, by some kind of approving response, and without necessarily realizing or intending it, *systematically endeavors to reinforce* certain types of patient response or behavior. The therapist's attitude is, 'There are some ways of looking at things or of behaving which are desirable for your adjustment, and I'd like to see you following these ways.' By the same token the therapist voices disinterest in or disapproval of what he regards as undesirable modes of behavior.

Self-confident

The therapist sounds as if *he* knows and believes in what he is doing, regardless of his particular method. (This is not a rating of the patient's response to the therapist, but of the way the latter sounds, independent of the patient.) The therapist conveys the attitude, 'I am confident that I can help you.'

Inspires confidence

This is a rating, not of the therapist's apparent confidence in himself, but *the confidence he inspires in you,* the judge. He makes you feel, 'This client is in good hands. I would refer people to him for help. I would go to him for help myself.'

Learning Through Human Encounters[1]

6

As a psychotherapist, I have learned to value a certain kind of human encounter. It is probably true also that, because I value a certain kind of human encounter, I am a psychotherapist. When I enter the college classroom, I take this valuing with me. I take it into an undergraduate course on Child Development, into a graduate course on The Psychotherapies, and into a seminar on Group Therapy with psychiatry residents and psychology interns. The setting may be a College of Arts and Sciences or a Medical School, a Home Economics Department or a Department of Psychiatry. In these different settings, within a traditional university, I have been able to operate freely with regard to grading, class size, course content and process, and to initiate new courses such as 'The Development and Actualization of the Self'.

These operations express certain characteristics of human encounter which I value. Some of these I here discuss. These are some of the principles of encounter which, as a psychotherapist, I value in interpersonal relationships in general and specifically, in the classroom. They provide the basis for some of the principles of *my* learning theory. Usually, learning theory is identified with stimulus-response, conditioning and behavior change conceptualizations. My belief, as a teacher, is that the principles of encounter which I have stated and will amplify lead to the most meaningful and, eventually, productive kind of learning. This paper is devoted to a clarification and amplification of ten principles, focusing on undergraduate teaching where the application would be the most difficult.

1. *I know who the other person is and he knows who I am.*
This means first of all that I rule out lecturing as a method of teaching because it does not give me adequate opportunity to know my students. It also eliminates large classes for the same reason. In a course which meets for one quarter, twice

---

1. The 'human encounter' aspects of learning are sympathetically portrayed by an Associate Professor of Psychiatry, Northwestern University. The author (BS, City College, College of the City of New York; MA, Ohio State; PhD, Chicago), did his clinical work under Carl Rogers.

Originally published in *Improving College and University Teaching*, (1975), *23*(2), 71–4. Reprinted with permission.

a week for one or two hours or once a week for three hours, and which engages mostly in group discussion, I have found that approximately 25 is my limit for feeling sure of the name of each student, to know something about his interests, and to have some feeling about him as a person. With this numerical limit, I can feel secure, too, about being able to perceive the existence of an acute or more than ordinary personal problem which might benefit from professional help.

In the smaller, discussion type group, I can feel more free to disclose myself as a person. In a human development course such as 'Family Relationships', I feel I can make a richer contribution and encourage a more meaningful exchange by expressing personal feelings and experiences.

I try to implement this first principle, as stated above, even before the beginning of a course, by meeting individually everyone who is interested in registering for the course, to learn something about the nature of his interest and to allow him to get some first-hand feeling for me and the course. I may talk to 50 or more people in this way and try to come out with 25 or so who like my approach and whom I evaluate as having an intrinsic interest in the course, in distinction from those who may find it convenient, or think it sounds interesting in a very general or superficial way, or who are looking for an 'easy' course. The result is usually a class in which the students are highly motivated, involved, and sometimes creative and productive in ways that are highly individual and unexpected.

2. *I am interested in people and in the meaning of the subject matter to them, not in subject matter itself.*
For this reason, and because I believe that human or humanistic learning is inextricably bound up with interest, I do not begin a course with a preconceived curriculum, which I could assume would be of some interest to the students who had selected the course. I allow the content of class interaction, projects, and productions such as papers to grow out of the individual and current interests of the students and of myself, recognizing that these may change during the course of the term. My overall concept of the course 'Problems in Human Development' is broadened from the subjects of physical handicaps, emotional disturbance, and mental retardation, to include other just as significant 'problems in human development' which concern individual students, such as the problems of being black or white in our society, and it focuses increasingly on personal problems experienced by the students in their own development. This more liberal concept has resulted in the transformation of what looks like a group of privileged happy-go-lucky young people into a real group of persons, with a full complement of very troublesome problems in their past and present lives, and with many unexpected sensitivities, sensibilities, and talents.

3. *I believe in human being-to-human being encounter rather than one based on professional role.*
The personal encounter promotes an involvement in the learning process where the student is an active agent, sensitive to what is going on inside and outside of

himself. The teacher who relates more as a professional, it seems to me, by contrast, encourages a more passive student posture, oriented to finding out what is supposed to be learned. In relation to *what* is learned, this can make the difference between trite generalizations and personally meaningful insights.

My own involvement as a teacher is also heightened, in the person-to-person type of relationship, because I am motivated to keep in touch with what is going on currently in my feelings and thoughts, because I participate in the excitement of not being sure what is going to come up in class, and because my behavior is congruent with my emotional life. Inasmuch as I am dealing in my courses with issues and problems in human development, I am helping to make the subject matter with which we deal come alive.

4. *I believe in encounters which are mutually interesting and meaningful.*
If I contribute to the class what is meaningful to me as a person, the encounter will be interesting and alive on my side of the interaction. How the students respond will indicate whether there is a mutuality of interest. I assume that learning and growth will not occur if my contribution is one which only I think is great or learned or insightful. By the same token, I want the experience to be fresh and interesting to me.

In the course 'Problems in Human Development' I used to interview a young blind man in class to convey, in an immediate and dramatic fashion, the problems experienced by a person without sight and to bring home the fact that there is a person, with all kinds of feelings, aspirations, abilities, etc., behind a handicap. In another course on 'The Individual, Marriage, and the Family', I would use a tape of an adolescent boy being interviewed by a noted psychotherapist. In both cases, these demonstrations, as I repeated them, took on a routine quality and decreased in interest for me, so I discontinued them.

The attainment of mutual or group interest involves risk and sometimes pain. It involves a process which is uncharted and has no known outcome, and almost always includes periods of silence which, in the beginning, for some of the participants are acutely uncomfortable.

5. *I value questions, insights, behavior which occur or develop spontaneously.*
I have found that out of spontaneous interaction come new learning and genuine growth. Prepared lectures or even demonstrations go together with preconceived learnings. These tend to be part of an authoritarian type of educational structure in which the student learns *for* the teacher, and the teacher is following a prepared script which is safe for him but is very unlikely to result in any growth for him. In the unstructured class, the learner may be any member of the group, including the instructor, the learnings or insights are unpredictable in content, and they are likely, if they occur, to be highly personal, meaningful, useful, and 'sharable'.

6. Each person in a group is a source of knowledge and insight; correspondingly, I recognize that I, like any other teacher, leader, or status figure, have areas of ignorance, doubt, uncertainty.

To view the teacher, or to set up the classroom situation, as if he is *the* one who determines *what* is to be learned and *how*, is to deny the truth of the above proposition. Not only do students know more about some areas than I do; through their experiences they can breathe life into observations, research findings, etc., translating 'objective' data into personal meaningfulness. In one class discussion about race relations, a student reported a personal experience in a North African community where a black preschool child, who had never before seen a white person, rubbed his fingers twice against her bare legs, looking to see if her pale pigmentation had come off on his hand. Another student arranged for a class discussion with one of the black power leaders on campus, still another with a member of Alcoholics Anonymous, contacts which I did not have. The more personal experiences shared by students, such as growing up in a family where the mother was in a mental hospital, or learning to cope with a body terribly scarred from burning, I certainly could not have originated.

I have also found that admitting ignorance or doubt, or introducing an issue about which I am confused, allows me to be an active learner in the classroom, and promotes a general atmosphere of evolving new clarifications and insights. This is a needed antidote for years of classroom experience in which the expectation is that you 'show what you know', and try to conceal what you do not.

7. It is up to each student to decide what would be meaningful for him to produce and whatever is produced is valued for its meaning to him.

The subjects I teach are broad in scope; there is no set curriculum I feel I must cover. I interpret the registration of a student for a course such as 'Child Development' or 'Problems in Human Development' as an expression of interest which will be defined on a very individual basis for each student. I recall that as a graduate student I enrolled in a course on the History of Psychology which was taught by a traditional kind of professor. To my surprise, he accepted my proposal to do a term paper on The Development of Nondirective Therapy, which was the aspect of psychology history in which I was most interested at the time. The result was a paper in which I poured a great deal of myself and which allowed me to make a contribution to the general field of psychology, coming out as my first publication. This provided the best 'apperceptive mass', too, for me to learn about the history of psychology in general.

As a result of giving my students the same kind of freedom, choice, and opportunity, some have written scholarly papers, others have produced beautiful poetry, others have had the growth experience under which they did not have to produce anything but could simply 'be' and relate to the others in class.

In a course which I have just completed in 'Family Relationships', one student created an eight-foot-high banner on the theme of love and sharing and individual risk-taking. Another presented to each member of the class a computer print-out, also about eight feet long, consisting of statements, questions, insights, expressed during the quarter, which were especially meaningful to this young man. Neither of these productions was required; each was unique and completely individual, unpredictable and non-traditional in form, and had the quality of a gift to the others in the class.

8. *What is produced is produced for the student himself and, if he wishes, to be shared by the group; it is not produced for me, a status figure.*
The examples I have just given of the banner and the computer print-out exemplify this principle. I regard the student's choice of production as being in his own service, not mine. This begins with words that are spoken in class; they are not for my benefit or for the others. It extends to anything that is written or made. For productions on paper, I have often provided a file box on a shelf, easily accessible to the class, in which any of us can place a statement, a reaction, a poem, or an article which we would like to share with the others.

I find that while students are entering my courses more ready for this kind of orientation to what they produce, it involves a considerable shift in their set, and for many it takes several weeks of experience in the classroom to believe that the responsibility for what they produce and how they share it is really theirs.

I have also found that, characteristically, students are more willing, at least at first, to make significant self-disclosures in writing, to me than to their fellow students. I understand and accept this, but encourage communication with the whole group, and practice this in my own behavior.

9. *What is produced is evaluated, not just by me, but by the student and, if shared by the other students, by them.*
A natural extension of the student working for himself is that he will be the judge of his product and effort. This overlaps with the issue of grading, but not completely. These questions come up with each new class I teach, either on the students' initiative or mine. Grading plans which have evolved from such discussions with students have typically included elements of self, peer, and instructor evaluation, with the student increasingly having the final responsibility. More significant to me, however, is the fact that, as a result of this kind of approach, many students are able to separate the course grade from their own evaluation of what they have done, with the grade assuming a subordinate position. (Most recently, with the University making it possible for almost all students to register for my courses on a 'pass–no pass' basis, I have encouraged this system.)

Self-evaluation at times extends far beyond the student's work in a particular class. Following a course on 'The Development and Actualization of the Self', one student changed her occupational goal from advertising to social service, another participated in a peace demonstration for the first time, a third decided that her engagement to a particular boy was largely a reflection of her parents' wishes and broke it up. All of these actions were seen by the students involved as bringing them closer in their living to what they really wanted, being more true to themselves, representing steps toward increased self-actualization.

Occasionally, I have felt 'burned' by self-evaluation, with a student giving himself a grade with which I strongly disagreed. In such instances, I have let the student know my feelings, but have left the final decision up to him.

Grading remains a difficult problem for me. I prefer the 'pass–no pass' system which leaves me and the student most free to participate in a learning relationship with sharply reduced artificial incentives. Where administrative conditions require me to give a grade, I believe that it is a learning experience both for me and my students at the time to examine the problem together, and to work out a mutually agreeable solution. I have deep convictions regarding both the deleterious effect of straight instructor evaluation and the growth opportunities afforded by self-evaluation. I believe any grading system should include the elements of evaluation by instructor, evaluation by peers, and evaluation by self. This evaluation may include a letter grade, but should not be restricted to this.

10. *It is up to each person to decide how personal, or self-disclosing he wishes to be.* I am dealing here, on the one hand, with my belief that the more personal involvement in the classroom situation, the more will occur in the way of significant learning and, on the other hand, that in enrolling for most of my courses, students have not made any commitment to self-disclosure. In an atmosphere of permission and sometimes encouragement to be self-revealing, but with an absence of pressure, and with the course set up on an impersonal subject basis rather than structured as group therapy, my experience has been that most of the students will at times make references to their personal lives in order to illustrate or support certain points. In this way, students will allude to divorce in their families, to prejudice, to the existence of a retarded brother or sister, to illegitimate birth, etc. I find that students respond in very diverse ways to the opportunity to be self-disclosing. Some take full advantage of it and apparently benefit a great deal. A very few are put off by it, in spite of having been told in advance that this is one of the possibilities of class experience. Quite a few volunteer comparatively little, but report that they have learned in a way that is very significant to them by being quiet and very attentive members of the group.

This is very different from the almost universal high level of self-disclosure present in group therapy. But I am glad to participate in the kind of educational experience which provides, over the course of years, hundreds of undergraduates with the learning possibilities in a classroom where one can be a person, relating to his classmates and teacher also as persons.

BECOMING — A THERAPIST, A PERSON, A PARTNER, A PARENT, A . . .

7

This article describes some important aspects of my own growth, the development of the Person-Centered Approach and connections I make between the two. In its early stages, Client-Centered Therapy contributed to my personal ideology of respect for persons and their capacity for self-direction and to the development of a professional skill in implementing this philosophy. At the same time it was non-threatening. This was followed by the recognition by Bown, Streich, Rogers and others that the person of the therapist must be expressed in the therapeutic process and by my own greater ability to do this. Self-awareness and self-expression have been easier for me within the context of psychotherapy than outside, however. While I have experienced growth as a person, outside the office, it has been a process which is painfully difficult and slow. The client-centered concept of congruence, genuineness or openness has been a guiding principle in my own growth and has facilitated my expressiveness as a person and as a therapist. Three 'client variables' in the personality theory accompanying Client-Centered Therapy have impressed me as especially potent in my own development as well as that of the field: self-concept, locus-of-evaluation and experiencing. They have resulted more in a process than in a product, characterized by many growing edges, for me and for the person-centered movement.

In the beginning — for me

I became a therapist before I became a person. I grew up, as in a dream, in a Jewish immigrant family which moved, during my childhood, from the lower East Side of Manhattan to progressively better apartments in the Bronx. There were milestones along the way in the achievement of comforts: our own bathroom, a refrigerator, telephone, steam heat, etc.

I did not think of myself as poor. There was always plenty of food, adequate heat and light and a high standard of cleanliness. There was also a deep, implicit sense of love and caring, which was often expressed in an attitude of over-protection. There was a consistent valuing of education; I was double-promoted five times, graduated from high school at 15, from college at 19 and had my master's degree at 20. My two older brothers and I all earned advanced degrees.

I was well cared for, but not in a way which promoted a sense of self. It

Originally published in *Psychotherapy, Theory, Research, and Practice,* (1978), *15,* 362–70. Reprinted with permission.

seemed a tremendous step to leave home to do graduate work at Ohio State in Columbus; this was made easier by my going out there with an undergraduate friend, with whom I shared a room. I think of myself then as a nice, pleasant boy, lacking in self-confidence, shy, hiding my inadequacies real or supposed, lacking many social skills, afraid of girls, ignorant of sex. I did not know how to dance or to drive a car.

I was intelligent, likable (although hard to get to know), liked to play ball, was interested in photography and politically idealistic. I had a lot of feeling for people who were poor, deprived, discriminated against, in pain. I hated war.

Somehow, working with Carl Rogers and learning the theory and practice of nondirective counseling filled a very central need for me. It seemed to give me a base on which to build a sense of self, it was very consistent with my idealism and desire to help others, and it provided a way of using myself which did not require a focusing on my own person. Perfect. I also learned to live away from home, to make new and valued friends with very different backgrounds (I think of Charles Gibbons from semi-rural south eastern Ohio and Bill Snyder from Chevy Chase), to develop clinical skills of testing and interviewing and to hold a job. (In spite of my family's relatively low economic position, I had never worked; as the youngest child, I was overprotected and I accepted the safety afforded by this treatment.)

Thus, my experience as a graduate student and, particularly, in nondirective counseling, was vital to my development as a person. Objectively, I had been developing as a person since my birth. Phenomenologically, my self-development began in this period of my life.

I developed skill rapidly as a nondirective counselor. Carl Rogers was beautifully clear about what the approach involved, I caught on quickly, the ideology appealed to me and I had lots of practice and people to talk to about it. Dr Rogers himself was interested, available and authentic.

It is meaningful to me to think of the client-centered therapist and Nat Raskin growing up in parallel fashion. At Ohio State, in the early 1940s, we both had a lot of skill and sensitivity to others, and a lack of attention to self. Within this kind of framework, there was a high level of confidence and articulateness.

World War II

We were also both caught up in World War II. Carl Rogers applied his skills to the USO (United Services Organization) and to returned servicemen. I became a Classification Officer with the Army Air Forces. As a First Lieutenant, I took on a lot of responsibility without exerting much authority. I took orders from men who had much less talent than I did, but were much more self-assertive.

After the war, Carl Rogers had moved to the University of Chicago as head of the Counseling Center and the teaching and research program in Client-Centered Therapy; I had obtained my master's degree from Ohio State and wanted to go on to my PhD. I applied to the new Veterans Administration Clinical Psychology Training Program headed by Dr James G. Miller and to the GI Bill of Rights and was accepted for graduate work with this kind of support at Yale University and the University of Chicago. This was a difficult choice for me. Yale meant being close to New York, my family, Ivy League status. Chicago meant the resumption of being a student with Carl Rogers and, in effect, continuing my development as a person. I chose Chicago.

The University of Chicago

There was a big leap in the development of nondirective counseling at the University of Chicago. While at Ohio State, Carl Rogers (1942) had written *Counseling and Psychotherapy*, a kind of primer on the nondirective method. While at Chicago, he published *Client-Centered Therapy*, containing much more theory, research and application (Rogers, 1951).

During my first year at Chicago, I worked for the VA, and took courses with Dr Rogers, Virginia Axline and other members of the Psychology Faculty and Counseling Center staff. For a course on the History of Psychology, I wrote a term paper on 'The Development of Nondirective Therapy'. I shared it with Dr Rogers and the Counseling Center people and, on the basis of it, was offered a job on the Center staff. I resigned from the VA, where I was having trouble reconciling my client-centered convictions with the practice of clinical psychology which relied heavily on the use of the Rorschach test and other diagnostic procedures.

My term paper became my first publication when it came out in the *Journal of Consulting Psychology* (Raskin, 1948). Part of my summary read: 'Rogers has given Rank's client-centered philosophy a definite technique and has made it more meaningful and complete by accepting the client's expressed feelings at the moment . . . and eliminating directive features of the Rankian method. Accompanying this more complete acceptance has been a greater concentration on the client's internal frame of reference. This has led to an increased emphasis on a nondirective *attitude* as opposed to nondirective techniques, to an appreciation of the self-concept as a factor in adjustment, to a greater stress on phenomenological methods of studying personality, and to the application of nondirective principles to other areas of human interrelationships.'

As a therapist at this time, then, I felt confident in my skills and derived support from a rationale and theory which underlay my practice. In this way I feel that I was growing with the movement, although, as I have indicated, as a person, I was just beginning to develop.

The next important phase in the development of the concept of the client-centered therapist occurred during the same period, toward the very end of the decade of the 1940s. This particular development, having to do with the person of the therapist, has the same type of central significance as Rogers' belief in the capacity of the client and the place of the self-concept in the personality theory of Client-Centered Therapy. In a chapter describing progress in client-centered counseling and psychotherapy, I quoted Oliver Bown's and Eugene Streich's informal writings as follows (Raskin, 1952):

Bown: . . . As therapist I can allow a very strong feeling or emotion of my own to enter the therapeutic relationship, and expect that the handling of this feeling from me by the client will be an important part of the process of therapy for him.

. . . a very basic need of the therapist can be satisfied legitimately (or I would rather say *must* be satisfied, if the relationship is to be healthy and legitimate) in his relationship with his client.

. . . the therapeutic interaction at this emotional level, rather than interaction at an intellectual cognitive level, regardless of the content concerned, is the effective ingredient in therapeutic growth.

Streich: When the therapist's capacity for awareness is thus functioning freely and fully without limitations imposed by theoretical formulations of his role, we find that we have, not an individual who may do harm, not a person who must follow certain procedures, but a person able to achieve, through the remarkable integrative capacity of his central nervous system, a balanced, therapeutic, self-growing, other-growth facilitating behavior as a result of all these elements of awareness. To put it another way, when the therapist is less than fully himself — when he denies to awareness, various aspects of his experience — then indeed we have all too often to be concerned about his effectiveness, as our failure cases would testify. But when he is most fully himself, when he is his most complete organism, when awareness of experience is most fully operating, then he is to be trusted, then his behavior is constructive.

Congruence and beyond

The therapeutic force in a freely-functioning therapist which Bown and Streich recognized was incorporated later in Rogers' (1951) inclusion of 'congruence' as one of three 'necessary and sufficient' conditions for psychotherapy. Perhaps because it was coupled with empathy and unconditional positive regard, 'congruence' may have represented a more formal, more impersonal, more professional, less free concept than the one Bown and Streich had in mind. In Rogers' (1970, 1972, 1977) later writings on the basic encounter group, on marriage and its alternatives, and on personal power, he depicts the therapist and facilitator increasingly as a freely functioning individual who can express himself emotionally and as a person. In *Becoming Partners* he writes as frankly about his own marriage as about the relationships of the other people in the book. Committing oneself in a relationship, communicating difficult thoughts and feelings, living by self-determined choices and developing a separate self are issues and problems for the therapist as they are for his clients (Rogers, 1972). And in his relationships with his associates and students, 'Dr Rogers' became 'Carl'.

Becoming a person (as a therapist)

It is clear that, in the 35–40 years of evolution of nondirective counseling to the basic encounter group, the concept of the counselor or therapist or leader or facilitator has grown from that of a basically sensitive and empathic professional to one who is still sensitive but also self-aware and self-expressive, willing to give vent to her emotions, willing to encounter, to break into another's frame of reference in terms of her own feelings, committed to being honest in her relationships.

I have found this changing conceptualization of the therapist to be personally meaningful. I have also found it easier to grow in such terms as a therapist than to do so as a parent, a partner, a person.

Therapeutic relationships are circumscribed in time; they are defined by the 50-minute hour, the two-hour group, the weekend encounter. In this way, they lend themselves to openness, to risk-taking, to frank and honest interaction, to disclosure of weakness, to the expression of love and anger, to warmth without possessiveness. Not that the struggle to be more personal, human and authentic as a therapist or as a client is easy. But I have found it easi-*er*. Easier to be more intimate and loving. Thus, I feel that I have thrived in the office and in the weekend retreat, as have many of my clients and my colleagues. I have experienced this in my own person both as a therapist and as a client, as a group leader and as a group member. In the therapeutic house, I believe that I can say accurately that I am generally perceived as warm and loving, able to be myself, quiet when I have nothing to say, honest when I feel stuck or confused, verbally and physically expressive, sometimes able to let go with tears or anger.

Becoming a person (outside the office)

My slowest growth has occurred as a person and in my personal relationships as a parent and as a partner. In these roles (which I use for want of a better term), I am amazed at how dumb I have been and how long it takes me to learn. I am aware of at least some of my main hang-ups in each area. As a person in general, I have difficulty in asserting myself, in enjoying myself and in revealing areas of weakness and ignorance. It has been very hard for me to work on this paper, principally because it is a form of self-assertion. It is easier for me to do an assignment and, with the pressures of deadlines, this has taken on the nature of an assignment. On the other hand, while I do chores more easily, I also hate them and so resist doing them.

My main hang-up as a parent has been to express the deep love I feel for my daughters by being overprotective, by making it harder for them to do things on their own, to make mistakes, to get hurt, to be separate selves. Fortunately, both of them, in their own ways, have shown tremendous strength to combat that part of my influence which is noxious, and they have helped me to learn to respect their strengths. I have also learned not to interpret their behavior for their benefit (which, as a client-centered therapist, I did not do at the office but saved up for them at home), not to insult them and not to sulk as much. I try to be less preoccupied and burdened with all the things I have to do and to be more available to them as a person.

As a partner, I feel my major hang-ups have been: (1) to expect myself, my children, my house, to be taken care of, in the way I wish, without asking and without being explicit, and (2) to be loved intimately, without being intimate myself. I fantasize about other relationships, as a way of avoiding the work of developing intimacy in my marital partnership, and stick to fantasy in order to avoid the risk of intimacy in these other relationships, and to avoid the risk of losing my wife.

Slowly, I have learned to ask to be held when I am afraid or anxious, to respond to expressions of warmth and affection, to initiate them, to share feelings of weakness and doubt which occur in other areas of my life, to say 'I want this for me', or 'I would rather not be with you right now'.

I would like in my marriage, or in any close relationship, to be more open, trusting and non-possessive. Having these qualities in an intimate relationship can be very threatening to one's self-esteem and one's security, and I think that is what makes it hard for me. I am afraid of being hurt and I am afraid of hurting. I suspect that I am also afraid of being left or of the consequences of leaving a wife and family on whom I depend deeply. So afraid that I do not want even to consider these possibilities. It is like being afraid of death and not writing a will, which is another non-action of mine.

I have grappled with these issues, alone, with my wife, and, both of us, with the help of a therapist. What I hope for, as with issues related to my self-concept, is a result that is not as nice and pretty, but has less illusion and more reality, less holding on for security's sake and more separation for self-fulfillment and enjoyment, and a deepening of love and intimacy.

Client-centered principles and me

The principles of Client-Centered Therapy and their evolution have always made a lot of sense to me. They have been extremely valuable to me as a guide and as a set of ideals, and at the same time very hard to learn and to practice in my own life, which seems to be a constant struggle to attain self-respect, to be open with others, to be open to what others communicate to me, to believe in my own experience of events and to risk asserting myself. There is constantly the temptation to seek psychological safety, by going along with others, by refraining from revealing feelings or taking stands, by taking refuge in institutions, by proceeding only so far in new relationships.

I have been very involved in group situations, therapy groups, supervisory groups, classes, etc. I seem to form relationships easily in these situations, and I get to know a lot of people in this way with whom I feel warm and friendly. I have become aware, however, that these relationships do not go beyond a certain level, and that this is a level which corresponds to a lack of intimacy which exists even in my 'close' relationships.

Another kind of interaction between client-centered principles and my personal behavior has to do with the issue of being good, nice, accepting, patient, empathic, etc. I grew up learning somehow that it was safe to be good. So I developed a pattern of nice behavior in which I never got angry or ruffled anybody. Even though I was shy, I developed the kind of social skill which put people at ease.

Learning to be a client-centered therapist strengthened my armamentarium for peaceful coexistence. I used the early concept of the client-centered therapist to bolster the inhibition of my anger, my aggression, etc. I got some feedback at that time that it was difficult for people, because I was so nice, to tell me things that were *not* nice, and that it was hard for people to get angry at *me*, but I did not get enough of this, or make enough of it, to change. Instead, I believe I deepened my commitment to accepting others, respecting them and being empathic.

When the concept of congruence, describing the therapist's genuineness, became a part of client-centered theory, it was coupled with the concept of unconditional positive regard (as well as empathy) which, in a sense, committed the therapist to a deeper acceptance of others (Standal, 1957). At the time of this development, in the latter half of the 1950s, I was physically separated from the center of the client-centered movement, but I believe that I was in a similar place psychologically, attempting the difficult and sometimes impossible task of being congruent and completely accepting at the same time.

One of the important aspects of the client-centered research project at the University of Wisconsin on therapy with schizophrenic patients had to do with the relationships among the three conditions postulated by Rogers (et al., 1967) as necessary and sufficient for personality change. Statistical analysis failed to demonstrate consistent relationships between congruence and the other two conditions. Partly this was a function of technical difficulties in making ratings with the Congruence Scale. There was also a 'complete divergence between Congruence Scale ratings and patient assessments of the quality of the therapy interaction' which 'highlighted the fact that ratings for present Congruence Scale could not be meaningfully anchored and were therefore, extremely difficult to interpret' (Rogers et al., 1967).

In an American Academy of Psychotherapists study, an analysis of 498 judgments of six expert therapists on twelve variables, yielded a low correlation of .22 between congruence and unconditional positive regard (Raskin, 1974).

In the Wisconsin study, perhaps even more significant than the statistical findings were the subjective reactions of a group of outside experts to their reading of representative samples of some of the more client-centered therapists with three of the more improved patients. The experts included the late Paul Bergman, O. Spurgeon English, William C. Lewis, Rollo May, Julius Seeman and Carl Whitaker. Truax and Carkhuff summarize some of their reactions (Rogers et al., 1967):

> Perhaps the most surprising and striking aspect of the commentaries by the 'outsiders' revolves around the construct of genuineness, self-congruence, or openness. The client-centered therapists, both individually and collectively, have advocated openness and freedom in the therapeutic relationship. They have emphasized as critically important the therapist's willingness for the patient to be himself in

his own manner. The outside theorists, in their attempts to describe the process of Client-Centered Therapy, often focus upon what they perceive as the therapist's rigid and controlling nature which closes him off to many of his own as well to the patient's experiences. If only one reviewer were to focus on this, it could be dismissed as a malperception, but clearly it is not. If it is in some sense a valid observation, how does this apparent rigidity interact with the intent to be open and the verbal communication of a willingness for the patient to take the lead? Is the patient, as suggested, in a difficult 'double-bind' situation when he encounters a therapist who verbally desires openness and freedom in the patient but cannot in actuality be free and open himself? Particularly striking was the observation by all the theorists that the client-centered process of therapy somehow avoids the expected and usual patient expressions of negative, hostile, or aggressive feelings. The clear implication is that the client-centered therapist for some reason seems less open to receiving negative, hostile, or aggressive feelings. Is it that the therapists have little respect for, or understanding of their own negative, hostile, or aggressive feelings, and are thus unable to receive these feelings from the patient? Do they simply 'not believe in' the importance of the negative feelings?

It seems very unlikely to me that client-centered therapists do not believe in the importance of negative feelings. I also agree with Truax and Carkhuff's attempt to resolve the dilemma they raise by hypothesizing that the two conditions of 'unconditional positive regard' and 'therapist congruence' represent two sides of the same coin of 'respect for human experiencing'. As an individual, I would say that I have this great respect for human experiencing, but I can apply it to others more easily than to myself, and also that I am more comfortable with positive than with negative feelings, both in myself and others.

In a publication on client-centered family therapy van der Veen and I (1970) stressed the importance of encounter emerging out of the therapist's personality as a development in Client-Centered Therapy. Rollo May, as one of the 'outside experts' in the Wisconsin study, 'sometimes got the feeling there were not two people in the room . . . A consequence of a misuse of the reflecting techniques . . . [is] . . . that we get only an amorphous kind of identity rather than two subjects interacting in a world in which both participate, and in which love and hate, trust and doubt, conflicts and dependency, come out and can be understood and assimilated.' May was concerned that the therapist's over-identification with the patient could 'take away the patient's opportunity to experience himself as a subject in his own right, to take a stand against the therapist, to experience being in an interpersonal world'. In those instances where the therapist did not merely reflect the patient but himself *added* something which came 'out of his subjective state, his own identity as one person in the relationship', May felt the occurrence of truly therapeutic moments in the three cases (Rogers et al., 1967).

It is more meaningful to me from my own experience, to describe a concentration on the client's frame of reference not as an over-identification but, if continued exclusively, as structuring an incomplete relationship, in which I do not feel completely honest or congruent. I see this as an example of deciding not to risk myself in the relationship, taking refuge in a form of institutionalization, in this case the institution of Client-Centered Therapy. For me, it is a dynamic similar to the one of taking refuge in my family as an institution when I lack the courage to venture out, or in Northwestern University or some other institution, when I am afraid of individual assertion or enterprise.

Wisconsin breakthroughs

Out of the work with schizophrenic patients at the University of Wisconsin, and with the development of the basic encounter group at the end of Rogers' stay in Madison, came some significant advances in the expressiveness of the therapist. One aspect of this was described by Gendlin (1963), who saw therapist expressivity as emphasizing the condition of congruence. Gendlin stated that the therapist 'can draw on his own momentary experiencing and find there an ever-present reservoir from which he can draw, and with which he can initiate, deepen, and carry on therapeutic interaction even with an unmotivated, silent, or externalized person.' 'Also,' Gendlin added, 'congruence for the therapist means that he need not always appear in a good light, always understanding, wise, or strong.' Rogers (1970), in later writings on the basic encounter group, describes the extension of his expressiveness in the realms of love and anger.

At the same time that these developments were occurring in Client-Centered Therapy, I moved off a plateau or came out of a rut in my own life. I was able to let go of my emotion in a way that was unprecedented for me, fell in love and got married. After two years in New York City, my wife and I moved to the Chicago area (the second time for me), away from both of our families. Our two daughters were born. I became involved with the American Academy of Psychotherapists, got into painful but growth-inducing workshop encounters, and my practice of psychotherapy, with individuals and groups, became freer to the extent that, for the first time, I felt like a unique individual therapist, rather than a competent practitioner of Client-Centered Therapy. I have described my personal growth in relation to Carl and to the Academy in an article in *Voices* (Raskin, 1971). In a poem in the same journal, I have communicated some of the ways I make life hard for myself (Raskin, 1973). I continue to try to be more free, to assert myself, to enjoy myself, to get closer to people, to love more deeply, to feel more keenly. I expect this to go on as long as I live.

'Client' variables and me

I have been focusing for the most part in this paper on the development of the concept of therapist functioning in Client-Centered Therapy and the relationship of this to my own growth. There have also been very significant changes in the concept of what happens to clients in the process of therapy or, to put it another way, in the personality theory accompanying Client-Centered Therapy.

I regard three concepts as particularly important in this regard, for the movement and for me, personally.

The first has to do with self-concept. While Rogers (1940) recognized early the importance of the client's view of himself, the person's concept of himself became the central construct in his personality theory (Rogers, 1959). Much of the original impetus for this came from Raimy's (1943) doctoral dissertation.

I have described the way I saw myself as a new graduate student. As I have become more generally self-aware; I have come to appreciate, often dramatically, the incongruities in my self-image and their nefarious effects. Three such incongruities come immediately to mind. One has to do with the dimension of passivity and aggression, a second with physical attractiveness, a third with my general importance.

The issue of aggression in myself comes out in some of these ways:

- I do not think of myself as aggressive. I am afraid I am passive; I do not want to be either.
- I impress others sometimes as quite passive, sometimes as quite strong and determined.
- I have seen myself on videotape in a characteristically passive posture, and do not like it.
- I have been told that I play tennis aggressively, which has not been my impression. However, I have been able, more and more, to experience my power in this situation, and to enjoy it. There has been some spread of this kind of acceptance and enjoyment of assertion of strength to other areas of my life.
- On the issue of passivity and aggression then, I see a pattern of lack of self-awareness, of denial, and of holding on to an inferior self-concept, together with a more recent expansion of my self-concept and a greater congruence between the concept of self held by me and by others.

Physical attractiveness is a second aspect of self-concept which has been very difficult for me. Some of the threads here follow:

- How I look is important to me. I want to look attractive to other people.
- I deceive myself about looks. In the mirror, I look younger and, to me, better-looking than in photographs or on videotape.
- The 'real' me seems to be much more attractive to other people than to me.
- It is very hard for me to believe people when they respond to me as physically attractive, but I am beginning slowly to be able to take in this kind of response and to enjoy it.

Here again, I see a pattern of holding on to an inferior self-concept, distorting reality to try to better it, and the beginning of a process of accepting what is real about me to others.

The third aspect, having to do with my feeling of general importance, has operated in a way that is very similar to the other two areas I have been considering. Again:

- I start out with an inferior concept, I have experiences which are discrepant from it.
- I try to hang on to my old, negative way and I am in the process of risking change and growth by incorporating positive feedback and acting in terms of it.

I hope that these three examples of the way in which my own self-concept has operated will convey the sense of its tremendous influence on me.

A second 'client' variable of great significance to the movement of Client-Centered Therapy as well as to me is that of relying on the self-interpretation of experience. There is no concept more central to Client-Centered Therapy, through its entire development, than this one; it has been expressed in many different ways. The very foundation for Rogers' client-centered method of treatment, his attitude toward facilitating basic encounter groups, his approach to problems in 'becoming partners' and in personal and group power, all are based on the deepest conviction, which I would paraphrase as, 'I believe in you. If I can help you to discover what is most "you", by understanding it as deeply as I can and by being the most "me" in a relationship with you, that would give me great satisfaction, and I will support you in what you choose for yourself.'

To me, this is the essence of Carl Rogers, his humanness and his warmth. It is his own special flame that has glowed with more and more light, warmth and color through the years. And, like the self-concept, the problem of listening to myself and following what I feel, has been and continues to be a most vital one. Carl has stated repeatedly that when he or his clients have listened to themselves and followed their convictions, the consequences have been gratifying and growth-producing. I have found this to be true, also. I am sure that it was my concern with the issue in myself that led to my choosing a doctoral dissertation on the concept of locus-of-evaluation, in which I found that success in psychotherapy was correlated with movement from others to self for the locus of standards and values which influence behavior (Raskin, 1952a).

One of the most significant ways in which this issue remains alive for me is in relation to my professional work. I feel that I have never really done 'my own thing', professionally. I have combined a part-time private practice, where I am autonomous, with affiliation with an institution, where I do much of what satisfies me, but where I rely on the power and authority which other people have to support my activities, and also devote a good deal of time and energy to differing, opposing and oftentimes suffering with policies with which I differ basically. I am loath to give up the security I feel I have in being part of an institution like a university or hospital, and am afraid of the risk that is involved in being completely on my own. The latter involves two clear alternatives in my mind: (1) a life with more time to do things that I enjoy which now I forego because of the pressure of doing all the things I 'have to' and (2) initiating a new professional organization for training, research (broadly conceived) and practice which would function in a way that would be more consistent with my values and beliefs and thinking and would challenge my capacity for leadership and cooperative responsibility.

I feel that, in this area, I have not taken the big leap or plunge, although I think I have made progress in practicing increasingly in accordance with my convictions, taking more time to do things I simply enjoy and being a more effective challenger and protagonist in conflict situations.

The third 'client variable' I wish to consider is that of 'experiencing' (Rogers et al., 1967). The development of this aspect of personality change occurred during the same period (1950s and 1960s) of defining and refining the 'necessary and sufficient' therapist conditions and the appreciation for greater therapist expressivity (Gendlin, 1963; Rogers, 1957).

Focusing on 'experiencing' in the client represented an advance over, or certainly an addition to, earlier formulations of client change described by accretions in insight, reductions in defensiveness, changes in self-concept and behavior, etc. A scale was developed to measure experiencing which went through several different revisions. An example of the most positive stage of the scale is: 'There is free movement in a continuing stream of felt referents. The client easily clarifies his own feelings and meanings by direct access to a continuous flow of inner events. He uses his felt referents as sure guideposts with reliance on his own free movement within his whole subjective field' (Tomlinson, 1961).

This is obviously a cognitive approach to an experiential concept. Since it was formulated, Rogers and his associates appear less concerned with such definitions and more interested in facilitating the free and full expression of feelings, often with people in other lands (Coulson, 1977; Rogers, 1977).

This is another personal issue for me. It is very hard for me to let go with my feelings in a public way. Privately I can feel extremely loving, furious, resentful, envious, lonely, ecstatic, etc. With people, I have to break through a wall of reserve.

I have been helped with this by some intensive experience as a client of Gestalt therapy and as a participant in peer groups with experientially oriented colleagues in the American Academy of Psychotherapists (Raskin, 1971, 1973). I have learned to overcome my inhibitions — to cry, to get angry, to love. And I have been able thereby to enrich my practice as a therapist. Still, the most important considerations continue to be to remain true to myself and respectful of others, appreciating the wonderful response I get from some and the less-than-wonderful I get from others. It is better to have a self with ragged and growing edges getting mixed reactions than a nice, apparently assured front trying to please everyone. And that gives other people — clients, students, spouse, children — a more real choice of how to relate to me.

I believe that here, too, there is a parallel with the movement of Client-Centered Therapy which also is not as neat-looking and organized as it used to be but, stemming from a core of deep conviction of respect for self and personhood, is being expressed by different people in different places in different ways.

References

Coulson, W. R. (1977) The foreignness of feelings. American Psychological Association Annual Convention, San Francisco.

Gendlin, E. T. (1963) Subverbal communication and therapist expressivity: Trends in client-centered therapy with schizophrenics. *Journal of Existential Psychiatry, 14.*

Raimy, V. C. (1943) The self-concept as a factor in counseling and personality organization. Unpublished doctoral thesis, Ohio State University.

Raskin, N. J. (1948) The development of nondirective therapy. *Journal of Consulting Psychology, 12,* 92–110.

Raskin, N. J. (1952a) An objective study of the locus-of-evaluation factor in psychotherapy. In W. Wolff and J. A. Precker (Eds.), *Success in Psychotherapy.* New York: Grune and Stratton.

Raskin, N. J. (1952b) Client-centered counseling and psychotherapy. In L. E. Abt and D. Brower (Eds.), *Progress in clinical psychology.* New York: Grune and Stratton.

Raskin, N. J. (1971) Who reveres the masters? *Voices: The Art and Science of Psychotherapy, 7,* 71–4.

Raskin, N. J. (1973) How do I screw myself, let me count the ways. *Voices: The Art and Science of Psychotherapy, 31,* 39.

Raskin, N. J. (1974) Studies of Psychotherapeutic Orientation: Ideology and Practice. Research Monograph No. 1. Orlando, Florida: American Academy of Psychotherapists.

Raskin, N. J. and van der Veen, F. (1970) Client-centered family therapy: Some clinical and research perspectives. In J. T. Hart and T. M. Tomlinson (Eds.), *New directions in client-centered therapy.* New York: Houghton Mifflin.

Rogers, C. R. (1942) *Counseling and psychotherapy.* Boston: Houghton Mifflin.

Rogers, C. R. (1951) *Client-centered therapy: Its current practice, implications and theory.* Boston: Houghton Mifflin.

Rogers, C. R. (1957) The necessary and sufficient conditions of therapeutic personality change. *Journal of Consulting Psychology, 27,* 95–103.

Rogers, C. R. (1959) A theory of therapy, personality, and interpersonal relationships as developed in the client-centered framework. In S. Koch (Ed.), *Psychology: A study of a science, Vol. III, Formulations of the person in the social context,* pp. 184–256. New York: McGraw-Hill.

Rogers, C. R. (1970) *Carl Rogers on encounter groups.* New York: Harper and Row.

Rogers, C. R. (1972) *Becoming partners: Marriage and its alternatives.* New York: Delacorte Press.

Rogers, C. R. (1977) *Carl Rogers on personal power*. New York: Delacorte Press.

Rogers, C. R., Gendlin, E. T., Kiesler, D. J. and Truax, C. B. (1967) *The therapeutic relationship and its impact: A study of psychotherapy with schizophrenics*. Madison: The University of Wisconsin Press.

Standal, S. (1957) The Need for Positive Regard: A Contribution to Client-Centered Theory. Unpublished PhD thesis. University of Chicago.

Tomlinson, T. M. (1961) The process approach to the analysis of personality change. *Psychiatric Institute Bulletin, 10(d)*. The University of Wisconsin: Wisconsin Psychiatric Institute.

THE CONCEPT OF THE SELF IN CLIENT-CENTERED THERAPY AND THE PERSON-CENTERED APPROACH 1940-1980

8

I began learning to be a counselor and psychotherapist in 1940, as a first-year graduate student at Ohio State University. I had been an undergraduate at the College of the City of New York, a psychology major, knew that I wanted to become a clinical psychologist and searched around for the best graduate program in the field. Initially I sent applications to Indiana University, the University of Iowa and the University of Minnesota. While these were being processed, I talked with Gardner Murphy, the new head of the Psychology Department at City College, the American psychologist with perhaps the broadest and deepest grasp of the field. Dr Murphy suggested I consider Ohio State University, which had recently hired a young and very promising man named Carl Rogers to replace the venerable Dr Goddard, known for the form board used in performance intelligence testing which was named after him.

I wrote to Dr Rogers, received an encouraging and welcoming response, applied to and was accepted at Ohio State, got my MA in 1941, and stayed on in Columbus as our country was getting involved in World War II. Subsequently, I spent three years in the army. After getting out, I decided to resume my graduate studies at the University of Chicago, to which Carl Rogers had moved after directing a counseling program for servicemen on leave and veterans.

I think it was during 1948, while I was working on my PhD and a member of the University of Chicago Counseling Center staff, I had an experience with a client which has remained indelible. She was an older woman, unprepossessing, poorly clothed, with a history of psychiatric hospitalizations and shock treatment. I had seen her only a few times, when she came in and related the following experience. She had boarded a rather crowded CIA bus, found a seat between two men and sat down, kind of hunching herself as she did so. She then had a reaction to this act of trying to make herself smaller and thought, 'No, I am entitled to as much room as these other people'. She squared her shoulders and in so doing, brushed up against one of the men next to her, who looked at her with annoyance. This did not deter my client nor result in an apologetic response. She

Presented at the Department of Psychiatry's Grand Rounds Conference, Northwestern University Medical School, Chicago, Illinois, April 9, 1980.

went on from this incident to take a series of steps which evidenced, for the first time at least in many, many years, a positive regard for herself.

I think of another client I saw, mostly in group therapy, more than 20 years later, around 1970. This woman was in her middle 30s, also with a traumatic history including a psychiatric hospitalization and a series of unsuccessful relationships with men in which she allowed herself to be used and abused. This woman really hurt and in sharing with our group the unhappy events of her life, gave the impression of a bottomless pit of endless suffering. She had an apartment in the Lincoln Park area which was potentially attractive but which she did not keep up. One day, after a particularly unhappy series of events which left her deeply disgusted with herself, she put up a poster on which she had printed, 'PRETEND to have self-respect'. She cleaned up her apartment and, like the lady I had seen in 1948, initiated a series of steps which evidenced self-regard. This culminated in her writing to a brother in California asking him to help her financially to move out and get settled in that state. He responded positively, she made the move, had some setbacks which only slowed her progress temporarily, and developed her own business.

I have another example of difficulty in believing in oneself, in which I was the principal. The woman of whom I have just spoken was a member of a group of four or five which met weekly for four hours at a time. My proposal to offer a conversation hour on this 'weekly four-hour encounter group' was accepted for the American Psychological Association Convention in Miami Beach in 1970. Our APA usually meets over Labor Day, which often falls toward the end of the convention, and my conversation hour was scheduled for late in the afternoon of Labor Day, I think 5 pm. I had run into two or three people who had told me they were planning to attend my program and, because of the scheduled hour (and my self-concept?), I expected a total of two or three to attend. When I walked into the meeting room, to my astonishment, there were two or three hundred! It took me a few minutes to get my bearings, and it turned into a good experience, but I like this example because of the neat mathematical ratio of my estimated value and the actual result, one to a hundred.

I think of a woman I saw just a few days ago for the first time, in individual therapy, whose difficulty in estimating her worth is also expressed numerically, in relation to her pay. She has a job in a small company in which she obviously occupies a central office management role. She discussed her marital history and social relationships in a way that made it clear that she asks very little for herself. In respect to her job she, a college graduate with computer skills and graduate school potential, is being paid less than $6.00 an hour and has not been given a raise in three years. This bothers her and she is especially annoyed now that the company is planning to hire additional part-time office help at a higher rate than she is being paid. In talking with me about steps she might take to improve her situation, she seriously proposed that she might ask for a raise to $6.50 an hour. As soon as she said this, she was struck by the absurdity of her level of aspiration and estimate of worth and she laughed. I am hopeful that, in the course of seeing me, this woman will revise her estimate of her worth, occupationally and interpersonally, sharply upwards.

I cite these examples in order to convey the way in which I think of the self-concept. While it can be described cognitively and while a fairly complex theory developed around it, it is primarily a phenomenological phenomenon which is conscious or close to the level of awareness, it is understandable to the client in his or her own terms, it can come out of immediate experience which the individual may or may not relate to his or her history.

The appreciation of the importance of self-esteem and related aspects of self-concept has become common. Aside from its emergence in psychotherapy, it has been exploited by Madison Avenue and by seemingly countless 'how-to' books on the development of self-confidence and looking after 'number one'.

Forty years ago, references to self were not so common. I ask you to journey back with me to 1940, when I was a psychology major at CCNY and a member of the class of 1940. My teachers and my courses were excellent. They helped me to appreciate the complexity of human behavior. Psychology was defined as the study of behavior, but I learned to appreciate that there was a lot more to understand than the stimulus-response connection. One had to understand the way the organism perceived or experienced the stimulus. Single stimuli had to be understood in relation to the other stimuli in the subject's total field. I developed some understanding of Freud and unconscious forces, of Kurt Lewin and field forces, of the Gestalt Psychology of Koffka, Kohler and Wortheimer, of biology's and society's impact on behavior. I do not remember any importance being attached to the self-concept in my undergraduate training; it is possible that it was not even mentioned. The likelihood of this is supported by Wylie's (1961) observation in her book, *The Self Concept*, that 'during the second, third, and fourth decades of the twentieth century, constructs concerning the self did not receive much attention from the behaviorist and functionalist psychologies which were dominating the American scene'. She adds that Freud, 'in his early theorizing, strongly emphasized the role of the id, and he did not explicitly formalize a self construct nor assign the closely related ego functions much importance, relatively speaking'.

I have described how, in the fall of 1940, I went out to Ohio State to begin graduate work in clinical psychology with Carl Rogers. Wylie cites Rogers as one of the phenomenological theorists who stressed the role of the conscious self-concept in determining a person's behavior. And, indeed, I experienced Rogers, in my own education, as introducing an entirely new and positive dimension into my thinking about human behavior. Even more exciting was learning that I could interact with people as a counselor and facilitate their awareness of themselves and observe how this resulted in changes of behavior. This was tremendously exciting, like learning to fly, I imagine.

Looking back, I think that Rogers' contribution was most impressive and remarkable, in view of the economic, political and sociological times. Let me say something of their nature. I was born, and like Rogers went to college, soon after the end of World War I, with its incredible destruction of human life and values. The year 1929 saw the tragedies wrought by the Great Depression, and a few years later Hitler began his rise to power, culminating in the invasion of Poland in 1939.

In this country, racial and religious prejudice were widespread. Lynchings of blacks in the South were still a way of having fun on Saturday night. Growing up in a city (New York) with a large Jewish population, which was rapidly getting more educated, I was spared the everyday prejudice to which blacks were subject. But not spared entirely. My oldest brother, with an outstanding undergraduate pre-medical education, was not able to get into any of the medical schools to which he applied; all of them followed the practice of having very restricted quotas for Jewish applicants. Many of his friends, as a result, went abroad for their medical educations. One of his best friends went to Munich and, ironically, found himself in the middle of Hitler's rise to power, but managed to graduate and return home.

At Ohio State, I was passed over for an assistantship which was given to a person of Anglo-Saxon heritage, learned that there was an advanced graduate student who had anglicized his name on the advice of his experimental psychology professors because he was interested in a career in academic psychology, and on my third date with a 'co-ed' named Katz, was told that she was sorry but that she was not allowed to go out with Jewish boys.

This might be funny in retrospect but what I am trying to bring out is that the human climate of 1940, dominated by the spread of war and fascism and by widespread prejudice in this country towards blacks and Jews, was not conducive to the positive view of human nature which was connoted by the meaning of the concept of self in the client-centered approach.

Rogers (1953) was very aware of the implications of his positive belief in people, and how it ran against the tide:

> This point of view is so foreign to our present culture that I do not expect it to be accepted, and it is indeed so revolutionary in its implications that it should not be accepted without thorough-going inquiry. But even if it should stand these tests, it will be difficult to accept. Religion, especially the Protestant Christian tradition, has permeated our culture with the concept that man is basically sinful . . . In psychology, Freud and his followers have presented convincing arguments that the id, man's basic and unconscious nature, is primarily made up of instincts which would, if permitted expression, result in incest, murder and other crimes. The whole problem of therapy, as seen by this group, is how to hold these untamed forces in check in a wholesome and constructive manner, rather than in the costly fashion of the neurotic. But the fact that at heart man is irrational, unsocialized, destructive of others and self — this is a concept accepted almost without question . . .

Later in the same paper, Rogers (1953) stated in one powerful sentence his contrasting view:

> When man's unique capacity of awareness is thus functioning freely and fully, we find that we have, not an animal whom we must fear, not a beast who must be controlled, but an organism able to achieve through the remarkable integrative capacity of its central nervous system, a balanced, realistic, self-enhancing, other-enhancing behavior as a resultant of all these elements of awareness.

How did the concept of self specifically express a positive view of men and women? It was positive in the first place in that the therapist took seriously and as valid working material the client's own, conscious attitudes toward himself. Raimy's unpublished doctoral dissertation, 'Self-Reference in Counseling Interviews,' which was completed in 1943, is cited by Wiley as the first use by a psychologist of the method of coding interviews with respect to expressed attitudes toward the self. He established the reliability of coding the unit represented by everything the client said between two counselor responses, six categories being employed: positive self-attitude, negative self-attitude, ambivalent self-reference, ambiguous self-reference, other or external reference, and informational question.

Raimy described his thinking in this way: 'The Self-Concept is the map which each person consults in order to understand himself. The approval, disapproval, or ambivalence he feels for the self-concept is related to his personal adjustment. A heavy weighting of disapproval suggests distress or disturbance. When successful personality reorganization takes place we may also expect a shift from self-disapproval to a self-approving balance.'

Raimy's results supported his hypothesis; cases judged successful showed predicted shifts while in cases judged unsuccessful such shifts were not found.

At the same time, as Seeman and Raskin (1953) note, the main significance in Raimy's study is probably not to be found in his empirical results but rather in the comprehensive formulation of an important aspect of self-theory. Raimy focused on learnings about the self as being the key type of learning in therapy. He saw the self-concept as functioning both inductively and deductively. It serves to regulate behavior and may serve to account for observed uniformities in personality. At the same time, it is itself altered and restructured by behavior and unsatisfied needs.

Also, like George Mead (1934), the noted sociologist, Raimy believed that the self-concept 'undoubtedly has its source in the social interactions of the person beginning with the immediate family and continuing on through life'.

While Raimy pioneered research into self-concept in counseling and psychotherapy, Rogers' (1931) own doctoral dissertation, twelve years earlier, demonstrated the importance he attached to phenomenological experience and its measurement. He devised 'A Test of Personality Adjustment', for boys and girls aged 9 to 13, consisting of six sections, four of which relied heavily on the child's conscious attitudes toward self and/or ideal.

Barrett-Lennard (1979) summarized the development of self-theory in client-centered therapy, from the 1940s to the 1960s as follows:

The development of self-theory had begun with Raimy's dissertation and was first focussed on by Rogers in an address he gave in 1947 — as retiring President of the American Psychological Association — under the title 'Some observations on the organization of personality.' By 1948, Raskin was able to say that 'The client's concept of self is now believed to be the most central factor in his adjustment and perhaps the best measure of his progress in therapy.' Two articles, by Elizabeth Sheerer and by Dorothy Stock, in the 1949 'parallel studies' project focussed directly on self-attitudes and feelings, and Hogan's dissertation and Haigh's report on defensive behavior in therapy effectively drew on the developing self-theory. Rogers' nineteen-proposition statement was a further order of development and established his school of therapy as a new source of an articulated, psychological perspective on human personality and nature.

Further, research focussing on the self-concept, in the 1950s and 1960s, notably by John Butler and collaborators has further illuminated the nature and functional significance of the self-concept, self-ideal and related constructs and variables. Most of the principles of self-theory as such are embodied also in later, broader-based theoretical statements, such as that of Rogers in the mammoth series *Psychology: A study of a science.*

Rogers' nineteen-proposition statement, cited by Barrett-Lennard constituted the last chapter of *Client-Centered Therapy* (1951). Examples of the propositions, each of which is amplified, are:

Reality is, for the individual, the field as perceived.

Our best opportunity of understanding behavior is from the internal frame of reference.

A portion of the total perceptual field becomes differentiated as the conscious self.

Perceptions are either organized into a consistent conscious system related to self, ignored or denied because inconsistent with concept of self.

When the self-concept is safe from threat, it can examine contradictory perceptions and take them into a revised concept of self.

Much of the research on self-concept in the 1950s was based on the Q-technique, developed by William Stephenson (1950). The client sorted 100 self-descriptive statements on cards in nine piles ranging from 'most characteristic of me' to 'least characteristic'. Typical statements were 'I am a submissive person', 'I have an attractive personality', 'I am afraid of what other people think of me'. The number of cards permitted to go in each pile was fixed to approximate a normal distribution. Each time the client did a self-sort, another one was obtained based on the self he or she would like to be, the ideal self. Clients followed this procedure before, during, at the end of therapy and often a follow-up period, with results such as the following:

Perceived self changes more during therapy then during a period of no therapy, and to a degree significantly greater for clients than for control group subjects.

There is a significant increase in congruence between self and ideal, during therapy.

The direction of change in the perceived self is in a direction which expert judges would term adjustment.

Qualitative analysis reveals that clients see themselves as more self-confident and self-reliant, understanding themselves better, experiencing more inner comfort, more comfortable relationships with others, feeling less guilty, less resentful, less driven and insecure, and experiencing less need for self-concealment.

Representations of ideal self are much more stable than representations of perceived self. Perceived self exhibits greater change then ideal self, but ideal self becomes more discrepant from the 'adjustment score'. In other words the self-ideal has become less perfectly 'adjusted', or more attainable. (Rogers and Dymond, 1954)

I think it is apparent that the concept of self, starting with Raimy's relatively simple conceptualization had become strikingly more differentiated by the middle of the '50s. Soon after the completion of the very large research undertaking at the University of Chicago, with its careful planning for assessing outcomes in self-attitudes, 'adjustment' and behavior, utilizing two different kinds of controls, and culminating in the volume edited by Rogers and Dymond (1954), Rogers (1954) went back to an intensive qualitative study of therapy interview data and came out with this cluster of concepts:

The experiencing of feeling
The discovery of self in experience
Openness to experience
Trust in one's organism
An internal locus-of-evaluation
Willingness to be a process

Each one of these concepts is personally meaningful to me, and I have dealt with several of them in a previous publication (Raskin, 1978). I would like here to relate them to myself on a current basis.

The experiencing of feeling

I remember an American Academy of Psychotherapists workshop at Lake Arrowhead 15–20 years ago. I was in a small group led by Laura Perls and I wound up in the 'hot seat' with Laura asking me to get in touch with my feelings. The experience was excruciatingly difficult, painful and embarrassing. I stuck with the AAP workshops, however, and participated in hundreds of hours of other group experiences which helped me to get in touch with and to express my feelings. Within the past month, in a weekend group of three couples and a single person, I opened up a crucial emotional blockage in my relationship with my wife. I was able to cry and to release deep feelings of affection and love.

The discovery of self in experience

In relation to the concept of self, I can say about this experience, that an important part of my self came into awareness, was expressed, was accepted by me, by my wife who is close to me and by significant others. The net result was a rise in self-esteem and in my being open to more experiences. When this kind of event occurs, as Rogers (1954) says, 'it means that the real self is something which is comfortably discovered in one's experiences, not something imposed upon it'.

Openness to experience

The meaning of this to me is that I can incorporate into my self-concept a variety of experiences. I think I have improved in my ability to do this. I used to behave as if I had to win every game of tennis I played, and play an errorless game. Now I can accept losing as well as winning. I do not need every client or every student to choose me for therapy or for a course. Some of my colleagues like and respect me, others do not. If I am able to take in these varied reactions to me, I can in turn be more open to all my experiences. I do not need to deny or distort them.

Trust in one's organism

If I can allow myself to experience a greater range of my own feelings and a mixture of reactions from other people, then I have a sounder basis for making choices which feel right for me. As Rogers (1954) puts it, 'I am giving my organism more data with which to work'. In addition, it makes it less crucial whether or not I make one decision or another, because I can 'swing with' the outcome, one way or another. I do not have to be right all the time.

An internal locus-of-evaluation

This concept is intimately related to the others and is of particular interest to me, being the subject of my doctoral research, in which I presented evidence that the overall success rating and the positive movement of individuals in psychotherapy on a number of relevant variables was significantly related to a shift from an external to an internal locus-of-evaluation. I have always been and continue to be sensitive to the evaluation of others. But I am not shattered if I fail to live up to someone else's expectations. I believe that more and more of my values and standards are centered in me. As a result, I find myself more sure of what is important to me: interpersonal relationships, opportunities to be creative, experiencing the beauty of nature, music and art.

Willingness to be a process
As Rogers (1954) points out, this involves the ability to give up fixed goals and expectations. I do not expect to be *the* perfect therapist, *the* efficient administrator, *the* perfect husband or parent, the *most* loyal friend. All of these ways of relating to others are important to me, but I realize that I will do better with them if I 'go with the flow', rather then achieve an impossible goal, anyway.

I realize that this 'willingness to be a process', since my exposure to client-centered therapy and the person-centered philosophy (which fortunately was early) has always characterized my approach to teaching and to psychotherapy, where I do not impose a predetermined outline or set of procedures. Rogers (1954) also cites the frightening aspects of this approach to experience but, in spite of the fact that I can be quite fearful, I have always chosen the open road in teaching and therapy to the safe but dull route. Without the protection of the professional situation, I think I tighten up in interpersonal relationships. But to the extent that I have been able and willing to be 'a process', in either context, I have given myself the opportunity to grow genuinely stronger.

The self-concept and the process of becoming a person
I think it is significant that the results of Rogers' qualitative study of recorded therapy interviews which were categorized under the headings of 'Openness to Experience', 'Trust in One's Organism', an 'Internal Locus-of-Evaluation' and 'Willingness to be a Process' were reported in a talk given at Oberlin College in 1954 entitled *What It Means to Become a Person* which, in turn, appears in the book *On Becoming a Person*.

I believe what is signified is a shift in interest from an analysis of statistical relationships between perceived self and ideal self, between perceived self and an adjustment score, etc., to a focusing on the concept of experiencing and on the process of 'becoming a person'. This included the person of the therapist as well as the client.

This does not represent a complete departure from the concept of self because, as I have tried to show, there is an intimate relationship between self-concept and concepts such as 'openness to experience' and 'willingness to be a process'.

After twelve focal years at the University of Chicago, Rogers moved to the University of Wisconsin where, from 1957 to 1963 he, with Gendlin, Kiesler, Truax, van der Veen and others carried out a large scale research project on psychotherapy with a schizophrenic population. The main patient variable studied was the degree of immediacy of experiencing, or 'the degree to which the client is open to his feelings, able to own them, and to explore them in search of their personal meaning' (Rogers et al., 1967). Gendlin (1963) and Rogers (op. cit.) reported separate experiences in reaching out to extremely withdrawn patients and Rogers began to formulate the 'basic encounter group', an intensive experience ranging from a weekend to a week in length and which had its antecedents in intensive group experiences devised by Rogers and his associates at the University of Chicago in 1946 and 1947 for the purpose of training Veterans Administration personal counselors (Blocksma, 1951).

In 1963 Rogers left the university world and traveled to La Jolla, California where, first at the Western Behavioral Sciences Institute and, since 1967, at the Center for Studies of the Person, he has, with a large number of associates, worked with thousands of people in a variety of group situations. These have included individuals working in the same school or other organizational system, medical students, faculty, administrators and their spouses, person-centered workshops in Brazil, Mexico, Chile, Venezuela, Japan, England, Holland, Germany, Italy, Poland and other countries, with some of these having multinational, multicultural and multi-lingual membership. Some of the meetings in this country and abroad have included many hundreds of people, in some instances more than a thousand. The common thread in these groups is that the leaders work to facilitate self-awareness, self-expression and the development of community by the participants themselves. They rely on the person-centered philosophy of trust in the self-directive capacities of individuals and groups, and challenge the prevalent assumption of education, government, business and much of religion and family life that people must be told what to do and systematically, sometimes secretly, checked on.

In contrast, I recently tried to summarize Rogers' contributions to the concept of the 'person'.

A person should be listened to, sensitively, respectfully.

A person merits a unique kind of respect regardless of age, degree of intelligence or social status.

A person's perception of himself is central to the way he behaves and relates to others.

A person has strength, great capacities which can be loosed if he or she experiences empathy in a non-possessive, caring and genuine relationship.

A person has choices which can represent increasingly the expression of her own unique self and which deserve to be supported.

Each person can be a rich source of experience for himself and others.

Each person has the potential to be a powerful social influence.
(Raskin, 1978)

Until last August (1979), I had only read or heard about, but never been in any of the very large groups led by Rogers and his associates. When they volunteered to facilitate a 12-hour starting experience for the 2,000 or so people attending the Association for Humanistic Psychology's 1979 Annual Convention on the Princeton campus, I took advantage of the opportunity. The group met out of doors in an area called Blair Meadow. What I learned the first evening was that lots of people had many diverse ideas about what they wanted to do, as individuals or as a group, and that it was important to 'go with the flow'. I wound up meeting off campus with about 10 of the people who had been sitting near me and getting to know each other better.

The following morning, Sunday, the majority of the group had reassembled on the meadow. With the aid of multiple microphones, various individuals made short unrelated speeches to the assemblage, and then an American Indian member led the entire group in a service which emphasized the connectedness between us and the unity of life on earth.

At our final session on Sunday afternoon, the floor was again open to anyone who wished to speak, and an amazing groupness developed around the common fear experienced by individuals as they tried to get up the courage to come to the microphone to express their thoughts and feelings. I was one of these. I felt it was terribly important to get up and speak to the assemblage about how I felt personally and about the meaning of the experience. I felt very much on display as I stood up and walked the twenty yards or so to the microphone. When I spoke I was open about my fear and the importance of facing it. I saw great significance in the common fear that was felt, by many individuals like myself with lots of experience in group participation and leadership. I ascribe this difficulty to the training all of us get in our families, in our education and then in our work, to look for external guidance and leadership. I experienced the situation as a tremendous challenge to my concept of self which, with considerable struggle, was able to assert in effort, 'I can and will do it. My thoughts and feelings are important, even in this large group.'

I have thought of the situation in which I found myself at Princeton as a microcosm of the world situation. With gigantic problems besieging us, the threat of nuclear war, inflation, terrorism, the energy shortage, it is so easy to feel helpless and to look to a few leaders, and then blame them for their lack of success. I believe it is a real challenge to each of us, as individuals, to think, to feel, to express ourselves, to make our contribution to the collective thought and will. I believe most strongly that we need to stretch our concepts of ourselves and to broaden radically the base of participation in government. If we can do this, perhaps we can survive, and survive with dignity.

References

Barrett-Lennard, G. T. (1979) The client-centered system unfolding. In F. J. Turner (Ed.), *Social work treatment: Interlocking theoretical approaches*, pp. 177–241. New York: Free Press. Second edition.

Blocksma, D. D. and Porter, E. H. Jr. (1947) A short-term training program in client-centered counseling. *Journal of Consulting Psychology, 11,* 55–60.

Gendlin, E. T. (1963) Subverbal communication and therapist expressivity: trends in client-centered therapy with schizophrenics. *Journal of Existential Psychiatry, 4,* 105 ff.

Mead, G. H. (1934*) Mind, self and society*. Chicago: University of Chicago.

Raimy, V. C. (1943) The self-concept as a factor in counseling and personality organization. Unpublished doctoral thesis, Ohio State University.

Raskin, N. J. (1948) The development of nondirective therapy. *Journal of Consulting Psychology, 12,* 92–110.

Raskin, N. J. (1978a) Becoming — a therapist, a person, a partner, a parent, a . . . *Psychotherapy: Theory, research and practice, 15,* 352–70.

Raskin, N. J. (1978b) A 'Voices' editorial amalgam. *Voices, 14,* 12–13.

Rogers, C. R. (1931) *Measuring personality adjustment in children nine to thirteen.* New York: Teachers College, Columbia University, Bureau of Publications.

Rogers, C. R. (1947) Some observations on the organization of personality. *American Psychologist, 2,* 358–68.

Rogers, C. R. (1951) *Client-centered therapy: Its current practice, implications, and theory.* Boston: Houghton Mifflin.

Rogers, C. R. (1953) Some directions and end points in therapy. In O. H. Mowrer (Ed.), *Psychotherapy: Theory and research,* pp. 44–68. New York: Ronald Press.

Rogers, C. R. (1954) Becoming a person. Oberlin College Nellie Heldt Lecture Series. Oberlin: Oberlin Printing Co. Also in C. R. Rogers, (1961) *On becoming a person*, pp. 107–24. Boston: Houghton Mifflin.

Rogers, C. R. (1957) The necessary and sufficient conditions of therapeutic personality change. *Journal of Consulting Psychology, 21,* 95–103.

Rogers, C. R. (1959) A theory of therapy, personality, and interpersonal relationships as developed in the client-centered framework. In S. Koch (Ed.), *Psychology: a study of a science, Vol. III. Formulations of the person and the social context*, pp. 184–256. New York: McGraw-Hill.

Rogers, C. R. (1961) *On becoming a person.* Boston: Houghton Mifflin.

Rogers, C. R. (Ed.) (1967) *The therapeutic relationship and its impact: a study of psychotherapy with schizophrenics.* Madison: University of Wisconsin Press.

Rogers, C. R. (1977) *Carl Rogers on personal power.* New York: Delacorte.

Rogers, C. R. and Dymond, R. F. (Eds.) (1954). *Psychotherapy and personality change.* University of Chicago Press.

Rogers, C. R. and Raskin, N. J. (1949) A co-ordinated research in psychotherapy. *Journal of Consulting Psychology, 13,* 149–219 (whole issue).

Seeman, J. and Raskin, N. J. (1953) Research perspectives in client-centered therapy. In O. H. Mowrer (Ed.), *Psychotherapy: Theory and research*, pp. 205–34. New York: Ronald Press.

Standal, S. (1954) The need for positive regard: a contribution to client-centered theory. Unpublished doctoral thesis, University of Chicago.

Stephenson, W. (1950) The significance of Q-technique for the study of personality. In M. L. Reymert (Ed.), *Feelings and emotions*. New York: McGraw-Hill.

Wylie, R. C. (1961). *The Self Concept: A critical survey of pertinent research literature*. Lincoln, Neb: University of Nebraska Press.

CLIENT-CENTERED GROUP PSYCHOTHERAPY, PART I: DEVELOPMENT OF CLIENT-CENTERED GROUPS

9

The client-centered approach began as a one-to-one method of counseling and psychotherapy in the early 1940s. By the end of that decade, it was being applied to group situations in ways that symbolized its broader meanings and implications for group therapy, classroom teaching, affective-cognitive learning in workshop settings, and organizational development and leadership. The development of intensive groups added new dimensions to the theory and practice of client-centered group methods. The approach was used with some success with groups numbering hundreds of people, often with a diversity of languages and cultures. Such experiences are providing data for understanding how cross-cultural and international differences may be resolved in the process of developing a person-to-person kind of empathy and understanding making for a caring community.

In this article, the early broadening of Client-Centered Therapy to a method and philosophy of working in a variety of group situations will be described. Even before the end of the 1940s, this application had taken many forms: group therapy that was simply an extension of one-to-one Client-Centered Therapy, group play therapy with children, courses conceptualized and carried out in a student-centered manner, workshops sensitive to the affective component of learning, and institutions incorporating a process of open and shared responsibility and leadership.

As Client-Centered Therapy evolved into a more generally conceived and applied person-centered approach, the intensive group movement came into being. I will summarize some of the main theories of intensive group process, including those of Rogers, Braaten, and Beck, and will attempt to bring out the similarities and differences between person-centered theories and other models of intensive groups.

As is true of Client-Centered Therapy with individuals, the application of this approach to groups has generated a significant amount of research. This began in the 1940s and, for the most part, has resulted in a confirmation of the efficacy of applying client-centered principles to groups (Barrett-Lennard, 1979; Devonshire and Kremer, 1980; Rogers, 1970). As with research on individual Client-Centered Therapy, the volume of such activity has declined since 1970, and much of the

Originally published in *Person-Centered Review* (1986) *1*(3), 272–90. Reprinted with permission.

slack has been taken up by European investigators. A second part of this article will review the research on client-centered groups and was published in this journal

Early development

Group therapy was an established method at the time Rogers' (1942) *Counseling and Psychotherapy* was published. In that book Rogers cites as a significant reference Durkin's (1939) paper on the application of 'Dr John Levy's relationship therapy' to a play group. Rogers noted that his newer concepts of psychotherapy that he termed 'nondirective' or 'client-centered' had been influenced by relationship therapy. Taft (1933), an important figure in that movement, defined relationship therapy succinctly as dealing with immediate experience rather than emphasizing analytic or intellectual aspects of the process, as traditional psychoanalysis did. The group described by Durkin (1939) in her article was a preschool play therapy group, with eight boys and girls two to five years of age, whom she met five mornings a week during two summer months. Although Durkin's orientation was based on the immediacy aspect of relationship therapy, her approach was primarily interpretive, in contrast to Rogers'. She wrote that the crucial factor upon which all therapeutic movement depended was the interpretation of the relationship between the patient and therapist and gave this example of a statement to a four-and-a-half-year-old girl who wanted Ms Durkin to go get toys with her:

> You are worried that I don't love you enough and may leave you alone. But I love you; I love all the children who come here. (Durkin, 1939)

Durkin's interpretative approach contrasts with Rogers', which emphasized the self-understanding capacity of his clients.

Rogers was a professor at Ohio State when he wrote *Counseling and Psychotherapy* (1942). As a student there, I recall reading about group therapy in periodicals like the *American Journal of Orthopsychiatry* and the *Journal of Consulting Psychology,* but the nondirective or client-centered approach was not being used outside of the one-to-one counseling context. This situation changed markedly soon after Rogers moved to the University of Chicago. In 1946, he was beginning to employ 'student-centered' teaching in the classroom. Also, the University of Chicago Counseling Center was organized by Rogers according to client-centered principles, with responsibility and power being vested in the staff. Meetings of staff members were characterized by attitudes of acceptance and respect and of trust in the capacity of the group to resolve problems and conflicts. Rogers and his associates at Chicago, in 1946 and 1947, used a group format to train Veterans Administration Personal Counselors in a series of six-week programs that promoted the awareness of 'attitudes which might be self-defeating in the counseling relationship' and their manner of relating to one another 'in ways that would be helpful and could carry over into their counseling work' (Rogers, 1970, p. 31). This pioneering program was described in detail by Blocksma and Porter

(1947), each of whom led a daily subgroup of about eight trainees, for one and a half hours. Although the balance of the program was largely didactic, Blocksma and Porter (1947, p. 58) stated that this experiential activity 'proved to be the core of the training program for most trainees. The observation of staff members confirmed the presumption that the course of learning largely paralleled the course of therapy as observed in individual counseling with client-centered procedures.'

The group leaders functioned by providing a permissive atmosphere, verbalizing clients' expressed attitudes and by understanding the points of view expressed in the group. As an example of the program's outcome, one graduate is quoted by Blocksma and Porter (1947, p. 59) as stating: 'It seems to me that nondirective therapy isn't just a technique but a whole philosophy of dealing with human beings.' The same student had the insight that 'one reason I couldn't trust clients more in the past was that I didn't fully trust myself' (p. 60). Evaluated as a very effective program, it was used as a prototype for summer workshops with other groups of trainees.

Another small-group experience that influenced Rogers took place late in the summer of 1950 around a daily demonstration interview observed by 12 students in a postgraduate seminar preceding the American Psychological Association convention. Rogers described the discussions that followed the daily interview, and that had begun on an academic note:

> As we got into it, sharing more and more deeply of our personal experiences, our failures, and our difficulties, it became a moving personal experience. (Kirschenbaum, 1979, p. 330)

Axline (1947, p. 85) applied nondirective principles to group as well as individual play therapy and believed that 'the child in a group seems to develop a feeling of confidence in the therapist sooner than . . . in individual therapy'. Axline felt that the group approach might be especially helpful where the child's problems focused around social adjustments. At the same time, she cautioned that the nondirective group should not be thought of as recreational or educational.

To pick up another strand in the line of development of client-centered groups, Hobbs (1951) contributed a chapter on group therapy to Rogers' *Client-Centered Therapy*. He contrasted 'group-centered psychotherapy' with analytic approaches, seeing the task of the client-centered therapist as communicating a sensitive understanding of the individual's perceptual field and feelings at the moment. Hobbs emphasized the therapist's acceptance and understanding of the individuals in the groups but also made the point that an advantage of group therapy was that the individual benefited from the therapeutic attitudes of other group participants.

> It is one thing to be understood and accepted by a therapist; it is a considerably more potent experience to be understood and accepted by several people who are also honestly sharing their feelings in a joint search for a more satisfying way of life. More than anything else, this is

the something added that makes group therapy a qualitatively different
experience from individual therapy. (Hobbs, p. 287)

Hobbs also clarified the group-centered therapist's lack of interest in diagnosis,
interpretation, cognitive insight, and transference attitudes that, he explained,
were handled like all other 'affect-laden expressions'. The term 'group-centered'
was an extension of 'client-centered' and did not imply an analysis of group
dynamics or processes.

   The following are examples of therapist responses extracted from Hobbs'
(1951, pp. 282–3) account of a group therapy session, which highlight the leader's
individually oriented stance:

You had a very warm relationship. He was almost your whole life.
It kind of overwhelms you.
Makes you feel pretty bad.
Makes you feel that you'd have to fight against her.
It stays with you pretty much of the time.

An examination of the client statements that preceded these responses also makes
it clear that the group therapist was consistently nondirective, working hard to
understand the clients' feelings and meanings but not going beyond what they
wished to communicate to the therapist and other group members. These
illustrations also suggested that the therapist might have been, consciously or
not, providing a model of empathic listening and response for the group members.

   Gordon (1951), in his contribution on leadership and administration to Rogers'
Client-Centered Therapy, conceptualized the group as a powerful and positive
entity. He posited that, given certain conditions, a group will actualize its 'adjustive
capacity' and increase its internal harmony and productivity. This basically positive
belief in groups contrasted with the distrust felt by Freud (1948), who is quoted
by Gordon (1951, p. 328):

A group is an obedient herd, which could never live without a
master. It has such a thirst for obedience that it submits instinctively
to anyone who appoints himself as its master.

The conditions set forth by Gordon to implement his positive philosophy
emphasized a group-centered leader who did not accept responsibility for the
group, but facilitated the members' assumption of responsibility through the
provision of the empathy, warmth, and acceptance conceptualized in Client-
Centered Therapy. In addition, Gordon delineated a 'linking function' in which
the leader connected the communications of individual members to those already
expressed. With this kind of facilitation, Gordon described the development of a
group process characterized by increasing positive attitudes and by a self-
responsible orientation.

   The principles of Client-Centered Therapy, as they were formulated by Rogers
(1951) and applied more specifically to therapy groups by Hobbs (1951) and

Gordon (1951) served as a base for employing the client-centered approach in a variety of groups. Examples of these in the 1950s and 1960s were groups for physically handicapped children, parents of physically handicapped children, parents of retarded children, mothers on public assistance, clients seen in private practice, psychiatry inpatients, residents of old people's homes, staff development groups for mental health professionals in hospitals and mental health agencies, and play therapy groups.

Typically, such groups would meet once a week for an hour and a half. *The basic contribution of the leader was an attitude of respect for the participants, implemented by disciplined empathic listening and communication.* This often resulted in an atmosphere characterized by the 'necessary and sufficient conditions' formulated by Rogers in 1957.

Development of the intensive group

Barrett-Lennard (1979, p. 206) noted that 'since the early 1960's, with the mushrooming development of growth-oriented groups associated, especially, with the human relations and human potential movements, the line between client-centered group therapy and client-centered forms of sensitivity-encounter group experience has become a very fine one.'

Rogers (1980) observed that whether persons come together because they are seeking help with serious problems (group therapy) or because they are seeking an enrichment experience (encounter group) the process is much the same.

In 1956, Rogers was elected the first president of the American Academy of Psychotherapists (AAP), an interdisciplinary group that also brought together therapists with diverse ideologies. Like the University of Chicago Counseling Center training program for Veterans Administration Personal Counselors (Blocksma and Porter, 1947) and Rogers' postgraduate seminar group preceding the 1950 convention of the American Psychological Association (Kirschenbaum, 1979), the AAP annual workshops began with a cognitive purpose (learning how other therapists worked, often in demonstrations with hospital patients), but became more and more personal. At the workshops, participants would meet for several hours a day in a small group (usually 3–8) over the course of 4 or 5 days. Interspersed with these small group meetings, which had continuity of membership and developed increasing closeness (during each workshop and over the years) were other meetings, often with a particular topic or theme. There were also opportunities for recreation, which were frequently useful for working out personal and interpersonal issues in another context. The entire workshop group of 50 to 150 would meet at the beginning and end of the 4–5 day period, as well as having most meals together.

The AAP workshops proved to be powerful experiences for enhancing personal awareness and self-esteem for the participating therapists. They stimulated me to arrange a weekend experience for four clients I was seeing individually in therapy (Raskin, 1966). We met at a college camp in the country, beginning Friday night for an hour-and-a-half session after an informal introductory meeting over coffee. We met both Saturday morning and afternoon, and had breakfast and lunch together. On Saturday evening, we went to town for bowling and pizza, and returned to the camp, meeting from 11 pm to 12.30 am. We ended at 3.30 Sunday afternoon, having talked for over 12 hours, all openly recorded on tape.

The issue with which the group began was, not surprisingly, that of whether or not other people could be trusted, be they friends or strangers. One of the participants remembered an incident in which, as a 9-year-old boy, a confidence had been betrayed by a friend, and he had felt humiliated. Experiences of sharing with others the fact of being in psychotherapy, at the risk of being stigmatized, were discussed.

On Saturday night, after the bowling and pizza in town, the atmosphere was light when the group reassembled at camp. It took a little while to get serious again and when we did, on a deeper level than before, the individuals in the group described basic tendencies toward depression, escape into fantasy, and withdrawal. I shared some very deep feelings I had about my brother, who was dying of cancer in New York. I expressed both my feelings of wanting to be open with the group about something that was very much on my mind and my misgivings about possibly hindering them. In return, I received a great deal of understanding and expressions like, 'It's refreshing that, as a professional person, you, too, are involved . . . It is not a burden . . . I am glad you can share with us . . . You had enough confidence in us to talk about it'.

At about this point, 'Loretta' said, 'I was thinking about how, as a group, in our first session, when we were hashing around about how are we going to trust each other; and how, in a short period of time, I think we've come a long way.'

'Al' said, 'I guess since Friday night we have come a long way. Since *last* night! It seems much longer.'

'Bill' said, 'It's been just about 26 hours since we started.'

'Alice' (Bill's wife) then wondered out loud, 'Why is it people can't get along on this basis? There is so much of this trying to impress, of a struggle for power.'

There was general agreement, aside from the issue of how it had come about, that the feeling of natural trust was something rare and precious. 'Loretta' said she had been thinking that 'if I could discover what has made this go, I would use it in my relationships with other people'.

In the last hours of the weekend, the discussion was mostly about the shortcomings of the participants' parents in providing love, an understanding of some of the reasons for these shortcomings, and an assumption of self-responsibility for breaking the cycle of deficient loving.

All of the people who participated in the group were 'doing well', several years later. *What seemed most meaningful to me about the experience was that the 'workshop' or 'basic encounter' arrangement of time and space can effectively help withdrawn and uncommunicative individuals to 'open up', and have a living experience of closeness and trust overpower a general attitude of distance and distrust.* Apparently this could happen in a remarkably short period of time, without employing gimmicks to get started, and without relying on a fatigue factor to break down defenses.

Some person-centered expressions of the intensive group movement

The therapy weekend just described represents one early example of an intensive person-centered group. It exemplified some of the conditions that make for intensity (meeting away from home, employing a multiday format, an informal kind of living together) and for person-centeredness (respect for each individual's way of participating in the group). It illustrated the development of a group feeling that transcends the individual participants and the way in which the leader can participate as a person.

Perhaps the best-known single group led by Rogers was documented in *Journey into Self* (McGaw, Farson, and Rogers, 1968). As an Academy Award winning film, it has been very widely viewed. Co-led by Farson, this small group exemplifies well a 'basic encounter' or 'I-Thou' experience, defined below, with a number of extremely moving episodes. Several of the participants made contact with covered-over feelings of loneliness, sadness, the need to be loved, and so on. Sharing these feelings resulted in responses of affectionate empathy. This group of ten, including the two facilitators, was mixed racially, occupationally, and, to a small extent, nationally (American and Canadian).

The intensive group became, and remains, one of the principal formats for the expression of the Person-Centered Approach. It has given rise to hundreds or even thousands of such experiences on an international scale. Only a small percentage of these would be labeled group therapy, but the process does not seem to be significantly different. Rogers (1970) described 15 steps in the process such as:

- milling around
- resistance to personal expression or exploration
- description of past feelings
- expression of immediate interpersonal feelings in the group
- the development of a healing capacity in the group
- self-acceptance and the beginning of change
- the expression of positive feelings and closeness
- behavior changes in the group

Barrett-Lennard (1979) suggested that Rogers' more detailed formulation of the process may be reduced to three phases:

- engagement
- trust and process development
- encounter and change

The core of the process may be what Rogers (1970) termed the 'basic encounter', where at least one person in the group responds with undivided empathy to another who is experiencing and sharing a very significant event with no holding back. Our language seems inadequate to describe such encounters; Rogers likens them to Buber's I-Thou relationships. Rogers (1970, p. 33) gives the example of a participant who, for the first time, fully experiences his grief over the loss of his child and the response of a fellow group member who, with tears in his eyes, states, 'I've never before felt a real physical hurt in me from the pain of another. I feel completely with you.'

Bebout (1974, pp. 376–7) related Rogers' 'basic encounter' experience to a concept of 'experiential communality', which has the following characteristics:
1. the sharing of feeling is *unpremeditated,*
2. it occurs in two members *simultaneously,*
3. the feelings shared are *functionally equivalent* — similar feelings are paired and result in greater closeness, and
4. the shared feelings constitute *affective-meaning* gestalts — 'each person discovers an identification between himself-as-experiencer and another self-as-experiencer'.

Bebout (1974, p. 377) points out that the 'identification' in point 4 is different from 'traditional concepts of identification, imitation or role-modeling, which require hierarchical, non-simultaneous, asymmetrical, or unconscious transactions between people . . . In experiential communality a *direct intimacy* between people is established — a direct 'feeling-together-with' another person — because the feelings are recognized as mutual in one existential moment'.

Bebout saw the empathic process as a precursor to and facilitator of experiential communality and the effortful, vicarious kind of empathy described by Raskin and cited by Rogers (1951, p. 29) as coming closest to experiential communality.

Rogers (1970) explored the part played by the leader or facilitator in intensive groups. To start with, he attributed great significance to the client-centered concepts of empathy, acceptance, and respect. He felt it was not only important to accept the individuals in the group, but to respect the entire group, even though the participants might seem to appear, at first, over intellectual, rigid, and superficial.

Rogers (1970) described, at some length, the importance he attached to being real, fully himself, and spontaneous in the group, which can be seen as an implementation of the therapist-offered condition of congruence, central to client-centered theory. He gave examples of how he himself had opened up in groups, which he believed contributed to his role as facilitator. He eschewed the term 'training', in connection with intensive groups for facilitator development, because he felt 'persons' cannot be trained, and because of the personal quality of the participation of the leader or staff.

Braaten (1974/75) summarized 14 formulations of the way in which intensive groups develop, including encounter groups, sensitivity groups, group therapy, and 'related intensive group experiences'. The theoreticians surveyed by Braaten were Bach, Bennis, Bion, Bradford, Gibb and Gibb, Mann, Mills, Ottaway, Rogers, Thelen, Tuckman, Whitaker and Lieberman, Whitman, and Yalom. From these, Braaten constructed a composite model in which four phases were distinguished following a *pregroup phase* having to do with the selection of participants and of an optimal physical setting, in addition to the preparation of the participants: (1) an initial phase — *forming,* in which the group leader 'must offer a minimal structure' while each participant 'must test the situation to size up his relationship to the leader and to the other participants' (p. 121); (2) an early phase — *storming*, where 'underlying differences in interests, values, norms and goals become apparent' and lead to frustration and conflict; (3) a mature work phase — *resolution and performing,* in which the individuals are willing to modify their original goals and behavior; there is increased self-disclosure as facades are dropped, and the interactions between group members are characterized by greater empathy; and (4) a *termination phase* with an emotional withdrawal from the group. Braaten also offered his own personal model (based on 25–30 teaching/learning groups with over 250 participants in a 10-year period) and compared it with his composite, finding them 'much the same'. He concluded that although 'substantial consensus' existed among the experts regarding a developmental phase model, the agreement was not complete. Braaten attributed the incompleteness of consensus to the extreme complexity of group process and differences in such variables as leadership style, group composition, goals, and methods. In my view, some of the unique aspects of the client-centered model are *(1) a relative lack of concern with the selection of the participants, (2) a focus on the individual feelings and attitudes of the members rather than a group task or work orientation, (3) the absence of a general expectation of intragroup conflict and confrontation of the leader and, (4) the view of the leader as a facilitator and personal participant.*

In addition to the theoretical models reviewed by Braaten, there is Beck's (1974, p. 423) formulation that she 'based on informal observation of a wide range of groups and careful observation of 13 small (N of 6–10) time-limited therapy groups conducted at the University of Chicago'. She presented her conception of an orderly group development process that is affected by such factors as the group's purpose, the personalities of the members, the roles and norms that evolve, the style of leadership, the emotional depth of group interaction, and the environment or context within which the group and its members exist. Beck defined 9 phases in the development of group structure that involve several early phases in which clients move closer together as a group, succeeded by some that stress the differentiation of group members in an atmosphere of greater freedom and fluidity, and finally termination and separation.

Beck described a successful group as moving toward distributed leadership, flexible roles, a concern with the here-and-now, cooperative communication and problem-solving, productive work on significant individual and group issues, a coordination of differences and partial overlap of goals and, finally, a strong sense of cohesion.

Application of the intensive group

The thinking about person-centered process and facilitation in intensive groups is directly applicable to client-centered group therapy. It has been implemented with a wide variety of persons including the following: therapy clients, counselors and psychotherapists, members of entire school systems, medical students, teachers, administrators, groups in conflict, drug users and their helpers, people representing different cultures and languages, and in ongoing learning programs in the Person-Centered Approach for people with varied occupations.

I discussed one particular format for an intensive person-centered group at an American Psychological Association annual convention:

> The author has conducted a 'four-hour group' since the fall of 1968, which has met regularly on Saturday mornings, and involves the same group of people each week.
>
> This arrangement combines the intensity of the short-term intensive group experience plus the continuity of relationship and followup which is often absent from the weekend encounter group.
>
> It provides the best application known to the author of the Basic Encounter type of group to an ongoing practice. It is a format which allows the therapist and other participants sufficient opportunity to know where each person is during each session and to learn how he or she functions and relates over a period of months. A deep, continuing sense of group identification and responsibility has been another important result of this method. (Raskin, 1970)

The participants in this group remained in meaningful contact with one another for many years. One unusual feature of the group was the rotation of the place of meeting for one series of sessions, so that a meeting was held in the house or apartment of each member with the participant's 'significant other' joining the group, if he or she were willing. There was also a weekend-away meeting that appeared to add significantly to the therapeutic value of the group.

The La Jolla Program and other large groups

A continuing project that has involved thousands of people in person-centered intensive groups is the La Jolla Program, which was initiated in 1966 (Coulson, Land, and Meador, 1977) for persons in a variety of professions who lead small groups in their work. For three-week periods, approximately 100 people experience small groups led by the staff, a daily community meeting of all the participants, and co-leadership of two weekend encounter groups composed of people in the community. Central to the philosophy of the program is the belief that each participant can discover within himself or herself an effective way of being a facilitator, a style that comes from the person's own experience, rather than from some external teaching.

The large-group community meetings that were part of the La Jolla Program received expanded expression in Person-Centered Approach workshops initiated in 1973 by Natalie and Carl Rogers, John K. Wood, Alan Nelson, and Betty Meador. These have been described by Rogers (1977), Bowen, Miller, Rogers, and Wood (1979), Wood (1980), and Wood (1984). They provided the opportunity for personal growth afforded by earlier smaller group experiences and, in addition, the extremely gratifying but usually difficult and painful creation of a community. I experienced one example of this in a 12-hour group of 2,000 people at the beginning of the Association for Humanistic Psychology's 1979 annual convention on the Princeton University campus, led by Carl Rogers and his associates. It was a good example of the evolution of a group from diversity and dissension to a cohesive atmosphere where one individual after another was heard with rapt attention and great respect.

Rogers (1980, p. 338) sees an answer to our world problems of the increasing maldistribution of wealth, and the growing alienation of millions, as coming from experiences such as the above in which the inner resources of individuals are recognized, respected, nurtured, and expressed in participatory decision making. 'A crowd can become participants in a unified way, given the right conditions.' Barrett-Lennard (1977), also believing in the power of trust in self and others to effect a positive group outcome, examined the meaning of community from an experiential person-centered standpoint. He hypothesized a relationship between effective community and open, direct self-presentation in addition to a caring interest in the experience and personhood of others. He believed that secrecy and hidden control are antithetical to such community, whereas trust and the acceptance of difference sustain it.

In recent years, one of the principal expressions of the intensive person-centered experience has been the group of ongoing learning programs in the Person-Centered Approach, in places as widely distributed as New York, California, Brazil, and Switzerland. The numbers involved are smaller than those in the Person-Centered Approach workshops described above, with up to 50 individuals in a particular program. They are characterized by continuity, with periodic meetings of the same group over a period of one or more years and a blending of cognitive and affective experiences. There is an exploration of various aspects of the Person-Centered Approach with opportunities for self-exploration. There are small group meetings and meetings of the entire community. Programs of this general nature, with distinctive individual features, have sprung up independently in many different parts of the world. Devonshire and Kremer (1980) have described some of these programs and other applications of the Person-Centered Approach to groups.

Conflict resolution
Charles Devonshire, Alberto Zucconi, Carl Rogers, Ruth Sanford, Gay Swenson, and many other practitioners of the Person-Centered Approach have, in recent years, made conflict resolution within and between national groups an intense focus of their efforts. In a 1984 American Psychological Association Symposium, Zucconi showed a videotaped interview with Rogers that described person-centered efforts at conflict resolution in Eastern Europe, Northern Ireland, and South Africa, Rogers' analysis of the Camp David accord, and his proposal for avoiding 'planetary nuclear suicide'. Raskin and Zucconi (1984) proposed that when a receptive group in conflict is provided with facilitative conditions akin to therapeutic empathy, congruence, and caring, negative stereotypes of the opposition weaken and are replaced by personal, human feelings of relatedness.

Rogers, Swenson, Zucconi and others facilitated a workshop outside Vienna in November 1985, on 'the Central American Challenge', which involved 50 participants from 16 countries; these individuals included high government officials, legislators, scholars, bankers, and foundation officials. Rogers was buoyed by the experience of this meeting as well as by a six-week immersion in South Africa in early 1986 that left him awed by the depth of feeling and intensity of conflict among blacks, whites, and individuals belonging to other groups. He came away with the conviction that none of the major groups want violence and that a reasonably peaceful solution would come out of a 'prolonged, facilitated, person-to-person meeting of all the real leaders of the different major groups' (Rogers, 1986, p. 17).

Conclusion

It is rather remarkable that a movement that began as a pragmatic, scientific alternative to the traditional methods of helping individuals with problems evolved into a strongly experiential way of working with large and small groups. Although most of these groups had a therapeutic focus, many others were developed to serve a variety of purposes. Over the years, the non-political character of the original activity has given way to a clear interest in reducing human suffering, and in cross-cultural and international conflict resolution.

How did these changes come about? Part of the answer may lie on the momentum generated by the continuous, intense interest in the experience of another human being. Another part of the explanation may be the inherent respect for self-directed growth and healing, and the caring implicit in the empathic activity. Inevitably, the therapist as a person became part of the process and significantly affected the nature of the group.

The spread of Client-Centered Therapy to the Person-Centered Approach with groups has been accompanied by a trust in group process paralleling the therapist's trust in the individual. The increased interest in working with groups has also been characterized by a greater reliance on experiential and intuitive processes and less on cognitive processes.

There are, however, unanswered questions regarding the Person-Centered Approach to groups. Sometimes the group does not respond to the facilitator-offered conditions. Conflicts exist between leaders of competing educational programs. Client-centered therapy and the Person-Centered Approach made a significant impact, in part, because the data of human experience were subjected to careful observation and research. Carl Rogers once reacted to some research results that seemed to contradict the basic client-centered hypothesis by saying that the facts were friendly. The continued development of person-centered groups and of our ability to resolve conflicts will be enhanced by critical self-evaluation as well as respect for the theory and practice of other orientations.

References

Axline, V. M. (1947) *Play therapy.* Boston: Houghton Mifflin.

Barrett-Lennard G. T. (1977) Toward a person-centered theory of community. Paper presented at the annual convention of the American Psychological Association, San Francisco.

Barrett-Lennard G. T. (1979) The client-centered system unfolding. In F. J. Turner (Ed.), *Social work treatment: Interlocking theoretical approaches* (2nd edn.) New York: Free Press.

Bebout, J. (1974) It takes one to know one: Existential-Rogerian concepts in encounter groups. In D. A. Wexler and L. N. Rice (Eds.), *Innovations in client-centered therapy.* New York: John Wiley.

Beck, A. P. (1974) Phases in the development of structure in therapy and encounter groups. In D. A. Wexler and L. N. Rice (Eds.), *Innovations in client-centered therapy.* New York: John Wiley.

Blocksma, D. D. and Porter, F. H. Jr. (1947) A short-term training program in client-centered counseling. *Journal of Consulting Psychology, 11,* 55–60.

Bowen, M., Miller, M., Rogers, C. R. and Wood, J. K. (1979) Learnings in large groups: Their implications for the future. *Education, 100,* 108.

Braaten, L. J. (1974/5) Developmental phases of encounter groups and related intensive groups. *Interpersonal Development, 5,* 112–29.

Coulson, W., Land, D. and Meador, B. (Eds.) (1977) *The La Jolla experiment: Eight personal views.* La Jolla: Landmark.

Devonshire, C. M. and Kremer, J. W. (1980) *Toward a person-centered resolution of intercultural conflicts.* Dortmund, West Germany: Pedagogische Arbeitsstelle.

Durkin, H. E. (1939) Dr. John Levy's relationship therapy applied to a play group. *American Journal of Orthopsychiatry, 9,* 583.

Gordon, T. (1951) Group-centered leadership and administration. In C. R. Rogers, *Client-centered therapy.* Boston: Houghton Mifflin.

Hobbs, N. (1951) Group-centered psychotherapy. In C. R. Rogers, *Client-centered therapy.* Boston: Houghton Mifflin.

Kirschenbaum, H. (1979) *On becoming Carl Rogers.* New York: Delacorte.

McGaw, W. H., Farson, R. and Rogers, C. R. (Producers). (1968). *Journey into self* [Film]. Berkeley: University of California Extension Media Center.

Raskin, N. J. (1966) A therapy weekend. Paper presented at the annual convention of the American Psychological Association, New York.

Raskin, N. J. (1970) The weekly four-hour encounter group. Paper presented at the annual convention of the American Psychological Association, Miami Beach.

Raskin, N. J. and Zucconi, A. (1984) Peace, conflict resolution, and the person-centered approach. Symposium presented at the annual convention of the American Psychological Association, Toronto.

Rogers, C. R. (1942) *Counseling and psychotherapy.* Boston: Houghton Mifflin.

Rogers, C. R. (1951) *Client-centered therapy.* Boston: Houghton Mifflin.

Rogers, C. R. (1957) The necessary and sufficient conditions of therapeutic personality change. *Journal of Consulting Psychology, 21*, 95–103.

Rogers, C. R. (1970) *Carl Rogers on encounter groups.* New York: Harper and Row.

Rogers, C. R. (1977) *Carl Rogers on personal power.* New York: Delacorte.

Rogers, C. R. (1980) *A way of being.* Boston: Houghton Mifflin.

Rogers, C. R. (1986) Journal of South Africa Trip, January 14 – March 1, 1986. A personal communication to family and friends.

Taft, J. (1933) *The dynamics of therapy in a controlled relationship.* New York: Macmillan.

Wood, J. K. (1980) Person-centered group therapy. In G. Gazda (Ed.), *Basic approaches to group psychotherapy and group counseling.* Springfield, IL: Thomas.

Wood, J. K. (1984) Community for learning: A person-centered approach. In R. F. Levant and J. M. Shlien (Eds.), *Client-centered therapy and the person-centered approach.* New York: Praeger.

CLIENT-CENTERED GROUP PSYCHOTHERAPY, PART II: RESEARCH ON CLIENT-CENTERED GROUPS

10

Rogers' formulation of individual Client-Centered Therapy was extended to group therapy as early as 1945. Research on the group process followed that paralleled that on individual therapy. Verbatim typescripts replaced impressionistic notes, therapist and client behavior were measured, client-centered group therapists were found to respond differently from directive ones, and there was confirmation of the therapeutic effectiveness of conditions such as empathy, congruence, and warmth, even with very disturbed populations. The emergence of interest in intensive groups was accompanied by some research, but it is noted that with this development, there was a decline in research activity and in the general impact of the client-centered school on psychotherapy research. This is related to Rogers' departure from a major university setting, to a heightened interest in the concept of experiencing and in the therapist's own experiencing, and to the difficulties of implementing, up to now, the alternative model of science and of psychological research that Rogers espouses.

Client-Centered Therapy, which began in the early 1940s as a one-to-one method of helpng people, in a few years broadened into a method and philosophy of working in group situations. One of the contributions of the client-centered approach was to 'take therapy out of the closet', by using verbatim accounts of sessions for teaching and research purposes. This also applied to group therapy. A significant amount of research on client-centered groups was published between 1946 and 1950.

Early studies

Hobbs and Pascal (1946) pioneered with 'a method for the qualitative analysis of group psychotherapy'. Using verbatim typescripts of group sessions, they compared authoritarian, eclectic, and nondirective approaches. The investigators categorized client and counselor responses and, on the basis of separating the latter into therapeutically positive and negative forms of verbal behavior, concluded that the eclectic and nondirective approaches were more effective than the authoritarian.

Fleming and Snyder (1947) reported on 'social and personal changes following

Originally published in (1986) *Person-Centered Review*, *1*(4), 389–408. Reprinted with permission.

nondirective group play therapy'. The investigators measured the occurrence of such changes using pre- and post-therapy tests within two experimental groups and a control group. One of the experimental groups, a girls' group, showed marked and statistically significant changes on a test of personality adjustment, on behavior ratings by peers, and on a sociometric test.

Recording six sessions of a therapy group with seven graduate students in counselling and psychotherapy, Peres (1947) found significant differences on a number of objective measures between those individuals who felt they had benefited and those who felt they had gained little. Categorizing the interview protocols, the benefited group verbalized an increasing proportion of statements indicating understanding and insight, and an increasing number of reports of plans and actions, which held up in a three-month follow-up. In the statements collected at this point following therapy, Peres also found in the benefited group greater acceptance of self and willingness to be oneself.

Gorlow, Hoch, and Telschow (1952) published a monograph covering three related studies of nondirective group psychotherapy. Hoch (1950) provided evidence for a generalized process in client-centered group therapy, comparing verbatim protocols from three groups with three different therapists. Group gestalts held while individuals varied in their manner of self-expression. Hoch concluded that the atmospheres were very similar in the three groups, and that one aspect of this allowed for individuals to express themselves in their own ways.

Hoch also discovered a pattern of increasing frequency of positive statements (regarding self, others, insight, and planning) and a decline in negative statements (toward self and others, defensiveness, and confusion) over the course of therapy. One feature of the pattern, however, was that negative statements actually peaked around the middle sessions. Also, members kept bringing up problems throughout, so that there was not a significant decline in the categories of 'statement of problem' or 'elaboration of problem'. Another finding was that when the second half of each group session was compared with the first half, there was an increase in the expression of positive attitudes. Finally, there was a confirmation of Peres' findings that the group participants who gained the most avoided intellectualizing and externalizing and showed more concern for the others in their groups.

Telschow (1950) studied the role of the group leader in client-centered group therapy. He also analyzed individual statements and found a high index (r = .86) of therapist responsiveness to content and feeling initiated by the group members. Telschow discovered a difference, however, in the way individuals responded to the therapist's efforts to understand, with those participants who did not profit from the therapy responding defensively. *Diaries kept by group members indicated that those who did gain had a positive response of feeling understood, in a nonintrusive manner, by the therapist.*

Gorlow (1950) analyzed the therapeutic behavior of group members. He discovered that, as a group, the participants became increasingly therapeutic in their behavior as the sessions continued. He also found significant differences among clients, with those profiting most from therapy exhibiting more permissive and accepting behavior and less interpretive and evaluative behavior. Another difference discovered by Gorlow was that those members initially categorized through Rorschach protocols as more anxious and hostile, made more negative statements (evaluative and critical) and fewer positive ones (accepting, clarifying, encouraging, and so on).

Haimowitz and Haimowitz (1952) measured the effects of psychotherapy on 56 individuals in the University of Chicago community. They compared 17 people receiving individual treatment, 27 in group therapy, 15 who experienced both modes concomitantly, and 15 people in a no-therapy control group. Their instrument was the Rorschach test, which they used to measure ten personality characteristics thought to be central:

Quality of reality orientation
Anxiety feelings
Feelings of dependence-independence
Attitude toward the self
Quality of affectivity
Adequacy of intellectual functioning
Spontaneity-flexibility
Personality integration
Attitudes toward others
Adjustment to emotional problems

In a carefully conceived manual, each of these variables was defined and specific criteria were delineated to detect the presence or absence of the variable in the Rorschach record. Ratings of 1 to 7, representing a range from extreme maladjustment to a highly adequate level of adjustment, were assigned for each of the 10 variables based on the individual's Rorschach responses.

As a second basis for Rorschach analysis, Haimowitz and Haimowitz employed a modification of the Harrower-Erickson neurotic signs method, and the same seven-point scale for the ten personality dimensions. A higher degree of reliability was established for this second method, but both methods resulted in the same conclusions: based on pre- and post-therapy Rorschachs, the therapy population in general showed small but consistent changes in the direction of better adjustment. Statistically significant improvement was reflected on 5 of the 10 variables, with the control group showing no significant change. Comparing the findings for the three different therapy modes, there was little difference in the overall effectiveness of each. The investigators felt that the three modes might be useful in different specific dimensions of adjustment and recommended further research on this question.

The studies summarized here, published between 1946 and 1952, are noteworthy for several reasons:

1. They carried on, in the area of group therapy, the pioneering effort in individual Client-Centered Therapy to study both therapy process and outcome objectively.

2. Their analyses were based largely on verbatim typescripts of group sessions, rather than therapist notes or impressions. In addition, they employed tests of personality adjustment, including the Rorschach, behavior ratings, and sociometric ratings.

3. They provided supporting evidence for both sides of the therapeutic equation hypothesized by Rogers in that period: (a) behavior of client-centered group therapists, as distinguished from authoritarian and eclectic therapists, was indeed characterized by recognition and acceptance of feelings, and (b) clients as a group responded with behavior that was increasingly positive in attitude, insightful, planful, and more sensitive to others, including other group members.

4. Behavior changes in the group were correlated with changes outside the therapy situation.

5. Attitudes toward self made up an important aspect of client behavior, lending support to the emerging theory of personality change that emphasized self-concept.

6. More successful clients could be distinguished from less successful ones in specific ways, for example, level of defensiveness in response to therapists' recognitions of feeling.

Research on hospital patients and other groups

Baehr (1954), in a retrospective study of 66 patients who had been discharged from a Veterans Administration Hospital, after receiving nondirective therapy, obtained no significant differences comparing 17 people who received predominantly group therapy, 16 who received predominantly individual treatment, and 33 who received approximately equal amounts of both. Baehr's criterion of change was a discontentment scale devised by himself, which resulted in a measure of discontent from 230 potential disagreement-arousing experiments. All three modes had some degree of effectiveness, in this decreasing order: group plus individual, individual, group. The differences among them were not significant, however, and it is not known how many patients who received the different forms of therapy were not discharged and were therefore not part of the sample.

Ends and Page (1957) compared four therapy groups experienced by 63 hospitalized alcoholics: client-centered, learning theory, neoanalytic, and social discussion (the control group). The groups were made up of six individuals and met three times a week for 15 weeks. The Butler-Haigh Q-sort was used as a measure of self-concept; alcoholic episodes and rehospitalization were recorded during an 18-month follow-up. The client-centered group exhibited the greatest amount of change, both at the end of treatment and in the follow-up period. The psychoanalytically oriented group improved less in both time periods. The controls showed some deterioration and the learning theory group showed even more negative change, lasting into the follow-up period.

Ends and Page (1959) carried out a second study, with two groups of 28 patients in a general alcoholic treatment program. Of the groups, one was randomly assigned to six weeks of Rogerian group therapy, comprising 30 daily sessions led by experienced therapists. The MMPI and self-ideal Q-sorts were the criteria of change. The therapy group improved significantly on 7 of 8 Q-sort indices, compared with only 3 for the control group. The MMPI did not distinguish significantly between the groups, but it was concluded that client-centered group therapy was an effective adjunct to the general treatment program.

Saltz and Baraff (1962) compared three groups of 'nonchronic psychotics' who had been in a state hospital for an average of 12 days. One experimental group of four received 13 hours a week of occupational therapy for 10 weeks. A second experimental group received the same treatment and also two hours a week of client-centered group therapy. A control group of eight received neither form of therapy. The criterion of change was self-ideal Q-sort discrepancies. Congruence between self and ideal increased for two of the four individuals in the combined therapy group, for one of the four receiving occupational therapy alone, and for six of the eight controls. These results went counter to the hypothesized benefit of client-centered group therapy, but are clouded by the very small number of subjects.

Truax (1961) also studied group therapy with hospitalized patients. His study was extremely ambitious and complex, aiming to clarify the effect on patient self-exploration of different kinds of therapist input and of 'certain characteristics of the group atmosphere'. The population in Truax's study was made up of 39 patients in three groups led by three different therapists, whom Truax described as differing in their psychotherapeutic orientation 'along almost all dimensions'. Truax described the groups as quite effective: 25 of the 39 were discharged from the hospital at the time of a one-year follow-up. Most of the others were described as moderately improved; however, one patient regressed during group therapy and a second who seemed to respond well committed suicide two months after the termination of group therapy.

Thirteen judges rated 3-minute samples obtained randomly from middle segments of typewritten transcripts of 126 tape recorded group sessions. Truax devised 9-point rating scales to measure 7 'therapist conditions (e.g. accurate empathy, genuineness, leadership)', 6 'group conditions controlled by the therapist (e.g., concreteness or specificity of expression, empathic understanding)', and 3 'group conditions indirectly influenced by the therapist (genuineness of group members, group cohesiveness, ego involvement in the discussion)'.

Truax hypothesized that each of the 16 conditions, which he drew from a variety of therapeutic orientations and defined carefully, would show a positive relationship to the patients' interpersonal exploration, for which he employed three measures: the Rogers and Rablen Process Scale (Rogers, 1959), an Insight Scale and a Personal Reference Scale. Truax saw the Process Scale, which employed a seven-stage continuum from rigidity and fixity of experiencing to flow and spontaneity, as representing an overall measure of the extent of intrapersonal exploration, with the other two measuring specific aspects of this dimension. Truax used a variety of statistical procedures to analyze his data, but the general results were predominantly confirming of his hypotheses, with 12 of the 18 therapeutic conditions significantly related to intrapersonal exploration in the predicted direction.

Later in the 1960s Truax and different associates carried out and published a series of research projects on group therapy. The setting of these studies for the most part was the University of Arkansas Rehabilitation Research and Training Center. Outcomes were correlated with perceived therapist-offered conditions of empathy, nonpossessive warmth, and genuineness, and with the patient dimensions of silent-verbal participation and of level of adjustment-disturbance at the beginning of therapy. There was a variety of group therapy populations included in these studies: hospitalized mental patients, institutionalized juvenile delinquents, psychotherapy outpatients, and vocational rehabilitation clients. The perception of the therapist-offered conditions was measured by a 141-item Relationship Questionnaire adapted by Truax from the Relationship Inventory (Barrett-Lennard, 1962). Level of adjustment or disturbance was assessed by a combined measure of psychological test results and behavior, Outcome levels were determined by MMPI scores, the Q-sort, and projective test evaluations. In addition, the number of days institutionalized during a one-year follow-up was used as an outcome measure for the mental hospital patients and the institutionalized delinquents. The vocational rehabilitation clients were measured for work attitudes and efficiency.

Some of the main findings summarized by Truax and Carkhuff (1967) were: (1) except for the mental hospital population, there were significant positive relationships between outcome and perceived accurate empathy, nonpossessive warmth and genuineness; (2) the 3 therapeutic conditions, both combined and separately, tended to be effective with both verbal and nonverbal clients; and (3) these perceived client-centered variables were of equal importance in producing positive personality change in the most and the least disturbed clients.

Bednar and Kaul surveyed 'Experiential Group Research: Current Perspectives' for the 1978 revision of the *Handbook of Psychotherapy and Behavior Change* (Bednar and Kaul, 1978). A few of the studies reviewed by them pertain to the client-centered or Person-Centered Approach.

Abramowitz, Abramowitz, Roback, and Jackson (1974) investigated the effects of 'directive' and 'nondirective' group therapy on 26 college students varying on the dimension of internal-external locus of control. The results were that 'as hypothesized, persons given a group therapy more closely matched to their locus of control orientation fared better than their fellow students whose treatments had not been fit to their personality . . . overall outcome was more favorable among externals matched with a directive, and internals matched with a nondirective, group modality than among externals assigned to a nondirective, and internals assigned to a directive, one' (p. 851). Outcome measures covered expectations for attaining independence, academic recognition and affection, feelings of isolation, alienation, guilt, and shame, state-trait anxiety, self-esteem, and a 'client-report focal-problem seriousness index'. It is noteworthy that both types of groups were led by the same person, one of the investigators, who is described as a licensed clinical psychologist. The authors state also that the nondirective mode was 'not necessarily Rogerian'. This was confirmed by the finding that both 'directive' and 'nondirective' groups had 'comparable levels' of perceived client-centered conditions, as measured by the Relationship Inventory (Barrett-Lennard, 1962).

Kilmann and Howell (1974) also investigated the relationship between therapeutic structure and locus of control in the participants. Their subjects and mode of therapy were quite different from the Abramowitz et al. project just reviewed: they studied the outcome of 'direct' and 'nondirect' marathon groups offered to 84 institutionalized female drug addicts. 'Collectively, the findings suggest that internals are better therapeutic risks than externals, regardless of a direct or nondirect therapist technique' (p. 912). As with the Abramowitz et al. investigation, there is reason to doubt that the 'nondirect' therapeutic mode can be equated with Client-Centered Therapy.

Kilmann, Albert, and Sotile (1975) employed a 16-hour marathon format in one study, and a traditional therapy format in which groups met twice weekly, 2 hours each time, for 4 weeks, for an equal total of 16 hours. Both formats were offered in a structured and unstructured version, 'the only difference being the degree of therapist control over member participation' (p. 588). The same therapist led all groups. Outcome was measured on the Personal Orientation Inventory, and was similar to the Abramowitz et al. study. External locus of control subjects gained most from the structured, spaced group. Internal clients achieved maximum gains in the minimal control and structure mode.

Dies (1973) and May and Thompson (1973) both reported significant positive correlations between therapist self-disclosure and group members' ratings of their helpfulness. The Dies' subjects were described as college students in '10 different therapy groups', May and Thompson's as college students in 'encounter groups'. While the results in both studies were quite clear-cut, the investigators in both were cautious in their interpretations. Dies concluded that 'a therapist must be sensitive to the potential influence he has upon group members and give careful attention to the timing of his therapeutic interventions — including his own transparency' (p. 347). May and Thompson state that 'the positive and negative effects of self-disclosure may have a curvilinear relationship to mental health . . . it is conceivable that in some groups both high and low self-disclosures could be ranked low on mental health and low on helpfulness in the case of the group leader' (pp. 351–2).

Strassberg et al. (1975) found, in the context of group therapy with 18 male psychiatric inpatients, that patients who rated the therapist as more caring on the Relationship Inventory (Barrett-Lennard, 1962) were significantly more self-disclosing. The self-disclosure score was based on ratings of patient statements during group therapy sessions by judges trained and experienced in rating discrete patient statements as personal or impersonal. At the same time, Strassberg et al., using a complex of personality and behavior outcome instruments, found 'in contrast to earlier findings', patients who were more self-revealing made less therapeutic progress than their counterparts who divulged less personal material. This failure to replicate was tentatively attributed to the limited ability of psychotic persons to integrate social feedback. 'The results underscore the delicacy of the psychotherapeutic undertaking with schizophrenics' (p. 1259).

Braaten (1982) carried out a methodological pilot study to explore individually perceived group atmosphere as a predictor of outcome. The therapy group was composed of ten mental health professionals who met with the investigator as leader over the course of a year. The Silbergeld Group Atmosphere Scale was employed, while a Therapy Project List 90 devised by the investigator and the Derogatis Symptom Check List 90 were the measures of outcome. The Group Atmosphere Scale includes such factors as affiliation and support (aspects of cohesiveness, autonomy, and tolerance of aggression). Examples of 'therapy projects' are the constructive solution of a crisis in an intimate relationship, a reduction in excess self-sufficiency, and the acceptance of certain contradictions in oneself. Braaten concluded (1) that the Group Atmosphere Scale is very promising, especially as a measure of group cohesiveness, (2) individually perceived cohesiveness early in therapy predicts symptom reduction toward the end of treatment, but does not forecast the number of successes in projects during a year of treatment, and (3) there is a significant positive correlation between the number of successes in projects and reduced psychopathology as measured by the SCL-90.

Westermann, Schwab, and Tausch (1983) evaluated intensive (2½ days duration) person-centered group therapy carried out with 164 clients with 'psychoneurotic disturbances', by 16 'highly qualified person-centered psychotherapists'. There were 18 groups, each with approximately 10 clients and 2 therapists. The clients were psychodiagnostically tested prior to the therapy, then four weeks and six months later. Forty-five clients who waited for therapy for eight weeks constituted a control group. Of the experimentals, 85% improved after four weeks in comparison with only 18% of the controls. The six-month follow-up was positive, as well. The investigators reported a correlation between positive outcome and the success of the clients in experiencing Rogers' 'necessary and sufficient conditions'.

The studies in this section appear to be significant in several ways:
1. The client-centered group approach can be effective with seriously disturbed populations.
2. Evidence is lacking that either individual or group Client-Centered Therapy, or the combination, is significantly more effective.
3. Positive outcomes with client-centered group therapy correlate with therapist-offered conditions such as empathy, genuineness, and warmth. Group atmosphere, related to cohesiveness, is a concept that derives from group rather than individual therapy, and shows promise as a correlate of participant progress.
4. The progress shown by more seriously disturbed populations experiencing client-centered group therapy may be delineated in terms of changes in self-

concept and in quality of experiencing (from fixed and rigid to spontaneous and open).

5. There is evidence of a relationship between the degree of directiveness in a therapy group and the dimension of locus of control in the participants. Specifically it appears that group members with an internal locus of control respond better to less directive groups. It is not clear, however, that groups characterized as nondirective in the relevant studies are equivalent to client-centered groups.

6. Therapist self-disclosure is related to the perception of the therapist as caring and to positive group therapy outcome. The investigators are cautious, however, in generalizing from these findings, believing that self-disclosure, on the part of both therapists and group members, may sometimes be nontherapeutic.

7. The locus of control and the self-disclosure findings came from studies that included encounter groups or marathons as well as the traditional format once-a-week therapy group.

Basic encounter, large community, and conflict resolution groups

Starting with the mid-1960s, largely coinciding with Rogers' move from the University of Wisconsin to the Western Behavioral Sciences Institute in La Jolla, California, there was a great increase in interest on the part of Rogers and his associates in working with intensive groups meeting over a weekend, several days, or an entire week. The experiences began with what Rogers termed Basic Encounter Groups, numbering 8 to 18, and grew to include large community groups with hundreds of participants. A common focus of these groups has been an interest in learning more about Client-Centered Therapy and the Person-Centered Approach. Rogers and his associates have also had a particular interest in cross-cultural meetings and conflict resolution. The range of participants in these contexts is very great — as few as nine Irish Catholics and Protestants in one group and as many as 300 or so in a workshop located in Hungary.

It is clear from the testimony of hundreds of participants (including my own) that these meetings have resulted in personal learning and growth, and in experiences of group understanding and communality that seem invaluable. The amount of formal research in this area has been very small, particularly against the background of the immense contribution of the client-centered approach to psychotherapy research.

Rogers (1970) reported on follow-up questionnaires he administered to 481 persons who had been 'in groups I had conducted, or in large workshops for which I was responsible' (p. 126). This constituted an 82% rate of return, 2 to 12 months following the group experience although, for most of the respondents, it was 3 to 6 months. Of the total, 75% reported that the group experience had been very helpful; most of these checked the option, 'a deeply meaningful, positive experience'. In relation to effect on behavior, 57% of the total reported a continuing positive difference. Rogers was not only interested in whether the results of the group experience were lasting but in whether damage resulted from such encounters. Only 2 of the 481 felt the outcome for them was 'mostly damaging'. The alternative, 'more unhelpful than helpful', was checked by 6 individuals and 21, or 4%, checked 'neutral' or 'made little difference'. This left 452 persons, or 94%, who checked one of the clearly positive categories.

Bozarth (1981) reports on the use of Rogers' survey form with 46 participants in a 9-day Person-Centered Approach workshop in which the community group was the major activity. Comparing their responses with those of 110 participants in a 5-day Person-Centered Approach workshop led by Rogers and associates, Bozarth presents 'remarkably similar' percentages on items having to do with changes in behavior in important interpersonal relationships, in awareness of feelings, and in the impact of small and large groups in the workshops. While Bozarth concludes that the results were very positive in reaction to both meetings, he notes the 'paucity of direct research evidence of the Community Group' (p. 125).

Meador (1971) analyzed movement on the Rogers' (1959) Process Scale for eight participants in the weekend group documented in the film *Journey into Self* (McGaw, Farson, and Rogers, 1968). Thirteen raters applied the Process Scale (measuring the extent to which experiencing is rigid and fixed as opposed to free-flowing and spontaneous) to ten randomly distributed 2-minute film segments for each of the eight group members. The judges were 'blind' as far as knowing when the segment occurred in the five sessions or in the 16 hours of meeting time. Meador found that each of the eight participants moved significantly toward the positive end of the scale.

A well-known project from this period was carried out by Lieberman, Yalom, and Miles (1973), who studied the outcomes of groups conducted by 16 leaders representing nine 'widely used group technologies'. The participants were drawn from a population of 200 undergraduates enrolled in an encounter group course. One of the leaders was described as Rogerian. The evaluation of outcome was based on self-ratings of the experience, leader estimates of member learning, a social network estimate of change (descriptions of behavior, ways of relating to others, and so on by three to five people nominated by the participant as able to describe his or her behavior), and co-participants' ratings of learning.

While 78% of those who completed all 17 groups thought the experience was constructive, the investigators rated the overall gain as 'modest', and emphasized the frequency of negative outcomes. They found great variations in results for groups with different kinds of leaders. Quantitatively, in terms of the number of dropouts, casualties, negative changers, those unchanged, moderate changers and high learners, the 'Rogerian'-led group showed little change. It was 13th out of 17 on the basis of the participants' ratings. However, Lieberman, Yalom, and Miles' description of the leader's behavior makes it clear that he was not client-centered in his approach.

Rogers (1980) and Devonshire and Kremer (1980) have reported on a number of research projects in Germany in which a variety of populations participated in person-centered encounter groups. These included:

- 132 emotionally disturbed individuals taking part in 2½-day encounter groups (Brun et al., 1976).
- 108 people averaging 70 years of age also experiencing 2½-day person-centered encounter groups, with younger people also taking part (Bergeest et al., 1977).
- 63 of the most neurotic pupils selected from a school population of 358 randomly assigned to a 'talk group', a 'sport group', and a control group (Thiel et al., 1978).

Positive results were reported in all of these studies. In the last one, the helpers in the 'talk group' (which showed significantly more benefit than the other two) were peers who had been specially trained in a person-centered approach. The degree of self-exploration of the participants in the 'talk group' was found to be significantly related to the amount of empathy expressed by the trained helpers. Devonshire and Kremer (1980) describe successful results from similar experiences in populations of prison inmates and judges, and teachers of special education.

Solomon (1986) presented a quantitative evaluation of a four-day meeting of 50 participants from 17 nations on 'The Central American Challenge'. The participants included many past and present governmental officials and legislators, in addition to individuals from universities, institutes, foundations, and other organizations. Emphasis was placed on the fact that all of these individuals were present unofficially, simply 'as persons'. The meeting was staffed by Rogers and eight facilitators who tried to express acceptance and respect for all opinions and feelings and thus work toward a general climate of safety, trust, and personal regard.

Each of two facilitators rated the participants in their small groups at the end of each day's small group meeting on 'Empathy, Listening, Respect, Trust, and Involvement', as well as on a seven-point process or freedom of experiencing scale. There was an end of workshop questionnaire in which the participants, on a six-point scale, rated their overall feeling about the workshop and, on a five-point scale, the impact of the Person-Centered Approach in helping them deal with future conflict situations. The facilitators' ratings show a daily improvement in the participants; it is recognized that the ratings may reflect a bias.

The participants' evaluation of the meeting was very high, averaging better than five, on the six-point scale, for their overall feeling, and around four, on the five-point scale, for the estimated impact of the Person-Centered Approach. Other more informal and personal responses buttressed the conclusion that this meeting had been an effective approach to conflict resolution.

Discussion
The history of research on client-centered group therapy basically parallels that in the individual sphere. Verbatim typescripts were introduced as a basic source of data, client-centered therapists were found to be behaviorally different from those with an authoritarian orientation, clients changed by becoming more positive,

insightful, and planful (as hypothesized by earlier client-centered theory) and by becoming more self-congruent and more free in their experiencing (in terms of later theory). External measures, such as the Rorschach, were employed in addition to those based on an internal frame of reference, for example, the client's self-attitudes. Evidence was advanced that extremely disturbed individuals could be helped by client-centered group therapy and that patient progress was related to the provision of conditions such as empathy, congruence, and warmth.

This type of research flourished while Rogers was at a major university with faculty associates and a strong group of graduate students working on dissertations and staff projects. It diminished after Rogers became affiliated with the Western Behavioral Sciences Institute in 1964 and later with the Center for Studies of the Person, which he helped establish. While Rogers' departure from academia is being advanced here as contributing to a decline in research on groups, it should be noted that he himself has expressed the view, with some passion, that graduate study in psychology, with its many external requirements, stifles research and creativity.

Another pertinent element was Rogers' rapidly increasing interest in the intensive group during the latter phase of his years at the University of Wisconsin and the beginning of his new life in La Jolla. It has been shown in these articles that a strong interest in client-centered groups, and in studying them, dated at least from the middle 1940s at the University of Chicago. The major effort of Rogers and his associates, however, at Chicago and Madison, was to contribute to the scientific understanding of the process of individual personality growth that accompanied the provision of a person-centered climate.

Even as this task went on, the involvement of the therapist as a person and the freeing up of the client's process of experiencing were increasingly emphasized in client-centered theory and research. Both of these trends gathered momentum as Rogers and his associates became increasingly involved in intensive groups.

In the university setting, for client-centered faculty and graduate students, there was typically a blend of the experience of doing therapy, teaching, and research. With the move to California, and with the major activity having become the intensive group, the balance shifted sharply away from study, analysis, and research and toward experiencing. Analysis was less satisfying and, in addition, seemed an intrusion and to lack validity.

This was not true for Rogers personally. Characteristically his immersion in an experience was followed by a careful description and interpretation. There has been a constant flow of papers, articles, and videotapes, and every few years, a significant book. Indeed, part of Rogers' intention in moving from the University of Wisconsin to the Western Behavioral Sciences Institute was to advance learning and knowledge of growth processes by working in an environment that was hospitable to newer philosophies of science and to psychological research that was humanistically oriented and not bound by tradition and conventionality.

At this point, this hope has not been fulfilled, beyond Rogers' own work and that of a few other investigators in the United States and abroad. The picture has been in marked contrast to the major impact of client-centered theory on psychotherapy research for 25 or 30 years. Kirschenbaum (1979) has tried to explain this in terms of a lack of concrete examples that make clear the alternative approach to science and research that Rogers was advocating, and that he had always provided in his professional career.

Recently, in keynoting the 25th anniversary of the Association for Humanistic Psychology, Rogers (1985) addressed the problem of the lack of impact of the humanistic approach on mainstream psychology in American higher education. In this talk, he portrayed a 'burgeoning' of books and articles that provide new models of science, models that accept imprecision in life experiences and behavior and recognize the importance of understanding meanings, motivations, intentions, and so on, from the inside. Rogers follows this with many specific instances of research that are not well-known but that exemplify the alternative models. To extend such research he recommends strengthening the less-established universities that are humanistically inclined, rather than trying to change those that are more established.

Group phenomena are extraordinarily complex. It makes sense that a more flexible and phenomenologically deeper approach is needed to understand and influence them. Also not to be overlooked is the possibility that individual clients or group participants will, out of the crucible of their experience, find helpful answers. The professional role, in this case, may turn out to be that of equal participant and appreciative observer, one very much in keeping with a person-centered approach.

References

Abramowitz, C. V., Abramowitz, S. I., Roback, H. B. and Jackson, C. (1974) Differential effectiveness of directive and nondirective group therapies as a function of client internal-external control. *Journal of Consulting and Clinical Psychology, 42,* 849–53.

Baehr, G. O. (1954) The comparative effectiveness of individual psychotherapy, group psychotherapy and a combination of these methods. *Journal of Consulting Psychology, 15,* 179–83.

Barrett-Lennard, G. T. (1962) Dimensions of therapist response as causal factors in therapeutic change. *Psychological Monographs, 76* (43, Whole No. 562).

Bednar, R. L. and Kaul, T. J. (1978) Experiential group research: Current perspectives. In S. L. Garfield and A. E. Bergin (Eds.), *Handbook of psychotherapy and behavior change* (2nd edn.), New York: John Wiley.

Bergeest, H. G., Steinbach, I. and Tausch, A. (1977) Personliche schwierigkeiten alter menschen. *Z. Gerontologie, 10,* 511.

Bozarth, J. D. (1981) The person-centered approach in the large community group. In G. M. Gazda (Ed.), *Innovations to group psychotherapy.* Springfield, IL: Charles C. Thomas.

Braaten, L. J. (1982, July) Individually perceived group atmosphere and goal attainment: A methodological pilot study. *Proceedings of the First International Forum on the Person-Centered Approach,* Oaxtepec, Mexico.

Brun, M., Tausch, R. and Westermann, H. (1976) *Psychische anderungen bei seelisch beeintrachtigten personen in personenzentrierten encounter gruppen.* Hamburg: Hamburg Universitat.

Devonshire, C. M. and Kremer, J. W. (1980) *Toward a person-centered resolution of intercultural conflicts.* Dortmund, West Germany: Pedagogische Arbeitsstelle.

Dies, F. R. (1973) Group therapists self-disclosure: An evaluation by clients. *Journal of Counseling Psychology, 20,* 344–8.

Ends, E. J. and Page, C. W. (1957) A study of three types of group psychotherapy with hospitalized male inebriates. *Quarterly Journal of Studies in Alcohol, 18,* 263–77.

Ends, E. J. and Page, C. W. (1959) Group psychotherapy and concomitant psychological change. *Psychological Monographs, 73,* (Whole No. 1480).

Fleming, L. and Snyder, W. U. (1947) Social and personal changes following nondirective group play therapy. *American Journal of Orthopsychiatry, 17,* 101–16.

Gorlow, L. (1950) Nondirective group psychotherapy: An analysis of the behavior of members as therapists. Unpublished doctoral thesis, Columbia University Teachers College.

Gorlow, L., Hoch, E. L. and Telschow, E. F. (1952) *The nature of non-directive group psychotherapy.* New York: Bureau of Publications, Columbia University Teachers College.

Haimowitz, N. R. and Haimowitz, M. L. (1952) Personality changes in client-centered therapy. In W. Wolff and J. A. Precker (Eds.), *Success in psychotherapy.* New York: Grune & Stratton.

Hobbs, N. (1951) Group-centered psychotherapy. In C. R. Rogers, *Client-centered therapy.* Boston: Houghton Mifflin.

Hobbs, N. and Pascal, G. (1946) A method for the quantitative analysis of group psychotherapy. *American Psychologist, 1,* 297.

Hock, C. L. (1950) The nature of the group process in non-directive group psychotherapy. Unpublished doctoral thesis, Columbia University Teachers College.

Kilmann, P. R., Albert, H. M. and Sotile, W. M. (1975) The relationship between locus of control, structure of therapy, and outcome. *Journal of Consulting and Clinical Psychology, 43,* 588.

Kilmann, P. R. and Howell, R. J. (1974) Effects of structure of marathon group therapy and locus of control on therapeutic outcome. *Journal of Consulting and Clinical Psychology, 42,* 912.

Kirschenbaum, H. (1979) *On Becoming Carl Rogers.* New York: Delacorte.

Lieberman, M. A., Yalom, I. D. and Miles, M. B. (1973). *Encounter groups: First facts.* New York: Basic Books.

May, D. P. and Thompson, C. L. (1973) Perceived levels of self-disclosure, mental health, and helpfulness of group leaders. *Journal of Counseling Psychology, 30,* 349–52.

McGaw, W. H., Farson, R. and Rogers, C. R. (Producers) (1968) *Journey into self* [Film]. Berkeley: University of California Extension Media Center.

Meador, B. (1971) Individual process in a basic encounter group. *Journal of Consulting Psychology, 18,* 70–6.

Patterson, C. H. (1984) Empathy, warmth and genuineness in psychotherapy: A review of reviews. *Psychotherapy: Theory, Research and Practice, 21,* 431–8.

Peres, H. (1947). An investigation of nondirective group therapy. *Journal of Consulting Psychology, 11,* 159–72.

Rogers, C. R. (1959) A tentative scale for the measurement of process in psychotherapy. In E. A. Rubenstein and M. B. Parloff (Eds.), *Research in psychotherapy.* Washington, DC: American Psychological Association.

Rogers, C. R. (1970) *Carl Rogers on encounter groups.* New York: Harper & Row.

Rogers, C. R. (1980) Client-centered psychotherapy. In H. J. Kaplan, B. J. Sadock and A. M. Freedman (Eds.), *Comprehensive textbook of psychiatry, III.* Baltimore: Williams & Wilkins.

Rogers, C. R. (1985) Toward a more human science of the person. Address at 25th anniversary meeting, Association for Humanistic Psychology, San Francisco.

Saltz, P. and Baraff, A. S. (1962) Changes in the relation between self-concepts and ideal-concepts of psychotics consequent upon therapy. *Journal of General Psychology, 67,* 291–8.

Solomon, L. N. (1986) The person-centered approach to international conflict resolution: A quantitative evaluation. Unpublished manuscript.

Strassberg, D. S., Roback, H. B., Anchor, K. N. and Abramowitz, S. I. (1975) Self-disclosure in group therapy with schizophrcnics. *Archives of General Psychiatry, 32,* 1259–61.

Telschow, E. F. (1950) The role of the group leader in nondirective group psychotherapy. EdD project, New York: Columbia University Teachers College.

Thiel, G., Steinbach, I. and Tausch, A. (1978) Schuler fuhren gilfreiche Gesprache mit Schulern. *Psychologie in Erziehung und Unterricht, 25,* 75.

Truax, C. B. (1961) The process of group psychotherapy: Relationships between hypothesized therapeutic conditions and intrapersonal exploration. *Psychological Monographs, 75*(14) (Whole No. 511).

Truax, C. B. and Carkhuff, R. R. (1967) *Toward Effective Counseling and Psychotherapy.* Chicago: Aldine.

Westermann, B., Schwab, R. and Tausch, R. (1983) Auswirkungen und prozesse person-zentrierter gruppen psychotherapie bie 164 blienten einer psychotherapeutischen beratungsstelle. *Zeitschrift fur Klinische Psychologie, 12,* 273–92.

SOME MEMORABLE CLIENTS AND WHAT MAKES THEM SO

11

An account of clients who made striking changes in their lives as a result of sudden dramatic shifts in their self-image. Others also stand out in my memory — including one who was mentally retarded yet accomplished so much, and another who made tremendous progress in spite of great emotional instability.

I felt the impact of the first two of my memorable clients because they made striking changes in their lives associated with sudden and dramatic shifts in their self-concepts. I described them in a talk on a 40-year history of the concept of self in Client-Centered Therapy and the Person-Centered Approach (Raskin, 1980).

The first occurred during 1948 while I was working on my PhD and was a member of the University of Chicago Counseling Center staff. I had an experience with a client that has remained indelible. She was an older woman, unprepossessing, poorly clothed, with a history of psychiatric hospitalizations and shock treatment. I had seen her only a few times, when she came in and related the following experience. She had boarded a rather crowded bus, found a seat between two men and sat down, kind of hunching herself as she did so. She then had a reaction to this act of trying to make herself smaller and thought, 'No, I am entitled to as much room as these people'. She squared her shoulders and in so doing, brushed up against one of the men next to her, who looked at her with annoyance. This did not deter my client nor result in an apologetic response. She went on from this incident to take a series of steps which evidenced, for the first time at least in many, many years, a positive regard for herself.

My second memorable client, I saw mostly in group therapy more than 20 years later, around 1970. This woman was in her middle 30s, also with a traumatic history including a psychiatric hospitalization and a succession of relationships with men in which she allowed herself to be used and abused. This woman really hurt and in sharing with our group the unhappy events of her life, gave the impression of a bottomless pit of endless suffering. She had an apartment which was potentially attractive but which she did not keep up. One day, after some

Originally published in W. Kir-Stimon and M. Stern (Eds.) (1986), *The memorable patient*. Binghamton, New York: Hawthorn Press, p. 107–13. Reprinted with permission.

particularly unhappy events which left her deeply disgusted with herself, she put up a poster on which she had printed, 'PRETEND to have self-respect'. She cleaned up her apartment and, like the lady I had seen in 1948, initiated a series of steps that evidenced self-regard. This culminated in her writing to a brother in California asking him to help her financially to move out and get settled in that state. He responded positively, she made the move, had some setbacks which slowed her progress only temporarily, and developed her own business.

I think of a third client who also turned her life around and made a bold move geographically and psychologically. I remember her because of years of difficult struggle in the first phase of our therapeutic relationship in which I feel I was a real partner. I remember her, too, because of my regard for her genuineness. Much of the time she spent with me was in silence. There was a quality in that silence I still have difficulty articulating. It had something to do with her not saying anything she did not really feel or mean. It had something to do also with an assumption of responsibility for her own difficulties; this expressed a kind of self-containment. She was close to her family, a family that was hard on her and her siblings. She found it difficult to move away from them, and from employment in an organization which, like her family, provided security but not very good treatment. Soon after one of her first moves to an apartment of her own, which was only a few blocks away from her parental home, she broke down, and I helped effect one of only two or three psychiatric hospitalizations in my long career as a psychotherapist. Over the course of a few years, she succeeded in moving, successfully, farther and farther away from her family. Then she took the really bold and courageous step of moving across the country, to a sun-belt city. She loved the out-of-doors, but continued in an office job in her new locale. After a year or two, she took an outdoor job, and I have visited her and enjoyed the external radiance that now accompanies her inner beauty.

I had always believed this client to be employed beneath her capabilities. Recently, she wrote and asked for my support for graduate study in a field that was consistent with her interests and would utilize her full intellect. This client is memorable because of her difficult and successful struggle toward greater and greater self-actualization and because, I am sure, I shared in the struggle.

The issue of intellect reminds me of another client who is memorable because she accomplished so much and was mentally retarded. In another context, I have written about her and about another client who made tremendous progress against a background of great emotional instability.

Jim

'Jim' was referred to me in 1968 by the psychiatric service of a local hospital, which felt that he needed outpatient psychotherapy. He was in his early 20s. I felt immediately, on both sides, a difficulty in the establishment of trust. It was a period of a number of political assassinations, and given Jim's close-shaven head, strong physique, and violent manner in speech and appearance, I sometimes experienced in our early contacts fear of a personal attack. He expressed hatred for a particular race and prejudice toward my own religious group. He described bar-room brawls that he commonly instigated. He looked to be, and described himself as, a blue-collar worker, and gave the impression of being anti-intellectual. On the other hand, Jim had definite educational, occupational, and economic aspirations. He wished to get a college degree and to become a United States Senator and a millionaire by the age of 30.

Jim's social relationships also presented some problems. He had no close male friends, and he conceptualized his relationships with women solely in terms of obtaining sexual satisfaction.

His father was dead and his mother had remarried. He had an older married sister, but none of the existing family relationships were warm or close.

In the first few months of therapy, I saw Jim two or three times a month; in succeeding months, this was reduced to once or twice a month. The frequency of our contacts was left up to him; the fee was based on what he thought he could afford. In our interviews, Jim brought up what he wished to talk about or thought was important, and I tried to be as empathic as possible, including instances where he would ask personal questions. At the same time I tried to understand his curiosity or whatever attitude accompanied his questions; I felt comfortable in answering them, so he learned something of my work, my family, where I lived, and so on.

A few months into our meetings, Jim talked of his memories of his father. As he recounted numerous occasions when his father had been caustically critical and physically brutal, his voice and emotion rose to a fevered pitch and he would seem out of control for several minutes. This happened in the course of a series of interviews and, without verbalizing any insights, he seemed to be done with this traumatic part of his emotional development and returned to current concerns.

One thing Jim often talked about was his tendency to exaggerate his accomplishments in conversing, for example, with men with whom he drank in bars. He would lie about his income, occupational level, and extent of his possessions. He was concerned about his need to do this. He was persistent in instigating violent scrapes, and his relationships with women continued to be characterized by lack of confidence, brevity, and narrow sexual purpose. He worked at a variety of physical and intellectual jobs. Along the way, he completed his college requirements, and took graduate courses at the local state university campus in both the physical and social sciences. He regarded any non-physical work as a very easy way of life.

Jim stopped talking about becoming a United States Senator and amassing a million dollars while still young, but it remained important to him to set economic and occupational goals for himself. I appreciated the importance he attached to achieving security and also 'making it big'.

About 5 years after the beginning of therapy, while continuing the once-or-twice-a-month frequency of meetings, Jim's social and occupational life grew more stable and substantial. He courted a woman in a social-service profession, and they were married. She worked while Jim went on with a combination of jobs, and they planned their future together. In the next few years, they had two children, and Jim invested much time and emotion in being a father. His family life, in general, clearly gave him much security.

Jim continued to see me. By 1980, the frequency of our meetings had dropped to once a month or less. I had arranged a sabbatical that year in another part of the country that allowed me, however, to return home each month. Thus, I was in a position to see him as often as I had been doing. However, while I saw my other clients on these return visits, Jim did not schedule an appointment with me until I had returned from my sabbatical, when he went back to seeing me about once a month. Some months later, when I raised the question, Jim confirmed that he had a great deal of feeling about my year away. He then resumed the exploration of his current problems. At the time of writing, I am seeing Jim about once every other month. He seems significantly more accepting of himself, happier with his life as it is, with less need to strive for achievements to impress others. He would like to learn to take more risks at work, feeling he would then be able to come closer to his real potential. His family life continues to be stable and satisfying.

Ginny

I was a therapist in a hospital outpatient group from 1972 to 1976, during which time I met Ginny. She was a graduate of the local high school's program for mentally retarded students. While she read only at a third or fourth grade level and was shy and uncertain of herself, once she achieved some security with me and the other group members, she expressed herself with some facility. She had some trouble with vocabulary, occasionally using one word or phrase when she meant another.

Ginny was in her early 20s when I first met her, and very attractive in spite of the poor clothes dictated by her economic circumstances. She had had a brief, unsuccessful marriage with a high school classmate of her own race, then lived with a minority group member, which resulted in the birth of a son, who was three when I first met Ginny. The reason she gave for being interested in therapy was that she wanted to be as good a parent as possible; she was afraid that without therapy, she might be responsible for her son growing up with problems.

Ginny had a bad relationship with her own mother who drank, had health problems, and was always trying to get Ginny to do things for her, as Ginny experienced it. Ginny had very warm feelings for her father, who was quite old and infirm and lived apart from Ginny's mother. An older sister lived in another state, and Ginny's contact with her was irregular.

The group was led in a client-centered fashion. One of the milestones for Ginny was sharing with the others that the group with which she had gone through high school was retarded. While Ginny was already an active participant in the group, after the admission of her intellectual-educational classification and as the group experienced some turnover in membership, she was able to assume increasingly a leadership role. She had worked on her own feelings of inferiority and had developed a high sensitivity to and ability to articulate issues of self-esteem. In this way Ginny was helpful to and gained the obvious respect of college graduates and even graduate students whose IQs may have been double her own.

One of the ways in which Ginny had evidenced a lack of self-regard at the time she began group therapy was in her relationships with both the father of her little boy and with a male friend of his who subsequently became interested in her. In those relationships, Ginny tolerated broken promises, dishonesty, infidelity, and so forth. As she explored her feelings about such experiences, she began to feel that she deserved better. She terminated these relationships and met a man of her own race who treated her with great love and respect. He had a child of his own from a previous marriage and related to Ginny's son with much warmth and caring. He proposed, they were married, and they continue to have a successful relationship as they near a decade of marriage. After the termination of the group, Ginny stayed in touch with some of the members, including one who responded to Ginny's request for help with her reading skills.

Art

I first saw Art in 1970. There was considerable strain in his marriage, centering on an eating disorder on his wife's side and chronic unemployment on his. He also drank a lot, but the extent of this was not clear, and he complained about pain and sensory disturbances that would occur at different times in different parts of his body, and would cause him great distress.

After a series of meetings which included Art and his wife and which served to reduce the tension between them, I began to see him individually. I experienced Art as a demanding client. He wanted relief from his pain, asked for advice, telephoned between appointments, and sought assurances that therapy would help him. My response to all this was to be empathic and congruent. I tried to convey my appreciation for his suffering and feelings of desperation, and expressed my hope that therapy would be helpful while refraining from offering advice or false reassurance.

Art derived some help from this process but not enough to satisfy him. As a result, a pattern emerged where he would see me for a few months, interrupt for a year or more, and then return for several months again. He had many other sources of help: medical or dental specialists, spiritual retreats, yoga, exercise, and so forth. Often, at night, he would have a six-pack with a friend, and he smoked a lot at the same time. I did not think of him as an alcoholic, however. He was a man who suffered a lot, looked for physical relief and emotional solace where he could find it, and did not seem interested in an insight-oriented approach to his problems.

Art's wife overcame her eating disorder; his difficulty in seeking and obtaining employment continued, although he managed some temporary and part-time work.

A turning point occurred when I was looking for someone to be interviewed for a course on Clinical Interviewing. The format I had evolved was for the same person to be interviewed by six or seven psychotherapists who represented different orientations. The therapist would explain his or her approach and conduct an interview in front of the class, followed by the reactions of the therapist, the interviewee, and the class.

I had a feeling that Art would be interested in this kind of opportunity. I telephoned him and he asked for some time to think about it. He called back a few minutes later to say he would like to do it.

Art was interviewed in turn by two client-centered therapists, two psychoanalysts, a Gestalt therapist, a psychiatric social worker with a bioenergentics orientation, and a behaviorist. Each interview had its own individual character. Not only was each interviewer distinct in his or her approach, but Art related differently to each, much as 'Gloria' did to Rogers, Perls and Ellis in the well-known film, *Three Approaches to Psychotherapy* (Shostrom, 1965).

Art was a participant in the discussion which followed each interview and in several class sessions which were interspersed between the demonstrations. He expressed satisfaction with each interview, but nothing spectacular occurred within any of them or immediately following. There was a cumulative result which occurred, however, in the weeks and months following this sequence of interviews which did seem remarkable.

Art decided to enter a hospital treatment program for alcoholism. He carried this out successfully and participated in the follow-up aspects of the program. He has remained alcohol-free in the many years that have since elapsed. In addition, he completed the graduate degree that had been in suspension since his first interviews with me and obtained significant employment. He returned for individual therapy with me for a period of about one year and, for the first time, showed an interest in and ability to perceive relationships between his physiological symptoms and psychological variables.

Another memorable client is a woman plagued for many years by difficulties with her heart and bladder and injuries sustained in accidents. In addition to this set of problems, she went through a divorce from her husband of over 30 years, occasioned by his surreptitious relationship with another woman. She came out badly in the divorce settlement, and the judge was later revealed to be dishonest.

This woman was terribly hurt and shaken by these developments, which turned upside down the reality she had experienced and the emotions she had invested for more than three decades. In spite of continued bouts of illness, and all kinds of externally-caused problems with her house and job, she has persevered. Showing remarkable fortitude, she has not only continued with her regular job but has taken on extra work. She has traveled, is working through the difficult readjustment of forming relationships with men she has not known, and has made plans for an active retirement.

The thoughts of one memorable client lead to thoughts of another and I could go on writing. The process clarifies my appreciation for the part I have played in helping others. It is a role very consistent with my person-centered orientation: I have been a facilitator, an emotional companion, a source of nonpossessive caring and support to whom these people could turn in their own ways. Our contacts, depending on the individual, have been regular and irregular, have varied in frequency and also made use of different modes of communication — talking in person, writing and telephoning.

It has been gratifying to me as a psychotherapist, to be a witness, in hundreds of meaningful relationships, to the tremendous strength of human beings to cope with adversity and to their inspiring capacity to adapt and grow, to learn to accept and to have regard for themselves and others. My many memorable clients have enriched my work and my person.

References

Raskin, N. J. (1980) Client-centered therapy. In S. J. Lynn and J. F. Garske (Eds.), *Contemporary psychotherapies: Models and methods.* Columbus, OH: Charles E. Merrill.

Shostrom, E. (Ed.) (1965) *Three approaches to psychotherapy* [Film]. Santa Ana, CA.

CARL ROGERS AND CLIENT/PERSON-CENTERED THERAPY (WITH FRED M. ZIMRING)

12

The 50 years that have elapsed since the beginning of Client-Centered Therapy are divisible into four periods, each of which starts with the publication of a work by Carl Rogers. In the first two periods, the main focus of Rogers' work was on individual psychotherapy. In the latter periods, the focus changed to new contexts in which the basic client-centered attitudes were applied: groups, education, and conflict resolution. These changes in context necessarily resulted in changes in the operations used to implement Rogers' basic principles.

First period

The first period of the client-centered approach was initiated when Rogers addressed the Psi Chi chapter (an undergraduate psychology honor society) at the University of Minnesota in December 1940 on 'Some Newer Concepts of Psychotherapy'. Rogers had begun a professorship at Ohio State University in that year and was in the process of delineating emerging trends in the child guidance field. He had described these trends in the book, *The Clinical Treatment of the Problem Child*, published in 1939. Rogers was already expert in the use of tests and interviews with children and parents, and he communicated these skills in a practicum course he taught at Ohio State.

Even as he was practicing and teaching, however, Rogers was refocusing his professional interest from working with children and their parents to therapy with adults. One outcome of the diagnostic process in which child guidance clinics engaged was the decision to offer treatment. In the late 1930s, at institutions such as the Judge Baker Guidance Center in Boston and the Rochester (New York) Guidance Center which Rogers administered, treatment resulted for approximately one third of the cases assessed. For Rogers, there was an abrupt shift from being a clinician who employed some diagnostic methods to being a therapist who eschewed diagnosis. As he was moving rapidly toward centering his efforts on therapy with adults, he made no significant distinction between 'counseling' and 'psychotherapy'.

Originally published in D.K. Freedheim (Ed.), *History of psychotherapy: A centruy of change (*1992). Washington DC: American Psychological Association, p. 629–56. Reprinted with permission.

One expression of the change being described here is that approximately one third of Rogers' book, *Counseling and Psychotherapy* (Rogers, 1942), is devoted to the verbatim account of an eight-interview treatment course with an adult, 'Herbert Bryan'.

Beginning with this volume, Rogers employed a hypothetical format which persisted throughout his career: 'if we do this, then such and such will follow'. In *Counseling and Psychotherapy*, the hypothesis took the following form: if the therapist accepts, recognizes, and clarifies the feelings expressed by the client, there will be movement from negative feelings to positive ones, followed by insight and positive actions which are initiated by the client.

Rogers placed particular stress on two aspects of the therapist's role. One was the importance of responding to feelings rather than content. The other was the acceptance by the therapist of the feelings expressed, whether they were positive, negative, or ambivalent.

In *Counseling and Psychotherapy* (1942), Rogers illustrated the difference between responding to feeling and content. A student (S), in his first contact with the counselor (C), states his problem as follows (phonographic recording):

S: I've always realized that my methods of study, my study habits, are wrong. I don't feel as though I am a very brilliant person, but I don't think I am as stupid as my brains indicate (p. 133).

Rogers states that it is plain that the student 'is feeling disappointed at the discrepancy between his ability and his grades and concerned lest his grades be taken to represent the true measure of his ability'. To make some response to this feeling would have been a move toward deeper revelation of the problem, but the counselor responds:

C: Well, how bad are your grades? I thought they were pretty good.
S: My cumulative average is about 2.3 or 2.4. I had a 3.1 last quarter (pp. 133–4).

This response to content by the counselor clearly has the effect of keeping the student on a content level and makes it difficult for him to go further with the feeling that he was developing.

Rogers gave a comparable instance where there 'is more adequate response to the feeling expressed'. The student in this case is describing the difficulty of writing to his parents to inform them that his grades have worsened:

S: I don't know if they're going to condemn me. I think so, because that's what they've done in the past. They've said, 'It's your fault. You don't have enough willpower, you're not interested'. That's the experience I've had in the past. I've been sort of telling them that I improved in this respect. I was alright [sic] the first quarter. Well, I wasn't entirely all right, but I just got worse. (Pause)
C: You feel that they'll be unsympathetic and they'll condemn you for your failures.

S: Well, my — I'm pretty sure my father will. My mother might not. He hasn't been — he doesn't experience these things; he just doesn't know what it's like. 'Lack of ambition', is what he'd say. (Pause)

C: You feel that he could never understand you?

S: No, I don't think he is — is capable of that, because I don't get along with him, don't at all! (Rogers, 1942, pp. 135–6)

It is clear that this counselor's response to the student's feelings has facilitated a process of exploration and expansion of feeling, of sharing, and perhaps of awareness.

The counselor's acceptance of the client's feelings

Rogers believed that at the same time that the counselor attended to feeling rather than content, the counselor's *acceptance* of whatever feelings were expressed was crucial. He emphasized both the difficulty and the importance of accepting negative feelings, the kind of feelings which often dominate the early phases of therapy (Rogers, 1942). Here is a particularly cogent passage:

> When the client is thoroughly discouraged, when he feels that he is 'no good', when his fears are overwhelming, when he hints that he has thought of suicide, when he pictures himself as completely unstable, completely dependent, entirely inadequate, unworthy of love — in short, when he is expressing any type of negative feeling toward himself, the natural tendency on the part of the inexperienced counselor is to try to convince him that he is exaggerating the situation. This is probably true, and the counselor's argument is intellectually logical, but it is not therapeutic. The client feels worthless, no matter how many good qualities may be objectively pointed out to him. He knows that he has contemplated suicide, no matter how many reasons may be pointed out for not doing so. He knows that he has worried about going insane, no matter how unlikely that possibility may be made to appear. The counselor is giving more genuine help if he assists the client to face these feelings openly, recognize them for what they are, and admit that he has them. Then, if he no longer has to prove that he is worthless or abnormal, he can, and does, consider himself more comfortably and find in himself more positive qualities. (Rogers, 1942, p. 144)

Rogers then gave an example of this principle of acceptance from an interview with a student (S) by a counselor (C):

S: I — uh — have the opinion that I'm inferior. That's the — that's the opinion I have.

C: You just know darn well that you don't measure up, is that it?

S: That's right. (Pause)

C: Want to tell me some more about that?

S: Well, I'll tell you. I've been interested in anthropology to some extent, and especially criminal anthropology. (Pause) Well, I continually compare physiques of people, and I feel that mine is inferior, and I don't stop — I don't — I also believe that the behavior of an individual is an approximation of his physique, you might say. That's what my belief is. I've read too much of Hooton (laugh). Did you ever hear of him? (C nods.) I expected you did.

C: And — uh — as you look about on other physical types, you just feel that yours is inferior, the lowest of the low.

S: No, not exactly, I wouldn't say that.

C: But you're far down in the scale?

S: Yes, (laugh) that's the way I feel. And I'd have to have some real basis to change my mind about it.

The counselor continues his consistent acceptance of the student's negative feelings, and toward the end of the interview, there is this exchange:

S: I do have abilities and I realize some — among them I have a certain knack for mathematics. I think I do. And I've always been more advanced than my fellow students in that, I think I can safely say.

C: Then there's one thing at least in which you really excel most of the students that you work with. (Rogers, 1942, pp. 144–6)

This excerpt exemplifies the expression of positive attitudes following the counselor's consistent acceptance of negative feelings. Rogers points out that 'when the counselor overstates' the student's attitude, suggesting that he feels he is 'the lowest of the low', the student objects, 'already giving a hint of the fact that his evaluation of himself is not all negative' (1942, p. 146).

Accepting ambivalent feelings
Rogers (1942) also emphasized the importance of accepting ambivalent feelings:
Where the client is conflicted in his feelings, where both love and hostility, attraction and repulsion, or both sides of a difficult choice, are being expressed it is particularly important to recognize this clearly as an ambivalent attitude. Some of the sorts of recognition which may be given are exemplified in such statements as, 'You feel you should go into commerce, but music is the thing you really like'; 'in spite of your bitterness toward your father, you do like him'; 'You want to come for help, yet still at times you feel it is too difficult'. . . A forward step in therapy is made when such ambivalences are definitely clarified. The client is well along toward solution when the client feels it to be a conflict with clear-cut choices. On the other hand, to recognize only one aspect of such muddled feelings may retard therapy . . . To recognize only an attitude of hostility toward a parent, when elements of affection are also being

expressed, may make it difficult for the client to bring out more fully these positive feelings. Consequently, ambivalent attitudes need to be brought into the discussion as openly as positive or negative feelings, since it is through their clarification that the client is enabled to find a solution to them. (Rogers, 1942, pp. 147–8)

The clarification of feelings

Rogers, in 1940 and 1942, talked of 'accepting, recognizing, and clarifying feelings'. In view of the nondirective nature of this orientation, it seems important to clarify the concept of clarifying. A good example occurs in the third interview of the case of 'Herbert Bryan' (Rogers, 1942) a young man in his late twenties (S in following):

S: Well, I feel that sex is very fundamental in life and that the least a man can do is be a good copulater; that should be one of the fundamentals. Of course, he should be a lot more, of course, if he does have the potentialities, but at least any animal can do that.

C: That's one of the reasons why it strikes you so hard if there is — if you have some doubt or some uncertainty as to your own abilities along those lines.

S: Yes, I feel that there's something fundamentally wrong there — something wrong with the very foundation, as it were — that any other achievement I might have would not be adequate compensation for a blocking in that fundamental field. I used to think that perhaps I would become an ascetic — go in entirely for intellectual life, and so forth, but I couldn't bring myself to value that wholeheartedly. I had the definite conviction that no intellectual achievement could make up for that fundamental blocking there. (Pause) I want to be a healthy animal first of all, then I feel that the super-elements there will grow out of that healthy foundation. I feel that any achievement that was the result of overcompensations would be pretty unsatisfying, no matter how great the achievement, no matter how great the world's applause. My private knowledge of that fundamental blocking would bring me down so much that the world's applause wouldn't make up for it.

C: In other words, you've got to have some respect for yourself on a pretty fundamental basis, in order to have any achievements in any line.

S: M-hm. Of course, I overvalue sex now as a direct result of my inhibition. That is I think more about it than I would if I didn't have the inhibition, but I want to put it somewhere between food and music. It has — well, you could make the analogy that it is somewhat like food; it's sort of a physical gusto, and on the other hand, it also has the artistry of music about it. And I feel that it can have an important place without being dwelt on, as it were. (Rogers, 1942, pp. 329–30)

Rogers saw his last response in the preceding excerpt as a particularly good clarification of a complex conversation which brings the client to a very significant insight. In his last statement he 'realizes quite frankly that he overvalues sex and places too much stress upon his thinking about sex. This is a result which would not have been obtained if the counselor had been in any way judgmental' (1942, p. 330).

It is clear that Rogers wished to clarify the client's responses in a manner which did not go beyond the client's own meanings and feelings. There were, in fact, many instances in the case study of 'Herbert Bryan' where Rogers went further, but he was critical of those instances. His practice was catching up with his theory, and even his theory still had elements of directiveness. He wrote that 'the cautious and intelligent use of interpretive techniques can increase the scope and the clarity of . . . self-understanding' (1942, p. 216). This may surprise many therapists. More surprising is the fact that the term *empathy* is not to be found in *Counseling and Psychotherapy* (1942). Rogers' 'acceptance, recognition and clarification of feelings' phrase does, however, contain the roots of the client-centered empathic attitude and technique.

The basic hypothesis formulated by Rogers (1942) at the time was: effective counseling consists of a definitely structured, permissive relationship which allows the client to gain an understanding of himself to a degree which enables him to take positive steps in the light of his new orientation. In the course of the book, Rogers makes clear that the increase in self-understanding which comes from successful therapy involves the 'recognition and acceptance of the self'.

In this first period of Client-Centered Therapy, then, the main therapeutic technique was the clarification of feelings with the emphasis on the client obtaining insight into those feelings. The goal was for the client to be able to cope and to act more positively.

Second period

The second period lasted from the beginning of the 1950s, when *Client-Centered Therapy* was published (Rogers, 1951), to the early 1960s, when *On Becoming a Person* (Rogers, 1961) was published. At the beginning of this period Rogers made explicit his basic hypothesis for therapy. He also specified the necessary conditions and sufficient conditions for therapeutic change (Rogers, 1957).

In *Client-Centered Therapy* (1951) Rogers emphasized that, rather than any particular technique, the attitude and orientation of the therapist was central. The basic attitude of the client-centered therapist was, for Rogers, the belief in the capacity of the individual to deal with his or her psychological situation and to deal constructively with whatever comes into consciousness.

Central importance given to the world of the client

Early in the second period there was increased emphasis on the importance of the client's world as the client sees it. In *Client-Centered Therapy* (Rogers, 1951), some propositions were set out. Rogers' first proposition was that 'The individual exists in a continually changing world of experience of which he is the center' (p. 483). Proposition II was that 'The organism reacts to the field as it is experienced and perceived' (p. 484). The perceptual field is, for the individual, 'reality'. For Rogers, it was this world to which the therapist attends. It is not the true reality which is important, but rather the world as the client sees it. These propositions meant that Rogers did not try to understand the causes of the person's problem. Instead, Rogers attended only to the client's perspective. In Proposition VII he says, 'The best vantage point for understanding behavior is from the internal frame of reference of the individual himself' (p. 494). The internal frame of reference was later defined as 'all of the realm of experience which is available to the awareness of the individual at a given moment. It includes the full range of sensations, perceptions, meanings and memories which are available to consciousness' (Rogers, 1959, p. 210).

Self-actualization: the basic motivation for change

If the therapist only attends to the world of the client, why does change occur? For Rogers, there is a fundamental, basic motivating force for change. The function of the therapist is to facilitate the action of this basic motivating force. Rogers was convinced that when the individual clearly perceived all elements 'the balance seems invariably in the direction of the painful but ultimately rewarding path of self-actualization or growth' (from *Journal of Consulting Psychology, 4*, as quoted in Rogers, 1951, p. 490). How does the therapist facilitate this basic motivation for change? He or she must unconditionally prize and attend to the client's internal frame of reference.

The emphasis on the world of the client and on understanding the client's internal frame of reference shifts the emphasis from clarification of feelings to understanding the way the client sees his or her world. The following excerpt in which Rogers finds the client's meanings more important than her feelings is an example. It is from 'Mrs Ett', a series of therapy interviews recorded and transcribed in the late 1940s. (S represents the client, C, Carl Rogers.)

S244[1]: Yes, they are very strong, they're there. I'm getting so emotional I can't talk. What I meant to say is that they are there and I feel them very strongly and, ah, oh, I don't know, it's like little demons inside of me at work all the time, it doesn't give me a chance to sit and rest quietly to read, there's always conflict, it's either that or this. Such a great indecision; I can't tell you the — if I were to tell anybody the amount of indecision, it's almost pathological. I have a maid, a new maid now, and I'm very much upset about this. She's the epitome of efficiency and yet I hate her. I can't stand her, I think I'll have to let her go just because she's too efficient. She is, ah, taking away Bonnie from me. If I hold Bonnie in my arms, whoops, she's right out of my arms and she is re-diapering the baby, feeding her, and many times I

---

1. Number tags identify individual statements by each party according to sequence.

would tell her that these are her duties and those are mine, but she has entered as the matriarch of the house — a colored woman — very nice, the type of a person, we hired her because of her appearance, very efficient and intelligent, but I find — oh my God! It didn't occur to me until just now that she's beginning to represent a mother figure to me. Isn't that — I never thought of it until right now, that I resent her because she's domineering, she's oh, she's very much like my mother.

C244: So that you resent her not only for her efficiency and her struggle to take over Bonnie but perhaps even more deeply because she is a mother.

S245: Oh, yes. Well, not so much a mother person as perhaps the type of person my mother is, because I notice that if I tell her something she won't listen to me, but she will continue to do it her way, which is what I have as the problem with mother all the time. And yesterday, Mr L . . . towards the end of the evening I was in such a fog, I was so undecided and so unhappy without knowing why, and now, darn it, I see why it is, it's that. I think I'll have to get rid of her for that reason, or what do you think I should do? Should I hang onto her and fight it out myself and use this as a good opportunity to vent out a lot of my feelings? It might be the ideal opportunity to struggle within myself against mother and then ultimately win, or should I dismiss her because she is rubbing me the wrong way at a time when I shouldn't be rubbed the wrong way. I mean what would your opinion be, I'm sure you won't give me an opinion, because you always turn everything back to a question, but from a clinical —

C245: It's not a question, you mean, but it's to know how to go at it — because you see yourself all that I would see there — ah, you might get rid of her because she represents your mother and you dislike her, or conceivably you might be able to adjust to her, which would certainly be a step toward adjusting to your mother, but, ah —

S246: I might have an awful lot of struggle, a lot of tension. I think there would be. Because for the past two or three days there's been an awful lot of tension in — I didn't know it until just now that she represents the mother figure to me, which is sometimes acceptable, very acceptable, and desirable, but at the other time, which is so upsetting for me.

C246: You feel pulled two ways by it, as you do with your own mother.

Looking first at the beginning of S244, Mrs Ett says that she is getting very emotional at the moment and almost can't talk. Rogers could have responded to her feeling in the moment, her experience of getting very emotional. Rogers did not choose to emphasize this. She then goes to her experience of indecision which is like having little demons inside. Again, Rogers did not choose to respond to the feeling. She then talks about her new maid and comes to the present realization, which seems important to her, that she resents the maid as a mother figure. Note that if she had been involved in following the experience of the 'little demons', she might not have come to the realization of her resentment of the maid as a mother figure.

In C244, Rogers responds to her resentment. Notice that it is not the 'feel' or sensation of the resentment to which he responded. Instead, he chose to couple her present reaction, her resentment of her maid, with her present perception of her maid as mother. Rogers could have emphasized the feelings, the anger and loathing that Mrs Ett seemed to feel for the maid. Instead, Rogers was interested in the connection between the relationship that Mrs Ett saw between her present reaction and elements of her world (maid's efficiency and being a mother).

In S245, Mrs Ett is trying to decide what to do about the maid and is weighing the various alternative courses of action and the feelings to which each is connected. Rogers simply reflects these alternatives without trying to heighten their feeling aspects.

In S246 Mrs Ett repeats the connection between the tension of the past few days and the realization of the maid as a mother figure. In addition, she describes her ambivalence about the mother figure. It is this ambivalence which is responded to by Rogers, not her feeling of tension. Again, it is her present experience ('You feel pulled two ways') to the content of her perception ('as you do with your mother') that is of primary importance, not the qualitative or emotional aspects of her tension and struggle.

The therapist's congruence

As this period proceeded there was increased specification of what the therapist should do. In 1959, in an important chapter, Rogers (Rogers, 1959) discussed a theory of therapy, personality, and interpersonal relations. Here, among other conditions required for therapy to occur, he specified 'that the therapist is congruent in the relationship' (p. 213). This condition, which he also called genuineness, was one of the growing edges of the theory and meant that the therapist should accurately symbolize his or her experience of himself or herself in the relationship. This might include the therapist's limits in the relationship as it did in this brief excerpt from the case of Miss Tir (Rogers, 1951).

> C(*client*): I think emotionally I'm dying for sexual intercourse, but I don't do anything about it. The thing I want is to have sexual intercourse with you. I don't ask you 'cause I'm afraid you would have to be non-directive.
>
> T(*therapist*): You have this awful tension, and want so much to have relations with me.
>
> C: (Goes on in this vein. Finally asks the therapist.) Can't we do something about it? This tension is awful! Will you relieve this tension? Can you give me a direct answer? I think it might help both of us.
>
> T: The answer would be no. I can understand how *desperately* you feel,

but I would not be willing to do that. (Rogers, 1951, p. 211, original
emphasis)

Note that the therapist does not say that he is doing this for the good of the client.
Instead, he takes responsibility for his own behavior after indicating his
understanding of the client's experience.

Unconditional positive regard
In an article on the necessary and sufficient conditions of therapeutic change,
Rogers (1957) set out as one of the conditions of the therapy process that the
therapist must experience unconditional positive regard toward the client. The
therapist should not approve, or disapprove, of some things that the client talks
about more than others, even if what the client is talking about could, in another
framework, be seen as destructive. Take, as an example, the following excerpt
(Rogers, 1951) from the case of Miss Gill who has for a number of interviews
been sounding quite hopeless about herself.

C(*client*): I've never said this to anyone before — but I've thought for
such a long time — This is a terrible thing to say, but if I could just
— well (short bitter laugh; pause), if I could find some glorious
cause that I could give my life for I would be happy. I cannot be the
kind of person I want to be. I guess maybe I haven't the guts — or
the strength — to kill myself — and if someone would relieve me of
the responsibility — or I would be in an accident — I — I just don't
want to live.

T(*therapist*): At the present time things look so black to you that you
really can't see much point in living.

C: Yes — I wish I had never started this therapy. I was happy when I
was living in my dream world. There I could be the kind of person I
wanted to be — But now — There is such a wide, wide gap —
between my ideal — and what I am. I wish people hated me. I try to
make them hate. Because then I could turn away from them and
blame them — but no — It's all in my hands — here is my life —
and I either accept the fact that I am totally worthless — or I fight
whatever it is that holds me in this terrible conflict. And I suppose if
I accepted the fact that I am worthless, then I could go away
someplace — and retreat back to the security of my dream world
where I could do things, have clever friends, be a pretty wonderful
sort of person.

T: It's a really tough struggle — digging into this like you are — and at
times the shelter of your dream world looks more attractive and
comfortable.

C: My dream world or suicide.

T: Your dream world or something more permanent than dreams.

C: Yes. (A long pause. Complete change of voice.) So I don't see why I should waste your time — coming in twice a week — I'm not worth it — What do you think?

T: It's up to you, Gill — It isn't wasting my time — I'd be glad to see you — whenever you come — but it's how you feel about it — it's up to you.

C: You are not going to suggest I come in oftener? You're not alarmed and think I ought to come in every day — until I get out of this?

T: I believe you are able to make your own decision. I'll see you whenever you want to come.

C: (Note of awe in her voice.) I don't believe you are alarmed about — I see — I may be afraid of myself — but you aren't afraid of me.

T: You say you may be afraid of yourself — and are wondering why I don't seem afraid for you? (Rogers, 1951, pp. 46–7)

There were two aspects of this situation that the therapist accepted unconditionally. One was the client's discussion of, and positive feelings about, suicide. Even though the therapist occasionally hedged his response to the client, for example, by referring to her attitudes as existing 'at the present time', in the main he accepted her negative feelings. Even more impressive was his acceptance of her discussion about having less therapy and his belief that she could make her own decision.

In summary, this period started with a strong emphasis on the centrality of the world of the client. Rogers defined his basic hypothesis, his faith in the individual's capability. Rogers then became more explicit about the actualizing tendency as being the motivating force in the change of the client. This was followed by his becoming more specific about what the therapist should do to aid this tendency.

Third period
The third period started with the publication of *On Becoming a Person* in 1961. The book, a collection of papers by Rogers, has a theme, stated in the title, that conveys the direction in which Rogers moved from that time on. In the earlier periods the aim was that the person become congruent with his or her experience, that the self become based on this experience. In the latter period, the goal was to become a person, to become one's experiential organism. It is no longer sufficient to know your experience. Now you *become* your experience. 'To be that self that one truly is', one of Rogers' statements of the goal, involves the absence of a self-monitoring experience. Thus, Rogers says, 'Consciousness, instead of being the watchman over a dangerous and unpredictable lot of impulses, of which few can be permitted to see the light of day, becomes the comfortable inhabitant of a society of impulses and feelings and thoughts, which are discovered to be very satisfactorily self-governing when not fearfully guarded' (Rogers, 1961, p. 119).

In the following example a graduate student has been puzzling over a vague feeling which he gradually identifies as a frightened feeling, a fear of failing, of not getting his PhD. The interview continues:

C: I was kind of letting it seep through. But I also tied it in with you and my relationship with you. And one thing I feel about it is a kind of fear of going away; or that's another thing — it's so hard to get hold of — there's kind of two pulling feelings about it. Or two 'me's' somehow. One is the scared me that wants to hold on to things, and that one I guess I can feel clearly right now. You know, I kinda need things to hold on to — and I feel kind of scared.

T: M-hm. That's something you can feel right this minute, and have been feeling and perhaps are feeling in regard to our relationship too.

C: Won't you let me *have* this, because, you know, I kinda *need* it. I can be so lonely and scared without it.

T: M-hm, m-hm. Let me hang on to this because I'd be terribly scared if I didn't. Let me *hold* on to it. (Pause)

C: It's kinda the same thing — *Won't* you let me have my thesis or my PhD so then . . . Cause I kinda *need* that little world. I mean . . .

T: In both instances it's kind of a pleading thing isn't it? Let me *have* this because I need it so badly. I'd be awfully frightened without it. (long pause)

C: I get a sense of — I somehow can't get much further — It's the kind of *pleading* little boy, somehow even — What's this gesture of begging? (Putting hands together as if in prayer) Isn't it funny? Cause that —

T: You put your hands in sort of supplication.

C: Ya, that's right! Won't you do for me, kinda — Oh, that's *terrible*! Who, me, *beg*? (Rogers, 1961, pp. 112–13, original emphasis)

In this excerpt, the client *becomes* his feeling of begging. There is no separation between the self and the experience. In the therapy hour he became his process of experiencing. For Rogers, successful therapy resulted in movement away from the rigid structure of the self. The person becomes the process of experiencing. At first, this happens only for a short while and then the structural self reappears. This can be seen in the excerpt where after the client becomes his experiencing, his old self reappears and passes judgment.

    The person who emerges from this process of becoming one's experience has several characteristics. He or she is *open to experience*. That is, the person is able to take in reality without distortion. A self structure does not interpose itself between reality and the person. Late in therapy a man (C) is reporting on the changes he feels have occurred as a result of therapy:

C: It doesn't seem to me it would be possible for anyone to report all the changes you feel. But I have certainly felt recently that I have more respect for, more objectivity for my physical makeup. I mean I don't expect too much of myself. This is how it works out: It feels to me that in the past I used to fight a certain tiredness I felt after supper. Well, now I am pretty sure I really *am tired* — that I am not making myself tired — that I am just physiologically lower. It seems to me I was constantly criticizing my tiredness. (Rogers, 1961, p. 116, original emphasis)

A second characteristic of the person who emerges from therapy is that the person comes to *place trust in one's organism*. That is, the person is able to make decisions by weighing and balancing the data from all levels of his or herself, without being afraid of the mistakes that might result from his or her emotions.

A third characteristic is a change in the *locus-of-evaluation*. The person looks less and less to others for approval and disapproval and for standards to live by. Instead, the person increasingly feels that the locus-of-evaluation is within the self, that he or she is the locus of choice and evaluation.

Another characteristic of the emerging person is the *willingness to be a process*. The individual changes from wanting to be a product, such as something or someone 'successful', to being a person in process, that is, to be a stream of becoming rather than a finished product. Thus, a client at the end of therapy says:

I haven't finished the process of integrating and reorganizing myself, but that's only confusing and not discouraging, now that I realize this is a continuing process . . . It's exciting, sometimes upsetting, but deeply encouraging to feel yourself in action, apparently knowing where you are going even though you don't always consciously know where that is. (Rogers, 1961, p. 122)

The therapist also became one's experience. This is what is meant by *congruence*, a concept that became increasingly important. Here the therapist is in the relationship without facade. The therapist is openly being the feelings that are flowing in himself at the moment.

For Rogers, the person's experiencing was occurring continually and automatically. The goal was to become this experiencing. The emphasis on the primacy of the process of experiencing led, in some quarters, to techniques such as focusing (Gendlin, 1981), which are thought to aid the person to get in touch with his or her experiencing and which has led some therapists to practice experiential, rather than the more orthodox Client-Centered Therapy.

Fourth period
The fourth phase covers the 1970–1980 period. It is the period in which the basic hypotheses and attitudes about psychotherapy were used in other contexts. It emphasizes the application of the principles of Client-Centered Therapy to education, to groups, and to peace and conflict resolution. Carl Rogers wrote two editions of *Freedom to Learn* (1969, 1983), *Carl Rogers on Encounter Groups* (1970), and a number of articles on peace and conflict resolution. The phrase, *person-centered approach*, becomes meaningful and appropriate in this phase of the development of the client-centered movement, as client-centered principles are applied to education, industry, and other human relations contexts.

Person-centered education

Clear examples of the applicability of the client-centered philosophy and methodology to other interpersonal contexts were the changes Rogers made to the practice of teaching. One of this chapter's authors, Nathaniel Raskin, had been a student in many of Rogers' courses at Ohio State University in 1940–1941. Rogers was very respectful of students, but he clearly directed the course and assumed responsibility for the evaluation of the student. Later, at the University of Chicago, 'Dr Rogers' offered himself as just one learning resource, and even though he came across as an extremely competent and self-confident psychologist, he had clearly shifted the responsibility for learning and grading to the student. The initial reaction of most students was doubt and even resentment, but most came to believe that students were responsible for their own education.

Rogers' twelve years at Chicago (1945–1957) and six at the University of Wisconsin (1957–1963) deepened his convictions about student-centered learning. Moving to La Jolla, California, in 1964 to the Western Behavioral Sciences Institute accelerated his interest in going beyond the psychotherapy office and even the classroom to further develop and apply his ideas.

In his foreword to the first edition of *Freedom to Learn* (1969), Rogers wrote, 'The conceptions that I wanted to present broadened into the theoretical and philosophical realms' (p. v). This was a complete contrast to the Rogers at Ohio State who disdained theory in favor of what worked. He makes clear later in the foreword the extent and the depth of his trepidation.

> Let me state briefly some of the questions which concern me . . .
> Can education fulfill its central role in dealing effectively with the
> explosive racial tensions which are steadily increasing? . . . Can
> education prepare us to live responsibly, communicatively, in a world
> of increasing international tensions, increasingly irrational
> nationalism? . . . Can the educational system as a whole, the most
> traditional, conservative, rigid, bureaucratic institution of our time
> . . . come to grips with the real problems of modern life? (Rogers,
> 1969, pp. vi–vii)

So profound was Rogers' feeling about traditional education that he characterized the adjectives in the preceding sentence as descriptive rather than critical. In the prologue to the same book, he amplifies his views:

> . . . in the vast majority of our schools, at all educational levels, we
> are locked into a traditional and conventional approach which makes
> significant learning improbable if not impossible. When we put
> together in one scheme such elements as a *prescribed curriculum,*
> *similar assignments for all students, lecturing* as almost the only mode
> of instruction, *standard tests* by which all students are externally
> evaluated, and *instructor-chosen grades* as the measure of learning,
> then we can almost guarantee that meaningful learning will be at an
> absolute minimum. (Rogers 1969, p. 5, original emphasis)

Rogers described the way he changed his way of operating in the class at the University of Chicago and how he introduced a class (Rogers, 1983):

> I ceased to be a teacher. It wasn't easy. It happened rather gradually, but as I began to trust students, I found they did incredible things in their communication with each other, in their learning of content material in the course, in blossoming out as growing human beings. Most of all they gave me courage to be myself more freely, and this led to profound interaction. They told me their feelings, they raised questions I had never thought about. I began to sparkle with emerging ideas that were new and exciting to me, but also, I found, to them. I believe I passed some sort of crucial divide when I was able to begin a course with a statement something like this: This course has the title *Personality Theory* (or whatever), but what we do with this course is up to us. We can build it around the goals we want to achieve, within that very general area. We can decide mutually how we want to handle these bugaboos of exams and grades. I have many resources on tap, and I can help you find others. I believe I am one of the resources, and I am available to the extent that you wish. But this is our class. So what do we want to make of it? This kind of statement said in effect, we are free to learn what we wish, as we wish. It made the whole climate of the classroom completely different. Though at the time I had never thought of phrasing it this way, I changed at that point from being a teacher and evaluator, to being a facilitator of learning — [a] very different occupation. (Rogers, 1983, p. 26)

In his two editions of *Freedom to Learn*, (1969, 1983) Rogers illustrated the implementation of person-centered education by a number of individuals in a variety of settings: a 6th-grade class, a course on the fundamentals of psychology, a secondary school French class, and a special project in one school which allowed pupils ranging from slow learners in the 7th-grade to gifted 11th-graders to spend about one quarter of their school time learning what they wanted individually to learn, in their own way, to supplement and synthesize their regular schedule of required subjects.

In these diverse settings, a host of methods for implementing student-centered education are described. As in the field of psychotherapy, Rogers believed in the importance of backing up a theory or philosophy or belief system with specific practices. At the same time, the diversity of methods which are presented indicate the primacy of principles for Rogers.

Rogers believed strongly that the power relationship which exists in traditional education must be reversed in order for learning and personal growth to occur optimally. He also believed that the most fruitful education involves an integration of cognition and emotions. Therefore, he advocated both self-directed learning of external subject matter and the use of intensive groups in which individuals exchange feelings in the process of interacting as persons.

Such groups for administrators and teachers were key elements in two system-wide educational experiments in which Rogers was involved. He described (Rogers, 1983) how Superintendent Newman Walker employed groups in his attempt to revive the public schools of Louisville, Kentucky.

> During a six-month period in the spring and summer, he enrolled 1600 members of the system in week-long human relations workshops — intensive group experiences held in a residential retreat setting. Included were Walker himself, the whole board of education, principals, teachers, central office staff and clerical workers. In these labs people came to know each other as persons and to confront differences. They communicated informally and learned about themselves and how they were perceived by others. They were more open in expressing their feelings. The cognitive was not ignored. They learned new ways of working with students, new ways of promoting learning. (Rogers, 1983, p. 228)

Encounter groups were also used extensively by Rogers and associates from the Center for Studies of the Person in the Immaculate Heart system in Los Angeles.

Person-centered groups
It did not take long for the principles of Client-Centered Therapy to be applied to group situations. Before the end of the 1940s there were Client-Centered Therapy groups and client-centered play groups for children.

In the 1950s and 1960s, the client-centered approach was used in therapy groups for blind and other physically handicapped children, parents of handicapped children, and staff development groups for mental health professionals, to name some of the populations.

> Typically, such groups would meet once a week for an hour and a half. *The basic contribution of the leader was an attitude of respect for the participants, implemented by disciplined empathic listening and communication.* This often resulted in an atmosphere characterized by the necessary and sufficient conditions formulated by Rogers in 1957. (Raskin, 1986, p. 278, original emphasis)

With the advent of the intensive group, a new chapter was begun in the history of Client-Centered Therapy and the Person-Centered Approach. Intensive groups helped Rogers to learn increasingly to *operate in terms of his feelings*. He responded empathically, particularly to feelings of hurt. He thought it important to express persistent feelings toward an individual or group. He valued his *awareness* of different feelings and the choice of expressing them or not, if it felt inappropriate. He wished to express positive or loving feelings as well as negative ones; it was difficult personally for him to express affection or anger in a group, but he grew in his ability to do this and believed it was helpful to the group process.

When Rogers confronted individuals in a group, he did so on the specifics of their behavior, and with feelings he was able to claim as his own: 'I don't like the way you chatter on. Seems to me you give each message three or four times. I wish you would stop when you've completed your message' (Rogers, 1970, p. 58).

Although he had to overcome a feeling of professional conscience in doing so, Rogers favored *expressing a current personal problem* or feeling of distress in a group. He believed that if he held back, he would not listen as well and that, in addition, the group would pick up his disturbance and might feel they were somehow to blame.

Being sensitive to artificiality, Rogers *eschewed planned procedures, exercises*, or *gimmicks* in a group. He distinguished this kind of planned operation by the leader from something that might arise spontaneously in the group, like a participant's suggesting that role-playing might be helpful at a particular point. Rogers wrote that *spontaneity* was the most precious, and at the same time elusive, element that he knew.

Rogers also *avoided interpretive or process comments*. He did not wish to make group members self-conscious or to interfere with the spontaneous experience of the group. He viewed interpretations as high-level guesses that would also place him in an unwanted authoritative role. Similarly, he believed in making use of the therapeutic power of the whole group if a serious situation arose, such as a bizarre behavior on the part of a group member. He felt there was therapeutic advantage in a participant's relating to the problem member as a person over a leader's tendency to relate to the member as an object.

Finally, Rogers wrote of his increased ability to be *physically expressive* in a group and to provide *physical contact* (Rogers, 1970) 'when this seems real and spontaneous and appropriate . . . When a person is suffering and I feel like going over and putting my arm around him, I do just that . . . I do not try consciously to promote this kind of behavior. I admire the younger people who are looser and freer in this respect' (ibid., p. 63).

Peace and conflict resolution

As early as 1948, Rogers proposed the application of client-centered principles to dealing with social tensions (Rogers, 1948). In 1960, he suggested that a person-centered approach to the conduct of foreign policy might result in a much more fruitful kind of dialogue than is customary between nations. It would include a frank expression of selfish interests as well as idealistic purposes, of mistakes as well as achievements. His hypothesis was that a more honest initiative of this nature would result in a more honest response and a much more satisfying way of relating to other nations.

Sanford led conflict resolution groups with Rogers in South Africa and the Soviet Union. Rogers' peace and conflict resolution efforts were built on a foundation of years of experience of learning to build community in large intensive groups, work he shared with Bowen, Henderson, McGaw, Miller (later O'Hara), Rice, N. Rogers, Solomon, Swenson, and J. K. Wood, and in cross-cultural meetings in Europe, Asia, and Latin America with Devonshire, Zucconi, Tausch, Thorne, Lietaer, Segrera, and Tsuge.

Rogers' collaborators

Rogers' students also made vital contributions to theory and practice at Ohio State, Chicago, and the University of Wisconsin. During the Ohio State years, Covner (1942, 1944a, 1944b), a student of Rogers at both the University of Rochester and Ohio State, supplied the technical expertise for making phonographic recordings of interviews and then did research which showed their superiority over notes from memory. Porter (1943) completed a doctoral dissertation at Ohio State in 1941 by demonstrating that a system of classifying counselor responses in electronically recorded interviews could be used reliably and could bring out differences between counseling methods. Snyder (1945) developed categories for classifying both counselor and client responses in nondirective therapy and obtained findings which supported nondirective hypotheses (e.g., the acceptance by the counselor of client attitudes and feelings was followed, regularly, by client insights). Raimy (1948) was the author of another Ohio State dissertation in which he developed a theory of the self and applied it to self-references in recorded interviews. Virginia Axline, Arthur Combs, Charles Curran, Thomas Gordon, Donald Grummon, Nicholas Hobbs, Nathaniel Raskin, and Bernard Steinzor were some of the other Ohio State students who made important research contributions, many of which were published as books. Seeman and Raskin (1953) have summarized much of this research.

At the University of Chicago in the late 1940s, Raskin, Seeman, Haigh, Hoffman, Sheerer, and Stock analyzed the data from ten fully recorded cases and published the results in an entire issue of the *Journal of Consulting Psychology* (Rogers, Raskin et al., 1949). In the same period, Aidman (1951) and Bowman (1951) carried out studies which showed an increasing congruence between the client's present and ideal self as expressed in the course of nondirective therapy. Seeman was the coordinator of research at the University of Chicago Counseling Center during the time of an even more sophisticated cooperative effort backed by the Rockefeller Foundation and reported in a book edited by Rogers and Dymond (1954). This project was regarded as state-of-the-art in the field of psychotherapy research and included a Q-technique investigation by Butler and Haigh (1954) hypothesizing that Client-Centered Therapy would reduce the difference between the perceived self and ideal self.

Dymond (1954), using self-sorts, measured adjustment changes over therapy. Rudikoff (1954) compared changes in the concepts of the self, of the ordinary person, and of the self-ideal. Seeman (1954) studied counselor judgments of process and outcome. Gordon and Cartwright (1954) researched the effect of psychotherapy upon certain attitudes toward others. Tougas (1954) showed ethnocentrism to be a limiting factor in verbal therapy. Grummon (1954) studied personality changes as a function of time.

Other students and collaborators at Chicago were Barrett-Lennard, who devised the Relationship Inventory still widely used in research on psychotherapy of diverse orientations (1986), Bown, Gendlin, Shlien, Standal, Streich, and Zimring. Bown (1951) and Streich (1951) helped develop the concept of a freely functioning therapist. Gendlin and Zimring (1955) examined the dimensions of experiencing and their change. Shlien (1964) compared time-limited, client-centered, and Adlerian therapy. Standal (1954) contributed a doctoral dissertation on positive regard, which helped conceptualize unconditional positive regard as one of the three 'necessary and sufficient' therapist-offered conditions.

During Rogers' tenure at the University of Wisconsin from 1957 to 1963, the client-centered hypothesis was tested within a population of hospitalized patients diagnosed as schizophrenic; it was believed that 'the greater the degree to which the conditions of therapy exist in the relationship, the greater will be the evidence of therapeutic process or movement in the client' (Kiesler, Klein and Mathieu, 1967, p. 187). Rogers (1958) and Rablen had developed a Process Scale, and Gendlin and Tomlinson a scale of experiencing (Gendlin and Tomlinson, 1967, p. 509), regarded as a central component of process change. This large-scale project with schizophrenic subjects was reported in a volume edited by Rogers, Gendlin, Kiesler, and Truax (1967). Others who contributed to the development of the research design and the scales of measuring therapist conditions and patient process and who analyzed the data collected by these scales, included Ginzberg, Moursand, Schoeninger, Stoler, van der Veen, and Waskow.

Rogers' theory of therapy and of personality are important elements of basic texts in psychology, psychotherapy, and personality theory. The concepts of self and empathy and the client-centered conceptualization of the psychotherapeutic relationship have had an impact on the theory and practice of orientations as diverse as psychoanalytic and behavior modification. Self-esteem has become a concept with which the general population is conversant. Activities such as parent effectiveness training, peer counseling, and hot lines are based on empathic listening in the Rogerian tradition.

Several books published recently include summaries of theory and research. In *Client-Centered Therapy and the Person-Centred Approach* (Levant and Shlien, 1984), many aspects of Rogers' therapy were examined. Lietaer (1984) was concerned with unconditional regard and Bozarth (1984) with the reflection of feelings. Seeman (1984) was concerned with the fully functioning person and Rice (1984) with client tasks. In addition, Barrett-Lennard, Levant, and Guerney each wrote chapters (1984) about family therapy. Hackney and Goodyear were concerned about the client-centered approach to supervision (1984).

There have been some recent discussions of the technique of client or person-centered therapy. Mearns and Thorne's (1988) *Person-Centred Counselling in Action* is the first systematic text since *Client-Centered Therapy* and is proving very valuable for teaching. Raskin and Zimring's 1991 chapter describes the progress of a client over a number of interviews.

Prior to 1980, Rogers had discouraged the institutionalization of Client-Centered Therapy. He hoped to turn people on to their own self-directed patterns, rather than to develop followers or 'little Rogerians'. This attitude delayed for decades the initiation of an organization or journal promulgating his theories.

In the late 1970s, there was strong pressure both nationally and internationally for organization. Rogers, heeding this pressure, explained his support for the launching of the *Person-Centered Review* in 1986 by David Cain: 'There has . . . developed a large number of people in many nations — therapists, teachers, business people, doctors, social workers, researchers, lay people, pastors — who have a strong interest in the continuing development of a client-centered/person-centered approach' (Rogers, 1986 p. 4).

The *Review* has published articles about many aspects of Client-Centered Therapy. In addition, *Client-Centered and Experiential Psychotherapy in the Nineties* (Lietaer, Rombauts, and Van Balen, 1990) contains many papers about clinical problems of various populations. These sources have included papers about the client-centered response (Patterson, 1990; Zimring, 1990) as well as papers about Carl Rogers and his development (Bozarth, 1990; Cain, 1987; Raskin, 1990; Seeman, 1990). Also included are papers about the use of the client-centered or Person-Centered Approach with various populations. These are concerned with working with children and child therapy (Boukydis, 1990; Ellinwood, 1989; Gordon, 1988; Santen, 1990); family and couple therapy (Anderson, 1989a, 1989b; Bozarth and Shanks, 1989; Esser and Schneider, 1990; Gaylin, 1990; Rombauts and Devriendt, 1990); working with disturbed clients (Elliot et al., 1990; Hamelinck, 1990; Prouty, 1990; Prouty and Pietrzak, 1988; Teusch, 1990), and working with clients who are working with fears of death and dying (Tausch, 1988).

Carl Rogers died in February 1987, at the age of 85. The first International Conference on Client-Centered and Experiential Psychotherapy convened September 12–16, 1988, in Leuven, Belgium (Lietaer, Rombauts, and Van Balen, 1990). Yearly international meetings have continued, following the first successful conferences.

References

Aidman, T. (1951) An objective study of the changing relationship between the present self and the ideal self pictures as expressed by the client in nondirective psychotherapy. Unpublished PhD dissertation, University of Chicago.

Anderson, W. J. (1989a) Client/person-centered approaches to couple and family therapy: Expanding theory and practice. *Person-Centered Review, 4*, 245–7.

Anderson, W. J. (1989b). Family therapy in the client-centered tradition: A legacy in the narrative mode. *Person-Centered Review, 4*, 295–307.

Barrett-Lennard, G. T. (1984) The world of family relationships: Theory and research. In R. F. Levant and J. M. Shlien (Eds.), *Client-centered therapy and the person-centered approach* (pp. 222–42). New York: Praeger.

Barrett-Lennard, G. T. (1986) The relationship inventory now: Issues and advances in theory, method, and use. In L. S. Greenberg and W. M. Pinsof (Eds.), *The psychotherapeutic process: A research handbook* (pp. 439–76). New York: Guilford.

Boukydis, C. F. Z. (1990) Client-centered/experiential practice with parents and infant. In C. Lietaer, J. Rombauts, R. Van Balen (Eds.), *Client-centered and experiential psychotherapy in the nineties* (pp. 797–811). Leuven, Belgium: Leuven University Press.

Bowman, P. H. (1951) A measure of discrepancy between different areas of the self-concept. Unpublished PhD dissertation, University of Chicago.

Bown, O. H. (1951) An investigation of therapeutic relationship in client-centered psychotherapy. Unpublished PhD dissertation, University of Chicago.

Bozarth, J. D. (1984) Beyond reflection: Emergent modes of empathy. In R. F. Levant and J. M. Shlien (Eds.), *Client-centered therapy and the person-centered approach* (pp. 59–75). New York: Praeger.

Bozarth, J. D. (1990) The evolution of Carl Rogers as a therapist. *Person-Centered Review, 5*, 387–93.

Bozarth, J. D. and Shanks, A. (1989) Person-centered group therapy. *Person-Centered Review, 4*, 280–94.

Butler, J. M. and Haigh, G. V. (1954) Changes in the relation between self-concepts and ideal concepts consequent upon client-centered counseling. In C. R. Rogers and R. F. Dymond (Eds.), *Psychotherapy and personality change* (pp. 55–75). Chicago: University of Chicago Press.

Cain, D. J. (1987) Carl Rogers's life in review. *Person-Centered Review, 2*, 476–506.

Covner, B. J. (1942). Studies in phonographic recordings of verbal material: I and II. *Journal of Consulting Psychology, 6*,105–13,149–53.

Covner, B. J. (1944a) Studies in phonographic recordings of verbal material: III. The completeness and accuracy of counseling interview reports. *Journal of General Psychology, 30*, 181–203.

Covner, B. J. (1944b) Studies in phonographic recordings of verbal material: IV. Written reports of interviews. *Journal of Applied Psychology, 28*, 181–203.

Dymond, R. F. (1954) Adjustment changes over therapy from self-sorts. In C. R. Rogers and R. F. Dymond (Eds.), *Psychotherapy and personality change* (pp. 167–95). Chicago: University of Chicago Press.

Ellinwood, C. (1989) The young child in person-centered family therapy. *Person-Centered Review, 4*, 256–62.

Elliot, R., Clark, C., Kemeny, V., Wexler, M. M., Mack, C. and Brinkerhoff, I. (1990) The impact of experiential therapy on depression: The first ten cases. In G. Lietaer, J. Rombauts and R. Van Balen (Eds.), *Client-centered and experiential psychotherapy in the nineties* (pp. 549–78). Leuven, Belgium: Leuven University Press.

Esser, U. and Schneider, I. (1990) Client-centered partnership therapy as relationship therapy. In G. Lietaer, J. Rombauts, and R. Van Balen (Eds.), *Client-centered and experiential psychotherapy in the nineties* (pp. 829–

46). Leuven, Belgium: Leuven University Press.

Gaylin, N. L. (1990) Family-centered therapy. In G. Lietaer, J. Rombauts, and R. Van Balen (Eds.), *Client-centered and experiential psychotherapy in the nineties* (pp. 813–28). Leuven, Belgium: Leuven University Press.

Gendlin, E. (1981) *Focusing*. New York: Everest House.

Gendlin, E. and Tomlinson, T. M. (1967) A scale for the rating of experiencing. In C. Rogers, E. Gendlin, D. Kiesler and C. Truax (Eds.), *The therapeutic relationship and its impact: A study of psychotherapy with schizophrenics* (pp. 589–92). Madison: University of Wisconsin Press.

Gendlin, E. and Zimring, F. (1955) The qualities or dimensions of experiencing and their change. *Counseling Center Discussion Papers 1, #3*. Chicago: University of Chicago Counseling Center.

Gordon, T. (1988) The case against disciplining children at home or in school. *Person-Centered Review, 3*, 59–85.

Gordon, T. and Cartwright, D. S. (1954) The effect of psychotherapy upon certain attitudes toward others. In C. R. Rogers and R. F. Dymond (Eds.), *Psychotherapy and personality change* (pp. 167–95). Chicago: University of Chicago Press.

Grummon, D. L. (1954) Personality changes as a function of time in persons motivated for therapy. In C. R. Rogers and R. F. Dymond (Eds.), *Psychotherapy and personality change* (pp. 238–58). Chicago: University of Chicago Press.

Guerney, B. G. Jr. (1984) Contributions of client-centered therapy to filial, marital, and family relationship enhancement. In R. F. Levant and J. M. Shlien (Eds.), *Client-centered therapy and the person-centered approach* (pp. 261–77). New York: Praeger.

Hackney, H. and Goodyear, R. K. (1984) Carl Rogers's client-centered approach to supervision. In R. F. Levant and J. M. Shlien (Eds.), *Client-centered therapy and the person-centered approach* (pp. 278–96). New York: Praeger.

Hamelinck, L. (1990) Client-centered therapy and psychiatric crisis intervention following suicide attempts. In G. Lietaer, J. Rombauts, and R. Van Balen (Eds.), *Client-centered and experiential psychotherapy in the nineties* (pp. 579–97). Leuven, Belgium: Leuven University Press.

Kiesler, D. J., Klein, M. H. and Mathieu, P. L. (1967) Therapist conditions and patient process. In C. R. Rogers, E. T. Gendlin, D. J. Kiesler, and C. B. Truax (Eds.), *The therapeutic relationship and its impact: A study of psychotherapy with schizophrenics* (pp. 187–220). Madison: University of Wisconsin Press.

Levant, R. F. (1984) From persons to system: Two perspectives. In R. F. Levant and J. M. Shlien (Eds.), *Client-centered therapy and the person-centered approach* (pp. 243–60). New York: Praeger.

Levant, R. F., and Shlien, J. M. (1984) *Client-centered therapy and the person-centered approach*. New York: Praeger.

Lietaer, G. (1984) Unconditional positive regard: A controversial basic attitude in client-centered therapy. In R. F. Levant and J. M. Shlien (Eds.), *Client-centered therapy and the person-centered approach* (pp. 41–58). New York: Praeger.

Lietaer, G., Rombauts, J. and Van Balen, R. (1990) *Client-centered and experiential psychotherapy in the nineties*. Leuven, Belgium: Leuven University Press.

Mearns, D. and Thorne, B. (1988) *Person-centred counselling in action*. London: Sage.

Patterson, C. H. (1990) Involuntary clients: A person-centered view. *Person-Centered Review, 5*, 316–20.

Porter, E. H. Jr. (1943) The development and evaluation of a measure of counseling interview procedures. *Educational and Psychological Measurement, 3*, 105–26, 215–38.

Prouty, G. F. (1990) Pre-therapy: A theoretical evolution in the person-centered/experiential psychotherapy of schizophrenia and retardation. In G. Lietaer, J. Rombauts, and R. Van Balen (Eds.), *Client-centered and experiential psychotherapy in the nineties* (pp. 645–58). Leuven, Belgium: Leuven University Press.

Prouty, G. F. and Pietrzak, S. (1988) The pre-therapy method applied to persons experiencing hallucinatory images. *Person-Centered Review, 3*, 426–41.

Raimy, V. C. (1948) Self reference in counseling interviews. *Journal of Consulting Psychology, 12*, 153–63.

Raskin, N. J. (1986) Client-centered group psychotherapy, part I. *Person-Centered Review, 1*, 272–90.

Raskin, N. J. (1990) The first 50 years and the next 10. *Person-Centered Review, 5*, 364–72.

Raskin, N. J. and Zimring, F. (1991) Person-centered therapy. In R. J. Corsini (Ed.), *Five therapists and one client* (pp. 59–102). Itasca, IL: Peacock.

Rice, L. N. (1984) Client tasks in client-centered therapy. In R. F. Levant and J. M. Shlien (Eds.), *Client-centered therapy and the person-centered approach* (pp. 182–202). New York: Praeger.

Rogers, C. R. (1939) *The clinical treatment of the problem child*. Boston: Houghton Mifflin.

Rogers, C. R. (1942) *Counseling and psychotherapy*. Boston: Houghton Mifflin.

Rogers, C. R. (1948) *Dealing with social tensions: A presentation of client-centered counseling as a means of handling interpersonal conflict*. New York: Hinds, Hayden, and Eldredge.

Rogers, C. R. (1951) *Client-centered therapy: Its current practice, implications, and theory*. Boston: Houghton Mifflin.

Rogers, C. R. (1957) The necessary and sufficient conditions of therapeutic personality change. *Journal of Consulting Psychology, 21,* 95–103.

Rogers, C. R. (1958) A process conception of psychotherapy. *American Psychologist, 13*, 142–9.

Rogers, C. R. (1959) A theory of therapy, personality, and interpersonal relationships, as developed in the client-centered framework. In S. Koch (Ed.), *Psychology: A study of science: Vol. 3. Formulations of the person and the social context*. New York: McGraw-Hill.

Rogers, C. R. (1961) *On becoming a person*. Boston: Houghton Mifflin.

Rogers, C. R. (1969) *Freedom to learn: A view of what education might become.* Columbus, OH: Charles E. Merrill.

Rogers, C. R. (1970) *Carl Rogers on encounter groups*. New York: Harper and Row.

Rogers, C. R. (1983) *Freedom to learn for the 80s*. Columbus, OH: Charles E. Merrill.

Rogers, C. R. (1986) A commentary from Carl Rogers. *Person-Centered Review, 1*, 3–5.

Rogers, C. R. and Dymond, R. F. (Eds.) (1954) *Psychotherapy and personality change*. Chicago: University of Chicago Press.

Rogers, C. R., Gendlin, E. T., Kiesler, D. V. and Truax, C. (Eds.) (1967) *The therapeutic relationship and its impact: A study of psychotherapy with schizophrenics*. Madison: University of Wisconsin Press.

Rogers, C. R., Raskin, N. J., Seeman, J., Sheerer, E., Stock, D., Haigh, G., Hoffman, A. and Carr, A. (1949) A coordinated research in psychotherapy. *Journal of Consulting Psychology, 13*, 149–220.

Rombauts, J. and Devriendt, M. (1990) Conjoint couple therapy in client-centered practice. In G. Lietaer, J. Rombauts, and R. Van Balen (Eds.), *Client-centered and experiential psychotherapy in the nineties* (pp. 847–63). Leuven, Belgium: Leuven University Press.

Rudikoff, E. C. (1954) A comparative study of the changes in the concepts of the self, the ordinary person, and the ideal in eight cases. In C. R. Rogers and R. F. Dymond (Eds.), *Psychotherapy and personality change* (pp. 85–98). Chicago: University of Chicago Press.

Santen, B. (1990) Beyond good and evil: Focusing with early traumatized children and adolescents. In G. Lietaer, J. Rombauts, and R. Van Balen (Eds.), *Client-centered and experiential psychotherapy in the nineties* (pp. 779–96). Leuven, Belgium: Leuven University Press.

Seeman, J. (1954) Counselor judgments of therapeutic process and outcome. In C. R. Rogers and R. F. Dymond (Eds.), *Psychotherapy and personality change* (pp. 99–108). Chicago: University of Chicago Press.

Seeman, J. (1984) The fully functioning person: Theory and research. In R. F. Levant and J. M. Shlien (Eds.), *Client-centered therapy and the person-centered approach* (pp. 131–52). New York: Praeger.

Seeman, J. (1990) Theory as autobiography: The development of Carl Rogers. *Person-Centered Review, 5*, 373–86.

Seeman, J. and Raskin, N. J. (1953) Research perspectives in client-centered therapy. In O. H. Mowrer (Ed.), *Psychotherapy: Theory and Research* (pp. 205–34). New York: Ronald Press.

Shlien, J. M. (1964) Comparison of results with different forms of psychotherapy. *American Journal of Psychotherapy, 18*, 15–22.

Snyder, W. U. (1945) An investigation of the nature of nondirective psychotherapy.

Journal of General Psychology, 33, 193–223.

Standal, S. (1954) The need for positive regard: A contribution to client-centered theory. Unpublished PhD thesis, University of Chicago.

Streich, E. R. (1951) The self-experience of the client-centered therapist. Unpublished paper, The Counseling Center, University of Chicago.

Tausch, R. (1988) Reappraisal of death and dying after a person-centered behavioral workshop. *Person-Centered Review, 3*, 213–16.

Teusch, L. (1990) Positive effects and limitations of client-centered therapy with schizophrenic patients. In G. Lietaer, J. Rombauts, and R. Van Balen (Eds.), *Client-centered and experiential psychotherapy in the nineties* (pp. 637–44). Leuven, Belgium: Leuven University Press.

Tougas, R. R. (1954) Ethnocentrism as a limiting factor in verbal therapy. In C. R. Rogers and R. F. Dymond (Eds.), *Psychotherapy and personality change* (pp. 196–214). Chicago: University of Chicago Press.

Zimring, F. (1990) A characteristic of Rogers's response to clients. *Person-Centered Review, 5*, 433–48.

THE CASE OF LORETTA: A PSYCHIATRIC INPATIENT

13

Transcript

Carl Rogers (CR): *(Screaming in the background)* I'm Carl Rogers. This must seem confusing and odd, and so on, but I, I felt really sorry that the interview had been kind of cut short 'cause I sort of felt maybe there were other things you wanted to say.

Loretta: I don't know. I'm being moved all right, transferred. And I was just wondering if I'm quite ready for a transfer. I've mentioned that — it's annoying, that woman talking, uh, she's been yelling like that *(referring to patient who keeps screaming in the background)*. I really rather like it on my ward. (C R.: M-hm, m-hm.) And I have been helping . . . I had thought maybe I could go home from there. (CR: M-hm, m-hm.) I know being transferred means I'll probably be put to work in the laundry all day. *(Screaming in the background)* And I don't feel quite up to that.

CR: M-hm, m-hm. So that's one immediate thing of concern. 'Am I ready to face whatever's involved in moving away from the spot where I've — ?'

Loretta: You get kind of oriented to one place when you're here.

CR: M-hm, you get sort of used to it and —

Loretta: Oh, I meant to correct one thing. When I said 'no' before, I didn't mean I was tired of talking to that doctor. I just meant, 'no,' that I was ready to, that I wondered why I couldn't go home.

This interview with Loretta is Tape Number One in the Audiotape Library of the American Academy of Psychotherapists (1958). This transcript was prepared by Marco Temaner and emended by Nathaniel J. Raskin. In B.A. Farber, D.C. Brink and P.M. Raskin (Eds.), *The psychotherapy of Carl Rogers, Cases and commentary* (1996). New York: Guilford, pp. 44–56. Reprinted with permission.

CR: Yeah, yeah. That you felt he didn't quite understand you on that *(screaming in the background)*, that really —

Loretta: Maybe he thought I was being blunt *(loud screaming in the background)* . . . and that I meant 'no,' I didn't want to talk to him anymore. *(Loud screaming)*

CR: Uh-huh. *(Screaming continues intermittently)* And if I, if I sense some of your feeling now, it is, uh, a little tenseness that, that, uh, maybe he didn't really get that. Maybe he thought you were, sort of —

Loretta: I thought he thought I —

CR: Shutting him off, or something.

Loretta: Yes! That's what I had thought. (CR: Uh-huh.) And that isn't what I meant — (CR: Uh-huh.) Uh, I don't know. I'm wondering if that transfer is a good thing. I mean, they make you feel so important around here, and still you aren't, but — (CR: M-hm, m-hm.) Then when I go over to Two, I know that's an open ward, that's [a] dormitory, and I've been wearing not so many of my own clothes 'cause I don't like to launder them. Just wonder if I'm ready for that change.

CR: M-hm, and that —

Loretta: 'Cause my father and that don't come to visit me or anything, so I don't get out at all on weekends or anything.

CR: M-hm . . . And I'm not quite sure about this. Is it in the ward where you are now that you feel, yeah, they seem to make you so important, but then really you're not. *(Screaming in the background)* Is that — ?

Loretta: That's really it. I'm important, but I'm really not. (CR: M-hm.) I probably wouldn't be on the other ward, either. Well I know that, you're not very important when you move to that ward.

CR: I see. So that if you're not very important where you are right now, you feel then if you were transferred, even less so.

Loretta: Even less important.

CR: So that's something that concerns you.

Loretta: I think it means working all day in the laundry, too, and I'm not quite ready for that. I mentioned earlier that I had this tickling sensation in my knees when I was on Six C when I was getting Reserpine and a tranquilizer — (CR: M-hm, m-hm.) I think it was. And I asked the doctor at that time if he would move me, so I could go to work and work in the laundry. (CR: M-hm, m-hm.) And the transfer came today. I didn't ask to be transferred, though, this time.

CR: M-hm, m-hm. But it troubles you as to whether you're really ready to face some of the things that would be involved.

Loretta: I don't know, there isn't much to face, it's kind of confusing, I think.

CR: I see. It's more a question of facing the uncertainties, is that what you mean?

Loretta: I don't know what I mean (little laugh) . . . I just know that —

CR: Right now you feel kind of mixed up?

Loretta: Well, I know there's Anita on that ward that I didn't trust very far *(banging in the background)* because she's the one that put me on shock treatment.

CR: I see.

Loretta: Or I think she did, anyway. (CR: M-hm, m-hm.) And still she put her arm around my shoulder when I came back, but it . . . she was the one that told me I had to go on it and I had done nothing that I knew of to be put on that kind of treatment.

CR: So that there's something that's real confusing. It would be putting you next to a person who seemed to like you and put her arm around you and, by gosh, was responsible for shock treatment.

Loretta: That's right . . . Of course she said it was doctor's orders, but I hadn't talked to a doctor that I knew of at the time. (CR: M-hm, m-hm.) And I know that they gave them to . . . even though that was a work ward they had them go over to the treatment ward and then back to the work ward. (CR: M-hm, m-hm.) *(Screaming in the background)* And then to work.

CR: M-hm, sure you heard, the explanation was doctor's orders and all that, but you can't help but feel, 'Is she really trustworthy?' 'Cause here she seemed to —

Loretta: No, I don't trust people anyway, anymore. (CR: M-hm, m-hm.) That's why I don't want them to trust me. I either believe in them or I don't believe in them.

CR: M-hm, and all or none.

Loretta: And I don't quite think I believe in her very much.

C.R: M-hm, m-hm. And really with most people you feel, 'I don't think I trust 'em.'

Loretta: That's the truth, I don't trust 'em. *(Screaming in the background)* Either believe 'em or I don't believe 'em or I don't, I'm not quite certain whether I believe them yet or not. (CR: M-hm, m-hm.) But I don't believe in, trust anymore.

CR: M-hm, m-hm. That's one thing that you feel has really dropped out for you, that just to trust people. Not for you.

Loretta: No, I don't trust 'em . . . You can get hurt much too easily by trusting people.

CR: M-hm, m-hm. If you really believe in someone, and let your trust go out to them, then —

Loretta: I don't have any trust, that's why I can't let any trust go out to 'em.

CR: M-hm, but evidently your feeling is that when that has happened in the past —

Loretta: You just get hurt by it.

CR: That's the way you can get hurt.

Loretta: That's the way I *have* been hurt.

CR: That's the way you *have* been hurt.

Loretta: I don't mind being moved. I mean if it's, uh *(pounding in the background)* uh, another thing toward going home. (CR: M-hm.)

(Screaming in the background) But I don't get out anyway, and I don't, I don't know that he, my brother, I wrote a letter but I didn't get any answer from him. *(Screaming in the background)* (CR: M-hm, m-hm.) He never came.

CR: M-hm. It isn't that, at least what I understand you to be saying, is that it isn't the practical question of the move so much that, uh, but it's the question of —

Loretta: If I'm quite ready for that.

CR: Yeah, are you, are you ready for a next step, is that it?

Loretta: I don't think I'm going to like working in the laundry, that I know. 'Cause I didn't like it either [of] the other two times. *(Announcement on PA system in the background)* And I don't think I care too much [for] working on [the] food center over there either, because I worked there before, and I didn't care for it. (CR: M-hm, m-hm.) Well, I didn't have anything . . . I . . . the first day I worked alright, the second day I worked about a half an hour, and I blacked out, and I tried it 3 more days, and I blacked out each day, so . . . I just quit trying to work there. There was too much electricity or something.

CR: M-hm, m-hm. You feel something was wrong over there? Too much electricity or something, 'that really had a bad effect on me when I was working there.'

Loretta: It did. I blacked out, completely. If I hadn't gone to sit down, I would have fainted.

CR: M-hm, m-hm. You feel really you were in, in kind of a desperate way, at those points?

Loretta: No, I didn't feel desperate. I just, I didn't understand it, I didn't know why I blacked out.

CR: I see.

Loretta: It did frighten me, though. I just couldn't work, so —

CR: It was just something very odd happening to you.

Loretta: 'Cause I don't have epilepsy seizures or anything like that, so I couldn't imagine what it was. I don't, I'm not, I don't usually have fainting spells.

CR: M-hm. It just made you feel real puzzled. 'What is happening to me?'

Loretta: What it was, yeah, I tried, but I couldn't work, and they wanted me to work, so . . . sometimes I think you get put back on treatment if you refuse to work.

CR: Uh-huh. Well, maybe, maybe shock treatment is really something they may use for punishment if you don't do the things the way they want you to do?

Loretta: Well, it would appear that way from what everybody says, but I don't think I was even, I don't know why they even gave it to me in the first place. I was just beginning to come to, enough to realize that I was in an institution, I think. (CR: M-hm, m-hm.) And the next thing I knew, they said, 'You're ready, you're on treatment.' (CR: M-hm, m-hm.) And I said, 'Why? I didn't do anything. I haven't had any fight or anything with anybody.' (CR: M-hm, m-hm.) And they said, 'Well, doctor's orders.' And I said, 'Well, I haven't even talked to a doctor.' Because I hadn't talked to one. (CR: M-hm, m-hm.) At least I didn't know it if I had. (CR. : M-hm, m-hm, m-hm.) And so —

CR: So to you it seemed, 'Here I was just beginning to come to life a little, really to know a little bit what was going on.'

Loretta: I was just beginning to realize I was in the hospital — (CR: Uh-huh.) When they put me on it, and they put me to work the same day.

CR: And then you feel that for no reason you could discern, zingo, you were —

Loretta: And I began talking very badly and everything, and I still haven't forgotten some of the things I said.

CR: M-hm, m-hm, m-hm. It feels that, that sort of brought out the worst in you, is that what you mean?

Loretta: If I had a worst part. It was like it wasn't even me talking.

CR : Uh-huh. Almost seemed as though this —

Loretta: And then I went home weekends, and I got in trouble there, because I talked so much, Of course, I was getting Sodium Amytal, too, so it might have been the combination of the two, not just the one thing.

CR: But there, too, I guess I get the feeling that you're wishing you could understand that part of yourself; was it something that was not you talking, or was it just the effect of the drugs, or what was it that made you — ?

Loretta: It was the combination, I think. (CR: Uh-huh.) If you notice, my . . . I move my feet.

CR: Yes, I did notice.

Loretta: As I said, my knees tickle. (CR: M-hm, m-hm.) And I, I don't know if it's the drugs I'm getting or what, but it's something I can't help. It isn't that I'm so terribly nervous that I can't sit still, that isn't it. I do that at group meetings or anything, and I can't control them. It's rather embarrassing *(laughs nervously)*.

CR: And you would like me to understand that it isn't just tenseness or something, it's, uh —

Loretta: No.

CR: It's simply the —

Loretta: Something I can't control.

CR: Uncontrollable tickling sensations. *(Screaming in the background)*

Loretta: In my knees and that far up, and my feet just move. If I'm sitting up there in the corner alone, that isn't so much, but my knees still tickle. (CR: M-hm m-hm.) But when I get in a group, and that, my, I don't know, they just move.

CR: It seems as though being in a group makes this worse.

Loretta: Well, I have it when I'm alone sometimes, too. (CR: M-hm, m-hm.) I think it's the medication I'm getting.

CR: Well, probably it's just the drugs?

Loretta: I think it's the green medication I'm getting. I don't even know what it is, 'cause I haven't asked, but then — (CR: M-hm.) *(Pause)* I think these meetings are very enlightening *(little laugh)*.

CR: Do you?

Loretta: Well, if you can't think quite clear at the time, you can think about it later.

CR: M-hm, m-hm. And in that sense they, they're somewhat helpful in *(banging in the background)* making you think more clearly afterwards?

Loretta: I think I've been helped a lot by, more by talking than I have by the pills, and that.

CR: M-hm, m-hm. It really, it seems as though getting things out to some degree in talk —

Loretta: Seems to alleviate whatever the situation is. (CR: H-hm, m-hm.) If it's created a situation that seems to alleviate . . . I wish that woman would quit screaming.

CR: 'Why doesn't she stop?'

Loretta: She can't stop though, that's the worst of it . . . That gives you a terrible feeling, what's going to happen to you if you end up in a, like that.

CR: Yeah, yeah, part of the, part of the disturbance of that noise is the feeling, 'My god, could this happen to me?'

Loretta: Yes. (CR: M-hm, m-hm.) Exactly. And you think you could just about go out of your head just from hearing that all the time. That's been going on for 3 days now, and why did they give her that much, she, if it's who I think it is, she was up on the ward for one of those QIM clinics, and I sat next to her, and she said something about liking to talk, and all of a sudden she was, she just began talking and didn't quit.

CR: So this seems kind of awful, that here is this person and —

Loretta: She was all . . . perfectly all right then, calm; she wasn't talking or anything —

CR: Next to you and so on, and now here it's just going on and on —

Loretta: You should think, I thought they could relieve those, not make them worse.

CR: It's kind of discouraging in a sense to feel that they, it seems to you, that they aren't helping her.

Loretta: Yes, considering it's an admission ward, and they shouldn't be that far out of their heads. It's more like the drugs they're giving after they're here are doing it to them.

CR: Almost makes you feel, 'Are they making her worse with their drugs?' Is that — ?

Loretta: That's right.

CR: And that's kind of a disturbing —

Loretta: I think it is.

CR: Thought, too —

Loretta: Because after all, I'm getting drugs, too, and I wouldn't want to end up like that.

CR: M-hm, m-hm. It can't help but raise the question in you, 'Would the drugs they're giving me make me like that?'

Loretta: That's right. And then once you're that way, what can you do about it? Only, only I know what they're like and I can see it, so I have enough control to hang on to myself, enough to keep from just batting my head against the wall, like, uh . . . Some of them had that feeling, and they just can't control it. They . . . I've seen so much of it and heard so much of it that I can hang on to myself a little bit.

CR: Those things are kind of —

Loretta: I think that's why, pardon me, I think that's why my knees tingle, though, because rather than batting my head against the wall, I have that type of reaction.

CR: M-hm, m-hm. So in a sense, you can hold yourself in enough so you're not going to bat your head against the wall, and yet it's as though it has to come out somewhere, and it, uh —

Loretta: Comes out in the tickling. It's terrible!

CR: Comes out in the tickling of your knees.

Loretta: Because . . . well, I've seen on the outside, too, so I mean I know that . . . it's just futile to bat your head. Why anyway, I think my head's too valuable to bat against the wall *(laughs)*. It's my own head, and I like it.

CR: You feel by gosh, 'I'm not going to smash my head against walls.'

Loretta: That's right. After all, God gave me that head, that's the head I want. I'm not going to bang it against the wall, even if I like to, which I really wouldn't like to do, anyway . . . Well, why, how does that help that girl to be in . . . locked up like that and screaming like that? What, I mean what . . . beneficial aid is she getting out of that? Anything?

CR: I guess that's the question you're asking yourself, 'What earthly good — ?'

Loretta: No, I'm asking *you*.

CR: You're asking me. Well, I'm not on the hospital staff, and I really guess I wouldn't try to answer because I don't know her, and I don't know anything about it. But what I can understand is, is the way that affects you and the feelings that it stirs up in you. 'Cause it sounds as though with you that, that is disturbing not only from the noise from her but the things that it *(screaming in the background)* stirs up in you.

Loretta: I don't know. I'm all mixed up. I want to *(loud screaming in the background)*go to Building One, but I know Building One's not the next to home . . . But if I could go home from One, I'd be happy . . . But I've been there before. I know it's going to be a great change from this building. I hate to leave this building 'cause it's quite beautiful . . . But still, it, maybe it's better than listening to that girl screaming all day, every day.

CR: It's a real tough choice to make.

Loretta: But I hate to think that I'm going to have to go to work in the laundry room. I'd rather . . . and there isn't as much to do around that ward as there is here, that much I know.

CR: M-hm, m-hm. You feel that, uh —

Loretta: You can relax and just sleep, because you do have beds, but I don't think they do. I think they expect you to work if you can. (CR: M-hm, m-hm.) They don't go that far as to just let you rest like you're in a hospital for a rest. *(Screaming in the background)* Keep you working all the time.

CR: If it, if it represented a chance to rest, then you might like it, but if it's a chance just to work all the time, uh, then you're not sure that that's what you want.

Loretta: I don't think I'm ready for it. (CR: Uh-huh.) Because my knees tickle, maybe that's . . . I worked in the laundry before, and I know. I got along all right. I know I can get along now, but —

CR: 'I could do it, but, uh, am I really ready for it?'

Loretta: Though why?

CR: 'Why?' M-hm.

Loretta: I packed my own grip, so I'm all ready to go. I didn't say, 'No, I won't go,' because I'm always putting up a big fight about it. (CR: M-hm, m-hm.) If it's an improvement, well I'm willing to go along with it.

CR: M-hm. A chance you're willing to take although within yourself, you feel a lot of question about it.

Loretta: I rather like seeing them admitted, although I can't say that I like to see 'em get worse. But when they improve it's quite a joy to, to be where they're all coming in and going out.

CR: It kind of helps you inside, when they, when they —

Loretta: To know that others get well and can go home.

CR: M-hm, m-hm. So that you're sort of discouraged and encouraged by what happens to others.

Loretta: I had thought, I had thought that I'd go home from here because I hadn't done anything very serious — (CR: M-hm.) I hadn't, uh, had any violent struggle with anybody, or anything like that.

CR: That's part of your feeling all the way through, 'I haven't done anything wrong, I've held myself in, you know, I really have not been violent, I haven't broken many rules.'

Loretta: I haven't broken any, I don't think.

CR: You haven't broken any —

Loretta: And half the time you have to find out what the rules are, because they don't tell ya.

CR: M-hm, m-hm. But your feeling is, 'I've been good.'

Loretta: But I haven't been too good, though. *(Screaming in the background* You shouldn't go overboard about being good, too. (CR: M-hm.) I don't believe in that, either. (CR: M-hm.) I've been as good as I know how to be. (CR: M-hm.) And I'm not letter-perfect. I would like to be, but I'm not.

CR: But in terms of what you can do, you feel you've done the best you can do.

Loretta: I'm doing as good as I know how.

CR: M-hm. Loretta, I know that some of these people have got to go, and I expect we've got to call it quits. I appreciate this chance to talk with you.

Loretta: And thank you very much. I know that you're very important people. That's what I've heard, anyhow.

The interview and its context
'I'm Carl Rogers. This must seem confusing and odd, and so on, but I, I felt really sorry that the interview had been kind of . . . cut short 'cause I sort of felt maybe there were other things you wanted to say.' Thus does Carl Rogers open his interview with Loretta, a state hospital inpatient, diagnosed as paranoid schizophrenic, in the summer of 1958. The American Academy of Psychotherapists was in the middle of its 4-day Second Annual Workshop at the University of Wisconsin in Madison. The 30 on so participating therapists were gathered in a small auditorium of the hospital to observe one another in actual practice. Loretta

had been previously interviewed by Albert Ellis to demonstrate his rational-emotive approach and by psychiatrist Richard Felder to demonstrate the experiential method of his Atlanta group, which included Carl Whitaker, Tom Malone, and John Warkentin.

Ellis and Felder had had a difficult time with Loretta, and there was a clamor in this diverse group of experienced therapists for Rogers to try his hand with her. He was only too willing, as he had suffered through two interviews in which, from his point of view, this woman's expressed feelings and attitudes had not been responded to empathically. Ellis, the day before, had tried to help Loretta to see the irrationality of her behavior, and Felder, earlier on this day, had attempted to engage her in a person-to-person dialogue about, among other things, a dream he had had about her the night before. It was the interview with Felder to which Rogers referred when he said he thought Loretta might have felt cut short. After Rogers agreed to the interview, Loretta, who had returned to her ward, was asked how she felt about returning to talk to still another psychotherapist; her response was positive.

Aside from attending this workshop as the first president of the American Academy of Psychotherapists, Rogers had moved from the University of Chicago to the University of Wisconsin the year before for a joint professorship in Psychology and Psychiatry. This bears directly on the interview with Loretta, because Rogers saw his appointment at Wisconsin as providing an opportunity to test the hypothesis that Client-Centered Therapy would work with a schizophrenic population. This would be explored comprehensively in a large-scale research project (Rogers, Gendlin, Kiesler, and Truax, 1967); the interview with Loretta was a single clinical test of Rogers' hypothesis.

The significance of the interview

The case of Loretta is significant in at least two ways. First, it is one of the few verbatim recordings of a therapeutic interview, within any orientation, with a psychotic patient. Second, it provides a concrete example of the application of Client-Centered Therapy to a psychiatric inpatient diagnosed as paranoid schizophrenic. The interview shows how a deeply disturbed individual may respond positively to the therapist-offered conditions of empathy, congruence, and unconditional positive regard.

One stereotype of Client-Centered Therapy is that it is a superficial approach that works primarily with 'normal people', for example, college students with minor problems. Rogers may have contributed to this belief in *Counseling and Psychotherapy* (1942), his first book-length exposition of his approach, in which he stated, as one of the tentative criteria for attempting psychotherapy of any kind, that the individual be 'reasonably free from excessive instabilities' (p. 77). His position was radically different in his next book, *Client-Centered Therapy* (1951). Here he wrote:

> Present opinion on applicability must take into account our experience. A client-centered approach has been used with two-year-

old children and adults of 65, with mild adjustment problems, such as student study habits, and the most severe disorders of diagnosed psychotics . . . An atmosphere of acceptance and respect, of deep understanding, is a good climate for personal growth, and as such applies to our children, our colleagues, our students, as well as to our clients, whether these be 'normal', neurotic, or psychotic. This does *not* mean that it will *cure* every psychological condition, and indeed the concept of cure is quite foreign to the approach. (pp. 229–30)

The interview with Loretta lasted about 30 minutes. Some of the noteworthy occurrences in this brief encounter, each of which is amplified, include:
1. Loretta's explanation of her side of the process of ending the just-completed interview with Dr Felder. It was clear that the opportunity to clarify this was important to her.
2. Her exploration of the problem of an impending transfer to another ward. This was her 'presenting problem', a real one.
3. The transition from this specific issue to the question of whether she was able to trust people in general and whether she could trust the hospital staff in her treatment.
4. Her expressions of distress and confusion about the treatment of a patient heard screaming in the background continually throughout the interview.
5. Her descriptions of peculiar sensations of tickling in her knees and of a feeling of electricity in the air when she had worked in the hospital laundry.
6. Her emerging positive self-regard as the interview progressed.

Loretta explains her side of the process of ending the just-completed interview
After introducing the subject of her impending transfer to another ward, Loretta wishes to clear up a possible misunderstanding of her attitude about ending the interview just concluded with Dr Richard Felder. She makes it clear that the opportunity to clarify this is important to her: 'Oh, I meant to correct one thing. When I said "no" before, I didn't mean I was tired of talking to that doctor. I just meant "no", that I was ready to, that I wondered why I couldn't go home.' Rogers empathizes: 'Yeah, yeah. That you felt he didn't quite understand you on that really.'

At this point, screaming can be heard in the background, but Loretta responds to Rogers' comment: 'Maybe he thought I was being blunt and that meant, "no", I didn't want to talk to him anymore.' To which Rogers responds: 'Uh-huh. And if, if I sense some of your feeling now, it is, uh, a little tenseness that, that, uh, maybe he didn't really get that. Maybe he thought you were, sort of . . . shutting him off, or something.' Loretta agrees: 'Yes! That's what I had thought.'

Rogers' empathic responses in this dialogue facilitate Loretta's explanation, and, apparently satisfied that she has clarified her position, she then returns to the issue of the ward transfer.

Loretta explores the problem of an impending transfer to another ward
Loretta now begins to explain her concern, her presenting problem: 'I don't know. I'm being moved all right, transferred. And I was just wondering if I'm quite ready for a transfer . . . It's annoying, that woman . . . yelling like that *(refering to patient who keeps screaming in the background).* I really rather like it on my ward.'

The ward transfer is clearly an issue of great importance to Loretta. She devotes about one quarter of the interview with Rogers to it. To summarize some of her attitudes about it:

I don't know if I'm ready for the work that would be involved in the transfer. I'd hate to work in the laundry room; I'm not even keeping up with my own laundry now. And when I worked in the food center in that ward, I had real physical trouble. I blacked out.

Even though the hospital makes a pretense that the patients are important, I'm not really important on my present ward and would be less so on the new one.

At one time I wanted the transfer, but I didn't ask for it right now.

I'm confused.

If the transfer is a step closer to my discharge from the hospital, that would make me favor it more.

I like the building I'm in, because it's beautiful, and there's more to do here, but it would be nice to get away from that screaming girl.

I wouldn't mind going to the new ward if they let you rest there, but they keep you working all the time.

I was able to work in the laundry when I was there before. I know I can do it now, but I'm not sure I'm ready for it.

I won't refuse to go. I've even packed my own grip. If it's an improvement, I'm willing to go along with the move.

Rogers communicates his empathic understanding of these attitudes. Specifically, he recognizes Loretta's feelings of confusion and uncertainty about whether she is ready for this change in her life. He acknowledges that it is a tough choice to make and articulates Loretta's feeling that it might not be what she really wants. This seems to have the effect of helping Loretta, after considerable exploration, come to a resolution of a very difficult and troubling issue: she would be willing to give the transfer a try, even though she is not sure she is ready for it.

Loretta's exploration of the issue of the ward transfer leads her into the
question of whether she is able to trust people in general
After Rogers empathizes with Loretta's feeling of confusion ('Right now you feel kind of mixed up?'), she moves to a new issue: 'Well, I know there's Anita on that ward that I didn't trust very far . . . because she's the one that put me on shock treatment.' Later in this segment, responding to Rogers' understanding and acceptance of her distrust of one person, Loretta shares with him the breadth of

her distrust: 'I don't trust people anyway anymore.' A little later, she adds, 'You can get hurt much too easily by trusting people.' The attitudes she expresses in this segment can be summarized as follows:

I don't trust the staff person who I think was responsible for my getting shock therapy. She acted friendly and said it was done on 'doctor's orders', but as far as I know I hadn't talked to a doctor.

In a very general way, I don't trust people anymore. I've been hurt when I did.

I don't understand why they suddenly ordered shock therapy for me. I wonder if it was because I said I couldn't work and they didn't believe me.

All of a sudden, I was given shock and assigned to work.

Rogers deals with Loretta's difficulties in trusting people by consistently trying to appreciate her feelings and perceptions. For example, when Loretta expresses her lack of trust about the staff member who orchestrated her shock treatment, Rogers replies, 'So that there's something that's real confusing. It would be putting you next to a person who seemed to like you and put her arm around you and, by gosh, was responsible for shock treatment.' He also empathizes with her feeling that the shock treatment is used to get her to perform her duties: 'Well, maybe, maybe shock treatment is really something they may use for punishment if you don't do the things the way they want you to do?'

Implicitly, in the way he responds, Rogers invites Loretta to correct him when he has not gotten her feelings exactly right. This is exemplified when she begins to discuss her inability to trust people because it inevitably leads to getting hurt. When Rogers responds with what appears to be accurate empathy: 'That's the way you can get hurt', Loretta goes further and states: 'That's the way I have been hurt.' Whereupon Rogers accepts her clarification: 'That's the way you have been hurt.'

Loretta expresses distress and confusion about the treatment of a patient frequently heard screaming in the background during the interview

A dramatic aspect of the audiotape recording of this interview is the sound of another female patient screaming in the background. After mentioning it in her first statement, Loretta does not bring up the subject again until more than halfway into her dialogue with Rogers, even though the sound is piercing and rather constant: 'I wish that woman would quit screaming.' Rogers' empathic response is in the form of a question: 'Why doesn't she stop?' Loretta's answer takes her into a personal concern: 'She can't stop though, that's the worst of it . . . That gives you a terrible feeling, what's going to happen to you if you end up in a, like that.'

Some of the attitudes expressed by Loretta in this section are:

That woman's screaming really bothers me. You could go out of your head hearing that all the time.

I'm worried that I could end up like that.

I sat next to her, and she seemed perfectly all right. She was calm and not talking.

You would think the hospital could help somebody like that, not make her
  worse.
I think maybe it's the drugs they're giving her.
I'm getting drugs, and I'm worried I could end up like that.

In his usual way, Rogers responds with explicit empathic understanding to these concerns. He verbalizes Loretta's fear that what happened to this screaming woman could also happen to her, as well as her suspicion that the hospital staff had caused her disturbance rather than relieved it. Note, for example, the following empathic response: 'Almost makes you feel, "Are they making her worse with their drugs?"' On the basis of Loretta's participation in the dialogue, one may reasonably conclude that she feels understood regarding her misgivings about the treatment of the screaming patient and her fear that she could end up the same way.

Loretta describes sensations of tickling in her knees and a feeling of electricity in the air
Loretta explains her experiences as follows: 'I don't think I'm going to like working in the laundry, that I know. 'Cause I didn't like it either the other two times . . . And I don't think I care too much working on food center over there, either, because I worked there before, and I didn't care for it (CR: Mh-m, m-hm.) Well, I didn't have anything . . . I . . . the first day, I worked all right, the second day I worked about a half an hour, and I blacked out, and I tried it 3 more days, and I blacked out each day, so . . . I just quit trying to work there. There was too much electricity or something.'

To this, Rogers replies: 'M-hm, m-hm. You feel something was wrong over there? Too much electricity or something, "that really had a bad effect on me when I was working there".' And after Loretta describes how frightened she felt by her blackouts, Rogers responds, 'It was just something very odd happening to you', and then, 'M-hm. It just made you feel real puzzled. "What is happening to me?"'

A little later, Loretta describes another symptom: 'If you notice, my . . . I move my feet.' To which Rogers responds: 'Yes, I did notice.' And Loretta further explains: 'As I said, my knees tickle. (CR: M-hm, m-hm.) And I, I don't know if it's the drugs I'm getting or what, but it's something I can't help. It isn't that I'm so terribly nervous that I can't sit still, that isn't it. I do that at group meetings or anything, and I can't control them. It's rather embarrassing *(laughs nervously)*.'

Rogers listens respectfully to Loretta's experience that the sensations are specific to particular situations: 'It seems as though being in a group makes this worse.' He is also responsive to Loretta's belief that her symptoms are caused by her medication: 'Well, probably it's just the drugs?' Later Loretta comes up with another explanation for the sensations in her knees. She has been discussing the patient who screams: 'And then once you're that way, what can you do about it? Only, only I know what they're like and I can see it, so I have enough control to hang on to myself, enough to keep from just batting my head against the wall, like, uh . . . Some of them had that feeling and they just can't control it. They . . . I've seen so much of it and heard so much of it that I can hang on to myself a little bit . . . I think that's why my knees tingle, though, because rather than batting my head against the wall, I have that type of reaction.

Rogers then responds: 'M-hm, m-hm. So in a sense, you can hold yourself in enough so you're not going to bat your head against the wall, and yet it's as though it has to come out somewhere, and it, uh . . . ' Loretta finishes Rogers' sentence: 'Comes out in the tickling.' Rogers accepts her way of putting it: 'Comes out in the tickling of your knees.'

The striking feature of the interaction between Loretta and Rogers on the topic of her odd sensations is that he is just as respectful of this kind of experience on the part of a hospitalized schizophrenic as he would be of the everyday experience of a 'normal' client. His unconditional positive regard for Loretta, together with his empathy and genuineness, appear to facilitate her movement toward a rational explanation of what initially appeared to be bizarre symptoms.

Loretta expresses greater positive regard for herself as the interview progresses
The interview with Loretta illustrates a dynamic observed by Rogers from the earliest days of Client-Centered Therapy: if the therapist conveys an empathic understanding and acceptance of the client's negative feelings, the client is freed to experience positive aspects of self and others. For example, immediately after the dialogue about the tickling in her knees, Loretta says: 'it's just futile to bat your head. Why anyway, I think my head's too valuable to bat against the wall *(laughs)*. It's my own head, and I like it.' Here is a dramatic expression of Loretta's belief that she is a worthwhile person. Similarly, in her next exchange with Rogers, she says: 'That's right. After all, God gave me that head, that's the head I want. I'm not going to bang it against the wall, even if I like to, which I really wouldn't like to do, anyway . . . Well, why, how does that help that girl to be in . . . locked up like that and screaming like that? What, I mean what . . . beneficial aid is she getting out of that? Anything?'

Rogers reply here is, 'I guess that's the question you're asking yourself, "What earthly good . . . ?"' Loretta interrupts Rogers at this point and says, 'No I'm asking *you*.' Here, then, we see Loretta standing up to this noted psychologist, letting him know what she meant: she wants to know what he thinks of the treatment of the screaming patient. There are other examples in the interview of Loretta's insistence on being understood exactly. One such instance occurs when Loretta is describing her blackouts. One of Rogers' responses is 'M-hm, m-hm. You feel really you were in, in kind of a desperate way, at those points?' Loretta corrects Rogers' statement: 'No, I didn't feel desperate. I just, I didn't understand it. I didn't know why I blacked out.'

These examples of Loretta's insistence on being understood exactly are the second indication of her emerging self-regard in this interview. A third, somewhat more indirect, expression is reflected in her assertion that therapy has been helpful to her: 'I think these meetings are very enlightening *(little laugh)* . . . I think I've been helped a lot by, more by talking than I have by the pills, and that . . . seems to alleviate whatever the situation is.' Loretta's statement that talking to professionals is more helpful than medication suggests that her participation in the treatment process is valuable. The interview with Rogers provides an example of her active stance in such a situation.

It is noteworthy, too, that while talking to Rogers, Loretta expresses concern that others may perceive her as not being good or as acting antisocially, in some way. The first instance occurs soon after the interview begins, when Loretta notes that she wants to correct an impression she may have made: 'Oh, I meant to correct one thing. When I said "no" before, I didn't mean I was tired of talking to that doctor. I just meant, "no," that I was ready to, that I wondered why I couldn't go home.' She explains that her intention was not to be blunt, that she didn't mean to be insulting, and that she did not want to be perceived that way.

Another instance of her wish to be perceived as someone who behaves in an acceptable manner occurs during her discussion of having received shock therapy. She says: 'I had done nothing that I knew of to be put on that kind of treatment.' Implicitly she is expressing a concern that she is being perceived as having done something 'bad'. This hypothesis is confirmed by what she says a few minutes later: 'And the next thing I knew, they said, "You're ready, you're on treatment." And I said, "Why? I didn't do anything. I haven't had any fight or anything with anybody."'

Later in the interview, Loretta brings out her perception that the decision about her release is related to whether she has acted out: 'I had thought that I'd go home from here because I hadn't done anything very serious . . . I hadn't, uh, had any violent struggle with anybody, or any thing like that.' In his response, Rogers recognizes that this is an issue that has run throughout the interview: 'That's part of your feeling all the way through, "I haven't done anything wrong, I've held myself in, you know, I really have not been violent, I haven't broken many rules."' Loretta replies: 'I haven't broken any, I don't think.' And then she adds, 'And half the time you have to find out what the rules are, because they don't tell ya.' Rogers then reflects her underlying assertion: 'M-hm, m-hm. But your feeling is, "I've been good."'

Loretta's response at this point is interesting and significant: 'But I haven't been too good, though . . . You shouldn't go overboard about being too good . . . I don't believe in that, either . . . I've been as good as I know how to be . . . And I'm not letter-perfect. I would like to be, but I'm not.' Rogers replies: 'But in terms of what you can do, you feel you've done the best you can do.' And Loretta affirms this comment, 'I'm doing as good as I know how.'

Here is an issue important to Loretta that she resolves in a way that expresses positive self-regard. She articulates an impressive acceptance of self: she is only as good as she really is, that she is not perfect, and that she does not believe in going 'overboard about being good'.

Rogers' behavior in the interview

In the course of demonstrating how Loretta dealt with six areas of concern during this interview, many illustrations have been given of the way Rogers interacted with her. An examination of the entire interview reveals a remarkable consistency of empathic responsiveness on Rogers' part. Of all of his responses, there are perhaps only one or two in which Rogers did something other than try to convey to Loretta his understanding of what she was sharing with him.

Loretta was responsive to this empathic approach. She advanced from one area of discussion to another (e.g., from the presenting problem of a possible ward transfer to the issue of her lack of trust in the institution and in people in general), and she made progress within specific areas (e.g., resolving her conflict about moving by deciding that the transfer might be an improvement and that she would not fight it). In addition, Rogers' empathic approach seemed to facilitate increased self-understanding and acceptance as well as a greater ability to view problems more clearly. Finally, Loretta's responsiveness to Rogers' therapeutic style is evident in the comments she makes immediately following some of his responses, statements such as 'That's really it', 'Yes, that's what I thought' and 'That's the truth', all indicate that she truly felt understood.

In addition to a high degree of empathy, Rogers provided two other therapist characteristics included in his classic formulation of 'necessary and sufficient conditions of therapeutic personality change': unconditional positive regard and congruence. He accorded Loretta the same kind of respect he would any client; his motive for interviewing her was his sense that her feelings had been insufficiently understood and respected in the first two demonstrations. He displayed unconditional regard for her belief that there was electricity in the atmosphere of the laundry and for the ticking sensations she experienced in her knees. He respected her choice of topic, her manner of exploring each one, and her decisions to switch to other issues. I count 24 times in this short interview that Loretta took the initiative in introducing a new subject, going back to one she had been exploring earlier, coming up with an insight or new attitude, or exercising some other form of self-direction.

Another index of the client-centeredness of this interview is the number of lines in the printed transcript taken up by Loretta's statements (218) and the number taken up by Rogers' (131). Many psychotherapists pay lip service to respecting the strength of their clients. However an examination of typescripts, when they are available, characteristically show Adlerians, Jungians, Gestalt therapists, cognitive therapists family therapists, and others dominating the interaction between client and therapist. This is often true of psychoanalytically oriented therapists, as well. Client-centered therapists, because they eschew the role of expert, are consistently less verbose, in spite of the usual reliance on words to convey empathic understanding.

Some support for these assertions comes from an analysis of the interview material in *Case Studies in Psychotherapy* (Wedding and Corsini, 1989). This book includes cases treated by therapists from a variety of approaches. All cases

TABLE 13–I

Number of Transcript Lines Spoken by Therapists and Clients

Orientation	Therapist(s)	Therapist Lines	Client Lines
Adlerian	Mosak and Maniacci	268	227
Client-centered	Carl Rogers	165	401
Rational-emotive	Albert Ellis	554	290
Cognitive	Aaron Beck	398	182
Gestalt	Fritz Perls	200	540
Family	Peggy Papp	253	325

Note. Based on verbatim interview material contained in Wedding and Corsini (1989).

that included verbatim interviews were tallied for the number of lines spoken by the therapist and the number spoken by the client or patient. As Table 13–I indicates, the Adlerian, rational-emotive, and cognitive therapists out-talked their clients or patients by a significant margin. Qualitatively, they are also quite directive. This is true, for example, of Fritz Perls, the Gestalt therapist. Even though he does not dominate in the number of words spoken, his interview is replete with comments like, 'Say this to them', 'Now play the bedroom', 'Now be the kitchen again', 'Stay with what you experience now', 'Be phony'. Peggy Papp, the family therapist is also quite directive; she speaks for a 'Greek chorus' of observing therapists who are watching through a one-way mirror. (The 325 client lines in the table represent the output of all five members of the family being treated by Papp.)

By contrast, Rogers is consistently empathic with 'Mrs Oak', a client he saw over a long period of time in the early 1950s and whose interview with Rogers was the one included in Wedding and Corsini (1989). Furthermore, Brodley (1991), in classifying Rogers' responses in 34 interviews between 1940 and 1986, found 1,659 empathic responses out of a total of 1,928 responses of all kinds, for an 'empathy percentage' of 86. And, if Brodley's (1991) three 1940 interviews from the case of 'Herbert Bryan' (the eight-interview case that took up approximately two-fifths of *Counseling and Psychotherapy* [Rogers, 1942]) are omitted, Rogers' empathic responses rise to a remarkable 90%.

Rogers came to view congruence or genuineness as 'the most basic of the attitudinal conditions that foster therapeutic growth' (Rogers, 1980, p. 2158). I grant that the judgment of genuineness is very subjective. However, I was present at Rogers' interview with Loretta and I have carefully reread the typescript: from this I find Rogers to have been very much up front with Loretta and truly interested in her. He meant what he said and he responded to her on the level of another human being rather than from the pedestal of an expert.

As consistently empathic as he was, I noted one lapse in Rogers' responsiveness to Loretta. Loretta referred to her family on a couple of occasions. Early in the interview, she says: 'Cause my father and that don't come to visit me or anything, so I don't get out at all on weekends or anything.' Then, a few minutes later, Loretta remarks: 'I don't mind being moved, I mean if it's, uh, . . . uh, another thing toward going home. (CR: M-hm.) . . . But I don't get out anyway, and I don't, I don't know that he, my brother, I wrote a letter, but I didn't get any answer from him . . . (CR: M-hm.) He never came.'

While Rogers responds, 'M-hm' to Loretta's references to going home and to her brother's nonresponse, by returning to the issue of the move he does not add the explicit recognition he generally accords to Loretta's feelings and attitudes. If Loretta had pursued the topic, it is likely that Rogers would have come around, but at this point he failed to facilitate Loretta's going further with her disappointment about not seeing or hearing from her father and brother, and what appears to be a strong interest in being discharged from the hospital and going home.

Is this a significant failure in empathy? When one listens to the audiotape of this interview, as distinguished from reading the transcript, this and other errors do not appear so glaring. This is supported by the recorded discussion that followed Rogers' interview with Loretta. About 30 members of the American Academy of Psychotherapists, most of whom were not client-centered therapists, observed this interview and attended a question-and-answer session with Rogers immediately after Loretta left. While the reactions were polite, they were largely critical. Why had Rogers failed to support the staff of the hospital? Why had he not pointed out connections among some of the things Loretta had talked about? There were many other remarks of this sort, but nobody in this audience, which included a number of noted psychoanalysts, commented on Rogers' failure to respond to Loretta's references to her brother and father.

This said, it still may be worth speculating on the reasons that Rogers did not pursue this particular topic. Was there something in Rogers' life — in his background — that made him disinclined to follow up Loretta's references to her family? In Kirschenbaum's (1979) biography of Rogers he notes the following:

In my first interview with Rogers he told me, 'I hate old people who reminisce.' He has frequently made comments like, 'We could count on the fingers of one hand the people of our own age we really enjoy. The rest are all too stuffy.' When he worked on his 'autobiography' in 1965 for a collection of autobiographical essays by well-known psychologists, he said it took him and Helen [his wife] months to recover from spending that much time looking in the past. Both the scientist and the artist in him were operating here; both sides needed new challenges and could not be content with past accomplishments. Beyond this, for Rogers, an interest in the future also went hand in hand with his association with young people. He had always valued his contact with graduate students, and this continued after he left the university setting. As he described it,

'Probably the major factor in keeping me alive as a growing therapist is a continuing association with young people on a thoroughly equalitarian basis. I have always worked with young staff members; I have never found people my own age stimulating except for rare and fortunate exceptions. I find that younger people are full of new ideas, exploring the boundaries of our disciplines and raising questions about any sacred cows which I hold dear. This keeps me stimulated, moving, and I hope growing.' (p. 396)

Rogers' family relationships seem to be consistent with these attitudes. He was closest to Helen, his wife of 55 years, his children, David and Natalie, and his six grandchildren. His interest in some of his own siblings appeared to decline with the years, probably because of a lack of shared values and interests.

It may be, then, that in responding to Loretta, Rogers' own issues influenced his 'overlooking' Loretta's references to her brother and father; clearly, he was far more attentive to her current concerns such as her move and her difficulty in trusting the hospital staff. This lapse, however, detracts only slightly from an extraordinary interview — one that offers a superb example of the client-centered approach being applied successfully to a woman disturbed enough to be a patient in a psychiatric state hospital with a diagnosis of paranoid schizophrenia.

References

Brodley, B. T. (1991, July 1–6) Some observations of Carl Rogers' verbal behavior in therapy interviews. Paper presented at the Second International Conference on Client-Centered and Experiential Psychotherapy, University of Stirling, Scotland.

Kirschenbaurn, H. (1979) *On becoming Carl Rogers.* New York: Delacorte Press.

Rogers, C. R. (1942) *Counseling and psychotherapy.* Boston: Houghton Mifflin.

Rogers, C. R. (1951) *Client-centered therapy.* Boston: Houghton Mifflin.

Rogers, C. R. (1980) Client-centered psychotherapy. In A. M. Freedman, H. I. Kaplan and B. J. Sadock (Eds.), *Comprehensive textbook of psychiatry/III* (pp. 2153–68). Baltimore: Williams & Wilkins.

Rogers, C. R., Gendlin, E. T., Kiesler D. J. and Truax C. B. (Eds.) (1967) *The therapeutic relationship and its impact: A study of psychotherapy with schizophrenics.* Madison: University of Wisconsin Press.

Wedding, D. and Corsini, R. J. (Eds.) (1989) *Case studies in psychotherapy.* Itasca, IL: Peacock.

PERSON-CENTRED PSYCHOTHERAPY: TWENTY HISTORICAL STEPS

14

In this chapter a number of significant steps in the development of person-centred therapy will be described. These advances occurred in a special kind of atmosphere, which reflected the spirit of the person-centred movement and the characteristics of its founder. Carl Rogers formulated an approach to psychotherapy and human relations based on trust in the self-determining capacities of individuals and groups customarily seen as requiring direction, control and external authority — clients, children, students, workers. Rogers inspired his students and associates by hard work, conviction, intelligence, sensitivity and example. As a teacher, therapist and administrator, he was respectful, equalitarian, thoughtful, generous and unassuming. As a psychologist who was breaking new ground he confidently and skilfully debated with advocates of directive counselling, psychiatrists opposed to psychologists doing therapy and behaviourists who did not recognize the role of feelings or the concept of self. In his early forties he became the President of the American Psychological Association and later received that organization's highest scientific and professional awards.

Rogers' students and associates looked up to him and were aware that they belonged to a movement that was influencing traditional practices in a radical, even revolutionary, way. They were providing the building blocks of a new field of psychotherapy research, based on verbatim accounts of therapy cases, contributing to journals and publishing books. Programmes were organized at the annual conventions of the American Psychological Association. In 1948, for example, Rogers and some of his students organized a symposium on psychotherapy research and enlisted leaders from around the United States to lead small discussion groups on the subject. This was an entirely new concept in these national meetings. In 1949 an entire issue of the *Journal of Consulting Psychology* was devoted to a series of reports by Rogers and a group of students and staff making up the 'parallel studies' project, the first time a group of cases recorded verbatim were subjected to several different research analyses (Rogers et al., 1949). A strong *esprit de corps* has characterized the movement in the more than half-century of its history, during which time it has become more and

Originally published in W. Dryden (Ed.), *Developments in Psychotherapy: Historical perspectives,* (1996), (pp. 1–28). London: Sage. Reprinted with permission.

more an international phenomenon. It is this kind of atmosphere that has given impetus to the growth and development described in this chapter.

The birth of the movement

Several of the significant steps in the development of the Person-Centred Approach to psychotherapy were contained in the original formulation of the movement on 11 December 1940. On that date, towards the end of Rogers' first year as a psychology professor at Ohio State University, he addressed the University of Minnesota's chapter of Psi Chi, the national psychological honour society, on 'Some newer concepts of psychotherapy'. When, unexpectedly, the impact of the speech became clear, Rogers developed his ideas further into a book-length description of his approach entitled *Counseling and Psychotherapy* (Rogers, 1942). While he was presenting ideas and methods that were radically different, he gave credit to Otto Rank and some of his followers — Jessie Taft, Frederick Allen and Virginia Robinson — for supplying the roots of the newer concepts. The following are some of the historical steps contained in this early talk and book:

Step 1. *'Therapy is not a matter of doing something to the individual, or of inducing him to do something about himself. It is instead a matter of freeing him for normal growth and development, of removing obstacles so that he can again move forward'* (Rogers, 1942, p. 29).
The counselling programme at the University of Minnesota typified the prevalent concepts and practices of the time. These were based on gathering information through case histories and psychological tests and, on the basis of this data, guiding the client towards personal and vocational choices deemed by the counsellor to be appropriate and realistic.

In his talk, Rogers cited some of the techniques employed in this directive approach — ordering and forbidding, exhortation, suggestion, advice and intellectualised interpretation. Rogers quoted an advice-giving counsellor, who happened to be the programme chairman of the meeting he was addressing, describing his goal in working with a student: 'My job was to dissuade him from continuing in pre-business . . . I pointed out the competition in the professional School of Business . . . the courses in the . . . curriculum: statistics, finance, money and banking, theoretical economics . . . He finally agreed to think it over. I outlined a plan of action' (Rogers, 1942, p. 24).

Rogers emphasised that this way of trying to help people made the basic assumption that the counsellor knows best what the goals of the individual should be and he tries in various ways to get the client to achieve these goals. The goal of the newer approach was not to solve a problem; it was to promote the growth of the individual, to foster independence and integration so that the client would be able to solve not only this problem but future ones.

Step 2. *The newer approach stressed emotional or feeling aspects rather than intellectual elements, placed more emphasis upon the individual's immediate situation than upon the past, and valued the therapeutic relationship itself as a growth experience.*

Rogers gave the example of a student who says, in his first interview, 'I've always realized that my methods of study, my study habits, are wrong. I don't feel as though I am a very brilliant person but I don't think I am as stupid as my grades indicate.' The traditional counsellor, rather than communicating recognition of the student's feeling that he can do better, responds to an aspect of content in the student's statement: 'Well, how bad are your grades? I thought they were pretty good' (Rogers, 1942, p. 133). This approach can also lead to focusing on the past and helps to structure a relationship of distance between therapist and client because the therapist is setting himself up as knowing more. If the therapist had responded to the client's expressed feeling, he would be staying with the student in the present and contributing to a relationship of equalitarian understanding and closeness, a relationship which could make a contribution to the client's personal growth.

Step 3. *Implicit in the therapist's attention to the client's attitudes and feelings was the idea that the client's frame of reference, which came to be referred to as the IFR (internal frame of reference), was the therapist's basic consideration, rather than his own appraisal of what was going on.*

A few years later, in 1947, as outgoing president of the American Psychological Association, Rogers expressed the importance he attached to this point of view with some eloquence:

> Client-Centered Therapy has led us to try to adopt the client's perceptual field as the basis for genuine understanding. In trying to enter this internal world of perception . . . we find ourselves in a new vantage point for understanding personality dynamics . . . We find that behavior seems to be better understood as a reaction to this reality-as-perceived. We discover that the way in which the person sees himself, and the perceptions he dares not take as belonging to himself, seem to have an important relationship to the inner peace which constitutes adjustment. (Rogers, 1947, p. 368)

Step 4. *Rogers sought order in whatever he studied. In his 1940 talk and 1942 book, he described characteristic steps in the therapeutic process:*

'*The individual comes for help.*' It might be added, on his or her own initiative. The client might be influenced by a parent, teacher or friend, but it is a deterrent to the client-centred process if he or she does not accept the responsibility for continuing in therapy.

'*The helping situation is usually defined.*' The counsellor conveys in various ways that she does not have the answers but will try to help the client work out his own solutions. This might be done explicitly, but for the most part is done implicitly by the therapist's concrete behaviour, e.g., concentrating on conveying an understanding of whatever the client volunteers, the fact that the therapist does not take a case history or probe for information, the therapist handling the next appointment by making it clear that this is the client's decision.

'*The counselor encourages free expression of feelings in regard to the problem.*' These feelings may be positive or negative, loving or hostile, clear or ambivalent. The counsellor is open to all of these, although negative feelings and ambivalence tend to predominate at the beginning of counselling, e.g., a mother describing her adolescent son as impossible to influence, or a child using play therapy to get rid of his baby sister.

'*The counselor accepts, recognizes, and clarifies these negative feelings.*' By being fully accepting of negative feelings, the therapist helps to create an environment which facilitates the client's ability to accept such feelings as part of himself.

'*When the individual's negative feelings have been quite fully expressed, they are followed by the faint and tentative expressions of the positive impulses which make for growth.*' Rogers described this change in direction as 'one of the most certain and predictable aspects of the whole process. The more violent and deep the negative expressions (provided they are accepted and recognized), the more certain are the positive expressions of love, of social impulses, of fundamental self-respect, of desire to be mature' (Rogers, 1942, p. 39). He gives the example of a mother who, having experienced the acceptance of feelings toward her son of desperation, hopelessness, annoyance and despair over the course of more than one interview, states that there were times when the boy could be 'good as gold'.

'*The counselor accepts and recognizes the positive feelings which are expressed, in the same manner in which he has accepted and recognized the negative feelings.*' The counsellor does this without praise, just as the client's negative feelings are not met with disapproval. This encourages a free exploration of self and creates an optimal environment for the promotion of insight and self-acceptance.

'*This insight, this understanding of the self and acceptance of the self, is the next important aspect of the whole process.*' Rogers cites a graduate student who says with a great deal of feeling, 'I'm really just a spoiled brat, but I do want to be normal. I wouldn't let anyone else say that of me, but it's true' (1942, p. 40). The mother who has been very critical of her son says, 'Perhaps what would do him most good would be for him to have some affection and love and consideration entirely apart from any correcting' (ibid., p. 41).

'Intermingled with this process of insight — and it should again be emphasized that the steps outlined are not mutually exclusive, nor do they proceed in a rigid order — is a process of clarification of possible decisions, possible courses of action.' The counsellor communicates his or her understanding of the various options perceived by the client and his or her feelings (such as fear or uncertainty) about implementing them, but does not recommend particular choices or try to minimise any ambivalent feelings.

'Then comes one of the fascinating aspects of such therapy, the initiation of minute, but highly significant, positive actions.' Rogers gives the example of a very withdrawn secondary schoolboy who spends a whole session 'giving all the reasons why he would be too terrified to accept a social invitation', and leaves the office doubtful about going. The counsellor does not urge him, recognizing that he may not be able to take this step. The client goes to the party, which adds greatly to his self-confidence.

'There is . . . a development of further insight — more complete and accurate self-understanding as the individual gains courage to see more deeply into his own actions.'

'There is increasingly integrated positive action on the part of the client. There is less fear about making choices, and more confidence in self-directed action. The counselor and client are now working together in a new sense. The personal relationship between them is at its strongest. Very often the client wants for the first time to know something of the clinician as a person.'

'There is a feeling of decreasing need for help, and a recognition on the part of the client that the relationship must end.' The counsellor recognises and accepts these attitudes, neither urging the client to leave nor trying to prolong the therapy. The client may express personal feelings of closeness and appreciation, which the counsellor may reciprocate.

Again, Rogers points out that the steps he has outlined may vary. But he maintains his belief that the therapy he has described is an orderly and 'even a predictable process in its major outlines', one which applies to a variety of problems and situations — parents and children, marital counselling, difficult vocational choice and other individual conflicts — and a process which 'has sufficient unity to provide suitable hypotheses for experimental tests' (1942, pp. 44–5).

Step 5. *This last statement points to another significant step taken by Rogers, systematically following up the way therapy was practised with research done to confirm or deny the validity of the hypotheses on which the practice was based.* Rogers' 1942 book, *Counseling and Psychotherapy*, summarised research projects on phases of psychotherapy in the treatment of adolescent girls, on the relationship between some basic capacities of the individual and the effectiveness of counselling, and on the development of a measure to compare directive and nondirective counselling interviews. The latter was part of E. H. Porter Jr's 1941 PhD dissertation, 'The development and evaluation of a measure of counseling interview procedures', later summarized in a journal (Porter, 1943). Categorising the statements in nineteen phonographically recorded interviews, Porter unveiled sharp contrasts between directive and nondirective counselling approaches.

A number of other graduate students at Ohio State University made contributions to the investigation of client-centred hypotheses.

Bernard J. ('Bud') Covner was a student of Rogers in Rochester, New York and followed him to Ohio State University, where he was indispensable in setting up the technology for making sound recordings of interviews. Covner (1942, 1944a, 1944b) also documented, in his doctoral dissertation and in four published articles, the inadequacy of notes compared with electronic recording.

William U. Snyder (1945) studied client and counsellor data in nondirective therapy. He found that 'the nondirective therapist uses a clearly defined method of counseling and . . . that there is a predictable process of therapy for the client' (Seeman and Raskin, 1953). Gump, Curran, Raimy and other Ohio State students also carried out significant studies, many of which were summarised by Seeman and Raskin. These individual investigations were pioneering efforts in the establishment of the field of psychotherapy research. Later, at the University of Chicago and the University of Wisconsin, individual students and staff members worked on different aspects of the same data, so that the research became cooperative and programmatic.

Step 6. *Rogers believed in the importance of using verbatim recordings of interviews in conducting research on the process of counselling and psychotherapy.* In a radical departure from the usual abbreviated and subjective accounts of therapy, approximately 40 per cent of *Counseling and Psychotherapy* was made up of the word-for-word transcript of the eight-interview case of Herbert Bryan. Rogers summarised the feelings and attitudes expressed by the client in the first and last interviews and made dozens of observations throughout the course of treatment but, having access to the verbatim account, the reader was able independently to judge the validity of Rogers' conclusions.

Move to the University of Chicago
Following the attack on Pearl Harbor, the United States declared war on Japan in December 1941. Rogers was asked to serve as Director of Counseling Services for the United Services Organization. Part of his job was to set up training courses for volunteers which included basic counselling principles. During his year of service on this job, in 1944–5, he conducted workshops or gave talks and demonstrations to perhaps 5,000 workers. In the summer of 1944, Rogers had been a visiting professor at the University of Chicago. He greatly impressed Dean Ralph Tyler, who offered him the opportunity to establish a university counselling

centre, based on client-centred principles. Rogers accepted and he moved to Chicago during the summer of 1945, remaining there until 1957, when he accepted a position at the University of Wisconsin.

Several big steps were taken in the development of the client-centred approach during these years. Rogers' book, *Client-Centered Therapy,* published in 1951, documents these changes, and his Preface to the volume conveys their spirit:

> This book is about the suffering and the hope, the anxiety and the satisfaction, with which the therapist's counseling room is filled. It is about the uniqueness of the relationship each therapist forms with each client . . . This book is about the highly personal experiences of each one of us. It is about a client in my office who sits there by the corner of the desk, struggling to be himself, yet deathly afraid of being himself — striving to see his experience as it is, wanting to *be* that experience, and yet deeply fearful of the prospect. The book is about me, as I sit there with that client, facing him, participating in that struggle as deeply and as sensitively as I am able. It is about me as I try to perceive his experience, and the meaning and the feeling and the taste and the flavor that it has for him. It is about me as I bemoan my very human fallibility in understanding that client, and the occasional failures to see life as it appears to him, failures which fall like heavy objects across the intricate, delicate web of growth which is taking place. It is about me as I rejoice at the privilege of being a midwife to a new personality — as I stand by with awe at the emergence of a self, a person, as I see a birth process in which I have had an important and facilitating part. It is about both the client and me as we regard with wonder the potent and orderly forces which are evident in this whole experience, forces which seem deeply rooted in the universe as a whole. The book is, I believe, about life, as life vividly reveals itself in the therapeutic process — with its blind power and its tremendous capacity for destruction, but with its overbalancing thrust toward growth, if the opportunity for growth is provided . . . the book also expresses our growing conviction that though science can never make therapists, it can help therapy; that though the scientific finding is cold and abstract, it may assist us in releasing forces that are warm, personal, and complex; and that though science is slow and fumbling, it represents the best road we know to the truth, even in so delicately intricate an area as that of human relationships.

> Again the book is about these others and me as we go about our daily tasks and find ourselves compellingly influenced by the therapeutic experience of which we have been a part. It is about each of us as we try to teach, to lead groups, to consult with industry, to serve as administrators and supervisors, and find we can no longer function as we formerly did. It is about each of us as we try to face

up to the internal revolution which therapy has meant for us: the fact that we can never again teach a class, chair a committee, or raise a family without having our behavior profoundly influenced by a deep and moving experience which has elements of commonality for all of us. (Rogers, 1951a, pp. x–xi)

This deeply felt Preface signals the following four (Seven to Ten) significant steps in the history of this orientation:

Step 7. *Therapy is conceived as being more than a practical way of helping people; it has the potential to be a deeply moving experience for both client and therapist.* Rogers' Preface demonstrates powerfully the depth of the experience for the therapist. *Client-Centered Therapy* includes a long Chapter 3 (pp. 65–130) on 'The therapeutic relationship as experienced by the client'. Rogers cites the observations of a number of clients in their own words. Here is part of one woman's account written after the conclusion of therapy:

My memory of several interviews is so vivid that I have thought of them often since the final counseling session. I shall never forget the happiness, excitement, elation, and peak of self-satisfaction I felt during the first part of the seventh interview when I had just come from proving to myself that I could face in the presence of someone other than the counselor the feeling that had been with me for years; that everyone thought I had expressed homosexual tendencies. I felt that it was the first evidence of the fact that I could find out what I was apart from what people thought I was — or rather, apart from what I thought they thought I was. I remember how keenly I felt my own pleasure reflected in the eyes of the counselor whom I was looking at directly for the first time in any interview. That in itself was something I had wanted to do very much since the first hour. During this interview I thought for the first time of the end of counseling; before that I could not believe that anyone would willingly remove himself from such a safe, satisfying situation. (Rogers, 1951a, p. 84)

Step 8. *The client's struggle is conceptualised as going beyond the search for solutions to problems. It has to do with the struggle to be oneself, and to live one's experience.*
This represents a fundamental advance over the formulation of client progress contained in *Counseling and Psychotherapy* (1942), which was described in terms of gaining insight and taking actions to resolve problems with which the client began therapy or to redefine issues. *Client-Centered Therapy* (1951) puts forward in depth and detail, in theory and in practice, the idea that it is the modification of self-perception that represents the core change in psychotherapy. There were precursors. Rogers' (1931) doctoral dissertation, *Measuring personality adjustment*

in children nine to thirteen years of age, relied heavily on the child's conscious attitudes toward self. Victor Raimy completed a doctoral dissertation in 1943 at Ohio State University on 'Self-reference in counseling interviews'. Seeman and Raskin noted that 'the main significance in Raimy's study is probably not to be found in his empirical results' (which showed a shift from self-disapproval to self-approval in successful therapy) 'but rather in the comprehensive formulation of an important aspect of self-theory. Raimy focussed on learnings about the self as being the key type of learning in therapy' (1953, p. 209).

When Barrett-Lennard (1979, p. 184) summarised the development of self-theory in Client-Centred Therapy from the 1940s to the 1960s he wrote:

> The development of self-theory had begun with Raimy's dissertation and was first focused on by Rogers in an address he gave in 1947 — as retiring President of the American Psychological Association — under the title, *Some Observations on the Organization of Personality*. By 1948, Raskin was able to say that 'The client's concept of self is now believed to be the most central factor in his adjustment and perhaps the best measure of his progress in therapy.' Two articles, by Elizabeth Sheerer and by Dorothy Stock, in the 1949 'parallel studies' project focused directly on self-attitudes and feelings . . . Rogers' nineteen-proposition statement was a further order of development and established his school of therapy as a new source of an articulated, psychological perspective on human personality and nature.

Step 9. *Rogers put forward a nineteen-proposition theory of personality to accompany his theory of therapy.*

Barrett-Lennard was referring to the nineteen-proposition Theory of Personality and Behavior which constitutes Chapter 11 of *Client-Centered Therapy*. Most of the nineteen propositions are directly related to the self-concept. An example is Proposition IX: *'As a result of interaction with the environment, and particularly as a result of evaluational interaction with others, the structure of self is formed — an organized, fluid, but consistent conceptual pattern of perceptions of characteristics and relationships of the "I" or the "me", together with values attached to these concepts.'* It is through this kind of interaction that a child may conclude, 'I'm a bad boy'.

Proposition XVII shows how psychotherapy can facilitate the alteration of elements of the self-concept: *'Under certain conditions, involving primarily complete absence of any threat to the self-structure, experiences which are inconsistent with it may be perceived, and examined, and the structure of self revised to assimilate and include such experiences.'*

In his 1951 preface, Rogers writes of the client's struggle 'to be his experience'. He equates this with striving to be oneself. Later in the book, he gives the example of a client who can't believe people who say they are impressed with her intelligence, because her self-concept is so inferior. He describes another client with a strict moralistic upbringing who fights against the admission of his sexual cravings. As therapy proceeds, 'by means of the relationship and the counselor's handling of it, the client is gradually assured that he is accepted as he is, and that each new facet of himself which is revealed is also accepted' (Rogers, 1951a, p. 517); these inadmissible experiences can be taken in as part of an expanded and positive self-concept.

Step 10. *Rogers sees the growth force in the client as rooted in a drive for order in the universe.*
This idea was mentioned by Rogers in his Preface to *Client-Centered Therapy,* but was not developed in the main text of the book. In 1952 he participated in a conference on creativity at Ohio State University and later expanded his remarks into a paper which included the following: 'The mainspring of creativity appears to be the same tendency which we discover so deeply as the curative force in psychotherapy — *man's tendency to actualize himself, to become his potentialities.* By this I mean the directional trend which is evident in all organic and human life — the urge to expand, extend, develop, mature — the tendency to express and activate all the capacities of the organism, or the self' (Rogers, 1961, pp. 350–1). The topic was taken up by him again in a 1963 paper on motivation, was stimulated by a conference on humanistic psychology in the early 1970s, and then articulated in a 1978 article on 'The formative tendency'. In *A Way of Being* (1980), Rogers cites the impact of other disciplines on his thinking, expressing a special indebtedness to the biologist Albert Szent-Gyoergyi, and Lancelot Whyte, a historian of ideas. He concludes:

> Thus, without ignoring the tendency toward deterioration, we need to recognize fully what Szent-Gyoergyi terms 'syntropy' and what Whyte calls the 'morphic tendency', the ever operating trend toward increased order and interrelated complexity evident at both the inorganic and the organic level. The universe is always building and creating as well as deteriorating. This process is evident in the human being, too. (1980, p. 126)

Step 11. *The therapist's empathy for the client is seen as an absorbing struggle to appreciate the client's perceptions and feelings with as much depth and sensitivity as possible.*
When I was a developing therapist, the endeavour to be empathic was very meaningful to me and I wrote a paper on 'The nondirective attitude', from which Rogers quoted in *Client-Centered Therapy:*

> There is [another] level of nondirective counselor response which to the writer represents *the* nondirective attitude. In a sense, it is a goal rather than one which is actually practiced by counselors, But, in the experience of some, it is a highly attainable goal, which . . . changes the nature of the counseling process in a radical way. At this level, counselor participation becomes an active experiencing

> with the client of the feelings to which he gives expression, the
> counselor makes a maximum effort to get under the skin of the person
> with whom he is communicating, he tries to get *within* and to live
> the attitudes expressed instead of observing them, to catch every
> nuance of their changing nature; in a word, to absorb himself
> completely in the attitudes of the other. And in struggling to do this,
> there is simply no room for any other type of counselor activity or
> attitude; if he is attempting to live the attitudes of the other, he cannot
> be diagnosing them, he cannot be thinking of making the process
> go faster. Because he is another, and not the client, the understanding
> is not spontaneous but must be acquired, and this through the most
> intense, continuous and active attention to the feelings of the other,
> to the exclusion of any other type of attention. (Rogers, 1951a, p. 29)

Rogers points out that what is intended is immersion in an empathic process without
the counsellor experiencing the same emotions as the client.

Although the term was not used in *Counseling and Psychotherapy* (Rogers,
1942), empathy has been a core concept throughout the history of this approach.
Rogers summarised empathy theory, practice and research in a paper which became
Chapter 7, 'Empathic: an unappreciated way of being' in *A Way of Being* (1980,
pp. 137–63).

Step 12. *Client-centred principles were applied to the classroom, to the workplace,
to administration, to group therapy, and to play therapy, in effect constructing a
person-centred approach to areas of human relations outside of individual
counselling and psychotherapy, even though the phrase 'person-centred approach'
was not yet being used in 1951.*
At Ohio State University in the early 1940s, the client-centred approach was
employed just for one-to-one counselling. Rogers seemed interested in what worked
in that context. In his preface to *Counseling and Psychotherapy,* he stated his
conviction that 'counseling may be a knowable, predictable, understandable process,
a process which can be learned, tested, refined, and improved' (1942, p. ix). He
exhibited no interest in possible applications or implications of the nondirective
approach, and gave the impression of being aphilosophical and apolitical. By
contrast, some years later, he wrote of his teaching at the University of Chicago:

> I ceased to be a teacher. It wasn't easy. It happened rather gradually,
> but as I began to trust students, I found they did incredible things in
> their communication with each other, in their learning of content
> material in the course, in blossoming out as growing human beings.
> Most of all they gave me courage to be myself more freely, and this
> led to profound interaction. They told me their feelings, they raised
> questions I had never thought about. I began to sparkle with emerging
> ideas that were new and exciting to me, but also, I found, to them. I
> believe I passed some sort of crucial divide when I was able to

begin a course with a statement something like this: 'This course has the title "Personality Theory" (or whatever). But what we do with this course is up to us. We can build it around the goals we want to achieve, within that very general area. We can conduct it the way we want to. We can decide mutually how to handle those bugaboos of exams and grades. I have many resources on tap, and I can help you find others. I believe I am one of the resources, and I am available to you to the extent that you wish. But this is our class. So what do we want to make of it?' This kind of statement said in effect, 'We are free to learn what we wish, *as* we wish.' It made the whole climate of the classroom completely different. Though at the time I had never thought of phrasing it this way, I changed at that point from being a teacher and evaluator, to being a facilitator of learning — a very different occupation. (1983, p. 26)

I was a student in Rogers' 'Personality Theory' class and other courses at Chicago. At first, I did not like having the responsibility for my learning shifted to me. But it did not take long for this to make sense to me. Soon after, I became a college teacher myself, and was a student-centred educator for about forty years, substituting student-chosen tasks for assignments and examinations, and using self-evaluation as the basis for grades. I learned that I could trust students as I did clients, and my educational career has been as gratifying and as validating of the Person-Centred Approach as my work as a therapist.

Step 13. *The therapist was seen as participating as a whole person in the therapeutic relationship.*
In an address at the Menninger Clinic in 1946, Rogers had stated, 'Client-centered counseling, if it is to be effective, cannot be a trick or a tool. It is not a subtle way of guiding the client while pretending to let him guide himself. To be effective, it must be genuine.' In the early 1950s, two graduate students and Counseling Center staff members, Oliver Bown and Eugene Streich, and Rogers himself, went further and described the therapist as entering into the relationship in a much more full and personal manner (Raskin, 1952, pp. 240–1).

Streich (1951) put it this way:
When the therapist's capacity for awareness is thus functioning freely and fully without limitations imposed by theoretical formulations of his role, we find that we have, not a person who must follow certain procedures, but a person able to achieve, through the remarkable integrative capacity of his central nervous system, a balanced, therapeutic, self-growing, other growth-facilitating behavior as a result of all of these elements of awareness.

Oliver Bown, who died in July 1995, was bolder than other members of the Counseling Center staff half a century ago, believing that the term 'love' was the most useful 'to describe a basic ingredient of the therapeutic relationship'.

I [Bown] use this term purposely to convey a number of things:

First, that as therapist I can allow a very strong feeling or emotion of my own to enter the therapeutic relationship, and expect that the handling of this feeling from me by the client will be an important part of the therapy for him.

Secondly, that a very basic need of the therapist can be satisfied legitimately (or I would rather say *must* be satisfied, if the relationship is to be healthy and legitimate) in his relationship with his client.

And, thirdly, the therapeutic interaction at this emotional level, rather than therapeutic interaction at an intellectual cognitive level, regardless of the content concerned, is the effective ingredient in therapeutic growth.

This was quoted by Rogers in *Client-Centered Therapy* (1951a, p. 160). He thought so much of Bown's views that he devoted eleven pages of the book to quoting them. Rogers himself strongly supported the concept of the therapist being involved as a person in the therapeutic relationship:

Shall we view this individual [the client] as a complex and as yet unresolved equation, or shall we enter into a warm, personal, human relationship with him, a relationship meaningful to ourselves as well as to the client? Do we gain our personal satisfaction from the correct understanding and manipulation of a complex set of factors in the case, or from the experience of relating to another individual in a deeply personal way? (1951b, p. 171)

Step 14. *William Stephenson's Q-technique was adopted as a methodology to measure the client's perceived self, ideal self, and the quantitative correspondence between the two, as therapy progressed. Other techniques were employed, such as using the clients as their own controls, in a waiting period prior to therapy, to achieve a state-of-the-art methodology for research on therapy process and outcome.*

In the early 1950s a grant obtained by the Rockefeller Foundation allowed Rogers and his associates at the University of Chicago Counseling Center to set a new standard of sophistication for investigating psychotherapy process and outcome (Rogers and Dymond, 1954). When the results were published, they stimulated a wealth of other projects, within and outside of the client-centred orientation.

Stephenson, a British psychologist, was on the University of Chicago faculty at the time. When Rogers learned, from a graduate student, about the Q-technique as a way of quantifying self-concept, he was thrilled. The client sorted 100 statements such as 'I am a submissive person' and 'I am afraid of what other people think of me' into nine piles ranging from 'most characteristic of me' to 'least characteristic'. The number of cards permitted to go in each pile was fixed so that the frequencies approximated a normal distribution. Each time the client did a self-sort, another one was obtained for self-ideal. This was done prior to, at the beginning of, during, at the end, and at some point after therapy. Some of the findings were that:

- perceived self changes more during therapy than during a period of no therapy and more than for control subjects;
- there is a significant increase in congruence between perceived self and ideal self, associated with therapy;
- after therapy, clients see themselves as more self-confident, understanding themselves better, experiencing more inner comfort, having better relationships with others, being less driven, and having less need to hide aspects of self;
- with therapy, perceived self changes much more than ideal self, while ideal self becomes more attainable.

Step 15. *Growth in the client was seen as going beyond increased self-esteem and involving openness to experience and the willingness to be engaged in a process of becoming.*
Following the large-scale quantitative study of client perceptions of self carried out at the University of Chicago in the early 1950s, Rogers immersed himself in an intensive qualitative study of client transcripts and came out with a formulation on 'What it means to become a person', which included this cluster of concepts:

The experiencing of feeling
The discovery of self in experience
Openness to experience
Trust in one's organism
An internal locus of evaluation
Willingness to be a process (Rogers 1961, pp. 107–24)

Taken together, these concepts mean that the person is constantly evolving, taking in what happens as he or she interacts with people, and can make mistakes without general devaluation. There is an immersion of self in whatever is going on and less concern with the evaluation of others, consequently greater enjoyment of interaction with others, and more possibility of learning and growing. These ideas were contained in a talk given in 1954 by Rogers at Oberlin College in Ohio.

In 1957, after twelve years at the University of Chicago, Rogers accepted a position as a professor of both psychology and psychiatry at the University of Wisconsin, which he and his wife, Helen, had attended as undergraduates. 'Openness to experiencing' became the central concept in assessing client progress in the University of Wisconsin project which applied the Person-Centred Approach to a schizophrenic population. The focus was on 'the degree to which the client is open to his feelings, able to own them, and to explore them in search of their personal meaning' (Rogers et al., 1967, p. 74).

Step 16. *Rogers formulated the 'necessary and sufficient conditions of therapeutic personality change' (1957).*
There is probably nothing for which Rogers is better known than the triad of therapist-offered conditions of empathy, congruence and unconditional positive regard. Just as his very clear formulation of the client-centred approach had provided a basis for research, debate and discussion by therapists of diverse orientations, his 'necessary and sufficient conditions', a challenging set of concepts which were also carefully defined and capable of quantification, have stimulated hundreds of articles, convention programmes and research projects by theorists and practitioners of many different persuasions. Barrett-Lennard's Relationship Inventory, one of the instruments designed to measure these conditions, somewhat modified, has been used in hundreds of research projects, not just in the context of psychotherapy, but in parent-child, student-teacher, worker-employer, and other human relations applications (Barrett-Lennard, 1986).

Step 17. *Rogers (1959) wrote 'A theory of therapy, personality, and interpersonal relationships, as developed in the client centered framework' for Sigmund Koch's 'Psychology: A Study of a Science'.*
This was the most rigorous exposition of Rogers' theories. In a diagrammatical representation of his formulation, 'A Theory of Therapy' is shown at the centre, with four other sets of theories surrounding the central theory on four sides and growing out of it. These are 'A Theory of Interpersonal Relationships', 'A Theory of Personality', 'A Theory of the Fully Functioning Person', and 'Theoretical Implications for Various Human Activities'. These include Family Life, Education and Learning, Group Leadership, and Group Conflict. This cluster of applications demonstrates the importance Rogers attached to the implications of the core principles of Client-Centred Therapy and foretold the direction of his efforts during the remainder of his life, which ended in February 1987.

Move to California
After spending a total of twenty-three years at three major American universities (Ohio State 1940–44; Chicago, 1945–57; and Wisconsin, 1957–63) Rogers, a youthful sixty-one years of age, finally accepted the standing invitation of Richard Farson, who had been a student in Chicago, to join him at the Western Behavioral Sciences Institute (WBSI) in La Jolla, California. The institute was a non-profit organisation devoted to humanistically oriented research in interpersonal relationships, and to facilitating constructive changes in these relationships. The inducement was freedom, and Rogers had been feeling quite constrained in academia. Kirschenbaum (1979, pp. 316–17), in his important biography, *On Becoming Carl Rogers,* quotes Carl's second thoughts after rejecting still another invitation from Farson:

> What was a university, at this stage of my career, offering me? I realized that in my research it offered no particular help; in anything educational, I was forced to fit my beliefs into a totally alien mode;

in stimulation, there was little from my colleagues because we were so far apart in thinking and in goals. On the other hand, WBSI offered complete freedom with no bureaucratic entanglements . . . the opportunity to facilitate learning without becoming entrapped in the anti-educational jungle of credits, requirements, examinations, and . . . degrees.

In a letter addressed to friends, Rogers added:
It offers the complete and untrammeled freedom for creative thought of which every scholar dreams . . . It means freedom from all routine responsibilities — committees, department meetings, budgets, requisitions, and the like. It fits my desire . . . to devote myself more to study, thinking, stimulating personal interactions, a modest amount of group or individual therapy, and writing . . .

In the Institute we will also have the opportunity of approaching the whole problem of professional education (and perhaps education more broadly) from newer perspectives. Thus, personal experiential learning, as it is being developed in workshops, group dynamics labs and such, can be tried out experimentally . . . in a climate in which individuals are not subjected to the inhibiting effects of exams, grades, and degrees, which are so irrelevant to this type of learning. It should be an opportunity to develop a truly *integrated* professional learning, in which the cognitive and the affective are interwoven.

One of Rogers' last projects at Wisconsin was a week-long psychotherapy workshop in July 1963 in which 'the cognitive and the affective' were truly interwoven. The workshop represented a transition from the quantitative study of individual psychotherapy which had absorbed so much of Rogers' time and energy towards immersion in a group process, evaluated largely by the participants in their own terms.

Step 18. *Rogers made group experiences and educational reform his primary foci.*
In the foreword to *Carl Rogers on Encounter Groups* (1970, p. v), Rogers wrote:
For more than thirty-five years, individual counseling and psychotherapy were the main focus of my professional life. But nearly thirty-five years ago I also experienced the potency of the changes in attitudes and behavior which could be achieved in a group. This has been an interest of mine ever since. However, only in the past seven or eight years has it become one of the two primary foci of my work — the other being the crucial need for greater freedom in our educational institutions.

Rogers felt very strongly about the stultifying effects of traditional methods of education, with its top-down orientation. He was directly involved in efforts to transform two entire school systems, and published two editions of *Freedom to Learn* (1969, 1983). The first edition included a paper, 'Current assumptions in graduate education: a passionate statement', which had been rejected by the *American Psychologist* as being too controversial and potentially divisive! The second edition of the book, *Freedom to Learn for the '80s,* included a description of attempts to use person-centred principles to bring about changes in a number of educational organisations, including an inner city school system and a big city parochial complex. Rogers described himself as an active observer in the first and as one of a large group of facilitators from the Center for Studies of the Person in the second experiment.

In his 'passionate' paper on graduate education, Rogers was critical of the passive nature of the learning process, the emphasis on evaluation, the prevalence of orthodoxy and the lack of encouragement of creativity. With regard to the experiments in changing educational organisations, Rogers wrote in most detail about the two projects in which he had been most directly involved. He described his efforts and the others involved in a total of six undertakings as having short-lived success, offering this explanation of the disappointing results:

> When an organization is truly democratic, when persons are trusted and empowered to act freely and responsibly, this poses an enormous threat to conventional institutions. Our culture does not as yet believe in democracy. Almost without exception the 'establishment' — and the people — believe in a pyramidal form of organization, with a leader at the top, who controls his or her subordinates, who in turn control those further down the line. When some form of organization, other than authoritarian, flourishes and succeeds, it challenges a way of being that is deeply rooted in our society (1983, p. 245).

The general encounter group movement had considerably greater success than the educational experiments. In this book, characteristically, Rogers looked for order in the phenomenon he was observing. Some of the steps he distinguished in intensive groups were:

- milling around
- resistance to personal expression or exploration
- description of past feelings
- expression of immediate interpersonal feelings in the group
- the development of a healing capacity in the group
- self-acceptance and the beginning of change
- the expression of positive feelings and closeness
- behaviour changes in the group

Rogers often wrote in a personal style. But Chapter 3 of *Carl Rogers on Encounter Groups,* 'Can I be a facilitative person in a group?' is unusually frank and self-disclosing. He writes that he delayed for more than a year in producing it, because he backed away from writing a homogenised chapter on 'The facilitation of encounter groups', or even one on 'My way of facilitating a group', because that still had the ring of an expert. He wanted to express his strengths, his weaknesses and his uncertainties, and the fact that he was involved in an ongoing process that could best be captured in a question.

Rogers states that, while his basic philosophy in a group does not differ from what it had been for years in individual therapy:

> . . . my behavior is often quite different in a group from what it used
> to be in a one-to-one relationship. I attribute this to the personal growth
> experienced in groups . . . My hope is gradually to become as much a
> participant in the group as a facilitator. This is difficult to describe
> without making it appear that I am consciously playing two different
> roles. If you watch a group member who is honestly being himself,
> you will see that at times he expresses feelings, attitudes, and thoughts
> primarily directed toward facilitating the growth of another member.
> At other times, with equal genuineness, he will express feelings or
> concerns which have as their obvious goal the opening of himself to
> the risk of more growth. This describes me too, except that I know I
> am likely to be the second, or risking, kind of person more often in
> the later than in the earlier phases of the group. Each facet is a real
> part of me, not a role (1970, pp. 45–6).

Listening remains vital to Rogers in the group situation:

> I listen as carefully, accurately, and sensitively as I am able, to each
> individual who expresses himself. Whether the utterance is
> superficial or significant, I *listen.* To me the individual who speaks
> is worthwhile, worth understanding . . . I wish very much to make
> the climate psychologically safe for the individual. I want him to
> feel from the first that if he risks saying something highly personal,
> or absurd, or hostile, or cynical, there will be at least one person in
> the circle who respects him enough to hear him clearly and listen to
> that statement as an authentic expression of himself . . . I would like
> the individual to feel that whatever happens *to* him or *within* him, I
> will be psychologically very much *with* him in moments of pain or
> joy . . . I think I can usually sense when a participant is frightened
> or hurting, and it is at those moments that I give him some sign,
> verbal or nonverbal, that I perceive this and am a companion to him
> as he lives in that hurt or fear. (1970, pp. 47–8)

Later, Rogers declares that 'my attempt to understand the exact meaning of what the person is communicating is the most important and most frequent of my behaviors in a group' (ibid., p. 51). He also felt more free to express himself as a person in the group situation:

I have learned to be more and more free in making use of my own feelings as they exist in the moment, whether in relation to the group as a whole, or to one individual, or to myself . . . I trust the feelings, words, impulses, fantasies, that emerge in me. In this way I am using more than my conscious self, drawing on some of the capacities of my whole organism. For example, 'I suddenly had the fantasy that you are a princess, and that you would love it if we were all your subjects' (ibid., pp. 52–3).

This trust in self articulated by Rogers looks like a good example of historical Step 13 above: 'The therapist was seen as participating as a whole person in the therapeutic relationship', with supporting statements by Streich, Bown, and Rogers himself in the context of the individual therapy situation. Twenty years later, with the move to California, and as a facilitator of groups, he was able to live the principle more fully.

Step 19. *The concept of the 'person'.*
A number of the historical steps described above have dealt with the concept of self — its use in theory, practice and research. Steps 8, 9, 14 and 15 begin with work done in the 1940s in which self-concept was deemed the most central construct for understanding clients. The concept occupied a substantial part of Rogers' nineteen-proposition Theory of Personality, and embraced a large body of quantitative research, much of it utilising William Stephenson's Q-sort.

Step 15 marks a very significant development. It stemmed from Rogers putting aside the statistical data on self-concept and self-ideal and immersing himself in a qualitative study of client transcripts. The resulting formulation and talk at Oberlin College in 1954 were called 'What it means to become a person', and included a group of concepts which focused on a self becoming actualised, by reason of being increasingly open to the individual's experience of self and others, and trusting that experience. There was an image of an individual who is constantly evolving, taking in what happens as he or she interacts with people, who is able to make mistakes without self-disparagement. There is an immersion of self in whatever is going on and less concern with achievement and the evaluation of others.

A journal article by Rogers published in 1964, 'Toward a modern approach to values: the valuing process in the mature person', clarifies the link between the concepts of self and of person (the article was reproduced in *New Directions in Client-Centered Therapy,* 1970, edited by Hart and Tomlinson): The 'person' is an individual who is growing significantly in the ability to be more truly himself by virtue of changes in his value system. Rogers sees a 'surprising commonality' in the value directions of maturing clients:
- they tend to move away from facades . . .
- they tend to move away from 'oughts . . .'
- they tend to move away from meeting the expectations of others. . .
- being real is positively valued . . .

- self-direction is positively valued . . .
- one's self, one's own feelings come to be positively valued . . .
- being a process [rather than desiring some fixed goal] is positively valued . . .
- sensitivity to others and acceptance of others is positively valued . . .
- deep relationships are positively valued . . .
- perhaps more than all else, the client comes to value an openness to all of his inner and outer experience . . . (Rogers, 1964, pp. 165–6).

The concept of 'person' connotes both an individual who deserves respect and who, being more fully realized, is more interested in and able to contribute to others. In 1978 I summarised some of the ways the Person-Centred Approach had given meaning to the concept of the 'person':

A person should be listened to, sensitively, respectfully.

A person merits a unique kind of respect regardless of age, degree of intelligence, or social status . . .

A person has strength, great capacities which can be loosed if he or she experiences empathy in a non-possessive, caring, and genuine relationship.

A person has choices which can represent increasingly the expression of her own unique self and which deserve to be supported.

Each person can be a rich source of experience for himself and others.

Each person has the potential to be a powerful social influence. (Raskin, 1978)

When Rogers wrote about 'the person' it was usually in the context of 'the emerging person' or 'the person of tomorrow'. In *A Way of Being* he lists the qualities of the 'person of tomorrow':

- openness
- desire for authenticity
- skepticism regarding science and technology
- desire for wholeness
- the wish for intimacy
- process persons
- caring
- attitude toward nature
- anti-institutional
- the authority within
- the unimportance of material things
- a yearning for the spiritual (1980, pp. 350–2)

Julius Seeman built a distinguished professional career for well over a quarter of a century investigating personality integration. In addition to carrying out his own research, often in collaboration with associates and graduate students, he studied a variety of sources, not restricting himself to investigators identified with the Person-Centred Approach. He drew upon the work of Heinz Hartmann, Erik Erikson, Jane Loevinger, Marie Jahoda, Brewster Smith, Robert White and many others. His review of the literature and of his own research led him to an affirmation of 'the congruence between Rogers' original formulation [of the fully functioning person] and the subsequent empirical inquiry'. Consistent with Rogers' thinking, Seeman found that high-functioning persons are healthier, are more efficient in their perception of reality, have superior environmental contact, a high degree of self-esteem, confidence and trust in themselves, and possess a sense of autonomy that facilitates the development of caring and generative relationships (Seeman, 1984, pp. 150–2).

Step 20. *The concept of community.*
Just as the concept of self expedited the development of the concept of the person, the latter stimulated ideas about community in the Person-Centred Approach. The person, or fully functioning person, is seen as someone who cares about others, is interested in close relationships and values open, experiential process. A natural result is a community with shared interests and values.

The term or concept of community is used in at least six different ways in the person-centred movement:
- At a particular workshop or conference, there may be fifty, a hundred, or several hundred individuals who have come together for the weekend, a week, or some other time span. In addition to the specific activities (individual presentations, panels, small group meetings, meetings of the entire group), there is *the possibility of the group as a whole developing a sense of community during the course of the workshop or conference.* At person-centred meetings, many or most of the participants would have that expectation. Some would have more individual and discrete goals.
- As part of most person-centred meetings, provision is made for times when all the participants meet with no agenda and can use the time in any way they wish. Typically, these would be daily meetings lasting one or two hours. These are called *community meetings,* and while they are often felt to be terribly frustrating, they continue to be valued as unique opportunities to create experiences or communities of the group's own design.
- *There are certain shared values regarding the organization of person-centred activities.* For example, the Association for the Development of the Person-Centered Approach has functioned for many years with no officers or elections. Different individuals volunteer to take the responsibility for future conferences, organisation membership, the journal, the newsletter, etc. Any conflicts are negotiated. At most conferences, there is an assumption that the schedule may be altered, a participant may volunteer a presentation that is not in the programme, a new interest group may spring up, and so on. This is an aspect of person-centred community that has to do with organisation.

- Barrett-Lennard (1994) has advanced a set of propositions on a *person-centred theory of community,* drawing upon a variety of sources, including questionnaire data collected after his participation in a 136-person, 16-day person-centred workshop led by Rogers and eight associates in August 1975.
- Personal relationships in the movement have developed over the course of years, stemming mostly from individuals getting to know each other in different conferences and training programmes, such as cross-cultural workshops starting in 1972, six international forums on the Person-Centred Approach, three international conferences on client-centred and experiential psychotherapy, a series of Latin American conferences, annual meetings of the Association for the Development of the Person-Centered Approach since 1986, and a large number of training programmes in the Person-Centred Approach in Eastern and Western Europe. These relationships have been furthered by collaboration on an article or programme, the discovery of a shared interest (e.g. poetry, children, music), visits to one another's homes, an email network which started with five people in 1993 and exceeds 100 in 1996, with participants from Australia, Austria, Belgium, Brazil, Bulgaria, Canada, Denmark, England, Greece, Holland, Hungary, Italy, Japan, Mexico, Norway, Portugal, Russia, South Africa and Switzerland. Another important international stimulus has been the publications of people in the movement, particularly Carl Rogers. The result of this variety of activities and interactions is *a growing international person-centred community, with relationships that increase in breadth and depth, professionally and personally.*
- A discussion of the international aspects of the person-centred community must include the special area of *peace and conflict resolution,* Rogers' most passionate interest in his last years. In the autumn of 1986, a few months before his death, he and Ruth Sanford led highly successful workshops and large meetings in Moscow and Tbilisi, and were preparing for a third trip to South Africa, which was undertaken by Ruth Sanford in the summer of 1995.

  Searching for peaceful ways to resolve conflict between larger groups became the cutting edge of the person-centered movement in the 1980s . . . In some instances opposing groups have met in an intensive format with person-centered leadership. This has occurred with parties from Northern Ireland, South Africa, and Central America . . . One notion is central to all these attempts at peaceful conflict resolution: When a group in conflict can receive and operate under conditions of empathy, genuineness, and caring, negative stereotypes of the opposition weaken and are replaced by personal, human feelings of relatedness. (Raskin and Rogers, 1995, pp. 153–4)

An example is a weekend-long meeting of a group of four Roman Catholics and five Protestants from Northern Ireland facilitated by Rogers, Patrick Rice and

Audrey McGaw. The early interaction was characterised by argumentative discussion of who was to blame for the violence, with different participants pointing their fingers at the wealthy class, the working class or the British Army. Then Tom recounted an incident in which his sister had been blown to bits in a street altercation and, grief-stricken himself, he had the task of informing his son of his aunt's death and then his parents of their daughter's death. 'No, it wasn't . . . it was Margaret'. Margaret had been an especially dear member of her family. This story, told with great emotion, had the effect of transforming the group's interaction into an exchange of deeply felt fears, concerns and events, and resulted in the development of warm relationships among the participants lasting well beyond the weekend meeting. (This experience has become available as an hour-long videotape entitled *The Steel Shutter,* an expression which originated with a young teacher in the group who was describing his need to find a way to keep overwhelming emotions from interfering with his daily functioning.) (McGaw et al., 1973).

The Person-Centred Approach as a movement
In 1990 I tried to take stock of the first fifty years of the Person-Centred Approach, particularly in the United States (Raskin, 1990). I was of the opinion that, in the context of American academic and professional psychology, 'we are in a weak position. Compared to behavioral and psychoanalytic psychology, we have few adherents. We have hardly any doctoral training programs that allow a significant concentration in Client-Centered Therapy and the Person-Centered Approach. We have very little presence at general national meetings of psychologists. We are struggling to maintain a journal.' I went on to describe some positive aspects:

- The orientation is generally included in textbooks on theories of personality and approaches to psychotherapy.
- The concepts of self, self-image and self-esteem, which the movement developed in a seminal way, are in common usage.
- Programmes based on empathic listening and respect for the individual such as peer counselling and 'hotlines' for people in crisis are widespread.
- A large number of person-centred psychotherapists and educators have been successful and have won the respect of colleagues with other orientations.

I tried to account for the weakened position of the movement in the United States:

- Rogers' move from academia in 1964, and his distinctive position as a writer, leader, innovator and integrator, in relationship to other leaders of the person-centred approach who remained in university settings but did not have the same impact;
- the clarity, practicality and immediate usefulness of the techniques and research methodology of Client-Centred Therapy in the 1940s and 1950s, affecting clinical practice and the stimulation of large numbers of doctoral dissertations;

- changes in values in recent years, causing psychotherapy and other fields to become more task-oriented and mechanised.

While the academic and professional position of Client-Centred Therapy has declined in the United States, the same has not been true in other parts of the world. International meetings in this orientation attract significantly greater numbers than conferences in the United States. For many years, Charles Devonshire and Alberto Zucconi have had great success in organising person-centred training programmes in Italy and other European countries. In recent years Devonshire has helped initiate new courses in Eastern Europe and his annual cross-cultural workshops, started in 1970, have been meeting in that part of the world and continue to be extremely well attended.

In personal communications, Brian Thorne and Dave Mearns have pointed out that there are 'flourishing person-centred associations in Holland, Belgium, Austria, and Switzerland', that there is a 'huge number of client-centred therapists in Germany' and that the approach is 'gaining ground in France, Greece, and Portugal'. They also cite the stronger position of the movement in European universities, such as Hamburg, Leuven, Vienna, the University of East Anglia in England, and Strathclyde University in Scotland. Thorne (1992) and Mearns (1994) are themselves responsible for training programmes at the latter two institutions and have made important contributions to the literature on the Person-Centred Approach.

These advances in European academic and research activity are confounded by the tendency to make this orientation part of a more inclusive category, 'experiential psychotherapies'. Greenberg, Elliot and Lietaer (1994, p. 510) write: 'Advocates of the experiential approaches emphasize the importance of active, process-directive intervention procedures oriented toward deepening experience within the context of a person-centered relationship. This implies that the relationship may not be sufficient for change.'

A directive dimension also characterises the work of four Americans associated with the person-centred orientation who have had a major international impact:

- 'A felt shift' is a term for the bodily change and sense of release that accompanies the sudden new understanding of a previously unclear feeling (Gendlin, 1978).
- Tom Gordon's Effectiveness Training programs for parents, teachers and industrial managers are international in scope. Over a million parents enrolled in workshops since their inception in 1962 and more than 3.5 million books on parent effectiveness training have been sold. Effectiveness training programs have the purpose of teaching specific skills of listening and conflict resolution in various settings.
- Natalie Rogers' Person Centered Expressive Therapy Institute, based in California, also conducts programmes in other parts of the United States and in Russia, Greece, England, Mexico, Canada, and many other countries. Natalie (Rogers, 1995, p. 207) describes 'rebelling against sitting and *talking* about life experiences and . . . *extending* the person-centered process to

include the whole body and expression through the arts'. She describes the invention by herself and her associates of art projects, improvisations, guided visualizations and music to enact rage, grief, sorrow and celebration, and she has conceptualised a Creative Connection Process which makes use of different art forms to release layers of inhibitions leading to a sense of oneness.

- Garry Prouty of Chicago is well known in Europe for his pre-therapy work with difficult populations. He describes pre-therapy as a theory and methodology designed to develop or restore the reality, affective and communicative functions necessary for therapeutics with the psychotic/ retarded or chronic schizophrenic clients. It theoretically expands Rogers' contention that client and therapist need to be in psychological contact as the first necessary condition of a therapeutic relationship (Prouty, 1990). The techniques of contact reflections, contact functions and contact behaviours are utilised to achieve therapeutic readiness.

The introduction by Gendlin, Gordon, Natalie Rogers and Garry Prouty of systematic direction in their work raises an issue which divides adherents of the Person-Centred Approach. This is true even though the interventions do not force any particular idea, feeling or action on their students or clients, and even though their purpose is to further some goal which is seen as a desirable outcome of client-centred work, such as heightened awareness, increased empathy, greater creativity and readiness for therapy. While these innovators believe they are being consistent with client-centred ideology and that they are furthering a person-centred process, other students of the approach are of the opinion that they do violence to basic person-centred tenets. Barbara Brodley (1995), Jerold Bozarth (1992), Tony Merry (1988), Ruth Sanford (1996), John Shlien (1967) and others argue with conviction that the belief in the client's capacities articulated with great eloquence by Rogers and others rules out intentional and systematic direction, strategies of confrontation or the devising of special methods for dealing with clients based on diagnostic or psychopathological assessment. Without accepting uncritically Rogers' own formulations such as the 'necessary and sufficient conditions', these individuals have done much to clarify and to shore up the importance of concepts like empathy with the client's world and self-actualisation. Fred Zimring (1995) is a scientist-clinician who has creatively rethought and researched the therapy process using cognitive and experiential concepts without introducing therapist direction into the practice of therapy. C. H. Patterson (1984) has made important contributions towards validating the Person-Centred Approach as a unique orientation.

The very first historical step articulated in this chapter was: 'Therapy is not a matter of doing something to the individual, or of inducing him to do something about himself. It is instead a matter of freeing him for normal growth and development, of removing obstacles so that he can again move forward' (Rogers, 1942, p. 29). While it has also been brought out here that Rogers himself became more free in his behaviour as a therapist or group facilitator, this activity did not take the form of systematic direction.

At the same time he made it clear that he was put off by the notion of creating 'little Rogerians'. He had great respect for those of his students and colleagues who departed from the client-centred approach in some form or other because of what made sense in their own experience. Many of them did, starting with William U. Snyder and Victor Raimy, Ohio State University students who made outstanding contributions to client-centred theory and research and who later became 'rational therapists', and continuing into his California period where, for example, collaborators Maureen Miller O'Hara and Betty Meador embraced the Gestalt and Jungian schools, respectively.

Other individuals like Bohart (1990) and Kahn (1994) have worked assiduously at the task of integrating person-centred theory with other orientations. G. T. (Goff) Barrett-Lennard (1986) is greatly respected across schools for his Relationship Inventory which has been used in research comparing diverse therapeutic approaches, as well as for his continuing contributions to community theory and the empathic process.

While there continues to be controversy about what is 'really' person-centred, the differing parties continue to meet together, respectfully and collegially, at the International Conferences on Client-Centered and Experiential Psychotherapy, which were held in Leuven in September 1988, then in Stirling, Scotland in 1991 and Gmunden, Austria in 1994, with Portugal scheduled as the next host in 1997. The meetings tend to be more cognitive in tone than the International Forums on the Person-Centered Approach, which also attract participants with a range of ideologies. The forums, which schedule a daily meeting of the whole community, were initiated in the summer of 1982 by Alberto Segrera in Mexico and will assemble again in South Africa in 1998, for the seventh time.

Personal afterword

The 20 steps described here are necessarily somewhat arbitrary. The same material could have been apportioned differently, resulting in a different number. Zimring and Raskin (1992) divided the first fifty years of the Person-Centred Approach into four major periods. Other equally qualified students of this orientation would differ about what is significant historically. Unavoidably, I was influenced by my own experience; each of us has a store of personal knowledge derived from our own participation and observation. The fact that I have been part of the movement from its beginning is advantageous in that not only do I know *about* the Steps in its unfolding; I was present at or close to these events that have occurred over a span of 55 years. A close relationship with Carl Rogers for 47 years has provided a similar benefit.

Rogers' ideas, from the beginning, were revolutionary and, as a truly client-directed approach to counselling and psychotherapy, remain unique, perhaps even more than before, because of an increasing reliance on experts, and of pressures from insurance companies and health organisations to specify problems and treatments. Extremely impressive, too, is the fact that what began simply as a practical new way of trying to help an individual in therapy and seemed very much like an American phenomenon within a tradition of logical positivism, evolved into an international movement affecting education, organisational structure, and many other human relations settings, as well as a philosophy and a way of being for non-professionals. Notwithstanding a decline in influence in the United States, the importance of the concepts of self and of experiencing, of empathic listening, genuineness, and unconditional positive regard, and the usefulness of verbatim typescripts and tapes of individual interviews and group sessions, are unlikely to disappear from psychotherapy and other areas of human relations.

Support for this view comes from an unexpected source: psychiatrist Peter Kramer, author of the well-known book *Listening to Prozac* (1993). In an article called 'Rogers' due', Kramer (1995) asks, 'Why is he [Rogers] so much out of favor? Why, when we have adopted so many of his ideas, do we no longer read or teach Rogers? In his lifetime, peers rated Rogers the most influential American psychologist and the most influential psychotherapist. It seems odd that Rogers' star should be in eclipse today when his central belief, that empathy is the key to psychotherapy, is in the ascendant.'

Kramer goes on to express a profound appreciation for Carl as a person, crediting him with 'the massive infiltration of therapeutic concepts into ordinary life' and a lot more. After giving an example of one of Carl's very sensitive empathic responses, he writes, 'When we banish Rogers, we deprive ourselves of his music.'

An example of such music may be Rogers' answer to a statement by B. F. Skinner that 'The hypothesis that man is not free is essential to the application of scientific method to the study of human behavior.' The exchange occurs in 'The place of the individual in the new world of the behavioral sciences', the last piece in *On Becoming a Person* (Rogers, 1961). (Kramer is the author of the introduction to Houghton Mifflin's new edition of this work.) Rogers replied that:

> we can choose to use the behavioral sciences in ways which will free, not control; which will bring about constructive variability, not conformity; which will develop creativity, not contentment; which will facilitate each person in his self-directed process of becoming; which will aid individuals, groups, and even the concept of science, to become self-transcending in freshly adaptive ways of meeting life and its problems. The choice is up to us. (1961, p. 400)

Acknowledgement
Excerpts from Carl Rogers, *Client-Centered Therapy,* First Edition. Copyright © 1951 by Houghton Mifflin Company. Reprinted with permission.

References

Barrett-Lennard, G. T. (1979) The client-centered system unfolding. In F. J. Turner (Ed.), *Social work treatment: Interlocking theoretical approaches* (2nd edn.) (pp. 177–241). New York: Free Press.

Barrett-Leonard, G. T. (1986) The Relationship Inventory now: issues and advances in theory, method and use. In L. S. Greenberg and W. M. Pinsof (Eds.), *The psychotherapeutic process: A research handbook* (pp. 439–76). New York: Guilford.

Barrett-Lennard, G. T. (1994) Toward a person-centered theory of community. *Journal of Humanistic Psychology, 34*(3), 62–86.

Bohart, A. C. (1990) Psychotherapy integration from a client-centered perspective. In G. Lietaer, J. Rombauts and P. Van Balen (Eds.), *Client-centered and experiential psychotherapy in the nineties* (pp. 481–500). Leuven, Belgium: Leuven University Press.

Bozarth, J. D. (1992) Coterminous intermingling of doing and being in person-centered therapy, *The Person-Centered Journal, 1*, 12–20.

Brodley, B. (1996) Carl Rogers' note on congruence. Presentation at 11th Annual Conference of the Association for the Development of the Person-Centered Approach. May, Kutztown, PA, USA.

Covner, B. J. (1942) Studies in phonographic recording of verbal material: I. The use of phonographic recordings in counseling practice and research. II. A device for transcribing phonographic recordings of verbal material. *Journal of Consulting Psychology, 6*,105–13, 149–53.

Covner, B. J. (1944a) Studies in phonographic recording of verbal material: III. The completeness and accuracy of counseling interview reports. *Journal of General Psychology, 30*, 181–203.

Covner, B. J. (1944b) Studies in phonographic recording of verbal material: IV. Written reports of interviews. *Journal of Applied Psychology, 28*, 89–98.

Gendlin, E. T. (1978) *Focusing.* New York: Bantam Books.

Greenberg, L., Elliot, R. and Lietaer, G. (1994) Research on experiential psychotherapies. In A. E. Bergin and S. L. Garfield (Eds.), *Handbook of psychotherapy and behavior change* (pp. 509–39). New York: John Wiley & Sons.

Hart, J. T. and Tomlinson, T. M. (Eds.) (1979) *New directions in client-centered therapy.* Boston, MA: Houghton Mifflin.

Kahn, E. (1994) Is client-centered therapy a one-person or a two-person psychology? Presentation at 3rd International Conference on Client-Centered and Experiential Psychotherapy, September, Gmunden, Austria.

Kirschenbaum, H. (1979) *On becoming Carl Rogers.* New York: Delacourt Press.

Kramer, P. D. (1993) *Listening to prozac.* New York: Viking.

Kramer, P. D. (1995) Rogers' due. *Psychiatric Times,* May.

McGaw, W. H., Rice, P. and Rogers, C. R. (1973) *The Steel Shutter* [videotape], La Jolla, CA: Western Behavioral Sciences Institute.

Mearns, D. (1994) *Developing person-centred counselling.* London: Sage Publications.

Merry, T. (1988) *A guide to the person-centred approach.* London: Association for Humanistic Psychology in Britain.

Patterson, C. H. (1984) Empathy, warmth, and genuineness in psychotherapy: a review of reviews. *Psychotherapy, 21,* 431–8.

Porter, E. H. Jr. (1943) The development and evaluation of a measure of counseling interview procedures. *Educational and Psychological Measurement, 3,* 105–26, 215–38.

Prouty, G. F. (1990) Pre-therapy: a theoretical evolution in the person-centered/experiential psychotherapy of schizophrenia and retardation. In G. Lietaer, J. Rombauts and R. Van Balen (Eds.), *Client-centered and experiential psychotherapy in the nineties* (pp. 645–58). Leuven, Belgium: Leuven University Press.

Raskin, N. J. (1952) Client-centered counseling and psychotherapy. In E. L. Abt and D. Brower (Eds.), *Progress in clinical psychology* (pp. 236–48). New York: Grune & Stratton.

Raskin, N. J. (1978) A *Voices* editorial amalgam. *Voices, 14,* 12–13.

Raskin, N. J. (1990) The first 50 years and the next 10. *Person-Centered Review, 5,* 364–72.

Raskin, N. J and Rogers, C. R. (1995) Person-centered therapy. In R. J. Corsini and D. Wedding (Eds.), *Current psychotherapies* (5th edn.) (pp. 128–61). Itasca, IL: F. E. Peacock.

Rogers, C. R. (1931) *Measuring personality adjustment in children nine to thirteen years of age* (Teachers College, Columbia University Contributions to Education, No. 458). New York: Bureau of Publications, Teachers College, Columbia University.

Rogers, C. R. (1942) *Counseling and psychotherapy.* Boston, MA: Houghton Mifflin.

Rogers, C. R. (1947) Some observations on the organization of personality. *American Psychologist, 2,* 358–68.

Rogers, C. R. (1951a) *Client-centered therapy.* Boston, MA: Houghton Mifflin.

Rogers, C. R. (1951b) Where are we going in clinical psychology? *Journal of Consulting Psychology, 15,* 171–7.

Rogers, C. R. (1954) What it means to become a person. In C. R. Rogers, *On Becoming a Person* (pp. 107–24). Boston MA: Houghton Mifflin.

Rogers, C. R. (1957) The necessary and sufficient conditions of therapeutic personality change, *Journal of Consulting Psychology, 21,* 95–103.

Rogers, C. R. (1959) A theory of therapy, personality, and interpersonal relationships, as developed in the client-centered framework. In S. Koch (Ed.), *Psychology: A study of a science,* Vol. 3: *Formulations of the person and the social context* (pp. 184–256). New York: McGraw-Hill.

Rogers, C. R. (1961) *On becoming a person.* Boston, MA: Houghton Mifflin.

Rogers, C. R. (1964) Toward a modern approach to values: the valuing process in the mature person. *Journal of Abnormal and Social Psychology 68*(2), 160–7.

Rogers, C. R. (1969) *Freedom to learn.* Columbus, OH: Charles E. Merrill.

Rogers, C. R. (1970) *Carl Rogers on encounter groups.* New York: Harper & Row.

Rogers, C. R. (1978) The formative tendency. *Journal of Humanistic Psychology, 18*, 23–6.

Rogers, C. R. (1980) *A way of being.* Boston, MA: Houghton Mifflin.

Rogers, C. R. (1983) *Freedom to learn for the '80s.* Columbus, OH: Charles E. Merrill.

Rogers, C. R. and Dymond, R. F. (Eds.) (1954) *Psychotherapy and personality change.* Chicago: University of Chicago Press.

Rogers, C. R., Raskin, N. J., Seeman, J., Sheerer, E. T., Stock, D., Haigh, G. Hoffman, A. E. and Carr, A. C. (1949) 'A coordinated research in psychotherapy', *Journal of Consulting Psychology, 13*: 46–220.

Rogers, C. R., Gendlin, E. T., Kiesler, D. J. and Truax, C. B. (Eds.) (1967) *A Study of Psychotherapy with Schizophrenics.* Madison, WI: University of Wisconsin Press.

Rogers, N. (1995) 'The creative journey', in M. M. Suhd (Ed.) *Positive Regard: Carl Rogers and other Notables he Influenced.* Palo Alto, CA: Science and Behavior Books, pp. 175–224.

Sanford, R. (1995) 'On becoming who I am . . .', in M. M. Suhd (ed.) *Positive Regard: Carl Rogers and other Notables he Influenced.* Palo Alto, CA: Science and Behavior Books, pp. 373–438.

Seeman, J. (1984) 'The fully functioning person: theory and research', in R. F. Levant and J. M. Shlien (Eds.), *Client-Centered Therapy and the Person-Centered Approach.* New York, NY: Praeger, pp. 150–2.

Seeman, J. and Raskin, N. J. (1953) 'Research perspective in client-centered therapy', in O. H. Mowrer (Ed.) *Psychotherapy, Theory and Research.* New York, NY: Ronald Press, pp. 205–34.

Shlien, J. M. (1967) 'A client-centered approach to schizophrenia: a first approximation', in C. R. Rogers and B. Stevens (Eds.) *Person to Person: the problem of being human.* Lafayette, CA: Real People Press, pp. 150–65.

Snyder, W. U. (1945) 'An investigation of the nature of non-directive psychotherapy', *Journal of General Psychology, 33*: 193–223.

Streich, E. R. (1951) 'The self-experience of the client-centered therapist'. Unpublished paper, University of Chicago Counseling Center.

Thorne, B. (1992) *Carl Rogers.* London: Sage Publications.

Zimring, F. M. (1995) 'A new explanation for the beneficial resluts of client-centered therapy: the possibility of a new paradigm', *The Person-Centered Journal, 2*:36–48.

Zimring, F. M. and Raskin, N. J. (1992) 'Carl Rogers and client/person-centered therapy', in D. K. Freedheim (Ed.) *History of Psychotherapy: A century of change.* Washington, DC: American Psychological Associaion, pp. 629–56.

PERSON-CENTERED THERAPY (WITH CARL R. ROGERS)

15

Overview

Person-Centered Therapy is an approach to helping individuals and groups in conflict. Its essentials were formulated by psychologist Carl R. Rogers in 1940. A clearly stated theory accompanied by the introduction of verbatim transcriptions of psychotherapy, stimulated a vast amount of research on a revolutionary hypothesis: that a self-directed growth process would follow the provision and reception of a particular kind of relationship characterized by genuineness, non-judgmental caring, and empathy. This hypothesis has been tested over decades in situations involving teachers and students, administrators and staff, facilitators and participants in cross-cultural groups, as well as psychotherapists and clients.

Basic concepts

Perhaps the most fundamental and pervasive concept in Person-Centered Therapy is trust. The foundation of Rogers' approach is an *actualizing tendency* present in every living organism — in human beings, this tendency is most clearly reflected in movement toward the realization of an individual's full potential. Rogers (1980) described this actualizing force as part of a *formative tendency,* observable in the movement toward greater order, complexity, and interrelatedness that can be observed in stars, crystals, and micro-organisms, as well as in human beings.

On a practical level, the Person-Centered Approach is built on trust that individuals and groups can set their own goals and monitor their progress toward these goals. This has special meaning in relation to children, students, and workers, who are often viewed as requiring detailed and constant guidance and supervision. In the context of psychotherapy, a person-centered approach assumes that clients can be trusted to select their own therapists, to choose the frequency and length of their therapy, to talk or to be silent, to decide what needs to be explored, to achieve their own insights, and to be the architects of their own lives. Groups are believed to be capable of developing the processes that are right for them, and of resolving conflicts within the group.

One particular person-centered application of trust involves the therapist or

Originally published in R. J. Corsini and D. Wedding (Eds.), *Current psychotherapies,* (2000) (6th edn.) (pp. 166–67). Itasca, Ill: Peacock. Reprinted with permission.

facilitator. In the early days of the movement, the focus was entirely on the client. The therapist provided continuous and consistent empathy for the client's perceptions, meanings, and feelings. With experience came growing recognition that it was important for the therapist to be appreciated as a person in the relationship and to be regarded with trust, as is the client.

Eugene Streich formulated one of the earliest statements of this trust:

> When the therapist's capacity for awareness is thus functioning freely and fully without limitations imposed by theoretical formulations of his role, we find that we have, not an individual who may do harm, not a person who must follow certain procedures, but a person able to achieve, through the remarkable integrative capacity of his central nervous system, a balanced, therapeutic, self-growing, other-growth facilitating behavior as a result of all these elements of awareness. To put it another way, when the therapist is less than fully himself — when he denies to awareness various aspects of his experience — then indeed we have all too often to be concerned about his effectiveness, as our failure cases would testify. But when he is most fully himself, when he is his most complete organism, when awareness of experience is most fully operating, then he is to be trusted, then his behavior is constructive. (1951, pp. 8–9)

Some 30 years later Rogers, in more intuitive and spiritual language, expressed such trust in the therapist or group facilitator, referring to it as 'one more characteristic' of a growth-promoting relationship, supplementing the classical conditions of congruence, unconditional positive regard, and empathy:

> When I am at my best, as a group facilitator or a therapist, I discover another characteristic. I find that when I am closest to my inner, intuitive self, when I am somehow in touch with the unknown in me, when perhaps I am in a slightly altered state of consciousness in the relationship, then whatever I do seems to be full of healing. Then simply my presence is releasing and helpful. (1986a, p. 198)

Congruence, unconditional positive regard, and *empathy* represent basic concepts of Person-Centered Therapy. These are qualities the therapist provides. While distinguishable, these three concepts are intimately related (Rogers, 1957). Congruence refers to the correspondence between the thoughts and the behavior of the therapist; thus, genuineness describes this characteristic. The therapist does not put up a professional front or personal facade.

The therapist also possesses unconditional positive regard for the client. The client may be reserved or talkative, address any issue of choice, and come to whatever insights and resolutions are personally meaningful. The therapist's regard for the client will not be affected by these particular choices, characteristics, or outcomes.

The therapist expresses this quality of genuine regard through empathy. Being empathic reflects an attitude of profound interest in the client's world of meanings and feelings. The therapist receives these communications and conveys appreciation and understanding, assisting the client to go further or deeper. The notion that this involves nothing more than a repetition of the client's last words is erroneous. Instead, an interaction occurs in which one person is a warm, sensitive, respectful companion in the typically difficult exploration of another's emotional world. The therapist's manner of responding should be individual, natural, and unaffected. When empathy is at its best, the two individuals are participating in a process comparable to that of a couple dancing, with the client leading and the therapist following.

Basic concepts on the client side of the process include *self-concept, locus-of-evaluation,* and *experiencing.* In focusing on what is important to the person seeking help, client-centered therapists soon discovered that the person's perceptions and feelings about self were of central concern (Raimy, 1948).

A major component of self-concept is self-regard. Clients typically lacked self-esteem. Some of the earliest psychotherapy research projects showed that when clients were rated as successful in therapy, their attitudes toward self became significantly more positive (Sheerer, 1949).

Successful clients were also found to progress along a related dimension, *locus-of-evaluation.* At the same time that they gained in self-esteem, they tended to shift the basis for their standards and values from other people to themselves. People commonly began therapy overly concerned with what others thought of them — their locus-of-evaluation was external. With success in therapy, their attitudes toward others, as toward themselves, became more positive, and they were less dependent on others for their values and standards (Raskin, 1952).

A third central concept in Person-Centered Therapy is *experiencing,* a dimension along which successful clients improved (Rogers, Gendlin, Kiesler and Truax, 1967), shifting from a rigid mode of experiencing self and world to an attitude of openness and flexibility.

The three therapist qualities and the three client constructs described in this section have been carefully defined, measured, and studied in scores of research projects relating therapist practice to the outcome of psychotherapy. There is considerable evidence that when clients receive congruence, unconditional positive regard, and empathy, their self-concepts become more positive and realistic, they become more self-expressive and self-directed, they become more open and free in their experiencing, their behavior is rated as more mature, and they deal better with stress (Rogers, 1986a).

Other systems
Person-centered therapy evolved predominantly out of Rogers' own experience. There are both important differences and conceptual similarities between the Person-Centered Approach and other personality theories.

Self-actualization, a concept central to person-centered theory, was advanced most forcefully by Kurt Goldstein. His holistic theory of personality emphasizes that individuals must be understood as totalities and that they strive to actualize themselves (Goldstein, 1959). Goldstein's work and ideas preceded those of Abraham Maslow, a founder of humanistic psychology, who was opposed to the Freudian and behavioral interpretations of human nature.

Heinz Ansbacher, a leading proponent of Adlerian theory, joined Maslow (1968) and Floyd Matson (1969) in recognizing a host of theories and therapists 'united by six basic premises of humanistic psychology':

1. People's creative power is a crucial force, in addition to heredity and environment.
2. An anthropomorphic model of humankind is superior to a mechanomorphic model.
3. Purpose, rather than cause, is the decisive dynamic.
4. The holistic approach is more adequate than an elementaristic one.
5. It is necessary to take humans' subjectivity, their opinions and viewpoints, and their conscious and unconscious fully into account.
6. Psychotherapy is essentially based on a good human relationship. (Ansbacher, 1977, p. 51)

Among those subscribing to such beliefs were Alfred Adler, William Stern, Gordon Allport, the Gestalt psychologists (Max Wertheimer, Wolfgang Kohler, and Kurt Koffka), the neo-Freudians (Franz Alexander, Erich Fromm, Karen Horney, and Harry Stack Sullivan), post-Freudians, such as Judd Marmor and Thomas Szasz, phenomenological and existential psychologists, such as Rollo May, the cognitive theorist George A. Kelly, and of course, Carl Rogers (Ansbacher, 1977).

While some fundamental person-centered concepts and values are consonant with the proponents of other systems, Rogers and Sanford (1985) have listed a number of distinctive characteristics of Client-Centered Therapy:

1. The hypothesis that certain attitudes in therapists constitute the necessary and sufficient conditions of therapeutic effectiveness;
2. The concept of therapists being immediately present and accessible to clients, relying on moment-to-moment experiencing in each relationship;
3. The intensive and continuing focus on the phenomenological world of the client (hence the term 'client-centered');
4. A developing theory that the therapeutic process is marked by a change in the client's manner and immediacy of experiencing, with increasing ability to live more fully in the moment;
5. A concern with the process of personality change, rather than with the structure of personality;
6. Emphasis on the need for continuing research to learn more about psychotherapy;
7. The hypothesis that the same principles of psychotherapy apply to all persons, whether they are categorized as psychotic, neurotic, or normal;

8. A view of psychotherapy as one specialized example of all constructive interpersonal relationships;
9. A determination to build all theoretical formulations out of the soil of experience, rather than twisting experience to fit a preformed theory;
10. A concern with the philosophical issues that derive from the practice of psychotherapy.

Meador and Rogers (1984) distinguished Person-Centered Therapy from psychoanalysis and from behavior modification in these terms:

> In psychoanalysis the analyst aims to interpret connections between the past and the present for the patient. In Person-Centered Therapy, the therapist facilitates the client's discoveries of the meanings of his or her own current inner experiencing. The psychoanalyst takes the role of a teacher in interpreting insights to the patient and encouraging the development of a transference relationship, a relationship based on the neurosis of the patient. The person-centered therapist presents him- or herself as honestly and transparently as possible and attempts to establish a relationship in which he or she is authentically caring and listening.
>
> In Person-Centered Therapy, transference relationships may begin, but they do not become full-blown. Rogers has postulated that transference relationships develop in an evaluative atmosphere in which the client feels the therapist knows more about the client than the client knows about him- or herself, and therefore the client becomes dependent. Person-centered therapists tend to avoid evaluation. They do not interpret for clients, do not question in a probing manner, and do not reassure or criticize clients. Person-centered therapists have not found the transference relationship, central to psychoanalysis, a necessary part of a client's growth or change.
>
> In behavior therapy, *behavior change* comes about through external control of associations to stimuli and the consequences of various responses. In practice, if not in theory, behavior therapy *does* pay attention to the therapy relationship; however, its major emphasis is on specific changes in specific behaviors. In contrast, person-centered therapists believe behavior change evolves from within the individual. Behavior therapy's goal is symptom removal. It is not particularly concerned with the relationship of inner experiencing to the symptom under consideration, or with the relationship between the therapist and the client, or with the climate of their relationship. It seeks to eliminate the symptom as efficiently as possible using the principles of learning theory. Obviously, this point of view is quite contrary to Person-Centered Therapy, which maintains that fully functioning people rely on inner experiencing to direct their behaviour. (1984, p. 146)

Raskin (1974), in a comparison of Rogers' practice with those of leaders of five other orientations, found that Client-Centered Therapy was distinctive in providing empathy and unconditional positive regard. Psychoanalytically oriented and eclectic psychotherapists agreed with client-centered theory on the desirability of empathy, warmth, and unconditional positive regard, but examples of rational-emotive, psychoanalytically oriented, and Jungian interviews were ranked low on these qualities.

This study provided a direct comparison of audiotaped samples of therapy done by Rogers and by Albert Ellis, the founder of Rational-Emotive Behavior Therapy (REBT). Among 12 therapist variables rated by 83 therapist-judges, the only one on which Rogers and Ellis were alike was 'Self-Confident'. The therapy sample by Rogers received high ratings on the following dimensions: 'Empathy', 'Unconditional Positive Regard', 'Congruence', and 'Ability to Inspire Confidence'. The interview by Ellis was rated high on the 'Cognitive' and 'Therapist-Directed' dimensions. Rogers was rated low on 'Therapist-Directed', while Ellis received a low rating on 'Unconditional Positive Regard'.

This research lends support to the following differences between Person-Centered Therapy and Rational-Emotive Therapy.

1. Unlike REBT, the Person-Centered Approach greatly values the therapeutic relationship.
2. Rational-emotive therapists provide much direction, while the person-centered approach encourages the client to determine direction.
3. Rational-emotive therapists work hard to point out deficiencies in their clients' thought processes; person-centered therapists accept and respect their clients' ways of thinking and perceiving.
4. Person-Centered Therapy characteristically leads to actions chosen by the client; rational-emotive methods include 'homework' assignments by the therapist.
5. The person-centered therapist will relate to the client on a feeling level and in a respectful and accepting way; the rational-emotive therapist will be inclined to interrupt this affective process to point out the irrational harm that the client may be doing to self and interpersonal relationships.

While Rogers and Ellis have very different philosophies and methods of trying to help people, they share some very important beliefs and values:

1. A great optimism that people can change, even when they are deeply disturbed;
2. A perception that individuals are often unnecessarily self-critical, and that negative self-attitudes can become positive;
3. A willingness to put forth great effort to try to help people, both through individual therapy and through professional therapy and non-technical writing;
4. A willingness to demonstrate their methods publicly;
5. A respect for science and research.

Similar differences and commonalities will be found when Rogers is compared to other cognitive therapists, such as Aaron Beck.

History

Precursors

One of the most powerful influences on Carl Rogers was learning that traditional child-guidance methods in which he had been trained did not work very well. At Columbia University's Teachers College he had been taught testing, measurement, diagnostic interviewing, and interpretive treatment. This was followed by an internship at the psychoanalytically oriented Institute for Child Guidance, where he learned to take exhaustive case histories and do projective personality testing. It is important to note that Rogers originally went to a Rochester child-guidance agency believing in this diagnostic, prescriptive, professionally impersonal approach, and it was only after actual experience that he concluded that it was not effective. As an alternative, he tried listening and following the client's lead rather than assuming the role of the expert. This worked better, and he discovered some theoretical and applied support for this alternative approach in the work of Otto Rank and his followers at the University of Pennsylvania School of Social Work and the Philadelphia Child Guidance Clinic. One particularly important event was a three-day seminar in Rochester with Rank (Rogers and Haigh, 1983). Another was his association with a Rankian-trained social worker, Elizabeth Davis, from whom 'I first got the notion of responding almost entirely to the feelings being expressed. What later came to be called the reflection of feeling sprang from my contact with her' (Rogers and Haigh, 1983, p. 7).

Rogers' methodology and, later, his theory, grew out of the soil of his own experience. At the same time, a number of links to Otto Rank are apparent in Rogers' early work.

The following elements of Rankian theory bore a close relationship to principles of nondirective therapy:

1. The individual seeking help is not simply a battleground of impersonal forces such as id and superego, but has personal creative powers.
2. The aim of therapy is acceptance by the individual, of self as unique and self-reliant.
3. In order to achieve this goal, the client rather than the therapist must become the central figure in the therapeutic process.
4. The therapist can be neither an instrument of love, which would make the patient more dependent, nor an instrument of education, which attempts to alter the individual.
5. The goals of therapy are achieved by the patient not through an explanation of the past, which the client would resist if interpreted, and which, even if accepted, would lessen responsibility for present adjustment, but rather through experiencing the present in the therapeutic situation (Raskin, 1948, pp. 95–6).

Rank explicitly, eloquently, and repeatedly rejected therapy by technique and interpretation, stating:

> Every single case, yes every individual hour of the same case, is different, because it is derived momentarily from the play of forces given in the situation and immediately applied. My technique consists essentially in having no technique, but in utilizing as much as possible experience and understanding that are constantly converted into skill but never crystallized into technical rules which would be applicable ideologically. There is a technique only in an ideological therapy where technique is identical with theory and the chief task of the analyst is interpretation (ideological), not the bringing to pass and granting of experience. (1945, p. 105)

Rank is obscure about his actual practice of psychotherapy, particularly the amount and nature of his activity during the treatment hour. Unsystematic references in *Will Therapy* (1945) reveal that, despite his criticism of educational and interpretive techniques and his expressed value of the patient being his or her own therapist, he assumed a position of undisputed power in the relationship.

Beginnings

Carl Ransom Rogers was born in Oak Park, Illinois, on January 8, 1902. Rogers' parents believed in hard work, responsibility, and religious fundamentalism and frowned on activities such as drinking, dancing, and card playing. The family was characterized by closeness and devotion but did not openly display affection. While in high school, Carl worked on the family farm, and he became interested in experimentation and the scientific aspect of agriculture. He entered the University of Wisconsin, following his parents and older siblings, as an agriculture major. Rogers also carried on his family's religious tradition. He was active in the campus YMCA and was chosen to be one of ten American youth delegates to the World Student Christian Federation's Conference in Peking, China, in 1922. At that time he switched his major from agriculture to history, which he thought would better prepare him for a career as a minister. After graduating from Wisconsin in 1924 and marrying Helen Elliott, a childhood friend, he entered the Union Theological Seminary. Two years later, and in part as a result of taking several psychology courses, Rogers moved 'across Broadway' to Teachers College, Columbia University, where he was exposed to what he later described as 'a contradictory mixture of Freudian, scientific, and progressive education thinking' (Rogers and Sanford, 1985, p. 1374).

After Teachers College, Rogers worked for twelve years at a child-guidance center in Rochester, New York, where he soon became an administrator as well as a practicing psychologist. He began writing articles and became active at a national level. His book, *The Clinical Treatment of the Problem Child,* was published in 1939, and he was offered a professorship in psychology at Ohio State University. Once at Ohio State, Rogers began to teach newer ways of helping problem children and their parents.

In 1940, Rogers was teaching an enlightened distillation of child-guidance practices described in *The Clinical Treatment of the Problem Child*. From his point of view, this approach represented a consensual direction in which the field was moving and was evolutionary rather than revolutionary. The clinical process began with an assessment, including testing of children and interviewing of parents, and the results of assessment provided the basis for a treatment plan. In treatment, nondirective principles were followed.

Rogers' views became more radical. His presentation at the University of Minnesota, on December 11, 1940, entitled 'Some Newer Concepts in Psychotherapy', is the single event most often identified with the birth of Client-Centered Therapy.

Rogers decided to expand this talk into a book titled *Counseling and Psychotherapy* (1942). The book, which included an electronically recorded eight-interview case, described the generalized process in which a client begins with a conflict situation and a predominance of negative attitudes and moves toward insight, independence, and positive attitudes. Rogers hypothesized that the counselor promoted such a process by avoiding advice and interpretation and by consistently recognizing and accepting the client's feelings. Research corroborating this new approach to counseling and psychotherapy was offered, including the first (Porter, 1943) of what soon became a series of pioneering doctoral dissertations on the process and outcomes of psychotherapy. In a very short time, an entirely new approach to psychotherapy was born, as was the field of psychotherapy research. This approach and its accompanying research led to the eventual acceptance of psychotherapy as a primary professional function of clinical psychologists.

After serving as Director of Counseling Services for the United Service Organizations during World War II, Rogers was appointed professor of psychology at the University of Chicago and became head of the university's counseling center. The 12 years during which Rogers remained at Chicago were a period of tremendous growth in client-centered theory, philosophy, practice, research, applications, and implications. In 1957, Rogers published a classic 'necessary and sufficient conditions' paper in which congruence and unconditional positive regard were added to empathy as three essential therapist-offered conditions of therapeutic personality change. This was followed by a comprehensive and rigorous theory of therapy, personality, and interpersonal relationships (Rogers, 1959b). Rogers' philosophy of the 'exquisitely rational' nature of the behavior and growth of human beings was further articulated and related to the thinking of Søren Kierkegaard, Abraham Maslow, and others. The practice of Client-Centered Therapy deepened and broadened. The therapist was also more fully appreciated as a person in the therapeutic relationship. Psychotherapy research, which had begun so auspiciously at Ohio State, continued with investigations by Godfrey T. Barrett-Lennard (1962), John Butler and Gerard Haigh (1954), Desmond Cartwright (1957), Eugene Gendlin (1961), Nathaniel Raskin (1952), Julius Seeman (1959), John Shlien (1964), and Stanley Standal (1954), among others.

At Ohio State, there was a sense that client-centered principles had implications beyond the counseling office. At Chicago, this was made most explicit by the empowerment of students and the counseling center staff. About half of Rogers' *Client-Centered Therapy* (1951) was devoted to applications of Client-Centered Therapy, with additional chapters on play therapy, group therapy, and leadership and administration.

In 1957, Rogers accepted a professorship in psychology and psychiatry at the University of Wisconsin. With the collaboration of associates and graduate students, a massive research project was mounted, based on the hypothesis that hospitalized schizophrenics would respond to a client-centered approach (Rogers, Gendlin, Kiesler, and Truax, 1967). Two relatively clear conclusions emerged from a complex maze of results: (1) the most successful patients were those who had experienced the highest degree of accurate empathy, and (2) it was the client's, rather than the therapist's, judgment of the therapy relationship that correlated more highly with success or failure.

Current status

Rogers left the University of Wisconsin and full-time academia and began living in La Jolla, California, in 1964. He was a resident fellow for four years at the Western Behavioral Sciences Institute and then, starting in 1968, at the Center for Studies of the Person. In more than two decades in California, Rogers wrote books on a person-centered approach to teaching and educational administration, on encounter groups, on marriage and other forms of partnership, and on the 'quiet revolution' that he believed would emerge with a new type of 'self-empowered person'. Rogers believed this revolution had the potential to change 'the very nature of psychotherapy, marriage, education, administration, and politics' (Rogers, 1977). These books were based on observations and interpretations of hundreds of individual and group experiences.

A special interest of Rogers and his associates was the application of a person-centered approach to international conflict resolution. This resulted in trips to South Africa, Eastern Europe, and the Soviet Union, as well as in meetings with Irish Catholics and Protestants and with representatives of nations involved in Central American conflicts (Rogers and Ryback, 1984). In addition to Rogers' books, a number of valuable films and videotapes have provided data for research on the basic person-centered hypothesis that individuals and groups who have experienced empathy, congruence, and unconditional positive regard will go through a constructive process of self-directed change.

Since 1982, there have been biennial international forums on the Person-Centered Approach, meeting in Mexico, England, the United States, Brazil, the Netherlands, Greece, and South Africa. Alternating with these meetings have been international conferences on Client-Centered and Experiential Psychotherapy in Belgium, Scotland, Austria, and Portugal.

The *Person-Centered Review,* 'an international journal of research, theory, and application', was initiated by David Cain in 1986 with a worldwide editorial board. The *Review* was succeeded, in 1992, by *The Person-Centered Journal,* co-edited by Jerold Bozarth and Fred Zimring. Zimring and Raskin (1992), in a volume on the history of psychotherapy during the first hundred years of the American Psychological Association, wrote:

> The *Review* has published articles about many aspects of Client-Centered Therapy. In addition, *Client-Centered and Experiential Psychotherapy in the Nineties* (Lietaer, Rombauts, and Van Balen, 1990) contains many papers about . . . the use of the approach with various populations . . . children and child therapy . . . family and couples therapy . . . disturbed clients . . . and clients who are working with fears of death and dying.

Raskin (1996) formulated significant steps in the evolution of the movement from individual therapy in 1940 to the concept of community in the 1990s.

Personality

Theory of personality

Rogers moved from a disinterest in psychological theory to the development of a rigorous nineteen-proposition 'theory of therapy, personality, and interpersonal relationships' (Rogers, 1959b). On one level, this signified a change in Rogers' respect for theory. On another, this comprehensive formulation can be understood as a logical evolution. His belief in the importance of the child's conscious attitudes toward self and self-ideal was central to the test of personality adjustment he devised for children (Rogers, 1931). The portrayal of the client's growing through a process of reduced defensiveness and of self-directed expansion of self-awareness was described in a paper on the processes of therapy (Rogers, 1940). Rogers wrote here of a gradual recognition and admission of a real self with its childish, aggressive, and ambivalent aspects as well as more mature components. As data on personality changes in psychotherapy started to accumulate rapidly, with the objective analyses of verbatim interviews, Rogers found support for his belief that the facts are always friendly, despite some results at variance with his hypotheses.

As outgoing president of the American Psychological Association, Rogers summed up this perspective:

> Client-Centered Therapy has led us to try to adopt the client's perceptual field as the basis for genuine understanding. In trying to enter this internal world of perception . . . we find ourselves in a new vantage point for understanding personality dynamics . . . We find that behavior seems to be better understood as a reaction to this reality-as-perceived. We discover that the way in which the person sees himself, and the perceptions he dares not take as belonging to himself, seem to have an important relationship to the inner peace which constitutes adjustment. We discover . . . a capacity for the restructuring and reorganization of self and consequently the

reorganization of behavior, which has profound social implications. We see these observations, and the theoretical formulations which they inspire, as a fruitful new approach for study and research in various fields of psychology. (1947, p. 368)

Rogers expanded his observations into a theory of personality and behavior that he described in *Client-Centered Therapy* (1951). This theory is based on nineteen basic propositions:

1. Every individual exists in a continually changing world of experience of which he or she is the center.
2. The organism reacts to the field as it is experienced and perceived. This perceptual field is, for the individual, 'reality'.
3. The organism reacts as an organized whole to this phenomenal field.
4. The organism has one basic tendency and striving — to actualize, maintain, and enhance the experiencing organism.
5. Behavior is basically the goal-directed attempt of the organism to satisfy its needs as experienced, in the field as perceived.
6. Emotion accompanies and in general facilitates such goal-directed behavior, the kind of emotion being related to the seeking versus the consummatory aspects of the behavior, and the intensity of the emotion being related to the perceived significance of the behavior for the maintenance and enhancement of the organism.
7. The best vantage point for understanding behavior is from the internal frame of reference of the individual.
8. A portion of the total perceptual field gradually becomes differentiated as the self.
9. As a result of interaction with the environment, and particularly as a result of evaluational interaction with others, the structure of self is formed — an organized, fluid, but consistent conceptual pattern of perceptions of characteristics and relationships of the 'I' or the 'me,' together with values attached to these concepts.
10. The values attached to experiences, and the values which are a part of the self structure, in some instances are values experienced directly by the organism, and in some instances are values introjected or taken over from others, but perceived in distorted fashion, as if they had been experienced directly.
11. As experiences occur in the life of the individual, they are either (a) symbolized, perceived, and organized into some relationship to the self, (b) ignored because there is no perceived relationship to the self-structure, or (c) denied symbolization or given a distorted symbolization because the experience is inconsistent with the structure of the self.
12. Most of the ways of behaving which are adopted by the organism are those which are consistent with the concept of self.
13. Behavior may, in some instances, be brought about by organic experiences

and needs which have not been symbolized. Such behavior may be inconsistent with the structure of the self, but in such instances the behavior is not 'owned' by the individual.

14. Psychological maladjustment exists when the organism denies to awareness significant sensory and visceral experiences, which consequently are not symbolized and organized into the gestalt of the self-structure. When this situation exists, there is a basis for potential psychological tension.

15. Psychological adjustment exists when the concept of the self is such that all the sensory and visceral experiences of the organism are, or may be, assimilated on a symbolic level, into a consistent relationship with the concept of self.

16. Any experience which is inconsistent with the organization or structure of self may be perceived as a threat, and the more of these perceptions there are, the more rigidly the self-structure is organized to maintain itself.

17. Under certain conditions, involving primarily complete absence of any threat to the self-structure, experiences which are inconsistent with it may be perceived and examined, and the structure of self revised to assimilate and include such experiences.

18. When the individual perceives and accepts into one consistent and integrated system all his sensory and visceral experiences, then he is necessarily more understanding of others and is more accepting of others as separate individuals.

19. As the individual perceives and accepts into his self-structure more of his organic experiences, he finds that he is replacing his present value system — based so largely upon introjections which have been distortedly symbolized — with a continuing organismic valuing process. (pp. 481–533)

Rogers comments that:

> This theory is basically phenomenological in character, and relies heavily upon the concept of the self as an explanatory construct. It pictures the end-point of personality development as being a basic congruence between the phenomenal field of experience and the conceptual structure of the self — a situation which, if achieved, would represent freedom from internal strain and anxiety and freedom from potential strain; which would represent the maximum in realistically oriented adaptation; which would mean the establishment of an individualized value system having considerable identity with the value system of any other equally well-adjusted member of the human race. (1951, p. 532)

Further investigations of these propositions were conducted at the University of Chicago Counseling Center in the early 1950s in carefully designed and controlled studies. Stephenson's (1953) Q-technique was used to measure changes in self-concept and self-ideal during and following therapy and in a no-therapy control period. Many results confirmed Rogers' hypotheses, e.g., a significant increase in congruence between self and ideal occurred during therapy, and changes in the perceived self were toward better psychological adjustment (Rogers and Dymond, 1954).

Rogers' personality theory has been described as growth-oriented rather than developmental. While this is accurate, it does not acknowledge Rogers' sensitivity to the attitudes with which children are confronted, beginning in infancy:

> While I have been fascinated by the horizontal spread of the Person-Centered Approach into so many areas of our life, others have been more interested in the vertical direction and are discovering the profound value of treating the infant, during the whole birth process, as a person who should be understood, whose communications should be treated with respect, who should be dealt with empathically. This is the new and stimulating contribution of Frederick Leboyer, a French obstetrician who . . . has assisted in the delivery of at least a thousand infants in what can only be called a person-centered way. (Rogers, 1977, p. 31)

Rogers goes on to describe the infant's extreme sensitivity to light and sound, the rawness of the skin, the fragility of the head, the struggle to breathe, etc., and the specific ways in which Leboyer has taught parents and professionals to provide a beginning life experience that is caring, loving, and respectful.

This sensitivity to children was further expressed in Rogers' explanation of his fourth proposition (*The organism has one basic tendency and striving — to actualize, maintain, and enhance the experiencing organism*):

> The whole process (of self-enhancement and growth) may be symbolized and illustrated by the child's learning to walk. The first steps involve struggle, and usually pain. Often it is true that the immediate reward involved in taking a few steps is in no way commensurate with the pain of falls and bumps. The child may, because of the pain, revert to crawling for a time. Yet the forward direction of growth is more powerful than the satisfactions of remaining infantile. Children will actualize themselves, in spite of the painful experiences of so doing. In the same way, they will become independent, responsible, self-governing, and socialized, in spite of the pain which is often involved in these steps. Even where they do not, because of a variety of circumstances, exhibit the growth, the tendency is still present. Given the opportunity for clear-cut choice between forward-moving and regressive behavior, the tendency will operate. (Rogers, 1951, pp. 490–1)

One of Rogers' hypotheses about personality (Proposition 8) was that a part of the developing infant's private world becomes recognized as 'me,' 'I', or 'myself.' Rogers described infants, in the course of interacting with the environment, as building up concepts about themselves, about the environment, and about themselves in relation to the environment.

Rogers' next suppositions are crucial to his theory of how development may proceed either soundly or in the direction of maladjustment. He assumes that very young infants are involved in 'direct organismic valuing', with very little or no uncertainty. They have experiences such as 'I am cold, and I don't like it', or 'I like being cuddled', which may occur even though they lack descriptive words or symbols for these examples. The principle in this natural process is that the infant positively values those experiences that are perceived as self-enhancing and places a negative value on those that threaten or do not maintain or enhance the self.

This situation changes once children begin to be evaluated by others (Holdstock and Rogers, 1983). The love they are given and the symbolization of themselves as lovable children become dependent on behaviour. To hit or to hate a baby sibling may result in the child's being told that he or she is bad and unlovable. The child, to preserve a positive self-concept, may distort experience.

> It is in this way . . . that parental attitudes are not only introjected, but . . . are experienced in distorted fashion, *as if* based on the evidence of one's own sensory and visceral equipment. Thus, through distorted symbolization, expression of anger comes to be 'experienced' as bad, even though the more accurate symbolization would be that the expression of anger is often experienced as satisfying or enhancing . . . The 'self' which is formed on this basis of distorting the sensory and visceral evidence to fit the already present structure acquires an organization and integration which the individual endeavors to preserve. (Rogers, 1951, pp. 500–1)

This type of interaction may sow the seeds of confusion about self, self-doubt, and disapproval of self, as well as reliance upon the evaluation of others. Rogers indicated that these consequences may be avoided if the parent can accept the child's negative feelings and the child as a whole while refusing to permit certain behaviors such as hitting the baby.

Variety of concepts

Various terms and concepts appear in the presentation of Rogers' theory of personality and behavior that often have a unique and distinctive meaning in this orientation.

• Experience

Experience refers to the private world of the individual. At any moment, some of this is conscious; for example, we feel the pressure of the pen against our fingers as we write. Some of it may be difficult to bring into awareness, such as the idea, 'I am an aggressive person'. While people's actual awareness of their total experiential field may be limited, each individual is the only one who can know it completely.

• Reality

For psychological purposes, reality is basically the private world of individual perceptions, though for social purposes reality consists of those perceptions that have a high degree of communality among various individuals. Two people will agree on the reality that a particular person is a politician. One sees her as a good woman who wants to help people and, based on this reality, votes for her. The other person's reality is that the politician appropriates money to win favor, and therefore this person votes against her. In therapy, changes in feelings and perceptions will result in changes in reality.

• The organism reacts as an organized whole

A person may be hungry, but because of a report to complete, will skip lunch. In psychotherapy, clients often become more clear about what is more important to them, resulting in behavioral changes directed toward the clarified goals. A politician may choose not to run for office because he decides that his family life is more important.

• The organism's actualizing tendency

This is a central tenet in the writings of Kurt Goldstein, Hobart Mowrer, Harry Stack Sullivan, Karen Horney, and Andras Angyal, to name just a few. The child's painful struggle to learn to walk is an example. It is Rogers' belief and the belief of most other personality theorists that, given a free choice and in the absence of external force, individuals prefer to be healthy rather than sick, to be independent rather than dependent, and in general to further the optimal development of the total organism.

• The internal frame of reference

This is the perceptual field of the individual. It is the way the world appears and the meanings attached to experience and feelings. From the person-centered point of view, this internal frame of reference provides the fullest understanding of why people behave as they do. It is to be distinguished from external judgments of behavior, attitudes, and personality.

• The self, concept of self and self-structure

'These terms refer to the organized, consistent, conceptual Gestalt composed of perceptions of the characteristics of the "I" or "me" and the perceptions of the relationships of the "I" or "me" to others and to various aspects of life, together with the values attached to these perceptions. It is a Gestalt available to awareness although not necessarily in awareness. It is a fluid and changing process, but at any given moment it . . . is at least partially definable in operational terms' (Meador and Rogers, 1984, p. 158).

• Symbolization

This is the process by which the individual becomes aware or conscious of an experience. There is a tendency to deny symbolization to experiences at variance with the concept of self — e.g., people who think of themselves as truthful will tend to resist the symbolization of an act of lying. Ambiguous experiences tend to be symbolized in ways that are consistent with self-concept. A speaker lacking in self-confidence may symbolize a silent audience as unimpressed; one who is confident may symbolize such a group as attentive and interested.

• Psychological adjustment or maladjustment

This refers to the consistency, or lack of consistency, between an individual's sensory and visceral experiences and the concept of self. A self-concept that includes elements of weakness and imperfection facilitates the symbolization of failure experiences. The need to deny or distort such experiences does not exist and therefore fosters a condition of psychological adjustment.

• Organismic valuing process

This is an ongoing process in which individuals freely rely on the evidence of their own senses for making value judgments. This is in distinction to a fixed system of introjected values characterized by 'oughts' and 'shoulds' and by what is supposed to be right or wrong. The organismic valuing process is consistent with the person-centered hypothesis of confidence in the individual and, even though established by each individual, makes for a highly responsible socialized system of values and behaviour. The responsibility derives from people making choices on the basis of their direct, organic processing of situations, in contrast to acting out of fear of what others may think of them or what others have taught them is the way to think and act.

• The fully functioning person

Rogers defined those who rely on organismic valuing processes as fully functioning people, able to experience all of their feelings, afraid of none of them, allowing awareness to flow freely in and through their experiences. Seeman (1984) has been involved in a 25-year research program to clarify and describe the qualities of such optimally functioning individuals. These empirical studies highlight the possession of a positive self-concept, greater physiological responsiveness, and an efficient use of the environment.

Psychotherapy

Theory of psychotherapy

The basic theory of person-centered therapy is that if the therapist is successful in conveying genuineness, unconditional positive regard, and empathy, then the client will respond with constructive changes in personality organization. Research has demonstrated that these qualities can be made real in a relationship and can be conveyed and appreciated in a short time. Changes in self-acceptance, immediacy of experiencing, directness of relating, and movement toward an internal locus-of-evaluation may occur in short-term intensive workshops or even in single interviews.

After a four-day workshop of psychologists, educators, and other professionals conducted by Rogers and R. C. Sanford in Moscow, participants reported their reactions. The following is a typical response:

> This is just two days after the experience and I am still a participant.
> I am a psychologist, not a psychotherapist. I have known Rogers'
> theory but this was a process in which we were personally involved.
> I didn't realize how it applied. I want to give several impressions.
> First was the effectiveness of this approach. It was a kind of process
> in which we all learned. Second, this process was moving, without
> a motor. Nobody had to lead it or guide it. It was a self-evolving
> process. It was like the Chekhov story where they were expectantly
> awaiting the piano player and the piano started playing itself. Third,
> I was impressed by the manner of Carl and Ruth [Sanford]. At first
> I felt they were passive. Then I realized it was the silence of
> understanding. Fourth, I want to mention the penetration of this
> process into my inner world. At first I was an observer, but then the
> approach disappeared altogether. I was not simply surrounded by
> this process, I was absorbed into it! It was a revelation to me. We
> started moving. I wasn't simply seeing people I had known for years,
> but their feelings. My fifth realization was my inability to control
> the flow of feelings, the flow of the process. My feelings tried to
> put on the clothes of my words. Sometimes people exploded; some
> even cried. It was a reconstruction of the system of perception.
> Finally, I want to remark on the high skill of Carl and Ruth, of their
> silences, their voices, their glances. It was always some response
> and they were responded to. It was a great phenomenon, a great
> experience. (Rogers, 1987, pp. 298–99)

This kind of experience speaks against the perception of the Person-Centered Approach as safe, harmless, innocuous, and superficial. It is intended to be safe, but clearly it can also be powerful.

• *Empathy*

Empathy, in Person-Centered Therapy, is an active, immediate, continuous process. The counselor makes a maximum effort to get within and to *live* the attitudes expressed instead of observing them, diagnosing them, or thinking of ways to make the process go faster. Such understanding must be acquired through intense, continuous, and active attention to the feelings of others, to the exclusion of any other type of attention (Rogers, 1951).

The accuracy of the therapist's empathic understanding has often been emphasized, but more important is the therapist's interest in appreciating the world of the client and offering such understanding with the willingness to be corrected.

This creates a process in which the therapist gets closer and closer to the client's meanings and feelings, developing an ever-deepening relationship based on respect for and understanding of the other person.

Person-centered therapists vary in their views of the empathic understanding process. Some aim to convey an understanding of just what the client wishes to communicate. For Rogers, it felt right not only to clarify meanings of which the client was aware, but also those just below the level of awareness. Rogers was especially passionate about empathy not being exemplified by a technique such as 'reflection of feeling', but by the therapist's sensitive immersion in the client's world of experience. Brodley (1993) has documented the high proportion of 'empathic understanding responses' in Rogers' therapy transcripts.

• *Unconditional positive regard*
Other terms for this condition are *warmth, acceptance, nonpossessive caring,* and *prizing*.

> When the therapist is experiencing a positive, nonjudgmental, acceptant attitude toward whatever the client *is* at that moment, therapeutic movement or change is more likely. It involves the therapist's willingness for the client to *be* whatever immediate feeling is going on — confusion, resentment, fear, anger, courage, love, or pride . . . When the therapist prizes the client in a total rather than a conditional way, forward movement is likely. (Rogers, 1986a, p. 198)

• *Congruence*
Rogers regarded congruence as:

> . . . the most basic of the attitudinal conditions that foster therapeutic growth . . . [it] does not mean that the therapist burdens the client with all of his or her problems or feelings. It does not mean that the therapist blurts out impulsively any attitudes that come to mind. It does mean, however, that the therapist does not deny to himself or herself the feelings being experienced and that the therapist is willing to express and to be open about any persistent feelings that exist in the relationship. It means avoiding the temptation to hide behind a mask of professionalism. (Rogers and Sanford, 1985, p. 1379)

Correspondingly, an effective way of dealing with the common occurrence of therapist fatigue is to express it. This strengthens the relationship because the therapist is not trying to cover up a real feeling. It may also reduce or eliminate the fatigue and restore the therapist to a fully attending and empathic state.

• *Implied Therapeutic Conditions*
There are three other conditions in addition to the 'therapist-offered' conditions of empathy, congruence, and unconditional positive regard (Rogers, 1957):
1. The client and therapist must be in psychological contact.

2. The client must be experiencing some anxiety, vulnerability, or incongruence.
3. The client must receive or experience the conditions offered by the therapist.

Rogers described the first two as preconditions for therapy. The third, the reception by the client of the conditions offered by the therapist, sometimes overlooked, is essential. Research relating therapeutic outcome to empathy, congruence, and unconditional positive regard based on external judgments of these variables is moderately supportive of the person-centered hypothesis. If the ratings are done by clients themselves, the relationship to outcome is much stronger. Orlinsky and Howard (1978) reviewed 15 studies relating client perception of empathy to outcome and found that 12 supported the critical importance of perceived empathy.

Process of psychotherapy

The practice of person-centered therapy dramatizes its differences from most other orientations. Therapy begins immediately, with the therapist trying to understand the client's world in whatever way the client wishes to share it. The first interview is not used to take a history, to arrive at a diagnosis, to determine if the client is treatable, or to establish the length of treatment.

The therapist immediately shows respect for clients, allowing them to proceed in whatever way is comfortable for them. She or he listens without prejudice and without a private agenda. The therapist is open to either positive or negative feelings, speech or silence. The first hour may be the first of hundreds or it may be the only one; this is for the client to determine. If the client has questions, the therapist tries to recognize and to respond to whatever feelings are implicit in the questions. 'How am I going to get out of this mess?' may be the expression of the feeling, my situation seems hopeless. The therapist will convey recognition and acceptance of this attitude. If this question is actually a plea for suggestions, the therapist may reply that she or he does not have the answers, but hopes to help the client find the ones that are right for him or her. There is a willingness to stay with the client in moments of confusion and despair. There is a realization that reassurance and easy answers are not helpful and show a lack of respect for the client.

The therapist looks to the client for decisions about the timing and frequency of therapy. The therapist must respect her or his own availability, but is guided as much as possible by scheduling that feels right to the client. Person-centered therapists commonly share with their clients the responsibility for fee setting and manner of payment. In a money-oriented society, this is an opportune area for showing respect for the client.

Regard is also demonstrated through discussion of options such as group therapy and family therapy, in contrast to therapists of other orientations who 'put' the client in a group or make therapy conditional on involvement of the whole family. This is not to be interpreted as meaning that the client is allowed to dictate the circumstances of therapy, but to make clear that the client is a vital partner in determining these conditions. On many issues, the client is regarded as the expert.

An interview illustrating the process of therapy

It has always been characteristic of the Person-Centered Approach to illustrate its principles with verbatim accounts. This has the advantage of depicting the interaction between therapist and client more exactly and gives readers the opportunity to agree or to differ with the interpretation of the data.

The following is a demonstration interview carried out by Carl Rogers in 1983. Because of space limitations, the middle third of the interview has been omitted. Asterisks indicate words that could not be made out in the transcription (T = Therapist, C = Client).

T1:   OK, I think I'm ready. And you . . . ready?

C1:   Yes.

T2:   I don't know what you might want to talk about, but I'm very ready to hear. We have half an hour, and I hope that in that half an hour we can get to know each other as deeply as possible, but we don't need to strive for anything. I guess that's my feeling. Do you want to tell me whatever is on your mind?

C2:   I'm having a lot of problems dealing with my daughter. She's 20 years old; she's in college; I'm having a lot of trouble letting her go . . . And I have a lot of guilt feelings about her; I have a real need to hang on to her.

T3:   A need to hang on so you can kind of make up for the things you feel guilty about — is that part of it?

C3:   There's a lot of that . . . Also, she's been a real friend to me, and filled my life . . . And it's very hard *** a lot of empty places now that she's not with me.

T4:   The old vacuum, sort of, when she's not there.

C4:   Yes. Yes. I also would like to be the kind of mother that could be strong and say, you know, 'Go and have a good life,' and this is really hard for me to do that.

T5:   It's very hard to give up something that's been so precious in your life, but also something that I guess has caused you pain when you mentioned guilt.

C5:   Yeah, and I'm aware that I have some anger toward her that I don't always get what I want. I have needs that are not met. And, uh, I don't feel I have a right to those needs. You know . . . She's a daughter; she's not my mother — though sometimes I feel as if I'd like her to mother me . . . It's very difficult for me to ask for that and have a right to it.

T6:   So it may be unreasonable, but still, when she doesn't meet your needs, its makes you mad.

C6:   Yeah, I get very angry, very angry with her.
        (Pause)

T7:   You're also feeling a little tension at this point, I guess.

C7:   Yeah. Yeah. A lot of conflict . . .

T8:   Umm-hmm . . .

C8:   A lot of pain.

T9:   A lot of pain. Can you say anything more what that's about?

C9:   *(Sigh)* I reach out for her, and she moves away from me. And she steps back and pulls back . . . And then I feel like a really bad person. Like some kind of monster, that she doesn't want me to touch her and hold her like I did when she was a little girl . . .

T10:   It sounds like a very double feeling there. Part of it is, 'Damn it, I want you close.' The other part of it is, 'Oh my God, what a monster I am to not let you go'.

C10:   Umm-hum. Yeah. I should be stronger. I should be a grown woman and allow this to happen.

T11:   But instead, sometimes you feel like her daughter.

C11:   Umm-hmm. Yeah. Sometimes when I cuddle her, I feel I'm being cuddled.

T12:   Umm-hmm.

       (Pause)

       But you place a lot of expectations on yourself: 'I should be different.'

C12:   Yeah. I should be more mature. I should have my needs met so that I don't have to get anything from her.

T13:   You should find other ways and other sources to meet your needs, but somehow that doesn't seem to be happening?

C13:   Well, I feel I get a lot of my needs met, but the need from her is very strong — it's the need from a woman really, I think . . . It doesn't quite make up the needs I get from men **** . . .

T14:   There are some things that you just want from her.

C14:   Umm-hmm. Yeah. Just from her. *(Sigh)*

T15:   When she pulls back, that's a very painful experience.

C15:   Yeah, that really hurts. That really hurts. *(Big sigh)*

       (Pause)

T16:   It looks like you're feeling some of that hurt right now.

C16:   Yeah, I can really feel her stepping back.

T-17: Umm-hmm. Umm-hmm.

       (Pause)

T18:   Pulling away from you.

C17:   Yeah . . . Going away.

T19:   **** you feel her sort of slipping away, and you . . . and it hurts . . . and —

C18:   Yeah. I'm just sort of sitting here alone. I guess like, you know, I can feel her gone and I'm just left here.

T20:   Umm-hmm. You're experiencing it right now: that she's leaving and here you are all alone.

C19:   Yeah. Yeah. Yeah. I feel really lonely. *(Cries)*

T21:   Umm-hmm. Umm-hmm . . . If I understand right, not lonely in every respect, but lonely for her.

T22:   I'm not a good therapist — I forgot a box of Kleenex, but . . . I think I've got . . . *(Laughs)*

C20:   Thank you. *(Laughs)* I feel like I could cry a million tears about that. *(Laughs)*

T23:   Umm-hmm. It feels as if the tears could just flow and flow on that score.

C22:   Yeah. Never stop.

T24:   That just to have her leave, have her pull away is just more than you can take.

C23:   Yeah. Yeah. It's really hard to go on without her. *(Cries)*

T-25: It sounds as though that is almost the center of your life.

C-24: It's very close to that, you know. My husband, my children, my home . . . My work is important too, but there's something about the heart that's connected to her. *(Sigh)*

T26:   And there's a real ache in your heart with her leaving.

C25:   Yeah. Yeah. *(Cries)*
       (Pause)

C26:   Oh . . . I just don't want her to go.

T27:   I want to keep her as my daughter, as my little girl, as the one I can cuddle . . .

C27:   Yeah, yeah. The one I can cuddle. She likes to cuddle too.

T28:   Umm-hmm. Umm-hmm.

C28:   *(Cries)* And you know, I'm also scared for her. I'm scared for her out in the world. I'm scared for her to have to go through all the things that I did and how painful that is. I'd like to save her from that.

T29:   You'd like to protect her from that life out there and all the pain that you went through . . .

C29:   Yeah, yeah. And all the new stuff that all the young people are going through . . . It's very hard. She's struggling.

T30:   It's a hard world . . .

C30:   Yeah, very hard . . .

T31:   And you'd like to cushion it for her . . .

C31:   Yeah, make it perfect . . .

[Middle third of interview omitted]

T73:   Does that mean that you feel no one cares, no one accepts?

C73:   No. I feel like now that there are people who do, who care and accept and hear and value me. But there's that little —

T74:   So that the person who can't care and accept and value you is you.

C74:   Umm-hmm. Yeah. It's mostly me.

T75:   The person who sees those things as unforgivable is you.

C75: Yeah. Yeah. Nobody else is that hard on me.
T76: Umm-hmm. Nobody could be that cruel to you, or make such awful judgment.
C76: *(Sigh)*
T77: Or hate you so.
C77: Or hate me so. Yeah.
T78: Sounds like you're the judge, the jury, and the executioner.
C78: Yeah, my own worst enemy.
T79: You pass a pretty tough sentence on yourself.
C79: Yeah. Yeah, I do. Not a very good friend to me.
T80: No.
C80: **** —
T81: You're not a very good friend to yourself. Umm-hmm.
C81: Umm-hmm.
T82: And you wouldn't think of doing to a friend what you do to yourself.
C82: That's right. I would feel terrible if I treated anyone the way I treat me.
T83: Umm-hmm. Umm-hmm. Umm-hmm.
      (Pause)
T84: Because to you, your self is just unlovable.
C84: Well, there's a part of me that's lovable . . .
T85: OK. OK.
C85: Yeah.
T86: OK. So in some respects you do love yourself.
C86: Yeah. I love and appreciate the little child part of me —
T87: Umm-hmm —
C87: That's really struggled and come through —
T88: Umm-hmm —
C88: And survived —
T89: Umm-hmm —
C89: An awful lot.
T90: Umm-hmm. That's a damned nice little girl.
C90: Yeah. She's really special —
T-91: Umm-hmm.
C91: She's like my daughter.
T92: Uh-huh.
C92: *(Sigh)*
T93: And she's a daughter you can hold on to.
C93: Yeah. Yeah. I can still cuddle her. And tell her she's beautiful. And love her.
T94: And she's a survivor, and she's strong, and she's been through a lot, but she's OK.
C94: Yeah. Yeah, she is. She's real special.
      (Pause)

T95:   It must be nice to have such a special person in your life.

C95:   Yeah. It is. That is nice. Yeah. She's very nice.

T96:   Can she care for the other parts of you?

C96:   She's starting to **** —

T97:   She's starting to.

C97:   Yeah.

T98:   Umm-hmm.

C98:   Just beginning.

T99:   Umm-hmm. She's not as hard on you as the adult you.

C99:   No. That's right.

T100: Umm-hmm.

C100: She's much more understanding.

T101: Umm-hmm.

C101: And compassionate.

T102: Umm-hmm.

C102: *(Sigh)*
       (Pause)

T103: Sounds like she loves you.

C103: Yeah. She gives me all that unconditional love that I didn't feel
       like I got.

T104: Umm-hmm. Umm-hmm. Umrn-hmm. And she loves all of you.

C104: Yeah. Yeah. She loves all of me.

T105: To her, none of it is unforgivable.

C105: No. It's all OK.

T106: All OK.

C106: Yeah. *(Sigh)*
       (Pause)

T107: I like her.

C107: I like her too. *(Sigh)* She's going to save me.

T108: Hmm?

C108: She's going to save me.

T109: She's going to save you.

C109: *(Laughs)* From hurting myself anymore.

T110: Umm-hmm . . . She may really be able to keep you from being so
       hard on yourself. Really save you.

C110: Yeah. I think she will; I think she will; I just have to give her a
       little help too.

T111: Umm-hmm. Umm-hmm.

C111: Like we'll work together . . . **** save me.

T112: She's a good companion to have, isn't she?

C112: Yeah, she is. *(Sigh)* It's good to have a friend.

T113: Yeah. Umm-hmm. To have that kind of a friend inside really touches
       you.

C113: Yeah. It really does. It'll never go away.

T114: Umm-hmm.

C114: It'll always be there for me.

T115: Umm-hmm. She's not going to pull away and —

C115: Go out into the world and do her thing. Laughs. **** gonna stay home with Mama.

T116: Umm-hmm. Umm-hmm. And be a mother to Mama too, huh?

C116: Yeah. Yeah.

(Pause)

(Sigh)

T117: What's that smile?

C117: It's your eyes are twinkling. (Both laugh)

T118: Yours twinkle too.

(Laugh)

(Sigh)

Tape over. [1]

Commentary

The interview illustrates, in concrete form, many principles of the process of person-centered therapy:

In T2, Rogers makes it clear that he is leaving it up to the client to talk about what she wishes. He indicates that this can be a deep exchange but that it does not have to be.

T1 and T2 signify that Rogers is ready to enter immediately into a person-to-person exchange in which he will be 'very ready to hear' whatever the client chooses to bring up.

After this, his responses are consistent attempts to understand the client and to communicate, or check out, his understanding of her feelings. They show that he is open to whatever kinds of feelings the client verbalizes. In T6, he recognizes a negative feeling, anger; in T10, he responds to a mixture of feelings; in T23, he accepts her feeling that her tears are endless; in T85 and T86 and many succeeding responses, he conveys his recognition of positive self-attitudes.

The therapist's last two statements (T117 and T118) reveal a mutuality in the relationship implicit throughout the interview but often not obvious on the printed page.

The client's tears and frequent expressions of self-depreciation could provide a stimulus for reassurance. However, Rogers consistently does not do this; he is a reliable, understanding partner who stays with the client as she lives with her various negative feelings and accompanies her as she finds the strength to rise above them.

---

1. From a previously unpublished article by Carl Rogers given to me for this chapter. N.J.R.

Mechanisms of psychotherapy

The interview just quoted reveals many examples of the way in which change and growth are fostered in the Person-Centered Approach. Rogers' straightforward statements in opening the interview (T1 and T2) allow the client to begin with a statement of the problem of concern to her and to initiate dialogue at a level comfortable for her.

Just as he does not reassure, Rogers does not ask questions. In response to C2, he does not ask the myriad questions that could construct a logical background and case history for dealing with the presenting problem. Rogers does not see himself as responsible for arriving at a solution to the problem as presented, or determining whether *this* is the problem that will be focused on in therapy, or changing the client's attitudes. The therapist sees the client as having these responsibilities and respects her capacity to fulfill them.

In this excerpt from a person-centered interview are numerous examples of the client's expanding her view of the problem after the therapist recognized her stated percept, accepted it unconditionally, and communicated his understanding to her:

1. Rogers' recognition of the client's stated need to hang on to her daughter (T3) is followed by the client's recognition that her daughter has been 'a real friend to me' (C3).
2. The therapist's appreciation of the difficulty the client has in letting go of her daughter (T5) is followed by the revelation of anger felt toward her daughter because 'I don't always get what I want' (C5). The therapist's acceptance of the anger as stated (T6) helps the client to bring out the extent of the emotion (T6).
3. The therapist's continued recognition of the client's feelings (T7 and T8) helps her to express and share the extreme pain she feels (C8).

Another result worth noting is the experiencing of emotion in the moment, as distinguished from the recounting of the emotion. This comes out in the exchange (T15, C15) and continues into the tears that begin in C20.

In the final third of the interview, we see another result of the therapist's empathic way of being with the client. She has now shifted from her daughter to herself as the agent of bad self-treatment: 'That's right. I would feel terrible if I treated anyone the way I treat me' (C82).

The mechanism of therapist acceptance leading to change of self-attitude is shown operating powerfully in T84, C84: 'Because to you, your self is just unlovable.' 'Well, there's a part of me that's lovable . . . ' The client goes on to define that part as 'the little child part of me' (C86) and 'She's really special' (C90), relates that part of herself to her daughter (C91), and sees that she herself can provide all the caring feelings she has been seeking unsuccessfully from her daughter (C93). The remainder of the interview clarifies a reciprocal relationship in which she sees that a part of herself that she prizes and loves is also a part she can depend on as a permanent source of support.

The interview exemplifies empathy backed by genuineness and unconditional positive regard. It helps the client to (1) examine her problems in a way that shifts responsibility from others to herself, (2) experience emotions in the immediacy of the therapy encounter, (3) accept aspects of self formerly denied to awareness, and (4) raise her general level of self-regard.

Therapeutic change involves both cognitive and affective elements. The integration of intellect and feelings is occurring in the therapist and in his relationship with the client. He is grasping her perceptions of her external and internal worlds, doing so with warmth and genuine caring. The client is also looking at some of the most troubling aspects of her life, changing the way she looks at others and self, and experiencing anger, pain, loneliness, tearfulness, nurturance, disgust, tenderness, and compassion. The resolution that she introduces toward the end of the interview (C114), 'It'll always be there for me' (the part of herself that will never let her down), may be seen as the therapeutic blending of conation, cognition, and affect.

An early formulation

In a paper given at the first meeting of the American Academy of Psychotherapists in 1956, Rogers (1959a) presented 'a client-centered view' of 'the essence of psychotherapy'. He conceptualized a 'molecule' of personality change, hypothesizing 'therapy is made up of a series of such molecules, sometimes strung rather closely together, sometimes occurring at long intervals, always with periods of preparatory experiences in between' (p. 52). Rogers attributed four qualities to such a 'moment of movement':

> (1) It is something which occurs in this existential moment. It is not a *thinking* about something, it is an *experience* of something at this instant, in the relationship. (2) It is an experiencing which is without barriers, or inhibitions, or holding back. She is consciously *feeling* as sorry for herself as she *is* sorry for herself. (3) This is . . . an experience which has been repeated many times in her past, but which has never been completely experienced. In the past she has felt it at some physiological level, but has 'covered it up'. This is the first time that it has been experienced completely. (4) This experience has the quality of being acceptable. It is . . . not 'I feel sorry for myself, and that is reprehensible.' It is instead an experience of 'My feeling is one of sorrow for myself, and this is an acceptable part of me.' (pp. 52–3)

This mechanism of psychotherapy described by Rogers in 1956 closely matches the experience of the client just discussed: she has a full, emotional experience of a part of herself, a lovable child, of which she has been aware but also covered up; she now experiences that part of herself, and accepts the child completely as part of a newly integrated self. Her laughter and twinkling eyes express the great emotional gratification that accompanies this reorganization.

Applications

Problems

Person-centered therapists offer the same basic conditions to all prospective clients. These conditions do not include psychological tests, history taking, or other assessment procedures leading to diagnoses and treatment plans. Diagnostic labels take away from the person of the client; assuming a professional posture takes away from the person of the therapist. The therapist's task is uncluttered by the need to be an expert. Rogers clearly stated his position on this issue:

> We have come to recognize that if we can provide understanding of the way the client seems to himself at this moment, he can do the rest. The therapist must lay aside his preoccupation with diagnosis and his diagnostic shrewdness, must discard his tendency to make professional evaluations, must cease his endeavors to formulate an accurate prognosis, must give up the temptation to subtly guide the individual, and must concentrate on one purpose only: that of providing deep understanding and acceptance of the attitudes consciously held at this moment by the client as he explores step-by-step into the dangerous areas which he has been denying to consciousness. (1946, p. 420)

A consequence of this position is that the Person-Centered Approach has been used with individuals diagnosed by others as psychotic or retarded, as well as with people simply seeking a personal growth experience.

'James' was one of the patients in the Wisconsin study (Rogers et al., 1967). In the course of a detailed description of two interviews with this patient, a 'moment of change' is described in which the patient's hard shell is broken by this perception of the therapist's warmth and caring, and he pours out his hurt and sorrow in anguished sobs. This followed an intense effort by Rogers, in two interviews a week for the better part of a year, to reach this 28-year-old man, whose sessions were filled with prolonged silences. Rogers stated, 'We were relating as two . . . genuine persons. In the moments of real encounter the differences in education, in status, in degree of psychological disturbance, had no importance — we were two persons in a relationship' (Rogers et al., 1967, p. 411). Eight years later, this patient telephoned Rogers and reported continued success on his job and general stability in his living situation, and he expressed appreciation for the therapeutic relationship with Rogers (Meador and Rogers, 1984).

This clinical vignette emphasizes the person-centered rather than problem-centered nature of this approach. All people have feelings, like to be understood, and have issues of self-concept maintenance and enhancement. The Person-Centered Approach respects the various ways people use to deal with these issues. In this regard, it may work particularly well with people who are 'different'.

This nonconcern with a person's 'category' can be seen in person-centered cross-cultural and international conflict resolution. Empathy is provided in equal measure for Catholics and Protestants in Northern Ireland (Rogers and Ryback, 1984) and for oppressed blacks and troubled whites in South Africa (Rogers, 1986b). Conflict resolution is fostered when the facilitator appreciates the attitudes and feelings of opposing parties, and then the stereotyping of one side by the other is broken down by the protagonists' achievement of empathy.

Evaluation

The heart of evaluation in Person-Centered Therapy is the evaluative process in the client. The client evaluates whether therapy is useful and the specific ways in which he or she can use it. The client decides what to bring up, how much to explore any particular issue, the level of emotional intensity, and so on. The natural extension of this client-centered responsibility is that the client decides when it is time to terminate therapy.

Because the theory of personality development in Person-Centered Therapy is based on how clients experience change, there is a smooth transition from clients' descriptions of change and those of therapists or external judges. Victor Raimy's (1948) pioneering dissertation on self-concept at Ohio State University was based on self-references in counseling interviews and on simple quantitative analysis of changes in self-approval in 14 complete series of counseling interviews. He defined a *self-reference* as 'a group of words spoken by the client which directly or indirectly described him as he appears in his own eyes'. Self-ratings of this type were used extensively in the 'parallel studies' project analyzing the first ten completely recorded cases at the University of Chicago Counseling Center (Rogers et al., 1949). Rogers described his experience involving clients' perceptions of the importance of self:

> In my early days as a therapist, I tended to scorn any thinking about the self . . . [it] seemed so ephemeral . . . Another problem was that it had very different meanings for different people.
>
> But my clients kept pushing me toward its consideration. It cropped up so frequently in therapeutic interviews. 'I can't be my real self;' 'I think that underneath I have a solid self, if I could get to it;' 'I don't understand my self;' 'With my mother, I never show my true self;' 'I'm always afraid that if I uncover the real me, I'll find there is nothing there.' Clearly, it was important to find a way of defining, of thinking about, the self. But how? (1986c, p. 1)

Rogers eventually found an answer in William Stephenson's Q-sort technique. It was possible to study 'the self as perceived by the individual', with items such as 'I am assertive', 'I feel inadequate', or 'I am a responsible person'. One hundred such items were sorted by the client into nine piles in a continuum from 'most like me' to 'least like me'. This method allowed for quantified descriptions of self-concept and correlations between perceived self before and after therapy, between perceived self and ideal self, and so on.

After the formulation of 'the necessary and sufficient conditions of constructive personality change' (Rogers, 1957), considerable research was generated on the measurement of empathy, congruence, and unconditional positive regard and their effects on the outcome of psychotherapy. In the early 1970s, the relationship of outcome to the provision of person-centered conditions was generally regarded as impressive (Bergin and Garfield, 1971). By the late 1970s, some psychotherapy researchers concluded that the 'potency and generalizability' of the earlier evidence were 'not as great as once thought' (Mitchell, Bozarth, and Krauft, 1977). More recently, Patterson (1984), Raskin (1985), and Stubbs and Bozarth (1994) have challenged the basis for questioning the strength of the original conclusions.

Through all of these assessments, a consistent finding has been that when the measurement of the therapist-offered conditions is based on client perception rather than external judgement, the relationship to outcome is stronger. Most of this research has utilized the *Relationship Inventory* (Barrett-Lennard, 1986).

Treatment

The process of the Person-Centered Approach has been described particularly in the context of individual psychotherapy with adults, its original arena. The broadening of the 'client-centered' designation to 'person-centered' stemmed from the generalizability of client-centered principles to other areas of human relations.

• Play therapy

Rogers deeply admired Jessie Taft's play therapy with children at the Philadelphia Child Guidance Clinic and was specifically impressed by her ability to accept the negative feelings verbalized or acted out by the child, which led to positive attitudes in the child.

One of Rogers' graduate student associates, Virginia Axline, formulated play therapy as a comprehensive system of treatment for children. Axline shared Rogers' deep conviction about self-direction and self-actualization and, in addition, was passionate in her interest in helping fearful, inhibited, sometimes abused children to develop the courage to express long-buried emotions and to experience the exhilaration of being themselves. She used play when children could not overcome the obstacles to self-realization by words alone.

Axline made major contributions to research on play therapy, group therapy with children, schoolroom applications, and parent-teacher as well as teacher-administrator relationships. She also demonstrated the value of play therapy for poor readers, for clarifying the diagnosis of mental retardation in children, and for dealing with race conflicts in young children (Axline, 1947; Rogers, 1951).

Ellinwood and Raskin (1993) offer a comprehensive chapter on client-centered play therapy that starts with the principles formulated by Axline and shows how they have evolved into practice with parents and children in the 1990s. Empathy with children and adults, respect for their capacity for self-directed change, and the congruence of the therapist are emphasized and illustrated.

• Client-centered group process

Beginning as a one-to-one method of counseling in the 1940s, client-centered principles were being employed in group therapy, classroom teaching, workshops, organizational development, and concepts of leadership less than ten years later. Teaching, intensive groups, and peace and conflict resolution exemplify the spread of the principles that originated in counseling and psychotherapy.

• Classroom teaching

In Columbus, while Rogers was beginning to espouse the nondirective approach, he accepted the role of the expert who structured classes and graded students. At Chicago, he began to practice a new philosophy, which he later articulated in *Freedom to Learn:*

> I ceased to be a teacher. It wasn't easy. It happened rather gradually, but as I began to trust students, I found they did incredible things in their communication with each other, in their learning of content material in the course, in blossoming out as growing human beings. Most of all they gave me courage to be myself more freely, and this led to profound interaction. They told me their feelings, they raised questions I had never thought about. I began to sparkle with emerging ideas that were new and exciting to me, but also, I found, to them. I believe I passed some sort of crucial divide when I was able to begin a course with a statement something like this: 'This course has the title "Personality Theory" (or whatever). But what we do with this course is up to us. We can build it around the goals we want to achieve, within that very general area. We can conduct it the way we want to. We can decide mutually how we wish to handle these bugaboos of exams and grades. I have many resources on tap, and I can help you find others. I believe I am one of the resources, and I am available to you to the extent that you wish. But this is our class. So what do we want to make of it?' This kind of statement said in effect, 'We are *free* to learn what we wish, *as* we wish.' It made the whole climate of the classroom completely different. Though at the time I had never thought of phrasing it this way, I changed at that point from being a *teacher* and *evaluator,* to being a *facilitator of learning* — a very different occupation. (1983, p. 26)

The change was not easy for Rogers. Nor was it easy for students who were used to being led and experienced the self-evaluation method of grading as strange and unwelcome.

• The intensive group

The early 1960s witnessed another important development, the intensive group. Rogers' move to California in 1964 spurred his interest in intensive groups, and in 1970, he published a 15-step formulation of the development of the basic encounter group.

Rogers visualized the core of the process, the 'basic encounter', as occurring when an individual in the group responds with undivided empathy to another in the group who is sharing and also not holding back.

Rogers conceptualized the leader or facilitator's role in the group as exemplifying the same basic qualities as the individual therapist; in addition, he thought it important to accept and respect the group as a whole, as well as the individual members. An outstanding example of the basic encounter group can be seen in the film *Journey into Self* which shows very clearly the genuineness, spontaneity, caring, and empathic behavior of co-facilitators Rogers and Richard Farson (McGaw, Farson, and Rogers, 1968).

• Peace and conflict resolution
Searching for peaceful ways to resolve conflict between larger groups became the cutting edge of the person-centered movement in the 1980s. The scope of the person-centered movement's interest in this arena extends all the way to conflicts between nations. In some instances opposing groups have met in an intensive format with person-centered leadership. This has occurred with parties from Northern Ireland, South Africa, and Central America. A meeting in Austria on the 'Central American Challenge' included a significant number of diplomats and other government officials (Rogers, 1986d). A major goal accomplished at this meeting was to provide a model for person-centered experiences for diplomats in the hope that they would be strengthened in future international meetings by an increased capacity to be empathic. Rogers (1987) and his associates also conducted workshops on the Person-Centered Approach in Eastern Europe and the Soviet Union.

Rogers offered a person-centered interpretation of the Camp David accord and a proposal for avoiding nuclear disaster (Rogers and Ryback, 1984). One notion is central to all these attempts at peaceful conflict resolution: when a group in conflict can receive and operate under conditions of empathy, genuineness, and caring, negative stereotypes of the opposition weaken and are replaced by personal, human feelings of relatedness (Raskin and Zucconi, 1984).

Case example[2]
Introduction
In 1964 Carl Rogers was filmed in a half-hour interview with a woman client for a film series, *Three Approaches to Psychotherapy* (Rogers, 1965). That interview contains many of the elements of Person-Centered Therapy discussed in this chapter and is a typical example of the person-centered way of working.

Rogers had never seen the woman before the interview and knew his contact with her would be limited to a half-hour. In his introduction to the interview, he describes the way he will hope to be with her. He says he will, if he is fortunate,

---

2. This example is borrowed from Meador and Rogers, 1984, pp. 187–92.

first of all, be real, try to be aware of his own inner feelings and to express them in ways that will not impose these feelings on her. Second, he hopes he will be caring of her, prizing her as an individual and accepting her. Third, he will try to understand her inner world from the inside; he will try to understand not just the surface meanings, but the meanings just below the surface. Rogers says if he is successful in holding these three attitudes, he expects certain things to happen to the client. He expects she will move from a remoteness from her inner experiencing to a more immediate awareness and expression of it; from disapproving of parts of her self to greater self-acceptance; from a fear of relating to relating to him more directly; from holding rigid, black-and-white constructs of reality to holding more tentative constructs; and from seeing the locus-of-evaluation outside herself to finding the locus-of-evaluation in her own inner experiencing.

The fact that the interview lasted for only half an hour and the client was seen by the therapist only one time emphasizes that the Person-Centered Approach depends on the here-and-now attitudes of the therapist, attitudes as valid and constant in a brief interaction as over a long period.

The interview

The interview is with a young woman, Gloria, a 30-year-old divorcée. The first portion of the interview concerns the problem Gloria presents initially, that she has not been honest with her nine-year-old daughter Pammy about the fact that she has had sexual relationships with men since her divorce. Gloria has always been honest with her children and is feeling great conflict over having lied to Pammy. She wants to know whether telling Pammy the truth about her sexual relationships would affect Pammy adversely.

At the very beginning Gloria tells Rogers, 'I almost want an answer from you. I want you to tell me if it would affect her wrong if I told her the truth, or what.' Later, on two occasions, she asks again for a direct answer to her question. Clearly, she wants an 'authority' to tell her what to do. Rogers' responses assure her that he understands her dilemma and guide her to her own resources for answering. After each time that she asks the question and hears the response, Gloria explores her own feelings a little more deeply.

To her first request, Rogers replies, 'And it's this concern about her (Pammy) and the fact that you really aren't — that this open relationship that has existed between you, now you feel it's kind of vanished?' After Gloria's reply, he says, 'I sure wish I could give you the answer as to what you should tell her.' 'I was afraid you were going to say that,' she says. Rogers replies, 'Because what you really want is an answer.'

Gloria begins to explore her relationship with Pammy and concludes that she feels real uncertainty about whether or not Pammy would accept her 'devilish' or 'shady' side. Gloria finds she is not certain she accepts that part of herself. Again she asks Rogers for an answer: 'You're just going to sit there and let me stew in it and I want more.' Rogers replies, 'No, I don't want to let you just stew in your feelings, but on the other hand, I also feel this is the kind of very private thing that I couldn't possibly answer for you. But I sure as anything will try to help you work toward your own answer. I don't know whether that makes any sense to you, but I mean it.' Gloria says she can tell he really does mean it and again begins to explore her feelings, this time focusing more on the conflict she herself feels between her actions and her inner standards. Shortly, she again says, 'I want you very much to give me a direct answer.'

Rogers replies:

> I guess, I am sure this will sound evasive to you, but it seems to me that perhaps the person you are not being fully honest with is you, because I was very much struck by the fact that you were saying, 'If I feel all right about what I have done, whether it's going to bed with a man or what, if I really feel all right about it, then I do not have any concern about what I would tell Pam or my relationship with her.'

To this Gloria answers:

> Right. All right. Now I hear what you are saying. Then all right, then I want to work on accepting *me* then. I want to work on feeling all right about it. That makes sense. Then that will come natural and then I won't have to worry about Pammy . . .

This statement indicates that Gloria has assimilated a real insight, an understanding that the solution to her problem is in herself rather than in an authoritative opinion on how knowledge of her sex life will affect Pammy.

From this point in the interview she focuses on her inner conflict. She tells Rogers what she 'wishes he would tell her' and then says she can't quite take the risk of being the way she wants to be with her children 'unless an authority tells me that'. Rogers says with obvious feeling, 'I guess one thing that I feel very keenly is that it's an awfully risky thing to live. You'd be taking a chance on your relationship with her and taking a chance on letting her know who you are, really.' Gloria says she wishes very strongly that she could take more risks, that she could act on her own feelings of rightness without always needing encouragement from others. Again she says what she'd like to do in the situation with Pammy and then adds, 'Now I feel like "Now that's solved" — and I didn't even solve a thing; but I feel relieved.'

Gloria: I do feel like you have been saying to me — you are not giving me advice, but I do feel like you are saying, 'You know what pattern you want to follow, Gloria, and go ahead and follow it.' I sort of feel a backing up from you.

Rogers: I guess the way I sense it, you've been telling me that you know what you want to do, and yes, I do believe in backing up people in what they want to do. It's a little different slant than the way it seems to you.

Gloria's expressing the feeling, 'Now that's solved — and I didn't even solve a thing; but I feel relieved', exemplifies an awareness of inner experiencing, a felt meaning she has not yet put into words. She 'feels relieved', as though her problem is solved. Therapeutic movement has occurred in her inner self before she understands its explicit meaning. It is interesting that she says in the same speech, 'I feel a backing up from you'. She *feels* the support of Rogers' empathic understanding and acceptance of her. From the person-centered point of view there is a relationship between her feeling understood and valued and her movement from seeking the locus-of-evaluation outside herself to depending on her own inner feeling of 'rightness' for a solution to her problem.

The next portion of the interview involves Gloria's experience of her own inner valuing processes and the conflicts she sometimes feels. She explains her use of the word *utopia,* which refers to times she is able to follow her inner feelings: 'When I do follow a feeling and I feel this good feeling inside of me, that's sort of utopia. That's what I mean. That's the way I like to feel whether it's a bad thing or a good thing. But I feel right about me.' Rogers' response that in those moments she must feel 'all in one piece' brings tears to Gloria's eyes, for those moments are all too few. In the midst of her weeping, she continues speaking.

Gloria: You know what else I was just thinking? I . . . a dumb thing . . .
          that all of a sudden while I was talking to you, I thought,
          'Gee, how nice I can talk to you and I want you to
          approve of me and I respect you, but I miss that my father couldn't
          talk to me like you are.' I mean, I'd like to say, 'Gee, I'd like you
          for my father.' I don't even know why that came to me.

Rogers: You look to me like a pretty nice daughter. But you really do
          miss that fact that you couldn't be open with your own Dad.

Gloria is now quite close to her inner experiencing, allowing her tears to flow as she thinks of her rare moments of 'utopia' and then expressing a feeling that comes into awareness of positive affection for Rogers. She then explores her relationship with her father, as she says, 'You know, when I talk about it, it feels more flip. If I just sit still a minute, it feels like a great big hurt down there.'

Gloria looks at and feels her deep inner hurt over her relationship to her father. She has moved significantly from seeking a solution outside herself to a problem with her children to looking inward at a painful hurt. She says she tries to soothe the hurt through relationships with fatherly men, pretending they are her father, as she is doing with Rogers.

Rogers: I don't feel that's pretending.

Gloria: Well, you're not really my father.

Rogers: No. I meant about the real close business.

Gloria: Well, see, I sort of feel that's pretending too, because I can't
          expect you to feel very close to me. You don't know me that
          well.

Rogers: All I can know is what I am feeling, and that is I feel close to you in this moment.

Here Rogers presents himself as he really is, offering Gloria the experience of genuine caring, an experience she missed in her relationship with her father. Shortly after this exchange, the interview ends.

Evaluation

It is clear that the therapist's empathy, genuineness, and caring come through and are received by the client throughout the course of the interview. His acceptance helps her make important progress. For instance, she begins the interview looking for an authority to tell her what to do, and by its end has much greater faith in her own ability to make decisions. She moves from trying to keep some distance from her emotions to letting them be expressed without inhibition, going so far as to focus directly on the great hurt she feels about her relationship with her father. She also starts off not accepting part of herself, and then sees greater self-acceptance as an important task for future work. Her self-concept becomes more complete, her experiencing becomes less rigid, her locus-of-evaluation moves from external to more internal, and her self-regard increases. All the important qualities of the therapist and client are revealed in this brief interview.

The intensity of Rogers' genuineness and presence in the relationship is readily apparent from watching the film. The strength of his feelings comes through when he says, 'It's an awfully risky thing to live', and when he clearly expresses his inner self: 'All I can know is what I am feeling, and that is I feel close to you in this moment.'

The therapeutic movement the client makes follows the direction and manner that Rogers initially predicted. First, he says she will move from a remoteness from her feelings to an immediate awareness and expression of them. She does in fact begin the interview wanting an answer to a troubling question and does move to a point toward the end where her feelings are flowing into awareness and she is expressing them as they occur. At one point she says, concerning her wanting a father like Rogers, 'I don't even know why that came to me.' She is allowing her feelings to come into expression without censoring, questioning, or even knowing where they are coming from.

Rogers also predicts Gloria will move from disapproving of herself toward self-acceptance. In the beginning, Gloria says she is not sure she accepts her 'shady' or 'devilish' side. Later, she very explicitly asks to work on accepting herself and spends much of the remaining time exploring the nuances of her self-acceptance.

Initially, Gloria believes there is a true answer that will solve her problem. She construes reality in this black-and-white fashion. Later, she tentatively considers relying on her own inner experiencing for solutions as she says, 'I wish I could take more risks.' Finally, she describes the utopian experience of feeling so sure of herself that whatever she does comes out of her inner experience and feels 'right'. This same example demonstrates the therapeutic process of moving from finding the locus-of-evaluation outside oneself to finding it in one's inner self.

The quality of this interview is like a piece of music that begins on a thin persistent note and gradually adds dimension and levels until the whole orchestra is playing. The intuitive interaction and response of the therapist are not unlike the interplay in a creative improvisation. Whatever wisdom science can bring to how the instruments are made and which combinations make for harmony and growth will greatly enrich the players, but we must never lose sight of the primacy of the creative human beings making the music.

As a result of countless inquiries about Gloria from people who had viewed his interview with her, Rogers (1984) published a historical note in which he stated that for about ten years after the interview, Gloria wrote to him approximately once or twice a year. Her last letter was written 'shortly before her untimely death' 15 years following the interview. He also described her reactions at a weekend conference led by him a year or more after the interview, during which her interviews with Rogers and with Fritz Perls and Albert Ellis were shown. She expressed much anger about the fact that she had done all the things Perls had asked her to do and that she had given over her power to him. Having seen the interview at this point, she did not like it, which contrasted with her positive reaction soon after the interview.

Rogers also described Gloria's request, at the end of a luncheon with him and his wife, Helen, during the same weekend, that they allow her to think of them as 'parents in spirit', parents she would have liked to have had. 'We each replied that we would be pleased and honored to have that status in her life. Her warm feelings for us were reciprocated . . . In the ensuing years she wrote me about many things in her life . . . There were very good times, and there were tragic times . . . and she showed sensitivity, wisdom, and courage in meeting the different aspects of her experience.' Rogers concludes, 'I am awed by the fact that this 15-year association grew out of the quality of the relationship we formed in one 30-minute period in which we truly met as persons. It is good to know that even one half-hour can make a difference in a life' (pp. 423–5).

Summary

The central hypothesis of the Person-Centered Approach is that individuals have within themselves vast resources for self-understanding and for altering their self-concepts, behavior, and attitudes toward others. These resources will become operative in a definable, facilitative, psychological climate. Such a climate is created by a psychotherapist who is empathic, caring, and genuine.

Empathy, as practiced in the Person-Centered Approach, refers to a consistent, unflagging appreciation of the experience of the client. It involves a continuous process of checking with the client to see if understanding is complete and accurate. It is carried out in a manner that is personal, natural, and free-flowing; it is not a mechanical kind of reflection or mirroring. *Caring* is characterized by a profound respect for the individuality of the client and by unconditional, nonpossessive regard. *Genuineness* is marked by congruence between what the therapist feels and says, and by the therapist's willingness to relate on a person-to-person basis rather than through a professionally distant role.

The impetus given to psychotherapy research by the Person-Centered Approach has resulted in substantial evidence demonstrating that changes in personality and behaviour occur when a therapeutic climate is provided. Two frequent results of successful person-centered therapy are increased self-esteem and greater openness to experience.

Trust in the perceptions and the self-directive capacities of clients expanded Client-Centered Therapy into a person-centered approach to education, group process, organizational development, and conflict resolution.

The world at the dawn of the twenty-first century is characterized by forces of enormous magnitude that threaten life on earth and, at the same time, the significance of the individual. In psychotherapy, the client and the practitioner are being increasingly hemmed in by externally managed care. These magnify the power of institutions and regulations and reduce the importance of individuals, feelings, and experience. In one sense this weakens the Person-Centered Approach; in another it ensures its continued existence and growth as a scientifically based system prizing individual worth.

Annotated bibliography

Barrett-Leonard, G. T. (1998) *Carl Rogers' helping system: Journey and substance.* London: Sage Publications.
A comprehensive and scholarly presentation of the Person-Centered Approach to psychotherapy and human relations. It starts with the beginnings of Client-Centered Therapy and the social-political-economic milieu of the 20s and 30s and continues with a description of early practice and theory, detailed examinations of the helping interview and the course of therapy, applications to work with children and families, to groups, education, conflict resolution and the building of community, research and training; it concludes with a retrospective and prospective look at this system of helping.

Bozarth, J. (1998) *Person-centered therapy: A revolutionary paradigm.* Ross-on-Wye, UK: PCCS Books.
A collection of twenty revised and new papers by one of the movement's outstanding teachers and theoreticians. It is divided into sections: Theory and Philosophy; The Basics of Practice; Applications in Practice; Research; and Implications. The book reflects upon Carl Rogers' theoretical foundations, emphasizes the revolutionary nature of these foundations, and offers extended frames for understanding this radical approach to therapy.

Rogers, C. R. (1942) *Counseling and psychotherapy.* Boston: Houghton Mifflin.
This was the first book-length presentation of an approach to therapy relying entirely on the client's capacity to construct his or her own personality change.

Chapter 2 is a slightly revised version of the talk given by Rogers at the University of Minnesota on December 11, 1940, which is regarded as the beginning of Client-Centered Therapy.

Rogers, C. R. (1951) *Client-centered therapy.* Boston: Houghton Mifflin.
This book describes the orientation of the therapist, the therapeutic relationship as experienced by the client, and the process of therapy. It expands and develops the ideas expressed in the earlier book *Counseling and Psychotherapy.*

Rogers, C. R. (1961) *On becoming a person.* Boston: Houghton Mifflin.
Perhaps Rogers' best-known work, this book helped to make his personal style and positive philosophy known globally. The book includes an autobiographical chapter and sections on the helping relationship; the ways in which people grow in therapy; the fully functioning person; the place of research; the implications of client-centered principles for education, family life, communication, and creativity; and the impact on the individual of the growing power of the behavioral sciences.

Rogers, C. R. (1980) *A way of being.* Boston: Houghton Mifflin.
As the book jacket states, this volume 'encompasses the changes that have occurred in Dr Rogers' life and thought during the decade of the seventies in much the same way *On Becoming a Person* covered an earlier period of his life. The style is direct, personal, clear — the style that attracted so many readers to the earlier book.' There is a large personal section, including chapters on what it means to Rogers to listen and to be heard and one on his experience of growing as he becomes older (he was 78 when the book was published), as well as important theoretical chapters. An appendix contains a chronological bibliography of Rogers' publications from 1930 to 1980.

Case readings
Rogers, C. R. (1942) The case of Herbert Bryan. In C. R. Rogers, *Counseling and psychotherapy* (pp. 261–437). Boston: Houghton Mifflin.
This may be the first publication of a completely recorded and transcribed case of individual psychotherapy that illustrates the new nondirective approach. Rogers provides a summary of the client's feelings after each interview and additional commentary.

Rogers, C. R. (1954) The case of Mrs Oak. In C. R. Rogers and R. F. Dymond (Eds.), *Psychotherapy and personality change.* Chicago: University of Chicago Press. [Also found in abridged form in C. R. Rogers (1961) *On becoming a person.* Boston: Houghton Mifflin. Also in D. Wedding and R. J. Corsini (Eds.), (2000). *Case studies in psychotherapy.* Itasca, IL: F. E. Peacock.]
This is a classic case illustrating therapist empathy and client change in terms of Rogers' self theory.

Rogers, C. R. (1977) A person-centered workshop: Its planning and fruition. In C. R. Rogers, *Carl Rogers on personal power* (pp. 149–85). New York: Dell.
This is an account of a 16-day intensive workshop in the Person-Centered Approach. It is included because so much of the Person-Centered Approach has been expressed in a group context and because it was so meaningful to Rogers, who said, 'Of all the ventures in which I have ever been involved, this was the most thoroughly person-centered . . . it has been, for me, a thoroughgoing test of the value of person-centeredness.'

Rogers, C. R. (1967) A silent young man. In C. R. Rogers, G. T. Gendlin, D. V. Kiesler, and C. Truax (Eds.), *The therapeutic relationship and its impact: A study of psychotherapy with schizophrenics* (pp. 401–6). Madison, WI: University of Wisconsin Press.
This case consists of two transcribed interviews that were conducted by Rogers as part of a year-long treatment of a very withdrawn hospitalized schizophrenic patient who was part of a client-centered research project on Client-Centered Therapy with a schizophrenic population.

Rogers, C. R. (1986) The dilemmas of a South African white. *Person-Centered Review, 1*, 15–35.
This article includes the transcription of a 30-minute demonstration interview conducted by Rogers. It is followed by the client's and therapist's reactions, a presentation of the themes of the interview, and two follow-up statements from the client, the second one coming three years after the interview.

References

Ansbacher, H. L. (1977) Individual psychology. In R. J. Corsini (Ed.), *Current psychotherapies*. Itasca, IL: F. E. Peacock.

Axline, V. M. (1947) *Play therapy.* Boston: Houghton Mifflin.

Barrett-Lennard, G. T. (1962) Dimensions of therapist response as causal factors in therapeutic change. *Psychological Monographs, 76* (43, Whole No. 562).

Barrett-Lennard, G. T. (1986) The relationship inventory now: Issues and advances in theory, method, and use. In L. S. Greenberg and W. M. Pinsof (Eds.), *The psychotherapeutic process: A research handbook* (pp. 439–76). New York: Guilford.

Bergin, A. E. and Garfield, S. L. (Eds.) (1971) *Handbook of psychotherapy and behavior change: An empirical analysis.* New York: Wiley.

Brodley B. T. (1993) Some observations of Carl Rogers' behavior in therapy interviews. *Person-Centered Journal, 1*(1), 37–47.

Butler, J. M. and Haigh, G. V. (1954) Changes in the relation between self-concepts and ideal concepts consequent upon client-centered counseling. In C. R. Rogers and R. F. Dymond (Eds.), *Psychotherapy and personality change* (pp. 55–75). Chicago: University of Chicago Press.

Cartwright, D. S. (1957) Annotated bibliography of research and theory construction in client-centered therapy. *Journal of Counseling Psychology, 4,* 82–100.

Ellinwood, C. G. and Raskin, N. J. (1993) Client-centered/humanistic psychotherapy. In T. R. Kratochwill and R. J. Morris (Eds.), *Handbook of psychotherapy with children and adolescents* (pp. 258–87). Boston: Allyn and Bacon.

Gendlin, E. T. (1961) Experiencing: A variable in the process of therapeutic change. *American Journal of Psychotherapy, 15,* 233–45.

Goldstein, K. (1959) *The organism: A holistic approach to biology derived from psychological data in man.* New York: American Book (Originally published 1934).

Holdstock, T. L. and Rogers, C. R. (1983) Person-centered theory. In R. J. Corsini and A. J. Marsella (Eds.), *Personality theories, research and assessment.* Itasca, IL: F. E. Peacock.

Lietaer, G., Rombauts, J. and Van Balen, R. (1990) *Client-centered and experiential psychotherapy in the nineties.* Leuven, Belgium: Leuven University Press.

Maslow, A. H. (1968) *Toward a psychology of being* (2nd edn.). Princeton, NY: Van Nostrand.

Matson, F. W. (1969) Whatever became of the Third Force? *American Association of Humanistic Psychology Newsletter, 6*(1), 1 and 14–15.

McGaw, W. H., Farson, R. E. and Rogers, C. R. (Producers) (1968) *Journey into self* [Film]. Berkeley: University of California Extension Media Center.

Meador, B. D. and Rogers, C. R. (1984) Person-centered therapy. In R. J. Corsini (Ed.), *Current psychotherapies* (3rd edn.) (pp. 142–95). Itasca, IL: F. E. Peacock.

Mitchell, K. M., Bozarth, J. D. and Krauft, C. C. (1977) A reappraisal of the therapeutic effectiveness of accurate empathy, non-possessive warmth, and genuineness. In A. S. Gurman and A. M. Razin (Eds.), *Effective psychotherapy: A handbook of research* (pp. 482–502). New York: Pergamon Press.

Orlinsky, D. E. and Howard, K. L. (1978) The relation of process to outcome in psychotherapy. In S. L. Garfield and A. E. Bergin (Eds.), *Handbook of psychotherapy and behavior change: An empirical analysis* (2nd edn.) (pp. 283–329). New York: Wiley.

Patterson, C .H. (1984) Empathy, warmth, and genuineness in psychotherapy: A review of reviews. *Psychotherapy, 21,* 431–8.

Porter, E. H. Jr. (1943) The development and evaluation of a measure of counseling interview procedures. *Educational and Psychological Measurement, 3,* 105–26, 215–38.

Raimy, V. C. (1948) Self-reference in counseling interviews. *Journal of Consulting Psychology, 12,* 153–63.

Rank, O. (1945) *Will therapy, truth and reality.* New York: Knopf.

Raskin, N. J. (1948) The development of nondirective therapy. *Journal of Consulting Psychology, 12,* 92–110.

Raskin, N. J. (1952) An objective study of the locus-of-evaluation factor in psychotherapy. In W. Wolfe and J. A. Pecker (Eds.), *Success in psychotherapy* (pp. 143–62). New York: Grune and Stratton.

Raskin, N. J. (1974) Studies of psychotherapeutic orientation: Ideology and practice. *Research Monograph, No. 1.* Orlando, FL: American Academy of Psychotherapists.

Raskin, N. J. (1985) Client-centered therapy. In S. J. Lynn and J. P. Garske (Eds.), *Contemporary psychotherapies: Models and methods* (pp. 155–90). Columbus, OH: Charles F. Merrill.

Raskin, N. J. (1996) Person-centred psychotherapy: Twenty historical steps. In W. Dryden (Ed.), *Developments in psychotherapy: Historical perspectives* (Chapter 1). London: Sage Publications.

Raskin, N. J. and Zucconi, A. (1984) Peace, conflict resolution, and the Person-Centered Approach. Program presented at the annual convention of the American Psychological Association, Toronto.

Rogers, C. R. (1931) *Measuring personality adjustment in children nine to thirteen.* New York: Teachers College, Columbia University, Bureau of Publications.

Rogers, C. R. (1939) *The clinical treatment of the problem child.* Boston: Houghton Mifflin.

Rogers, C. R. (1940) The process of therapy. *Journal of Consulting Psychology, 4,* 161–4.

Rogers, C. R. (1942) *Counseling and psychotherapy.* Boston: Houghton Mifflin.

Rogers, C. R. (1946) Significant aspects of client-centered therapy. *American Psychologist, 1,* 415–22.

Rogers, C. R. (1947) Some observations on the organization of personality. *American Psychologist, 2,* 358–68.

Rogers, C. R. (1951) *Client-centered therapy.* Boston: Houghton Mifflin.

Rogers, C. R. (1957) The necessary and sufficient conditions of therapeutic personality change. *Journal of Consulting Psychology, 21,* 95–103.

Rogers, C. R. (1959a) The essence of psychotherapy: A client-centered view. *Annals of Psychotherapy, 1,* 51–7.

Rogers, C. R. (1959b) A theory of therapy, personality and interpersonal relationships as developed in the client-centered framework. In S. Koch (Ed.), *Psychology: A study of science: Formulations of the person and the social context* (pp. 184–256). New York: McGraw-Hill.

Rogers, C. R. (1965) Client-centered therapy. Part I. In E. Shostrom (Ed.), *Three approaches to psychotherapy.* Santa Ana, CA: Psychological Films.

Rogers, C. R. (1977) *Carl Rogers on personal power.* New York: Delacorte Press.

Rogers, C. R. (1980) *A way of being.* Boston: Houghton Mifflin.

Rogers, C. R. (1983) *Freedom to learn for the 80s.* Columbus, OH: Charles E. Merrill.

Rogers, C. R. (1984) A historical note — Gloria. In R. F. Levant and J. M. Shlien (Eds.), *Client-centered therapy and the person-centered approach* (pp. 423–5). New York: Praeger.

C. R. (1986a) Client-centered therapy. In I. L. Kutash and A. Wolf (Eds.), *sychotherapist's casebook: Therapy and technique in practice* (pp. 197–208). San Francisco: Jossey-Bass.

Rogers, C. R. (1986b) The dilemmas of a South African white. *Person-Centered Review, 1,* 15–35.

Rogers, C. R. (1986c) Measuring the self and its changes: A forward step in research. *Archives of Humanistic Psychology,* 1–13.

Rogers, C. R. (1986d) The Rust workshop: A personal overview. *Journal of Humanistic Psychology 26,* 23–45.

Rogers, C. R. (1987) Inside the world of the Soviet professional. *Journal of Humanistic Psychology, 27,* 277–304.

Rogers, C. R. and Dymond, R. F. (Eds.) (1954) *Psychotherapy and personality change.* Chicago: University of Chicago Press.

Rogers, C. R., Gendlin, G. T., Keisler, D, V. and Truax, C. (Eds.) (1967) *The therapeutic relationship and its impact: A study of psychotherapy with schizophrenics.* Madison: University of Wisconsin Press.

Rogers, C. R. and Haigh, G. (1983) I walk softly through life. *Voices: The Art and Science of Psychotherapy, 18,* 6–14.

Rogers, C. R., Raskin, N. J., Seeman, J., Sheerer, E. T., Stock, D., Haigh, G., Hoffman, A. E. and Carr A. C. (1949) A coordinated research in psychotherapy. [Special Issue]. *Journal of Consulting Psychology, 13*(3).

Rogers, C. R. and Ryback, D. (1984) One alternative to nuclear planetary suicide. In R. F. Levant and J. M. Shlien (Eds.), *Client-centered therapy and the person-centered approach: New directions in theory, research, and practice* (pp. 400–22). New York: Praeger.

Rogers, C. R. and Sanford, R. C. (1985) Client-centered psychotherapy. In H. I. Kaplan, B. J. Sadock, and A. M. Friedman (Eds.), *Comprehensive textbook of psychiatry* (4th edn.) (pp. 1374–88). Baltimore: William and Wilkins.

Seeman, J. (1959) Toward a concept of personality integration. *American Psychologist, 14,* 794–7.

Seeman, J. (1984) The fully functioning person: Theory and research. In R. F. Levant and J. M. Shlien (Eds.), *Client-centered therapy and the person-centered approach: New directions in theory, research, and practice* (pp. 131–52). New York: Praeger.

Sheerer, E. T. (1949) An analysis of the relationship between acceptance of and respect for others in ten counseling cases. *Journal of Consulting Psychology, 13,* 169–75.

Shlien, J. M. (1964) Comparison of results with different forms of psychotherapy. *American Journal of Psychotherapy 28,* 15–22.

Standal, S. (1954) The need for positive regard: A contribution to client-centered theory. Unpublished PhD dissertation, University of Chicago.

Stephenson, W. V. (1953) *The Study of behavior.* Chicago: University of Chicago Press.

Streich, E. R. (1951) The self-experience of the client-centered therapist.

Unpublished paper. Chicago: The University of Chicago Counseling Center.

Stubbs, J. P. and Bozarth, J. D. (1994) The dodo bird revisited: A qualitative study of psychotherapy efficacy research. *Journal of Applied and Preventive Psychology, 3*,109–20.

Zimring, F. M. and Raskin, N. J. (1992) Carl Rogers and client/person-centered therapy. In D. K. Freedheim (Ed.), *History of psychotherapy: A century of change* (pp. 629–56). Washington, DC: American Psychological Association.

THE HISTORY OF EMPATHY IN THE CLIENT-CENTERED MOVEMENT

16

Introduction

In the theory and practice of client-centered psychotherapy, there is no concept more important than empathy. It became clear that to be effective, it was necessary for empathy to be more than a technique for facilitating the expression by clients of their feelings and experiences. It was necessary for therapists to believe in the importance of being empathic in a profound way. As the theory of the client-centered approach developed under the leadership of its founder, Carl Rogers, empathy became part of a triad of 'therapist-offered conditions', the other two being genuineness or congruence and unconditional positive regard, a thoroughgoing acceptance of clients as they are. Rogers came to characterize empathic as 'an unappreciated way of being', and wrote a chapter with this title. This was just one of hundreds of articles, books, talks, audiotapes, and videotapes by Rogers and others describing and illustrating this core concept.

The term 'empathy' has been used by many other mental health practitioners, but it is believed that client-centered therapists are unique in the fidelity and consistency of this way of being with their clients.

Early history at Ohio State University, 1940-42

Carl Rogers did not use the term 'empathy' in his first full-length book on therapy, *Counselling and Psychotherapy* (1942), but, as part of delineating characteristic steps in a 'newer approach to psychotherapy', Rogers defined the basic hypothesis of the approach:

> Effective counselling consists of a definitely structured, permissive relationship which allows the client to gain an understanding of himself to a degree which enables him to take positive steps in the light of his new orientation. (1942, p. 18)

The new approach was significant in a number of ways:

In S. Haugh and A. Merry (Eds.) *Empathy, Volume 2 of Rogers' therapeutic conditions: Evolution, theory and practice* (2001). Ross-on-Wye: PCCS Books. Reprinted with permission.

- The counselor sought not only to help clients deal with the immediate, presenting problem but to become more independent, more responsible, less confused and, being more integrated, have an increased ability to cope with new problems.
- There was more stress on emotional and feeling aspects than intellectual elements.
- There was more of a focus on the immediate situation than the individual's past.
- The therapeutic relationship itself was seen as a growth experience.

While Rogers did not use the term 'empathy' in *Counseling and Psychotherapy*, he gave examples of how the counselor 'accepts, recognizes, and clarifies' the client's feelings. This 'recognition of feeling' response represented a specific implementation of the concept of empathy in the early years of the client-centered approach. It was a practical technique. As far as attitudes were concerned, *Counseling and Psychotherapy* contained a great deal about the attitudes of the client, but not those of the therapist.

Development of the concept at the University of Chicago, 1945–57

Not so in *Client-Centered Therapy* (1951), where Rogers wrote that the attitudinal orientation which appears to be optimal for client-centered counselors is one where they act consistently upon the hypothesis that clients are competent to direct themselves. The counselor, as much as possible, assumes the client's internal frame of reference, to perceive the world and the client's own self in the way that the client does, and to communicate this empathic understanding with the implicit attitude, 'Did I understand you correctly?'

This orientation was very meaningful to me as a graduate student and I wrote a paper trying to articulate it in 1947 entitled 'The Nondirective Attitude'. It was never published but Rogers quoted from it in his book, *Client-Centered Therapy*, (1951, p. 29) citing this passage:

> At this level, counselor participation becomes an active experiencing with the client of the feelings to which he gives expression, the counselor makes a maximum effort to get under the skin of the person with whom he is communicating, he tries to get within and to live the attitudes expressed instead of observing them, to catch every nuance of their changing nature; in a word, to absorb himself completely in the attitudes of the other. And in struggling to do this, there is simply no room for any other type of counselor activity or attitude; if he is attempting to live the attitudes of the other, he cannot be diagnosing them, he cannot be thinking of making the process go faster. Because he is another, and not the client, the understanding is not spontaneous but must be acquired, and this through the most intense, continuous and active attention to the feelings of the other, to the exclusion of any other type of attention.

Rogers pointed out that this description represented an empathic rather than an emotional identification with the client; the counselor is experiencing the different feelings of the client but not having those feelings himself. In a memorable formulation of his own of the client-centeredness of the relationship, he wrote:

> We have come to recognize that if we can provide understanding of the way the client seems to himself at this moment, he can do the rest. The therapist must lay aside his preoccupation with diagnosis and his diagnostic shrewdness, must discard his tendency to make professional evaluations, must cease his endeavors to form an accurate prognosis, must give up the temptation subtly to guide the individual, and must concentrate on one purpose only, that of providing deep understanding and acceptance of the attitudes consciously held at this moment by the client as he explores step by step into the dangerous areas which he has been denying to consciousness.
>
> I trust it is evident from this description that this type of relationship can exist only if the counselor is deeply and genuinely able to adopt these attitudes. Client-centered counselling, if it is to be effective, cannot be a trick or a tool. It is not a subtle way of guiding the client while pretending to let him guide himself. To be effective, it must be genuine . . . (Rogers, 1946)

In 1957, Rogers published a classic article on *The Necessary and Sufficient Conditions of Personality Change*, in which empathy was one of a triad of therapist-offered conditions, the other two being congruence or genuineness and unconditional positive regard for the client. He stressed the importance of the client experiencing or receiving the therapist's attitudes. This publication, because of its clarity and fundamental concepts, stimulated a vast amount of research.

The case of Loretta, a dramatic example of empathy, 1958
The Case of Loretta (Farber, Brink, and Raskin, 1996)

The woman known as 'Loretta' was a state mental hospital patient, diagnosed as being paranoid schizophrenic. She had agreed to be interviewed before an audience of about 30 members of the American Academy of Psychotherapists (including the author) as part of its annual workshop during the summer of 1958 on the campus of the University of Wisconsin. As part of a format in which members observed one another in actual practice, she was first interviewed by Albert Ellis demonstrating his rational-emotive approach and then by psychiatrist Richard Felder giving an example of the experiential method of his Atlanta, Georgia psychiatric group which included Carl Whitaker, Tom Malone, and John Warkentin.

Ellis and Felder had both experienced a difficult time with Loretta, and there was a clamor in this diverse group of experienced therapists for Carl Rogers to try his hand with her. Rogers was champing at the bit, as it were, having suffered through two interviews in which, from his point of view, Loretta had not been responded to empathically. Ellis, the day before, had tried to get Loretta to see the irrationality of her behavior and Felder, earlier on this day, had attempted to engage her in a person-to-person dialogue about, among other things, a dream he had had about her the night before.

Loretta agreed to return for another interview which Rogers began by saying in a soft voice, 'I'm Carl Rogers. This must seem confusing and odd, and so on, but I, I felt really sorry that the interview [with Felder] had been kind of cut short because I felt maybe there were other things you wanted to say.' Loretta was immediately responsive to this expression of empathy and unconditional positive regard, and she expressed her concern about an impending move to another ward. She explained, 'I meant to correct one thing. When I said "No", I wondered why I couldn't go home.'

Rogers: You felt he didn't quite understand you on that, that really . . .

Loretta: . . . he thought I was being blunt and that I meant I didn't want to talk to him any more.

Rogers: And if I sense some of your feeling now, it is a little tenseness that maybe he didn't really get that, that maybe he thought you were sort of shutting him off, or something.

Loretta: Yes, that's what I had thought, and that isn't what I meant.

Loretta had made it clear that it was important to her to explain what she had said at the end of her interview with Felder. Rogers lets her do this, while conveying a full appreciation of her feelings. Later in the interview, Rogers demonstrates the same respect for Loretta's experience of a sensation that many mental health professionals might have seen as one of her oddities:

Loretta: Did you notice, I moved my feet?

Rogers: Yes, I did.

Loretta: My knees tickle. And I don't know if it's the drugs I'm getting or what, but it's something I can't help. It isn't that I'm so terribly nervous I can't sit still. That isn't it. I do that at group meetings or anything and I can't control them; it's rather embarrassing.

Rogers: M-hm. And you'd like me to understand that it isn't just tenseness or something . . .

Loretta: . . . it's something I can't control.

Rogers: Uncontrollable tickling sensations.

Loretta: In my knees, that far up. And my feet just move.

Loretta expressed her appreciation for the Academy meetings in which she had participated, saying 'I think I've been helped a lot, more by the talking than I have by the pills and that.' Rogers' consistent and respectful empathy appears to facilitate the expression and clarification by Loretta of a number of different attitudes: (1) her apprehension concerning a proposal to move her to another ward, and her reasons for it; (2) her distrust of a particular person on the new ward and of people in general, brought on by repeated experiences of having been misled; (3) her disturbance in response to a woman who can be heard screaming in the background while Loretta is being interviewed, and her fear that, like this woman, she could be a victim of ineffective treatment.

Loretta goes on to express some strikingly positive attitudes toward herself and a possible insight about the tingling in her knees:

Loretta: After all, I'm getting drugs and I wouldn't want to end up like that.

Rogers: M-hm, m-hm. It can't help but raise the question in you: 'Will the drugs they're giving me make me like that?'

Loretta: That's right. Then once you're that way, what can you do about it? Only I know what they're like and I think I have enough control that I could hang on to myself, keep from beating my head against the wall. Some of them have that feeling and they just can't control it. But I've seen so much of it and heard so much of it that I can hang on to myself, a little bit.

Rogers: Those things are kind of . . .

Loretta: I think that's why my . . . pardon me . . . I think that's why my knees tingle. All because rather than banging my head against the wall, I have that type of reaction.

Rogers: M-hm, m-hm. So that in a sense, you can hold yourself enough so that you aren't going to bat your head against the wall. And yet because it has to come out somewhere, it comes out in the knees.

Loretta: Yes, it's just futile to bat your head. Anyway, I think my head's just too valuable for that *(laughs)*. It's my own head, and I like it.

Rogers: You feel that, by gosh, I'm not going to smash my head against the wall.

Loretta: That's right. God gave me that head; that's the head I want.

There seems to be evidence here of the power of empathy and unconditional positive regard when, even in a person as emotionally disturbed as Loretta, there is evoked a strong, unmistakable expression of self-regard.

Rogers' passionate statement about empathy, 1958

Following the interview with Loretta, the American Academy of Psychotherapists' observers gave their reactions, several of them questioning Rogers' approach. He made this statement:

I can't help but come back in here in the discussion. Most of the time, especially in a discussion during a workshop of this sort, I can really let other people have their way of working with people and realize, 'Sure, they're working in their own way'. Then it's surprising how deeply I feel in an actual specific situation, how much of a partisan I become. I can't help but feel disturbed by the fact that we are so convinced that all of the judgments have to be made in us. We know the answer — 'His ego is strong enough to be able to take this', and 'Shall I yield a little to her unconscious?', and 'Does she mean by peristalsis what I mean by it?'

'The hell you do!', I feel like saying to all that stuff. And my feeling is, there's an in-between kind of way. And curiously enough, it happens to be the way I work (general laughter). Take . . . combining the things you just said . . . 'When she was afraid you were hypnotizing her', I feel it really would have helped to have tried to understand. That would have led into this kind of thing . . . 'You were just saying . . . (I mean, if one had responded) . . . you really are scared that I may somehow exercise power over you' I'm sure it would have gotten into the kind of material you're talking about. And on this peristalsis thing. You can pick any angle. But there you don't know what she means; I don't know either. I have hunches, but I don't know. And I would have liked to have responded, 'Somehow this experience had real meaning for you. This is a term that somehow made some kind of sense to you,' and then I think she would have felt very much drawn to explain what kind of sense it did make to her. And then I would know whether she was talking about a positive experience with Al Ellis or whether, out of that experience or the total experience of being in the hospital or what not. And this is another meaning that occurred to me, that life does have a rhythm and things do digest and move on through.

And I just feel we would not need to make all the judgments and all the decisions in ourselves. Dammit, we have the best resource for knowledge right there in the other chair!

Rogers' comprehensive account of empathy and its effects in Koch's *Psychology: A study of a science*, 1959

Rogers (1959b) published the most comprehensive account of his thinking in Sigmund Koch's *Psychology: A study of a science*. This described the therapist's empathy and its receipt by the client as an essential ingredient of personality change. It listed many outcomes in the personality and behavior of the client:

- Increased congruence, openness to experience, less defensiveness
- Greater realism and objectivity
- Greater effectiveness in problem-solving
- Improved psychological adjustment due to a more open self-concept
- Reduced vulnerability to threat
- More realistic perception of and achievable self-ideal
- Greater congruence between perceived self and ideal self
- Reduced physiological and psychological tension, including anxiety
- Greater positive self-regard

- Perceived locus-of-evaluation in self rather than others
- More confidence and self-direction
- The achievement of an organismic valuing process
- A more realistic and accurate perception of others
- More acceptance of others
- More behaviors 'owned' as belonging to self
- Fewer behaviors felt to be 'not myself'
- Behavior perceived as being more within the person's control
- Behavior perceived by others as more socialized and mature
- Behavior more creative, adaptive, and expressive of the person's own purposes and values

Rogers cited the considerable research evidence for this theoretical statement of outcomes.

The case of Mike, another example of empathy and its effectiveness, 1960
The Case of Mike (Rogers, 1960)
Rogers conducted many demonstration interviews showing how he employed empathy and the other client-centered conditions. One of them, known as 'The Case of Mike', was carried out before an audience of counselors in the late 1950s. 'Mike' was 17 years old. Here is an excerpt:

Mike: Let's put it this way. My stepfather and I are not on the happiest terms in the world. And so, when he states something and, of course, she [Mike's mother] goes along, and I stand up and let her know that I don't like what he's telling me, well, she usually gives in to me.

Rogers: I see.

Mike: Sometimes, and sometimes it's just the opposite.

Rogers: But part of what really makes for difficulty is that you and your stepfather, as you say, are not . . . the relationship isn't completely rosy.

Mike: Let's just put it this way, I hate him and he hates me. It's that way.

Rogers: But you really hate him and you feel he really hates you.

Mike: Well, I don't know if he hates me or not, but I know one thing, I don't like him whatsoever.

Rogers: You can't speak for sure about his feelings because only he knows for sure what they are, but as far as you are concerned . . .

Mike: . . . he knows how I feel about it.

Rogers: You don't have any use for him.

Mike: None whatsoever. And that's been for about eight years now.

Rogers: So for about eight years you've lived with a person whom you have no respect for and really hate.

Mike: Oh, I respect him.

Rogers:	Ah. Excuse me. I got that wrong.
Mike:	I have to respect him. I don't have to but I do. But I don't love him. I hate him. I can't stand him.
Rogers:	There are certain things you respect him for, but that doesn't alter the fact that you definitely hate him and don't love him.
Mike:	That's the truth. I respect anybody who has bravery and courage, and he does.
Rogers:	I see.
Mike:	And I still, uh, though I respect him, I don't like him.
Rogers:	But you do give him credit for the fact that he is brave, he has guts or something.
Mike:	Yeah. He shows that he can do a lot of things that, well, a lot of men can't.
Rogers:	M-hm, m-hm.
Mike:	And also he has asthma and the doctor hasn't given him very long to live. And he, even though he knows he is going to die, he keeps working and he works at a killing pace, so I respect him for that, too.
Rogers:	M-hm. So I guess you're saying he really has . . .
Mike:	. . . what it takes.
Rogers:	. . . quite a few, yeah, he has what it takes in quite a few ways. He has a number of good qualities. But that doesn't mean you care for him at all. Quite the reverse.
Mike:	That is the truth. The only reason I put up with him being around is because for my mother's sake.
Rogers:	M-hm, m-hm.

In this example we see the therapist keeping the initiative with the client and attempting only to provide a full appreciative understanding of the feelings Mike is trying to convey to him. The result is that Mike differentiates his feelings about his stepfather in an increasingly refined manner. The therapist does not try to accomplish this for Mike; he has no way of knowing the exact nature of his feelings. By trying to understand Mike on his own terms, however, the therapist facilitates a process in which Mike progresses from a statement of mutual hatred to one-sided hatred, to an expression of respect, to the reasons for his respect, and to the clear differentiation that, though he respects his stepfather, he does not like him.

Empathy with schizophrenics, the Wisconsin Project, 1957–63

During the period of 1957 to 1963, Client-Centered Therapy was tried out with a new population, hospitalized schizophrenics in Madison, Wisconsin. A fundamental hypothesis was that, provided with empathy and the other 'necessary and sufficient conditions of personality change', the therapy process would be found to be the same with the schizophrenic person as with the 'normal'. The research results were mixed, but there were some positive findings — Client-Centered Therapy was helpful with at least some of the 'chronic' or long-term schizophrenic patients, high therapist conditions of empathy and congruence did correlate with successful outcome, when these conditions were low, patients deteriorated (Rogers, Gendlin, Kiesler and Truax (Eds.), 1967).

The case of Gloria, 1964

Rogers interviewed Gloria, in 1964, as part of a project by Shostrom (1965), in which three therapists of different persuasions interviewed the same client on the same day. Gloria was interviewed first by Rogers, then by Albert Ellis demonstrating the rational-emotive technique, and finally by Frederick ('Fritz') Perls illustrating Gestalt therapy. This film has probably been seen by more students of therapy than any other. Rosenzweig (1996) summarized Rogers' interview, and the present author has commented on her summary with respect to Rogers' employment of empathy and congruence, as follows: after greeting Gloria and conveying an appreciation of her nervousness, Rogers explained that they had just 30 minutes to talk but hoped that the session would be helpful.

It quickly became obvious that Gloria came to the interview with a problem for which she hoped she would get an answer. She was newly divorced and sometimes had men over. Her nine-year-old daughter had asked if she had ever made love to a man since her father had left. Gloria had lied to her and felt terribly guilty about doing this. She wanted Rogers to tell her if it would harm 'Pammy' if she told her the truth. Rogers responded with empathy and congruence, 'I sure wish I could give you the answer as to what you should tell her . . .'cause what you really want is an answer.' A little later in the interview, Gloria revealed another concern she has about her relationship with Pammy, that if she knew the truth about her behavior, could she accept her? Rogers continued to empathize, and Gloria said, 'I feel there are some areas that I don't even accept.' Rogers recognized this and then Gloria verbalized her fear that Rogers would just sit there and let her stew in her feelings but that she wanted him to get rid of her guilty feelings about going to bed with a single man, so she could feel more comfortable. Rogers replied congruently, 'And I guess I'd like to say, "No, I don't want to let you stew in your feelings but, on the other hand, I also feel this is the kind of very private thing that I couldn't possibly answer for you, but I as sure as anything will try to help you work toward your own answer. I don't know whether that makes any sense to you, but I mean it."'

Gloria said she appreciated what Rogers had said and that he sounded like he meant it but she just didn't know how to answer these questions on her own. He recognized the 'real deep puzzlement that you feel as to what the hell shall I do, what can I do?' After a while, Gloria talked about her frustration because of the wish to approve of herself but that her actions would not let her; she felt guilty when she slept with someone she did not love. Again she questioned Rogers, 'Do you feel that to me the most important thing is to be open and honest? . . . If, for example, I could say to Pammy, "I was, I felt bad lying to you, Pammy, and I want to tell you the truth now." And if I tell her the truth and she's shocked at me and she's upset, that that could bother her more? I want to get rid of my guilt, and that will help me, but I don't want to put that on her.' Rogers responded with congruence rather than empathy, 'I guess, I'm sure this will sound evasive to you, but it seems to me that perhaps the person you're not being fully honest with is you. Because I was very much struck by the fact that you were saying, "If I feel alright about what I have done — whether it's going to bed with a man or what — if I really feel alright about it, then I don't have any concern about what I would tell Pam or my relationship with her."'

Gloria then said, 'I want to work on accepting me then . . . then I don't have to worry about Pammy.' But then Gloria questioned how it is that she accepts her impulse to do things that seem so wrong to her, Rogers responded empathically, 'What you'd like to do is to feel more accepting toward yourself when you do things that are wrong, is that right?' When Gloria agrees, he said congruently that it sounded like a tough assignment. Gloria said she felt hopeless and told Rogers what she needed was for him to show her where to begin so that things would not seem so hopeless anymore. Once more, Rogers' response was a congruent one, asking her what she wishes he would say to her. She said she wanted him to tell her to go ahead and risk being open with Pammy, explaining, 'If she really knows what a demon I am and still loves me and accepts me, it seems like it would help me to accept me more, like it's really not that bad.' She wondered if her own mother had been more open with her about sex, whether she might have been more broad-minded. She said she wanted Pammy to see her as a full woman, with both a sweet and a more sexy, devilish side, but she also wanted to be fully accepted by her. Rogers responded congruently, 'M-hm. You don't sound so uncertain. What I mean is, you've been sitting here telling me just what you would like to do in that relationship with Pam.' Gloria said she did not want to take that risk unless an authority figure were to give her the OK. Rogers said that he understood that it was risky to live and specifically with her daughter, 'You'd be taking a chance on your relationship with her. You'd be taking a chance on letting her know what you are, really.' Gloria continued, 'Yeah, but then if I don't take a chance, if I feel loved and accepted by her, I'm never gonna feel good about it anyway.' Rogers asked, 'If her love and acceptance of you is based on a false picture of you, what the hell is the good of that? Is that what you are saying?'

Gloria agreed. She admitted to a feeling of jealousy that her ex-husband was regarded as 'all sweetness and light' by the children, and that he had not been honest with them. She described herself as more 'ornery' than him and more likely to do things of which they would disapprove. Rogers recognized that she would find it hard to believe they would really love her if they knew her. Gloria said she needed reassurance that she was doing the right thing before she could go ahead and take the risk. She agreed enthusiastically when Rogers recognized that she would like somebody to give her permission, 'It's so damn hard to really choose something on your own, isn't it?' Gloria spoke of her wish that she could just accept herself and that she could respect herself if she could say, 'No matter what you ask me, kids, at least I told you the truth. You may not have liked it but it was the truth.' Rogers responded that it sounded from the tone of her voice that she hated herself more when she lied than doing things of which she disapproved. Gloria confirmed this, saying the lie she told Pammy had been over a month ago, and she was still tormented by it. 'Now,' she said, 'I feel like that is solved, and I didn't even solve the thing. But I feel relief.'

Gloria told Rogers that she felt he was backing her up, giving her permission to follow her instincts. He responded, 'I guess the way I sense it is you've been telling me you know what you want to do, and yes, I believe in backing up people in what they want to do. It's just a little different slant than the way it seems to you.' He clarified this, 'See, one thing that concerns me is it's no damn good you're doing something that you haven't really chosen to do. That's why I'm trying to help you find out what your own inner choices are.'

Gloria said it was hard to tell which of her feelings was strongest. If she actually behaved in certain ways, she did not know whether it meant she felt strongly about it, because she often disapproved of herself afterward. Rogers recognized her confusion that she could feel comfortable about something she did at the moment, but this could be followed by discomfort, and she was left not knowing which course of action she should have followed.

Gloria said that when she left her husband, she knew she had made the right decision. She had not been conflicted about her choice and knew that she had been following her true feelings. Rogers said that it appeared that she knew perfectly well the feeling within herself when she was doing something that was really right for her. Gloria agreed and Rogers added, 'You can really listen to yourself sometimes and realize, "No, no, this isn't the right feeling. This isn't the way I would feel if I was doing something that I really wanted to do."' Gloria replied, 'But yet many times I'll go along and do it anyway, and say, "Oh well, I'm in the situation now, I'll just remember next time."'

Gloria said when she had a feeling that she knew was good for her, it felt like utopia. Rogers responded, 'I sense that in those utopian moments, you really feel kind of whole, you feel all in one piece.' Gloria agreed and said, 'It gives me a choked-up feeling when you say that because I don't get that as often as I'd like.' Rogers said he suspected none of us get that feeling as often as we would like. Gloria responded by saying she had also been thinking about how nice it was to talk to him. She said she missed that her father had not talked to her the way Rogers did. 'I mean, I'd like to say, "Gee, I'd like you for my father."' Rogers responds with congruence and empathy, 'You look to me like a pretty nice daughter . . . 'cause you really do miss the fact that you couldn't be open with your own dad.'

Gloria said her father had not listened to her. She realized the reason she always had to be perfect was because her father always wanted her to be better than she was. Rogers said, 'You're just trying like hell to be the girl he wants you to be.' Gloria said, 'Yeah, at the same time rebelling.'

She said she gloated at the idea of writing to her father that she was working as a waitress. She knew he would disapprove and she could hurt him by telling him this, but she also wanted him to accept her and love her regardless of what she did. Rogers said, 'I guess you feel really badly that you think there's very little chance he'll say that.' Gloria said her father did not hear her. She described how two years ago she had tried to talk to him about her feelings, that she loved him although she had been afraid of him. In response he had said things like, 'Honey, you know I love you. You know I've always loved you.' Rogers responded, 'M-hm. Never really known and loved you, and this somehow is what brings tears inside.' Gloria said that when she talked about it, she felt 'more flip', but when she sat still, she felt a great big hurt. Rogers replied, 'It's much easier to be a little flip because then you don't feel that big lump of hurt inside.'

Gloria said the relationship with her father was another hopeless situation. She had tried working on it, but felt it was one more thing she had to accept. Her father was just not the type of man with whom she could communicate. She said he cared, but not so they could cooperate or communicate with each other. Rogers described Gloria's feeling, 'Well, I'm permanently cheated.' Gloria said that was why she liked substitutes. She valued talking to Rogers and other men she could respect. She said she kept a feeling inside that she was very close to Rogers, that he was like a substitute father. Rogers said, 'I don't feel that's pretending,' and Gloria said, 'But you're not really my father.' He replied, 'No. I meant about the real close business.' Gloria said she felt it was pretending, that she couldn't expect him to feel that close to her because he didn't know her that well. The interview closed with Rogers saying, 'Well, all I can know is what I am feeling; that is, I feel close to you in this moment.'

The basic encounter group, 1967

Rogers (1967b) described the process of the 'basic encounter group', portraying the leader's responsibility as 'primarily the facilitation of the expression of both feelings and thoughts on the part of the group members'. A 'basic encounter' was one in which a person in the group shares a very meaningful experience with no emotional holding back; another group member responds with kindred emotion, conveying profound empathy for her confrère. In this kind of intensive group, characteristically, the participants begin by 'milling around' and resisting personal expression or exploration; this is followed by describing past feelings, expressing negative feelings, expressing and exploring personally meaningful material, expressing immediate interpersonal feelings in the group, developing a healing capacity in the group, becoming more self-aware and making changes in oneself, cracking facades (reflecting an impatience with defensive behavior), receiving feedback from group members, having a 'basic encounter' experience, expressing positive feelings and closeness, and changing behavior in the group (increasing spontaneity, genuineness, caring) (pp. 262–72).

Rogers (1970) included this description in *Carl Rogers on Encounter Groups* and expanded his view of the facilitator's role in these groups. He wrote that he hoped, gradually, to become as much a participant in the group as a facilitator, and that he listened:

> I listen as carefully, accurately, and sensitively as I am able, to each individual who expresses himself. Whether the utterance is superficial or significant, I listen. To me the individual who speaks is worthwhile, worth understanding . . . I wish very much to make the climate psychologically safe for the individual. I want him to feel from the first that if he risks saying something highly personal, or absurd, or hostile, or cynical, there will be at least one person in the circle who respects him enough to hear him clearly and listen to that statement as an authentic expression of himself. (p. 47)

Rogers stated that his attempt 'to understand the exact meaning of what the person is communicating is the most important and most frequent of my behaviors in a group' (p. 51). If a difference in feeling was being expressed, he wanted his understanding to extend to both sides. 'This helps to sharpen and clarify the significance of differences' (p. 52).

He wrote that he had learned to be increasingly free to make use of:

> my own feelings as they exist in the moment, whether in relation to the group as a whole, or to one individual, or to myself. I nearly always feel a genuine and present concern for each member and for the group as a whole . . . I believe I am quite sensitive to moments when an individual is feeling a readiness to speak or is close to pain or tears or anger . . . It is probably particularly to hurt that I respond with empathic understanding . . . I endeavor to voice any persisting feelings which I am experiencing toward an individual or toward the group, in any significant or continuing relationship . . . I trust the feelings, words, impulses, fantasies, that emerge in me . . . I want to be as expressive of positive and loving feelings as of negative or frustrated or angry ones . . . I find it difficult to be easily or quickly aware of angry feelings in myself . . . am slowly learning in this respect. I seem to function best in a group when my 'owned' feelings — positive or negative — are in immediate interaction with those of a participant . . . When asked a question, I try to consult my own feelings. If I sense it as being real and containing no other than the question, then I will try my best to answer it. I feel no social compulsion, however, to answer simply because it is phrased as a question. There may be other messages in it far more important than the question itself. (pp. 52–4)

An objective comparison of client-centered with other orientations, 1974

Raskin (1974) was interested in an objective comparison of different approaches to psychotherapy; were the claimed differences real? Rogers (1977) called the resulting monograph a 'landmark study', and summarized it as follows:

> Raskin took six recorded interviews, conducted by six widely known and respected therapists, each from a different school of

thought. Each therapist approved a selected segment of his interview as being representative of his way of working. These segments were rated by 83 therapists, who classified themselves as belonging to one of 12 different therapeutic orientations. The segments were rated on many variables drawn from differing therapeutic theories and practices. Looked at politically, those who rated high on such variables as 'therapist-directed' or 'systematically reinforces' are clearly therapists whose behavior is controlling, and who make important choices for the client. Those who rate high on such variables as 'warm and giving', 'equalitarian', and 'empathic' obviously leave power and choice in the hands of the client.

When these 83 therapists used the same variables to give a picture of the 'ideal' therapist, there was very substantial agreement, and the outstanding characteristics were all non-controlling. In other ways they desire to behave in ways that treat the client as an autonomous person.

Yet in practice the picture is very different. Of the six expert therapists rated, only two — the client-centered and experiential therapists — showed any great similarity to the ideal therapist. The other four — including the rational-emotive, the psychoanalytic, the Jungian — correlated negatively with the ideal, some sharply so. In other words, in practice four of the six were more opposite than like the ideal therapist as perceived by the 83 practising therapists. The politics of the therapeutic relationship thus not only differs sharply from therapist to therapist, but in the same therapist may show a sharp difference between the professional ideal of the group and the way she actually behaves. (pp. 19–20)

In this project, Raskin gave this definition of 'empathic':

The therapist is trying, as sensitively and accurately as he can, to understand the client, from the latter's own point of view. It is an understanding of what the client is aware of and trying to convey to the therapist, so if the latter is accurate in his empathic endeavor, the client will feel and may say, 'Yes, that's it! That's how I feel! That's what I meant! You really understand me.' This is an understanding different from the kind which relates the client's behavior to a theory of personality or adjustment which is held by the therapist and which may result in a client reaction such as, 'Let's see. Is that true? That may be right. I never thought of that.' The empathic attitude is, 'I want to know and to convey to you my understanding of how you see things, how you interpret your experience, how you feel about yourself and others.'

Empathic described as 'a way of being', 1975

Rogers (1975) published a re-examination and re-evaluation of what 'empathic' meant to him, describing it as 'one of the most delicate and powerful ways we have of using ourselves' and 'extremely important both for the understanding of personality dynamics and for effecting changes in personality and behavior' and at the same time 'a way of being that is rarely seen in full bloom in a relationship'. He feared the apparent ascendance of behavior modification and other directive orientations with the therapist in the role of expert. After expressing his appreciation to Eugene Gendlin for his concept of 'experiencing', Rogers offered a current definition of empathy:

> An empathic way of being with another person has several different facets. It means entering the private, perceptual world of the other and becoming thoroughly at home in it. It involves being sensitive, moment by moment, to the changing felt meanings which flow in this other person, to the fear or rage or tenderness or confusion or whatever that he or she is experiencing. It means temporarily living in the other's life, moving about in it delicately without making judgments; it means sensing meanings of which he or she is scarcely aware, but not trying to uncover totally unconscious feelings, since this would be too threatening. It includes communicating your sensings of the person's world as you look with fresh and unfrightened eyes at elements of which he or she is fearful. It means frequently checking with the person as to the accuracy of your sensings, and being guided by the responses you receive. You are a confident companion to the person in his or her inner world. By pointing to the possible meanings in the flow of another person's experiencing, you help the other to focus on this useful type of referent, to experience the meanings more fully, and to move forward in the experiencing.
>
> To be with another in this way means that, for the time being, you lay aside your own values in order to enter another's world without prejudice. In some sense it means that you lay aside your self; this can only be done by persons who are secure enough in themselves that they know they will not get lost in what may turn out to be the strange and bizarre world of the other, and that they can comfortably return to their own world when they wish.
>
> Perhaps this description makes clear that being empathic is a complex, demanding, and strong — yet also a subtle and gentle — way of being'. (pp. 142–3)

Conclusion

Since Rogers' death in February of 1987, Barrett-Lennard (1998), Bozarth (1998), Brodley (1996), and others in the movement he founded have continued to make significant contributions to the concept of empathy. Psychiatrist Peter Kramer

(1995) wrote that it 'seems odd that Rogers' star should be in eclipse today when his central belief, that empathy is the key to psychotherapy, is in the ascendant. He described Rogers' way of working as 'music'. Kramer's appreciation may indicate that the unprecedented attention to the concept of empathy by client-centered therapists for over half a century will have a lasting impact on the general field of psychotherapy research and practice.

References

Barrett-Lennard, G.T. (1998) *Carl Rogers' helping system, journey and substance.* London: Sage Publications.

Bozarth, J. D. (1998) *Person-centered therapy: A revolutionary paradigm.* Ross-on-Wye: PCCS Books.

Brodley, Barbara T. (1996) Empathic understanding and feelings in client-centered therapy. *Person-Centered Journal, 3,* (1), 22–30.

Farber, B. A., Brink, D. C. and Raskin, P. M. (Eds.) (1996) *The psychotherapy of Carl Rogers.* London and New York: Guilford Press.

Kramer, P. (1995) Rogers' due. *Psychiatric Times,* May.

Raskin, N. J. (1974) Studies of psychotherapeutic orientation, Ideology and practice. *Research Monograph No. 1.* Orlando, FL (now New Bern, NC): American Academy of Psychotherapists.

Rogers, C. R. (1942) *Counselling and psychotherapy.* Boston: Houghton Mifflin.

Rogers, C. R. (1946) Significant aspects of client-centered therapy. *American Psychologist, 1,* 415–22.

Rogers, C. R. (1951) *Client-centered therapy.* Boston: Houghton Mifflin.

Rogers, C. R. (1960) 'The Case of Mike', Audiotape No. 7, AAP Tape Library, Orlando, FL (now New Bern, NC): American Academy of Psychotherapists.

Rogers, C. R., Gendlin, E. T., Kiesler, D. J. and Truax, C.B. (Eds.) (1967a) *The therapeutic relationship and its impact: A study of psychotherapy with schizophrenics.* Madison: University of Wisconsin Press.

Rogers, C. R. (1967b) The process of the basic encounter group. In J.F.T. Bugental (Ed.) *Challenges of humanistic psychology* (pp. 261–76). New York: McGraw-Hill.

Rogers, C. R. (1970) *Carl Rogers on encounter groups.* New York: Harper and Row.

Rogers, C. R. (1975) Empathic: An unappreciated way of being. *The Counseling Psychologist, 5*(2), 2–10. Reprinted in C.R. Rogers (1980) *A way of being* (pp. 137–63). Boston: Houghton Mifflin.

Rogers, C. R. (1977) *Carl Rogers on personal power.* New York: Delacorte Press.

Rosenzweig, D. (1996) Summary of 'The case of Gloria'. In B. A. Farber, D. C. Brink and P. M. Raskin (Eds.), *The psychotherapy of Carl Rogers* (pp. 57–64). London and New York: Guilford Press.

Shostrom, E. L. (Producer) (1965) *Three approaches to psychotherapy* [Film], Orange, CA: Psychological Films.

INDEX

Rogers' Therapeutic Conditions:
Evolution Theory and Practice

This series traces the evolution and application of Carl Rogers' necessary and sufficient therapeutic conditions from 1957 to the present day. It contains the contributions of distinguished practitioners and theoreticians from all over the world. Common strands are followed in each of the four volumes: the historical perspective; client incongruence; new material; seminal papers; the connection of each therapeutic condition to the others and to resecarch.

Volume 1: Congruence edited by Gill Wyatt
• 2001 • pp. 242 + x • paperback 1898059292 • £18.00

Volume 2: Empathy edited by Sheila Haugh and Tony Merry
• 2001 • pp. 256 + x • paperback 1898059306 • £18.00

Volume 3: Unconditional Positive Regard edited by Jerold Bozarth and
Paul Wilkins
• 2001 • pp. 236 + xiv • paperback 1898059314 • £18.00

Volume 4: Contact and Perception edited by Gill Wyatt and Pete Sanders
• 2002 • pp. 300 + xiii • paperback 1898059322 • £18.00

——————— • • • ———————

A collection of the work of John Shlien

To Lead an Honorable Life:
Invitations to think about Client-Centered Therapy and the Person-Centered Approach
edited by Pete Sanders
• 2003 • pp. 234 + xvi • paperback 1898059462 • £17.00

This long-awaited book features Shlien's best-known work alongside lesser-known papers and some hitherto unpublished essays. John Shlien was one of the most influential of Carl Rogers' students and associates. He writes with a witty, often provocative style, and his insightful comments and creativity as a theorist shine through every page of this seminal book.

Person-Centred Approach
& Client-Centred Therapy
Essential Readers
Series editor Tony Merry

Person-Centred Therapy: *A Revolutionary Paradigm*

Jerold Bozarth 1998 ISBN 1 898059 22 5 234 x 156 pp 204+vi £16.00

Jerold D. Bozarth is Professor Emeritus of the University of Georgia, where his tenure included Chair of the Department of Counseling and Human Development, Director of the Rehabilitation Counseling Program and Director of the Person-Centered Studies Project.

In this book Jerold Bozarth presents a collection of twenty revised papers and new writings on Person-Centred therapy representing over 40 years' work as an innovator and theoretician. The book is divided into five sections:

- Theory and Philosophy
- Applications of Practice
- Implications
- The Basics of Practice
- Research

This important book reflects upon Carl Rogers' theoretical foundations, emphasises the revolutionary nature of these foundations and offers extended frames for understanding this radical approach to therapy. This book will be essential reading for all with an interest in Client-Centred Therapy and the Person-Centred Approach.

——————— • • • ———————

Experiences in Relatedness:
Groupwork and the Person-Centred Approach
edited by **Colin Lago** and **Mhairi MacMillan**
1999   ISBN 1 898059 23 3 234 x 156 pp 182+iv £16.00

This book is an international collection of specially commissioned papers. Contributors include Ruth Sandford (USA); Peggy Natiello (USA); John K. Wood (Brazil); Peter Figge (Germany); Irene Fairhurst, Tony Merry, John Barkham, Alan Coulson and Jane Hoffman (UK). This is the first substantial book within the person-centred tradition on groupwork since Carl Rogers' *Encounter Groups*. Topics include the history of the development of small and large groupwork within the PCA; theoretical principles of person-centred groupwork; working with issues of sexuality and sexism; the use of the group in training; and groups, organisations and the Person-Centred Approach.

The authors have uniquely caught the spirit of the person-centred approach in their various writing styles, which combine personal expression with disciplined reflections on experience. References to research studies sit comfortably alongside personal testimonies; philosophical reflections are underpinned by a wide range of references from other disciplines.

——————— • • • ———————

Women Writing in the Person-Centred Approach
edited by **Irene Fairhurst**
1999 ISBN 1 898059 26 8 234 x 156 pp. 217+ii £16.00

Edited by the co-founder of the British Association for the Person-Centred Approach (BAPCA), this book is the first anthology of women's writing informed by and focusing on the Person-Centred Approach. This uniquely themed collection includes contributions from all over the world, representing the wide range of developments in client-centred therapy and the Person-Centred Approach.

In person-centred counselling and psychotherapy training courses, women outnumber men by about eight to one, yet in our literature the opposite is the case. This book is not written specifically for women, or about women — it redresses the balance — it is a place for women with something to say to meet together, and, for some, to find their voice. Twenty-one papers from an impressive international list of contributors.

Person-Centred Approach
& Client-Centred Therapy
Essential Readers
Series editor Tony Merry

Understanding Psychotherapy: *Fifty years of client-centred theory and practice*

by **C.H. 'Pat' Patterson** *foreword by John Shlien*

2000 ISBN 1 898059 28 4 234 x 156 pp. 338+iv £17.50

'This weighty volume, collection of a life-time of work, constitutes a whole course of instruction in theory and practice. But how does it look, feel, sound, in action? There is at hand a wonderful answer.'   John Shlien

'C.H. Patterson is one of the most productive and observant scholars of psychotherapy in the twentieth century. He continues such work into the twenty-first century with new publications and reiteration of some of his classic writings. **Understanding Psychotherapy** contains the real 'gold standards' of psychotherapy and counseling.'   Jerold Bozarth

Aimed at everyone with a scholarly interest in psychotherapy and counselling whether client-centred or not, this substantial volume is a mine of essential reading. The style is direct and accessible, inviting the reader to consider many theoretical, practical and contextual issues that have vexed therapists for the past 50 years.

—————— • • • ——————

Family, Self and Psychotherapy:
A person-centred perspective
by **Ned L. Gaylin**

2001 ISBN 1 898059 36 5 234 x 156 pp. 190 £16.00

> **Required reading for all professionals and volunteers working with families, children and individuals.**

Family, Self and Psychotherapy provides a comprehensive person-centred look at the family as the essential element of society and is required reading for all professionals and volunteers working with families, children and individuals. Gaylin also explores our human need to be interconnected and its implications for both individual and family therapy.

The volume is informally divided into three sections. The first section deals with the centrality of the family to our species as a whole and to us as individuals. The next addresses the optimistic philosophical foundations of the person-centred approach: the tapestry of the self and its core drive towards psychological well-being. The last section — the heart of the book — deals with the principles and pragmatics of the person-centred approach to working with individuals and families.

In ***Family, Self and Psychotherapy*** Gaylin asserts that therapeutic relationships are more likely to thrive when viewed from this positive perspective especially when therapy operates within the individual's family context.

Ned L. Gaylin *is a Professor at the University of Maryland where he currently serves as director of the graduate program in Marriage and Family Therapy. He maintains an active interest in child and family therapy with a particular emphasis on both normal and abnormal development in the family context. He also is concerned with the evaluation of the process and outcome of psychotherapy — particularly family therapy, the application of Client-Centred theory and techniques to family therapy, and the study and enhancement of creativeness.*

PCCS Books
has the largest list of person-centred
titles in the world

www.pccs-books.co.uk

Features include:

• personal accounts

• discounts on all orders

• free p&p in the UK

• gift certificates

• browse by subject and authors

• the site's best-sellers

• easy navigation

• regularly updated news section

• links to other websites